Birdsong

BY THE

Seasons

INCLUDING CD RECORDINGS
OF THE
BIRDSONG SONAGRAMS
SHOWN IN THIS BOOK

Birdsong

BY THE

Seasons

A YEAR OF
LISTENING TO BIRDS

Donald Kroodsma

DRAWINGS BY NANCY HAVER

HOUGHTON MIFFLIN HARCOURT
BOSTON   NEW YORK
2009

www.hmhbooks.com

Library of Congress Cataloging-in-Publication Data

Kroodsma, Donald E.
  Birdsong by the seasons : a year of listening to birds / Donald
Kroodsma ; drawings by Nancy Haver.
      p. cm.
  Includes bibliographical references and index.
  ISBN-13: 978-0-618-75336-9
  ISBN-10: 0-618-75336-2
1. Birdsongs — United States. 2. Birds — Vocalization — United States.
3. Songbirds — Seasonal distribution — United States. I. Title.
  QL698.5.K757 2009
  598.159'4 — dc22   2008053293

Book design by Anne Chalmers
Typefaces: Minion, Miller Display, Futura, Futura Condensed
Illustrations by Nancy Haver

Printed in the United States of America
DOC 10 9 8 7 6 5 4 3 2 1

FOR KENDA, LARA, AND DAVID

Contents

Acknowledgments

I OFFER A hearty thank-you to all those who helped make these seasonal listening adventures possible: Ed Carlson at Corkscrew Swamp, for access to Corkscrew Swamp at odd hours; the late Glen Woolfenden of Archbold Biological Station, for sharing his Florida scrub-jays with me; Felipe Chavez-Ramirez of the Platte River Whooping Crane Maintenance Trust, for sharing his enthusiasm for the cranes on the Platte River; David Kroodsma of www .rideforclimate.com, for making my tropical pilgrimage possible; Lynda and Roger Mayhorn of the Buchanan County Bird Club and Virginia Society of Ornithology, for hosting me and sharing their backyard birds; Ed Talbot, Gene Morton, and Greg Budney, for trying to identify mimicry in white-eyed vireo songs; the Colorado Field Ornithologists, for hosting my visit to "the other" Colorado, especially the Pawnee grasslands; Dan Albano, for knowing kingfishers; the late David Stemple, for a quarter century of listening together; Bill Evans, who tutored me in the art of recognizing calls of night migrants; the Department of Conservation and Recreation at "the Quabbin," for a research permit granting access to the wilderness surrounding the reservoir that waters Boston; Philip Whitford, for his love of Canada geese; Greg Budney, curator of Cornell's Library of Natural Sounds, for giving permission to produce sonagrams from sounds in their collection (see figure 8, page 78, and figure 38, page 230); my group of birding consultants in my local Hampshire Bird Club, for their collective eyes and ears and knowing what is about; and the birds themselves, without whose songs our natural world would indeed be a quiet and far less interesting place.

For reading parts or all of the manuscript, I thank Janet Grenzke and Mary Alice Wilson. Bill McQuay (at Cornell's Library of Natural Sounds), you're a magician in the sound studio; thanks so much for all of your effort and expertise in assembling the sounds for the two CDs.

I owe a special thank-you to those who have fostered my interest in birdsong or shared their enthusiasm over the past 40 years. Near the top of the list, in rough chronological order, would be the late Olin Sewall Pettingill, Jr., John Wiens, Jared Verner, Peter Marler, Gene Morton, Nick Thompson, the late David Stemple, Bruce Byers and David Spector and Cindy Staicer (and other former graduate students as well), Julio Sánchez, Greg Budney, and Lang Elliott. Thanks, too, to countless amateur and professional bird listeners to whose collective knowledge I could add.

Thank you, also, to Margaret and Dick, Linda and Al, parents who gave everything; and to Melissa, for tolerating a spouse with the ultimate birdsong obsession.

At Houghton Mifflin Harcourt, Lisa White is the consummate editor, Anne Chalmers the artist who makes sonagram figures sing, and Taryn Roeder the publicist who makes sure the world hears the magic that is birdsong; thanks also to Teresa Elsey, production editor extraordinaire, and to Susan M. S. Brown, for a thoroughly wonderful copyediting job. Thank you, Russell Galen, for helping find a home for this book at Houghton Mifflin Harcourt. And Nancy Haver, I love your drawings that grace the text.

Important: Read Me First!

THE SEASONS OF BIRDSONG follow the seasons of the sun. As the sun dips low in the winter sky, the northern woods fall quiet; those few birds who remain call softly as they search for food to survive the short days and long, cold nights. As the sun makes its comeback, beginning in late December on the winter solstice, so too does song; gonads grow and hormones surge through transforming bodies, the urge to sing now irrepressible as the thoughts of these same birds turn to seeking mates for the coming spring. Following the sun, migrants from the Tropics soon flood the northern latitudes, culminating in a peak of sun and song by late May to early June. At the summer solstice in late June, the sun begins to slip away again, as does song. Migrants soon depart for southern latitudes, and those who stay behind retreat to survival mode, calling more softly as thoughts turn again to finding fuel to survive the short days and long, cold nights.

Outline of the 24 Accounts

Come follow these seasons of sun and song from New Year's Day through the winter solstice. In January, we visit the New England winter roost for a young female pileated woodpecker and for thousands of robins; following the sun to the south ourselves, we head to the Everglades to visit thousands of large wading birds in their winter roost. The Florida sun continues to beckon throughout February, with limpkins, scrub-jays, and anhingas. March is celebrated with the grand spectacle of migrating sandhill cranes on the Platte River in Nebraska. April brings a tropical pilgrimage to the ancestral home of so many of our North Temperate birds.

During May, June, and July, what a joy it is to listen to all that birds have on their minds throughout North America. Taking center stage in this peak season are birds that I found irresistible, birds that took over my life for hours or days at a time: brown thrashers and white-eyed vireos in Virginia; horned larks, Cassin's sparrows, lark buntings, and McCown's longspurs in the Pawnee grasslands of Colorado; Baltimore orioles, belted kingfishers, American crows, Blackburnian warblers, scarlet tanagers, indigo buntings, and more in my New England home.

The singing season largely over, August slows as waxwings finish their late-season breeding, but how fascinating now to listen to young songbirds of all kinds practicing their songs for next year. During September, listen to a wood thrush going to roost, then sit on a local hilltop and listen to countless nocturnal migrants calling overhead as they stream south. Come spend October with a ruffed grouse who drums throughout the month. In the quiet of November, we flash back to a summer spectacular, the singing of two hermit thrushes in June, then observe Thanksgiving with a mockingbird as she defends her winter territory. Last is a celebration of the winter solstice, and if you listen to the birds, they will tell you in song that this day is in fact the first day of spring, the very day that marks the beginning of a whole new cycle.

Those are the brief story lines for the 24 accounts that mark the changing of the seasons. Now let me explain how best to navigate and appreciate these seasonal adventures throughout the book.

The Two Compact Discs

One disc was simply not enough. This book is about using sounds not so much to *identify* birds as to *identify with* them; so much of the joy of listening is to linger and listen to one bird for an extended period. Listen to one of the most intelligent species, for example, as two American crows eloquently discuss life matters during a nine-minute session. Throughout the book, I refer you to specific tracks on the discs, with track 1-50 referring you to CD 1, track 50, for example, and track 2-1 referring you to the crows on CD 2, track 1. For instructions on how to listen to each of these audio tracks, see Appendix 1. The text there supplements the text in the accounts and describes in detail the content of the audio tracks.

How to Listen

I urge you to turn to page 277, the introduction to Appendix 1: The Audio Book. There I explain how best to listen to the sounds on the two compact discs. Although most people will probably start reading at the beginning of the book and listen to the sounds when each is referenced, I suggest that you could listen first and then read the book. Do whatever works best for you, but above all don't miss out on the detailed track descriptions in The Audio Book.

The Sonagram Is a Window on the Mind of a Singing Bird

(Note: You have my blessing to skip this section if you wish. Although I believe that *seeing* birdsong is half the fun, you can certainly enjoy the seasons of bird-song without sonagrams in your life.)

Sonagrams! I can't imagine a world without sonagrams; they are windows on the minds of singing birds. Without these visual images of bird sounds, we would know so little of what these feathered creatures are saying.

I do realize, of course, that just the sight of sonagrams scares some people, so let's try to fix that in this brief sonagram primer. It may help first of all to think of a sonagram as a musical score for birdsong. Hasn't the sonagram become far friendlier already?

But, to the fundamentals. The format for a sonagram is much the same as that for a score of human music: We read it from left to right, and frequency (or pitch) is on the vertical. In human music, we think in terms of octaves and doubling of frequencies, so that a sound at middle A on a piano vibrates the airwaves 440 times a second, the A above that at 440 × 2 = 880 times a second, the A below at 440 ÷ 2 = 220 times a second. For birdsong, instead of using this octave scale, we simply plot the actual frequency on the vertical axis and label the frequency in cycles per second, or hertz (the unit named after Dr. Heinrich Hertz, a German physicist who studied these things). The highest note on a piano, then, is about 4,000 cycles per second, also written as 4,000 Hz, or 4 kilohertz, abbreviated 4 kHz. The relative loudness of a note on a son-agram is indicated by darkness.

Those are the fundamentals. Now let's look at and listen to some examples. That's the key to appreciating sonagrams, by the way: Hearing what we simultaneously see, perhaps slowed down so that we can hear the details, makes all the difference. And you can "hear" most sonagrams in this book — just check the code in the time scale beneath the sonagram to find where to listen. For the first great blue heron call in figure 3 (page 28), for example, "T1-11, 0:35" means you can find this sound on CD 1, track 11, at 0:35.

Some sounds are harsh and not the least bit musical or tonal. A gunshot or a door slam, for example, would produce a vertical mark on a sonagram, because such a noise contains a wide range of frequencies (or pitches) at any given instant. Some bird sounds are similarly harsh and atonal. Consider the *fraaahnk, fraaahnk, fraak, fra* of a great blue heron, for example (figure 3, page

28); see in the sonagram how the sounds span the frequency spectrum from near 0 up to 6 kilohertz. Listen to these sounds on track 1-11, and you hear the nonmusical, grating effect of this heron's calls. Other such harsh calls are those of the Florida scrub-jay (see figure 6 on page 52, track 1-22, for example) or the CHRRR! of the northern mockingbird defending her winter territory (figure 45 on page 255; track 2-52).

Other sounds are far more musical, or tonal. A pure tone at middle A on a piano, for example, would be a horizontal line at 440 hertz across the sonagram. Some birds produce such pure tones that are held fairly constant in frequency. The opening whistle of a hermit thrush song is a striking example (figure 42 on page 244; track 2-6). Other examples include the beautiful whistles on the end of the Cassin's sparrow songs (figure 14, page 115; track 1-49; although the last notes in Songs A and C have a slight vibrato effect) and the whistled *see* notes of a cedar waxwing (figure 29, page 182, middle left; track 2-24).

Many bird sounds consist of a rather pure tone that is not held constant in frequency but rather is rapidly slurred through a range of frequencies. A favorite example is the song of the Baltimore oriole (figure 12, page 103; track 1-45) or the northern cardinal (track 1-60; not illustrated in a figure). The banded wren from the Neotropics also has such a beautiful song (figure 9, page 81; track 1-39).

Many bird sounds contain noticeable harmonics. Let's revisit that middle A string on a piano; when it vibrates, it produces a fundamental tone of 440 hertz, but because of the physics of a vibrating cord, also in the sound are harmonics at $440 \times 2 = 880$ hertz, $440 \times 3 = 1,320$ hertz, $440 \times 4 = 1,760$ hertz, and so on. An example of such harmonic structure in a bird sound is in the calls of the limpkin. In figure 4 (page 38), see the lowest fundamental note in each phrase and then all of the harmonic notes stacked above; in the third phrase of the third row in that figure is a picture-perfect "harmonic stack," for example, in which the fundamental note rises to about 1,600 hertz, and harmonics above that are in multiples of 1,600 hertz, at about 3,200 hertz, 4,800 hertz, 6,400 hertz, 8,000 hertz, and so on. When listening to such sounds, we don't hear the harmonic notes separately but instead hear them all together with a unique quality, or timbre. Other examples of harmonics in bird sounds can be found in the calls of a pileated woodpecker (figure 1, page 6; track 1-1), the great kiskadee (figure 8, page 78; track 1-38), and the white-breasted nuthatch (figure 46, page 268; track 2-65).

And what fun when the sonagrams reveal clearly how the bird uses his two voice boxes to produce two different sounds at the same time, sounds that are not harmonically related and therefore cannot be produced by one voice box alone. For the cedar waxwing, see figure 30 (page 186) for clear evidence that the calling bird uses both voice boxes. Another example is provided by the American robin (figure 48, page 273; track 2-66); in the three examples in that figure, the robin sings entirely different phrases above and below 5,000 hertz, again revealing the simultaneous use of the two voice boxes. Such simultaneous use of the two voices can be detected in sonagrams, but when a bird uses his two voices successively, there's no way to know if he's alternating quickly between his two voices or being especially acrobatic with just one.

And birds got rhythm. I just love following along in sonagrams as I listen to a bird leap through frequency and time. Some of my favorites are the songs of white-eyed vireos (figure 11, pages 94–95; track 1-43), lark buntings (figure 15, page 118; track 1-50), and especially Cassin's sparrows (figure 14, page 115; track 1-49). As I listen, I am the song, generated high in the brain and surging along the nerves down the sides of the neck to the two voice boxes; I am the air, beginning deep in the lungs, now pressurized and forced through the voice boxes; I am the two voice boxes themselves, my membranes vibrating in rhythm with the precision-guided puffs of air shunted to the left and the right passageways. I am as close to being the bird as I can imagine.

I invite you to listen and revel in the sight of these songs, as *any listening experience* is richer if the sound can be *seen* and *heard* at the same time. For an even richer listening experience, I encourage you to use the free Raven Lite software from Cornell University (www.birds.cornell.edu/brp/raven/Raven .html) so that you can watch the sonagrams and listen to any of the sounds on the two compact discs at any speed you wish. Slow the songs to half or quarter speed, or even down to one-eighth speed, as I have done for you with hermit thrushes (track 2-6; figure 42); at these speeds, I am convinced that we are hearing details in the songs that the birds themselves hear. And that is where I want to be, as close to being and experiencing a singing bird as possible.

How to Record Your Own Bird Sounds

Listening to birds and identifying with them is enormously satisfying, and the next logical step is capturing the sounds of birds and taking those sounds home with you. In Appendix 2, I offer some advice on how to do just that.

Concluding Thoughts

I feel compelled to add a brief comment here about the words "song" and "call." Birds of a given species have many different vocalizations, but one of them typically stands out because it is relatively complex, loud, and prolonged; it is used mostly by the males and typically from prominent perches, all in an effort, it seems, to impress females during the breeding season. That special vocalization we label a "song"; all of the others are "calls." That said, there are many exceptions, such as the cedar waxwing (see page 178 to explore these ideas further).

Only 24 accounts? you might ask. And why those 24? What a challenge it has been to whittle down the hundreds of potential accounts to only two dozen. My original plan was to distill the hundreds down to 52, one for each week of the year, but I soon realized that each would then be too brief and too shallow to appreciate each bird and each experience. So my filing cabinets are full of birds left behind, those awaiting their due attention. The survivors are the birds who spoke to me in some special way, the birds whose lives and mine intersected at some key, influential moment, creating for me enduring experiences that I am privileged to share with you.

JANUARY

1

A Pileated Woodpecker Goes to Her Roost on New Year's Day

New Year's Day, January 1, 6:30 A.M.,
Lawrence Swamp, Amherst, Massachusetts.
50 minutes until sunrise

I KNOW SHE'S in there. Off the edge of the paved rail-to-trail bike path where I sit, it's just 50 feet to the east across the open ice to the lone dead oak tree, then up the stump 10 feet to the five-inch-diameter hole. She's out of sight just below that entrance, and still sleeping, no doubt, as none of the other day birds are stirring yet either.

I hear only the great horned owls now, three pairs of them hooting back and forth to one another, getting in their last licks before daylight. Their hormones are flowing midwinter, as it's their breeding season, and soon they'll have eggs and young at what seems the oddest time of year. One pair is at least a quarter mile to the east, beyond the railroad tracks on the other side of this beaver-made lake; another pair is behind me toward South East Street; and the third is to my right in the depths of the Lawrence Swamp forest. In each pair I hear the female and male duetting, her *who whoo whoo whoohoho whoooo whoo* slightly higher-pitched than his.

Yes, I know she's in there because I saw her enter late yesterday afternoon, at 3:44 P.M. on New Year's Eve to be exact, almost three-quarters of an hour before the official sunset. It was a grand entrance, too, entirely unexpected. I was sitting quietly in my camp chair, watching the old oak that had housed a pileated family just this past summer and wondering if anyone was roosting in the cavity over the winter. By 3:20, with the goal of recording anything I might hear, I had started my recorder, pointed the microphone at the nest hole, and laid the recorder and mike on a pack beside me.

With binoculars in hand, I was poised to get a good look at the bird, if one appeared, and I knew exactly what to look for. There had been four in the family, two adults and two young, a male and female of each, and if I got a good look at the bird, I'd know exactly who it was. The adults would have bright yellow irises, but the young ones would still have dark eyes. And the males would have strikingly red crests, crowns, and malar stripes directly behind their bills; the females would have red crests, but their crowns would be yellowish brown, the malar stripes black.

Waiting here this New Year's morning, I replay yesterday afternoon's events:

Sitting, waiting, watching, listening on New Year's Eve, the last day of 2003 . . . a downy woodpecker calls, then a hairy woodpecker, and a crow caws in the distance. More birds chime in: white-breasted nuthatches, titmice, red-bellied woodpeckers, and a red squirrel, an honorary bird given its wonderful chatter.

On the bike path behind me are a few in-line skaters and cyclists, but mostly just people out for a leisurely stroll with either children or a dog, all curious about what would cause me to sit here, motionless.

"See any birds?" asks the woman with her young boy. "Not yet" [a true answer, given that I had only heard those birds, but an evasively simple answer, too, hoping that my guests wouldn't linger too long]. "What we're looking for is the beavers. I think they made a little dam over there, but I don't see their home." "Their home is just beyond the [huge] dam; can't miss it." "Was it where all those sticks were, because we were pulling sticks from that pile." "Yes, that's their home." [Embarrassed laughter.]

A starling whistles and begins singing off to the right. In his song I hear killdeer and kestrel sounds, starlings being superb but underappreciated mimics (see page 139).

"You going to see something?" "Maybe." "What are you seeing in the past?" "Woodpeckers." "Oh, woodpeckers! We are looking for beavers; a gorgeous day; you don't get cold sitting there?" "Not yet." "Happy New Year." "Yes, to you, too."

"Hello." "Hello." "You should build yourself a little bonfire, huh?" It's a cheerful New Year's Eve crowd.

Amtrak! Right on schedule. The distant whistle to the right is the first clue, but seconds later the train is roaring by, the LEDs on my recorder a screaming red to warn that the electronics are severely overloaded. With my ears momentarily shut down, I now see how yellow the light is just before sunset, the sun's rays filtered by the pines and oaks behind me and shining in yellow splotches on the whitish, limbless trunks of the drowned forest before me. Yes, the beavers have done their thing, damming the waters, killing the trees, creating this woodpecker heaven. In almost every tree I can see where the woodpeckers have worked, with nesting cavities for the downy and hairy and red-bellied and pileated woodpeckers, and for the northern flickers, too.

It is as if she waited for the brief lull that followed the train, and I am ever so grateful (track 1-1; figure 1). To the far left, the northeast, I first hear her, calling in flight, a wild *kuk-kuk-kuk-kuk-kuk-kuk-kuk,* seven or eight a second, and I then see her, too, in undulating flight, coming right toward me. It is a six-second announcement she makes as she approaches, *kuk-kuk-kuk-kuk-kuk-kuk-kuk,* and then *Thunk!* as she lands in a beanpole of a tree trunk perhaps 30 feet to the right of the nest cavity and about 20 feet up. She continues calling, *kuk-kuk-kuk-kuk,* more slowly now, and a little lower-pitched; my eyes are glued to her features. A female! A young female! Her scarlet red crest is raised and glowing in the evening sun, her malar stripe black, her pitch-black eye as intense as her calls are now wild and uneven, the spacing irregular, a loud, laughing, primeval cackle.

PILEATED
WOODPECKER

For a good half minute she perches there, calling just 20 yards away, flaunting all her features. What a magnificent creature, this largest of North American woodpeckers, the better part of a power-packed pound, 10 times the weight of the downy woodpecker that I heard earlier. Her outstretched wings span two and a half feet, all black except for the white patch at the base of her outer flight feathers. Ah, and look at those massive feet, two toes in front, two in back, the woodpecker's zygodactyl pattern. I note the stiffened tail feathers, propping her up against the vertical trunk; the distinctive head and neck pattern, black and white topped with a red crest, a yellowish brown crown between the crest and the bill. And the feature I most remember, the pitch-black eyes, confirming that she hatched just this past summer and is only half a year old.

And that chisel for a bill. And the tongue within, one of the wonders of the natural world. I have watched these woodpeckers feed, hammering away at some tree, then inserting the bill deeply into the tree, standing there motionless except for a quivering of the forehead. I could imagine that long,

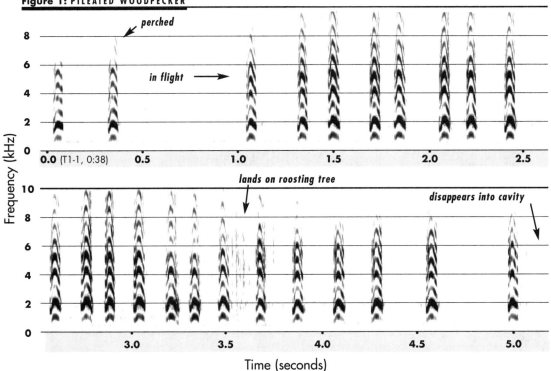

Figure 1: PILEATED WOODPECKER

Birdsong by the Seasons

sticky tongue protruding a good three inches beyond the bill and exploring the cavity within the tree. Anything not sticking to the tongue might be impaled on the barbs of the bony tip, then withdrawn into the bill and swallowed. What a marvelous tongue, lying on the floor of the closed mouth, extending to the back of the throat and then splitting into two, one half to each side of the neck. Small bones wrapped in muscles run to the back of the head, where they again become a single muscle envelope that then passes over the top of the head and down the forehead to the top of the bill. Although it is possible that a pileated woodpecker feeding on carpenter ants deep within a tree is wrinkling her forehead while thinking grand thoughts, it is the tongue muscles beneath the skin that make her brow quiver.

My lady woodpecker pauses in her calling for a second, utters a single *kuk,* pauses another second, and then, over just a few seconds, gradually picks up the pace and the pitch, followed by a two-second burst of her most intense calling as she launches from her perch and swoops down to her nesting cavity, calling briefly at the entrance at a more leisurely pace before popping inside.

I check my watch: 3:44 P.M.

"Good afternoon; whatcha seeing?" "A pileated woodpecker." "Hmmm; if you ever get to Gate 29, or was that 30, at Quabbin [Reservoir], plowed all the way down, I saw six turkeys down there."

There she is again, just her head sticking out of the entrance. It's 3:50 P.M. What's she up to now? I study her head again, confirming all the features I had seen before. It is a young female, almost certainly the one who was raised in this very hole during the summer and captured on film by countless photographers. And in three minutes she disappears into the cavity.

For another 45 minutes I sit, reflecting, watching, listening, and enjoying

Figure 1. The loud, cackling, primeval *kuk-kuk-kuk-kuk* of a young female pileated woodpecker on her final approach to her winter roosting cavity. She's been out foraging (and socializing, I'd like to think) for about eight and a half hours, but now she returns, calling loudly as she ends her day. In this sonagram, the first two calls are the last of a series given from a perch just 10 yards from the nesting cavity, and then she's airborne, flying the last 10 yards in a little over two seconds (from 1.0 to 3.5 seconds). See (and hear, on track 1-1) the foot noise at 3.6 seconds as she lands, and for another second and a half she calls, after which the scuffles of her feet on the cavity's entrance are the last sounds heard from her on this New Year's Day 2004. As with other sonagrams throughout the book, please note that the code in the lower left tells where you can listen to this particular sound; for this sonagram, "T1-1, 0:38" tells you that these sounds are on CD 1, track 1, beginning at 0:38.

the smiling faces of inquisitive passersby. This young pileated seems to be first to her roosting place, as I still hear all of the other birds in the area. A bluebird calls *tuwee tuwee,* and high overhead I hear *jip jip, jip jip jip,* calls of either a crossbill or a redpoll flying by.

"What's that guy doing?" asks the child with the woman. "He's sitting here watching that hole in the tree, because there's a great big woodpecker sleeping in that tree overnight." "Jingle bells, jingle bells [the little boy sings as they walk away], oh what fun it is to ride, in a one-horse open sleigh, HEY . . . HEY . . ." and into the distance he fades.

That was yesterday afternoon, almost 15 hours ago. Fifteen hours! What does she do in that cavity overnight for 15 hours? She sleeps some, no doubt, but for the entire 15 hours? I imagine being cramped in her small cavity, but she must be comfortable, cozy even. But now I wait for her, to hear how she greets the day. Will she emerge as emphatically as she went to roost? Or will she slip quietly into the day? I will soon know.

The great horned owls continue to call. I wonder where she goes during the day, how far? Does she meet any other pileateds? Does she have a prospective mate, a male she meets and spends much of the day with? Or is she still single? And just how does she find enough food during the day to sustain her through these long winter nights?

At 6:54 A.M., still 25 minutes before sunrise, I hear the first day birds awakening, a subtle chorus of high-pitched calls from what must be a junco flock that has roosted nearby. Two minutes later crows caw far to the east, followed soon by chickadees and nuthatches. They are my signal to begin recording, as I want to capture the sounds of her departure.

Recorder slung over my shoulder, headphones slipped over my ears, I aim the sight of my parabolic microphone at the cavity's entrance. I will now hear every peep from her, every scratch of those zygodactyl feet on her roosting cavity, and as she emerges any *kuk-kuk-kuk* will blow me away.

More birds awaken, the bluebirds and goldfinches and the red squirrel, as I hear the *tuwee tuwee* off to the left, the *per-chick-o-ree per-chick-o-ree* flight notes overhead, and the chatter behind me.

There's her head! It's 7:02, 17 minutes before sunrise. She faces to her left. With my binocular vision, I see only her, but as she eyes me with her right eye, she also sees everything on the other side of her head with her left eye. In 30 seconds she's gone, down into the cavity again.

At 7:10 she sticks her head out just briefly, for five seconds, then disappears again. She's getting restless, it would seem. A half minute later a hairy woodpecker calls; it's the first woodpecker I have heard. A minute later the redpolls or crossbills call *jip jip* overhead.

At 7:12 she's back. First it's her head, then half her body is poised at the cavity entrance. She swings her head to the left, then to the right, while I try to imagine what she sees with an eye on each side of her head. She then cocks her head, the right eye toward the ground, the left skyward. What does she see? What is she thinking? Does she hear how the world has awakened around her, the downy and hairy woodpeckers now both calling, starlings whistling and singing, nuthatches *yank*ing, goldfinches calling *per-chick-o-ree* as they commute overhead, crows cawing in the distance, the red squirrel behind me chattering away?

Five minutes of looking is apparently enough, and at 7:17 she erupts from the cavity, flying to her left, to the tree from which she swooped to the cavity 15½ hours ago. She taps the tree once with her bill, then climbs, tapping some more, until she's at perhaps twice the height of her roosting cavity, and then she launches into the air to the northeast, the direction from which she came yesterday, flying off into the distance and disappearing two minutes before official sunrise. Her only sounds have been those of her feet, her wings, and her bill. Not a peep did she utter as she greeted the new year.

I'm surprised, even disappointed. How could she greet the new day so unceremoniously? Shouldn't there be a loud *kuk-kuk-kuk-kuk-kuk-kuk-kuk-kuk* to announce the day, or a drumroll on a nearby tree? "Nope," I hear her say. Perhaps, I think, she has saved her theatrics for the distant place to which she flies. Perhaps. But if so, then why the grand entry here last night at her roosting cavity?

Now hooked on sharing this New Year's Day with this young woodpecker, I return in the late afternoon, stationing myself again at the roosting cavity. It's 3:20, and if she keeps the same schedule as yesterday, she'll arrive in 24 minutes. I lower the headphones over my ears, start the recorder, and aim the parabola in the direction from which I expect her to arrive. Now focused solely on the sounds about me, I hear overhead the jet airplane and the rustle of last year's oak leaves in the wind. In-line skaters whiz by behind me, a child yells in the distance, horns honk.

"You could probably be arrested for that." To my immediate left stands my friend John Green, ardent naturalist and photographer, commenting on my appearance and my no doubt nefarious activities. He quickly tells me how exciting a summer it was watching the woodpeckers in this nesting cavity, how on the Fourth of July he spent eight hours here. (I missed it all, as I spent the summer bicycling across the country.) There were two young birds, he explains, a male and a female, and their voices changed as they aged. And the adult male did most of the feeding. And—

I interrupt: "I'd love to talk more, but I need to excuse myself, as I don't want to miss what I hope will happen here. In just 10 minutes, at 3:44, she'll arrive. But no guarantees, you understand. You're welcome to stay, but please be as quiet as possible." As I turn away, another voice pops up. "What are you doing?" I ignore the question, hoping that John will quietly explain.

I return to listening, listening for any clue to her arrival. Behind me I hear the *swish-swish* of polyester, the *clomp-clomp* of walking steps. Another *swish-swish* and *clomp-clomp*, this one faster, jogging. Nuthatches. And the Amtrak! Drat, same time as yesterday, I should have known—please hurry, I think, get by us before she arrives. It seems an eternity, but the train passes, the horn soon blowing in the distance toward Amherst. In the relative quiet again, I hear a red-breasted nuthatch, distant traffic, a bicyclist behind me, the distant *beep-beep-beep* of something big in reverse. A child on a scooter behind me pauses, then apparently moves on, all heard over my headphones. "Trust me, she's my best friend, but . . . ," then silence as the couple passes, the conversation resuming in muffled tones down the path. I sense three shadows behind me, at least four of us standing here, waiting, watching, listening, though perhaps a larger crowd has now gathered. Whoever is behind me, they are quiet, and that's all that matters.

Kuk-kuk-kuk-kuk-kuk-kuk-kuk (track 1-1). There she is! Or, rather, where is she? The parabolic microphone and headphones don't give me the directional cues that my unaided ears would provide. I sense she's to the right of where I'm aiming, so I swing the parabola to the right, the *kuk-kuk-kuk-kuk-kuk-kuk-kuk* becoming louder and then fading as I pass her. I swing the parabola back to the loudest point, then raise and lower the parabola, looking for the "sweet spot" where she is the loudest. Quickly I'm on her, the sight atop my parabola pointing to the very tops of those distant trees, perhaps 100 yards away. I shift my head left, then right, trying to catch a glimpse of her, but to no avail. She's up there, though, I'm sure, as my trusty parabola, my big ear, doesn't lie.

When I first heard her, it was a frenzied burst of calling, high-pitched and fast-paced, lasting perhaps only two seconds, probably the last two seconds of her flight into those trees. Over the next five or so seconds, her calling tapered to four or five calls a second, then down to two as she now calls from the tops of the trees.

Then about 10 seconds of silence. Except in my headphones I can hear her tapping on the tree with her bill, scuffling her feet on the trunk.

She then resumes her wild calling, but she's still perched, giving at most five calls a second, sometimes two, an occasional second of silence, overall almost a minute of this irregular, untamed voice cackling into my ears.

Then silence again, almost a minute.

Shattering the silence is her frenzied in-flight calling, becoming louder in my headphones, and five or six seconds later I see her landing in a tree only 40 yards away. As she perches, the pace of calling quickly tapers to five, then four, then three or two a second.

She's perched only 10 seconds before she launches into the air again, making her final approach to the roosting hole. Flying above and to the right of the cavity, she calls loudly, banks to her right, the *kuk-kuk-kuk-kuk-kuk-kuk-kuk* from her bill and the *swoosh* of her wings louder and louder in my ears. She then swoops to the cavity, her feet hitting the entrance with a *thunk*. For a second she perches there, calling a few last times, then disappears into the cavity.

I search for words to describe what I have just seen and heard and felt. None come. In my searching, I remind myself that this is the first day of my retirement from the university, effective just hours ago, at midnight on New Year's Eve. I feel younger, 10 years younger, no, 30 or 40 is more like it. Joy. Rapture. Dancing down a yellow brick road and other wonderfully silly thoughts come to mind. Giddy. Excited. Happy. Content. Here is Life, celebrated in a single bird, a young bird who has the rest of a promising life ahead of her, as I realize that I do, too.

Deep inside, a riotous tumult of emotions celebrate the moment, but being the cool-headed professional that I am, I maintain my composure and hold the parabola aimed at the nest hole, thinking that there might be an encore of some kind. Ten seconds pass, 20, a minute, but I soon realize she's in for the night. I glance at my watch. It's 3:46 P.M., right on schedule.

As I lower my parabola, signaling the end of her performance, cheers and applause erupt from behind me.

2

The Harbingers of Spring (Robins) in Their Winter Roost

Monday, January 2, 3:00 P.M.
Whately, Massachusetts

I HAVE DRIVEN the half-hour from my Amherst home, across the Connecticut River on the Sunderland Bridge, south to Whately, then turned west onto a little-traveled road on the very western edge of the Connecticut River Valley. About a mile in, just before the road rises into the foothills of the Berkshires, I pulled off to the right, just beyond the old tobacco barn.

In front of me, 25-foot firs extend about 200 yards to the north and 100 yards east to west, so densely packed that it's impossible to walk among them. It is here, I say to myself in disbelief, in the shelter of these overgrown Christmas trees, where thousands upon thousands of robins will come to spend the night. *Robins*—the harbingers of spring, soon to be here, in midwinter, by the thousands.

I look about, admiring this winter scene. Just a few hundred yards to the west rises the 500-foot-high forested ridge that extends around to the north, protecting this winter roost from the worst of the winter winds. Behind me, across the road, is a smaller patch of these dense firs, and smaller scattered islands dot the landscape to the northeast, too, where some robins will settle for the night. Most of them, though, should be right here among these firs.

Today I begin my winter vigil with the robins. I am eager to see them roost and see them depart, but most of all I want to be here among the robins in the worst of winter conditions, when the Arctic winds attack. Now it is a balmy 36°F, but I will watch for one of those winter storms to beat all winter storms, my goal being to spend the night among the robins, to try to understand what it is like to be a robin wintering in western Massachusetts under such conditions.

There they come, the first flock of them, about 30 in all. I check my watch: 3:18 P.M. They fly from the east, overshooting the roost and landing in the tall trees to the southwest. Other flocks of 50, 100, and more soon follow in waves, all of them flying past the roost and into the tall trees beyond.

By 3:30, my friend Mary Alice has joined me, and we are overwhelmed. Clouds of robins drift overhead, often in layers, the upper cloud moving in one direction, the lower in another. Wave after wave arrives, mostly from the east, some from the southeast: "Look, over there . . . Oh my goodness . . . Wow . . . Look behind you . . . Here comes a huge flight from the east . . . Oh my gosh!"

With our binoculars, we look to the east, first at the nearest flock, then at the one beyond that, and as far as the resolving power of our binoculars allows, we can see specks of robins growing in the distance. It is like watching airplanes landing at a busy airport, for beyond each plane can be spotted yet another, and another. Or like the saying about the fleas that have little fleas upon them,

> Beyond the first wave of robins was another just behind 'em,
> The second wave followed by a third, and so on ad infinitum.

I watch a flock of about 200, a broad north-south front of robins arriving from the valley and moving west. Over the roost they shift directions together, first to the northwest, then to the southwest, with some disagreement as a splinter group begins a dive directly into the roost, but then all of them eventually fly northwest to the ridge.

By 3:45, the trees in the roost are adorned with robins calling *tut tut tut* and sometimes a sharp *piik piik,* but the vast majority of robins are staging in the trees to the west. At 4:00 and still at 4:15, the sky to the northeast is speckled with incoming robins. Others are hopping about on the open ground, some perching nearby in small deciduous trees — they are everywhere!

By 4:20, the tide has shifted, with birds now moving back into the roost from the staging areas. There the robins jockey for their night's position, the clamor intensifying (track 1-2), gentle *tut tut*s giving way to sharper *piik piik* calls, to some squeals, and often to bill snapping, a sharp, loud clapping sound used no doubt when two robins found themselves face-to-face in quarters too close. But no song — none of the sweet, melodious caroling of the robin's spring song. Ominously, a great horned owl hoots from the nearby woods to the south; it is a female, as indicated by the relatively high frequency and large number of notes in her hooting, and she's no doubt keen on feasting and nourishing her body to prepare for the eggs she will soon lay.

By 4:35, four minutes after the official sunset, we see no birds in the air, and in the roost they are quieting down, too, settling in for the night.

How many robins? During the Northampton Christmas Count, on December 19, the number of roosting robins had been estimated conservatively at 2,500. Very conservatively, we thought, as surely there were thousands upon thousands more.

Tuesday, January 3

I am by myself this evening, just wanting to take in the spectacle one more time. I watch from the road at first, but then work my way up the slope to the northwest, near one of the main staging areas. There the robins are feeding on the fruits of the Oriental bittersweet, and after the majority of birds arrive from the east, just like the day before, the masses depart for a direct flight into the firs. Thousands fly over my head, many so close I feel I can almost reach out and grab them.

ROBINS

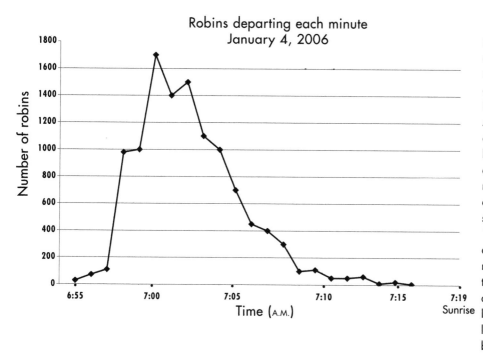

Robins departing each minute
January 4, 2006

Number of robins

Time (A.M.)

7:19 Sunrise

Figure 2. Robins departing their night roost on the morning of January 4, 2006. Beginning at 6:55 A.M., after a number of mourning doves had already departed, the exodus of robins started with a trickle and soon surged until well over 1,000 robins were departing each minute. The departure then tapered to a trickle again, the last of the robins leaving three minutes before the sun peeked over the horizon at 7:19.

Wednesday, January 4

A few hours later I am back, this time in the morning. I hope that the birds, after fasting all night, will make a direct flight from the roost toward their destination for the day. There should be some urgency in filling the stomach, I reason, and the birds should stream out of the roost in a way that lets me estimate their numbers more easily than when they arrive at night.

Sunrise is at 7:19 A.M., and by 6:30 I am waiting at the northeast corner of this fir stand, as I want to see the robins rise into the glowing sky to the southeast. Only Jupiter still shines brightly in the southern sky. With a gentle north wind and clear skies at 15°F, I'll rely on the robins to provide some warmth.

At 6:47, amid the loud *tut*s and *piik*s and squeals of the rustling robins, I hear the whistle of mourning dove wings and catch a glimpse of a single bird shooting out of the roost. In the next eight minutes I hear another 50 doves depart, the whistle of their wings giving them away.

At 6:55, the first robins depart. I count by twos — 2, 4, 6, 8, a total of 28 robins in a minute, all heading directly up into the southeast sky (figure 2).

I soon count by 10s, then by 50s, then try to lop off 100 robins at a time from the departing masses, estimating 72, 110, 980, and 1,000 for the next four minutes.

7:00. A hundred birds every three to four seconds! Seventeen hundred birds in this minute alone!

In the following minutes, I estimate 1400, 1500, 1100, 1000, 700, 450, 400, 300, 100, 119, 50, 50, 60, 10, 20, and 5 by 7:16 A.M. That seems to be it. A few robins linger in the firs, but no more are departing.

I stand motionless, searching for words to describe what I have just witnessed. Twenty-one minutes is what it took for this roost to unload. Who is that laughing? I realize that I am giggling out loud. The count comes to over 11,000. Dare I admit that number to anyone? Robins, the harbingers of spring, here, now, in the middle of winter, easily over 10,000 birds in this single stand of fir trees?

That evening I return with friends from the Hampshire Bird Club. We stand where I had the night before, just above the fir trees, up toward the ridge to the northwest, giving us a sweeping view of the valley. To the east, a gray cloud cover hugs the distant horizon, with a band of light blue sky above that, then a pink sky with grayish clouds intruding. Against a glowing backdrop of turquoise and lavenders and pastels, we watch the swarms of robins approaching. Trees beyond us are soon dripping with robins, those low in the underbrush feeding on the bittersweet fruits. Voices chime in almost continuously: "Look, look here! . . . It's incredible! . . . Like swarms of mosquitoes! . . . Oh, my golly! . . . Look at that! . . . They keep coming! . . . Look at this! Look at this! *Look at this!* . . . They're everywhere!" As the robins gather in the roost, a sharp-shinned hawk makes a pass, hoping for a late-afternoon meal. Other birds are around, too, a small flock of cowbirds calling from a nearby tree, flocks of cedar waxwings flying about and preparing to roost, and a lone red-tail screaming as it glides along the ridge.

How many robins? Thousands upon thousands. We agree that 10,000 is not an unreasonable estimate.

Saturday, January 7

I need to experience these robins in yet another way, not to stand back and count but rather to be *among them* as best I can when they depart. By 6:30 A.M., I have positioned myself adjacent to the roost, just to the east. The *tut*s and *piik*s and squeals and bill snapping surge until 6:54, when the birds begin boiling from the roost and streaming directly over me. Eyes closed, I listen, imagining myself among them, squabbling over airspace, the dull roar of hundreds and then thousands of robins whirring and squealing all about me (track 1-8). I hear an occasional mourning dove and waxwing and cowbird in the exodus; a great horned owl hoots in the distance, and a few blue jays and cardinals and juncos and chickadees call from the firs nearby. But mostly it is the robins, thousands upon thousands of them, with me among them, the departure slowing to a trickle by 7:15, just a few minutes before sunrise.

Sunday, January 8

From how far do these robins come to roost here? It's eight miles east across the valley to the Pelham hills, but another large robin roost is there. My long-time birding friend Dave Stemple (see page 133) and I hatch a small plan. He'll watch from his home in Hatfield Center, about three miles southeast of the roost, and I'll watch two miles beyond that, at the Connecticut River. I see no robins heading toward the roost, but at 3:55 P.M. about 50 robins appear in Dave's yard. A total of about 380 robins stop there, Dave reports, all eventually departing northwest toward the roost.

The next night Dave watches again. No birds stage in his yard this night; instead, they fly directly by, again heading toward the roost. Altogether, he estimates that he saw about 387 birds.

Friday, January 13

Never enough. After out-of-town trips that I could not cancel, I return, this time with Dave and his son Jason. We come with two video cameras, hoping somehow to capture the essence of the departure. Jason, a professional photographer, runs his camera continuously; I am sufficiently flustered that I capture only a couple of minutes.

Back at the Stemple house, we play our videos on the large-screen television, gawking at what we see. In the foreground are masses of robins taking flight, launching skyward, boiling up out of the fir trees; behind them are other robins, beyond them others, and so on, until in the distance there appears to be a grayish smoke in the air and swirling overhead, all robins. Many of them make a beeline out of the roost, but others reorient overhead, choosing to leave in a direction other than that in which the masses emerge from the roost. Over and over we play these videos to endless exclamations, never tiring of the spectacle.

How many? we inevitably ask ourselves. Thirty thousand seems a conservative estimate. More and more robins are using the roost this winter, the numbers having swollen in the last three weeks alone.

Sunday, January 15, 3:15 P.M.

Sunset is at 4:43, almost an hour and a half from now.

I have watched the weather for weeks now, waiting for a night like this. Already it is 13°F, and overnight it'll drop to 0. Add the northwest wind howling at well over 20 miles an hour, and the wind chill will make it feel much colder. Yes, I need to see and hear this classic harbinger of spring under these worst of winter conditions, as I sense that it is especially for a night like this that the robins come to their communal roost.

Knee-deep in snow, I walk down a narrow lane into the roost, stretching the 125-foot microphone cables from the car where I will listen to the point where my stereo microphones are perched atop my tripod. I'm amazed, as it's dead calm deep in the dense firs even though the wind howls above me. The birds have chosen their roost wisely, I sense; although it will be cold tonight, the robins will feel little wind chill, as the howling winds will pass over the firs but not through them.

And who will come to dine tonight? In an Arkansas roost during the late 1920s, barred owls, great horned owls, bobcats, and feral housecats ate themselves silly. Would I hear the "almost terrifying snarl" of a bobcat making a kill, or the barred owl's "unearthly hoots, squawks, and screams that sounded as if the demons of Pandemonium were paying a personal visit"? The author of those words felt that the robins defeated themselves, because they were easy prey in such a roost. Yes, the robins were easy prey, but each robin's chances of surviving the night were no doubt better when it joined other robins. This Hatfield roost lies within the territory of a single pair of great horned owls, for example, and one pair of owls can do just so much damage; if these robins were spread out through the entire valley and among many owl territories, the overall carnage would be much greater, and each individual's chances of survival would be poorer.

"The Whately roost." The words come easily now, but in robin-time this roost is quite recent. In all of Massachusetts from 1901 to 1950, when robins were true harbingers of spring, only two robins were seen on the annual Christmas Bird Count. Over 100 were first documented in 1951, over 1,000 in 1976, over 10,000 in 1995, over 50,000 in 1999 throughout the state, and I'm sure there are at least 30,000 in this roost alone this year, 2006. Smart farmers, these robins, as they eat the fruits of plants like Oriental bittersweet and distribute the seeds all over creation, ensuring more and more food as the years pass.

But where are these robins today? Back on January 2, the first robins appeared at 3:18 P.M., and we were overwhelmed with them by 3:30. Today there are no robins at 3:30, none at 3:45, none at 4:00, and none at 4:15. Except for the howling wind, it is deathly quiet. *There,* at 4:21, I hear the *tut* and *piik* from a few robins overhead; I spot them well above the roost, struggling against the northwest wind, and they drop directly into the roost. These robins *are* late: compared with January 2, sunset is 12 minutes later today, but the first robins are 63 minutes later. Others begin streaming into the roost now, too, all of them flying directly in, forgoing what had seemed a rather leisurely stop at the staging areas to the west on previous days. It was a tough day, I sense, with snow and cold through the night before, the winds and biting cold of today.

Listening through my headphones now, it is as if I stand with eyes closed in the roost itself, the robins arriving all around me (track 1-3). The wind roars in the treetops and up on the ridge to the west, but over that roar I can hear the *whoosh* of wings as the robins funnel in. One lands just to my left, *tut tut tut,* another to my right, *piik, piik,* giving way to a squeal as another flies in. A flock of mourning doves whistles by. By 4:40 the wing noises are continuous, now outroaring the wind itself, but relatively few birds are actually calling. The roar of wind and wings continues, minute after minute, with an occasional call and some bill snapping, but, oh my, the wings, the wings, as thousands upon thousands of birds are now coming in. Increasingly I hear more calling and loud thrashing about, no doubt the result of head-to-head clashes as so many robins crowd into so small a space.

By 5:00, 40 minutes after the first robins arrived, the roost is quieting, the roar of the wind gaining ground. Yes, by 5:05 it's definitely quieter, though single robins still fly about, and by 5:15 it is so quiet that I could never know by listening that I stand among so many robins. *Pffft,* to my right. A robin sneezing? Footsteps! Just to the left I hear something moving in the snow, then silence. In the wind and the cold, a tree snaps to my left up on the ridge, cracking sharply above the dull roar of the winter wind.

Other than the wind, it is silence that once again rules. Silence, among thousands and thousands of robins, not a peep out of them.

I'm getting colder here in the car, even though I have all of my winter layers on and am wrapped in a down sleeping bag to boot. I'll warm myself by going to see the almost full moon rise, I decide, walking up the ridge. A little before 6:00, right on schedule, there it is, but I'm no warmer for the effort.

At 6:20, back in the car, I settle in, listening some more. . . . Footsteps, and I startle, sitting up and looking warily out the window, only to remind myself that, with the headphones on, I am listening inside the roost, of course, not where I am sitting, so realistic are the microphones in capturing the sounds there. Something walks in the snow, from left to right (track 1-4). And what fantastic howling in the wind, as it surges and fades, only to come back again with a vengeance.

By 7:00, I know that I'm not going to make it. My plan was to outlast the robins, to listen the night through, but I'm getting colder and colder, my feet already numb. What hardy beasts they are, and what a wimp I am. I concede. Reluctantly, I put the recorder into the "cooler" I have brought for just this contingency. With four gallons of water in the bottom and two sleeping bags tucked around it, the cooler should stay warm enough here beside the barn until the morning, I reason, giving the recorder ample time to finish capturing sounds of the roost until shortly after midnight, when the recording disc will be full. I'll go home now and come back for the morning departure. Besides, all is quiet now, and perhaps there will be no action until daybreak.

Monday, January 16

Martin Luther King Day, I note. It's 5:30 A.M. I'm back. The car thermometer reads 3°F, and the winds have died considerably. Sitting in the car, I hook up a fresh recorder to the microphones and put the headphones on. Wow, what a contrast to the night before, what silence. After five minutes there's a small *peep* to the right, a sound I would have dismissed as nothing had I not known that thousands of robins were about me.

At 5:40, there's the distant noise of what sounds like a small avalanche of snow falling from a fir tree, the robins there erupting with *tut*s and *piik*s and many exploding into the air. The calling continues for one, two, three minutes, and then the robins quiet down. I hear one just to my right scratch itself, the leg no doubt reaching under the wing to scratch its head.

A few birds call, and there are the *pffft*s of what sound like sneezing robins all about me. Occasionally a lone robin flies about the roost. Trees up on the ridge explode in the frigid weather, some with a deep resonance echoing throughout the valley, others with a sharper, more hollow *pop*.

Overall, it is so quiet. I hear what must be a mouse chewing on something, an occasional robin adjusting its position on a perch, *tut* and *piik* calls in the distance and a few nearby. Another tree snaps . . . small *peep*s, sounds of seeming contentment . . . a soft warbling, as if a robin dreams of spring song.

By 6:30, I sense an increasing restlessness, with more calls and more fluttering about on the perches. A fit of that sneezing sweeps contagiously through the nearby robins. A great horned owl hoots, the first I've heard this morning. Tension seems to build, the owl hooting again, and again, five times over five minutes, the robins' calls becoming louder and more continuous, and at 6:38 I hear the roar of wings, then another roar, and another, as great hordes of robins lift off simultaneously (track 1-7). This is it! This is the moment! Accompanied by the continued hooting of the owl, thousands of robins now burst from the firs, streaming overhead, the roar of wings and continuous calling almost deafening in my headphones (track 1-8).

By 6:55 the majority have departed, and by 7:00 it is far quieter. I listen until 7:20, hearing also a few cowbirds, waxwings, and carduelines, perhaps crossbills or redpolls.

Walking around the roost, I find tracks of rabbits, squirrels, and a larger four-legged creature, perhaps a bobcat. A few robins linger, one hopping about in the lower branches, a casualty of perhaps the cold or some nighttime encounter. Other than that, the roost appears tidy.

Back home now, headphones on, I sit at my computer and listen eagerly to those five hours that I recorded between 7:00 P.M. and midnight. Then I listen to the good parts again. Wow, what a night!

What fantastic howling of the wind; every once in a while the gusts are so strong it seems that the entire world is going to blow away, trees up on the ridge snapping in the bitter blasts, some large trees thundering to earth. Through some of these blasts, the robins are mum, in others a wave of *tut*s sweeps through the roost, and in one there's a wave of sneezelike *pfft*s. Sitting in my office, I put on a vest to stay warm.

At 9:20 P.M., two snowmobiles pass by and head into the woods to the northwest, returning an hour and a quarter later, the robins quiet to both passes.

But it is the restlessness within the roost that most intrigues me, the first episode beginning just a little before 8:00 after a relative calm for the previous three hours. In the howling winds, robins dash about the roost, thrashing and resettling, and seven minutes after the first flights, I hear what must be a robin squealing in its death throes (track 1-5). Five such mass disturbances occur in the 25 minutes between 7:49 and 8:15 P.M.

And then it is only the howling wind and snapping trees and an occasional single robin flying about or sounding off, until 10:29 P.M., when once again there's a massive disturbance, panicked robins soon hurtling past the microphones and resettling within the roost. Again and again I hear that odd mini-avalanche sound followed by a burst of robin wings on the air, seconds later the *swoosh* of robins flying past the microphones, the *tut*s and *piik*s of discontent sweeping through the roost.

Who whooo whoooooo who who, in the distance, and at that instant I realize what I have been hearing. The source of the robins' consternation is a great horned owl, of course, and now I can both hear and see the entire sequence. The mystery sound is the owl flying into a fir tree, making a grab for a perched robin; that's the sound I had mistaken for a small avalanche of snow falling from a tree. Then nearby robins hurtle into the air, resettling about the roost and flying past my microphones. Again and again I hear these mass disturbances, the most telling occurring just two minutes before midnight: I hear the distant attack, robins taking flight and seconds later flying past my microphones, and 40 seconds after the attack, a great horned owl hoots near the microphone (track 1-6). As I listen to this sequence again and again, I hear more of a chortle than a hoot from this owl. Two more times the owl attacks before my recorder gasps its last, turning off at 12:10 A.M., leaving what happened during the early-morning hours to the imagination.

3

An All-nighter Among the Wading Birds in the Everglades

Shark Valley, January 29–30
Everglades National Park

GREAT BLUES AND little blues, tricolors and greens, great and snowy egrets, black-crowned and yellow-crowned night-herons, white and glossy ibis, and wood storks, oh my! As I bike north along the tram road, they swarm about me in an early-morning frenzy, flushing from the road before me and from the canal on the left and the wet prairie on the right, hundreds upon hundreds of big, flashy south Florida birds, the unearthly squawks of the great blues escorting me, the birds protesting loudly as they have all night long.

Yes, *all night long,* and what a night it has been! It was just last year that I learned of the wading bird roost at the end of the tram road at Shark Valley in the Everglades, and I knew then that I needed to spend a night here, listening from the time the birds arrived until the time they departed the next morning. I learned, too, that the park gate closes at 6:00 P.M. but that bicyclists are welcome anytime, so late yesterday afternoon I left the car outside the gate and then biked the seven miles south to the end of the road, where the observation tower overlooks the roost and the saw grass prairie extends in all directions. In tow behind my take-everywhere, folding Bike Friday was its airline suitcase, which becomes a trailer, now well stocked with recording gear and various supplies that would see me through the night.

It's now about 8:00 on the morning of January 30, and I have left the roost and am biking back to civilization, trailer in tow, the birds of the night having also left the roost and now flying and foraging all about me. Yes, what a night, dizzying, euphoric. My thoughts are racing among the sounds and sights of this nightly gathering in a desperate attempt to secure them all in long-term memory. I try to control the process, replaying the highlights of these last 18 hours in sequence in the hope that an orderly filing of the memories will lead to better retrieval later.

I remember the alligators as I biked in yesterday afternoon. Road hazards, they line the road, little ones and big ones and monsters. It is a bit humbling to know how fast they can run and how powerful they are, but comforting to know that they usually just lie there. They are reptiles, "lower" vertebrates, my subconscious tells me. But I remind myself that by some standards birds are also reptiles, merely dinosaurs with feathers, much closer relatives to these alligators than one would think at first glance.

The waders. Yes, they are everywhere I look to the left and right of the tram road, and little do they know that we will spend the night together, along with thousands upon thousands of others that I hope will converge at the roost from all over creation.

Turkey vultures. Drifting lazily over the prairie, they sniff for a meal as they glide on the gentle south wind, some near and some mere specks floating in the distance, some low and some enjoying what must be a magnificent vista from on high.

Tourists abound. It's Sunday, after all, but the last tram load will be gone by about 5:00 P.M., and then, except for a few lingering cyclists, I'll no doubt have the place to myself. It's a new moon, the sky dark and heavily overcast with a threat of rain. Who could possibly want to be out here under such conditions?

The observation tower. Walking up the spiral rampway onto the viewing platform high above, I sweep my eyes slowly from east to south to west, seeing nothing but saw grass prairie and isolated hummocks where a few trees huddle. White birds decorate the prairie; a few great egrets are aloft, bouncing along on slow wingbeats. Below me is the pond, arcing from the left to the right, then extending north, and trees, wonderful trees, a veritable forest of them in this man-made roosting oasis.

I look and listen, breathing in this scene. Four painted turtles squeeze up on a log in the pond below. A soft-shelled turtle swims as gracefully underwater as the cormorant nearby, both so awkward on land but so slick underwater with those foot-propellers out behind. A kingfisher rattles, followed minutes later by a splash and a catch, the bird retreating to a perch to toss its prey into the air and swallow it, yes, headfirst. A purple gallinule forages on the lily pads, magically walking on water. Isolated large early birds of all kinds perch here and there in the roost. I hear the occasional sharp *skeow* of a green heron, the deep, hoarse trumpeting of a great blue, *fraaahnk, fraaahnk, fraak, fra.* Gnatcatchers wheeze, cardinals chip, yellowthroats *cjerp,* crows caw, grackles grackle, red-winged blackbirds *konk-la-ree.* There's a *killdeer.* Small splashes in the water down below. A considerable south wind still blows, but it will die through the night, I'm sure.

And anhingas (track 1-29). Both males and females perch in the open just across the water in the trees below me; most are paired, and as one sits on the nest, the mate perches nearby. Among them there's an almost constant click and chatter, undulating, *chitter chitter chitter chee cheur chitter chitter,* intensifying when mates trade places on the nest or when a squabble over perch rights breaks out. And there's what sounds like the loud *whirrrrrrrrrrrrr* of fish line pulled out over the drag on a spinning reel—also an anhinga. What heavy and labored wingbeats, too, so much effort to loft this sleekest of underwater swimmers into the air, so much body-chaos and thrashing about as it returns to perch.

The arrival. At first it is just a trickle, beginning a little after 5:00—there are egrets and herons of all kinds, singly for the most part, but they're overshadowed by the white ibis, a few singles at first, then a dozen or more together, soon streaming in from all directions. They're mostly the adults, all white with black-tipped wings and reddish bills and legs fore and aft; they're strong fliers, coming in just over the treetops, hundreds upon hundreds of them, largely silent on the wing, but what a commotion of grunts and groans they make as they perch and settle in, at times sounding like a barnyard of bleating lambs. Snow-white birds against a darkening sky, against the darkening prairie, streaming past me, the groaning and moaning and bleating—never to be forgotten. Almost lost in this spectacle are the hundreds of brown and white young birds from last summer, but I work to secure them in memory, too.

Also incoming, a tricolored heron over the water from the left, quietly, though its swooping and looping and darting flight speaks volumes, a sheer exuberance for life, for simply *being* here and now . . . but perhaps I read too much into it.

Snail kites arrive silently, one by one, the white patches at the bases of their tails glowing in the twilight, six of them coming to land in the same tree, just off to the left.

And the departure of night-herons (tracks 1-9, 1-10). Amid the growing commotion of the day birds arriving, the darker night-herons leave, birds of the day and night crossing at dusk, now a steady exodus of barking *quork*s and *quark*s and *what*s streaming past me, mostly low-pitched, of the black-crowned variety. But some are higher, and some in between. Some must be yellow-crowned, I reason, as they sound a bit more crowlike. Can I be sure? Black-crowns lower, yellow-crowns higher? In the growing darkness, I strain to see these birds, glimpsing mostly the stocky black-crowns, their gull-like, rapid flight so different from that of other herons.

By sunset, about 6:10 P.M., it is already dark under these heavy clouds, and most of the roosting birds seem to be in their places, though a few ibis still arrive and a few night-herons depart.

Birds of a feather . . . squawk together. About 20 minutes after sunset, in the gathering calm of the roost, off to the left a green heron sounds off, *skeow,* followed by another, and another, their *skeow*s sweeping through the marsh, the last one just barely audible in the distance. I tallied about 25 calls over a half minute or so, at least a dozen individuals involved, and then they were silent. Though this roost is a mix of species, birds of a kind seem to stick together, vocally if not physically.

And great blue herons, too (track 1-11; figure 3). One roosts just below me to the south, others nearby to the left and right, still others scattered through the roost. Their trumpeting is also contagious; rarely does one sound off without the others. *Fraaahnk, fraaahnk, fraak, fra!* Each rendition seems slightly different in the number of notes and the quality of their delivery, sometimes nearly a piercing shriek, sometimes low and throaty. What unearthly sounds from these creatures, so expressive, so prehistoric-sounding, so like a mortally wounded bird in its death throes.

By 7:00, the insects dominate the soundscape, in a high-pitched, continuous chorus of males seeking mates, though I must work to hear them, as my ears are trained to hear the birds through and beyond such noise. Fireflies *dah-dah-dah-di-di-dit* as I read their code, several long glows followed by several shorter ones. What interesting sounds they would add to the night if only each flash were a brief whistle.

About 8:00, there's a screech-owl, no, two (track 1-12). The male sings just below me — it's the "bounce" song, a series of about a hundred rapidly repeated whistles, all on the same pitch, over roughly three seconds. The female responds in kind, though on a slightly higher pitch, back to the northeast.

By 9:00, I take one last look before settling in for the Big Listen. To the east, the horizon glows with the lights of Miami; to the north the lights of the Miccosukee village shine brightly along the Tamiami Trail; but to the south and west the horizon is dark, as is the sky overhead. In the roost, though, I can see the ibis glowing in the dark. They have settled into three groups, two smaller ones to the left and right just in front of me, and a third group with well over 2,000 birds another 100 yards beyond them.

Okay. Enough looking—now it's time to just listen. I mount the stereo parabolic microphone on the tripod and aim it south into the roost. The microphone cable leads back to the recorder and headphones under the mosquito netting, where I can now rest comfortably. With the headphones on and my eyes closed, the sensitive microphone will whisk me away on sound journeys throughout the night.

And what a symphony of sound it is! Small splashes in the water speak of, what, fish splashing about? Or night-herons working the shoreline? The leopard frogs are warming up, just a few at a time—there should be a resounding chorus later. And those occasional loud popping sounds? What are they? They're unlike any bird noise that I know, like tiny balloons exploding. Fish. Must be fish. The huge splashes tell of alligators, as no other beast I've seen out here could possibly move that much water. Ibis moan and flutter about in the roost, great blues trumpet, and . . .

Rails. King rails. There's an occasional outburst of calling, a descending, accelerating *cheup-cheup-cheup-chep-chep-chep-chp-chp-chp-chp*, and it's never just one, but instead the contagious calling sweeps through the marsh, each pair of rails responding from its own territory (track 1-9).

Limpkin mania. Wow, what a racket. What unearthly screams and wails by the males now, up to a dozen within earshot, I'd say, but the closest are a few hundred yards away. I hear the females chime in, too, *gon, gon*. I must get to know these birds better, I vow (see "The Limpkins of Corkscrew Swamp," page 34). Like the rails, these limpkins are territorial, each pair on its own territory and not flocking here to the roost like the other birds.

Drifting off now, suspended in the soundscape, floating lightly about, I listen, taking in each creature in turn, the soft splashes down below of the fish and frogs, the insects humming, the ibis moaning and fluttering, herons . . . And a

GREAT BLUE HERON

split second is all it takes to achieve full consciousness again, that primitive fight-or-flight response kicking in, adrenaline surging through the body, for right beside me must be — what? — a roaring bear or, no, an alligator. The body says run, but the mind holds sway, though barely. No alligator could have climbed the spiral concrete ramp of this tower to be here beside me, I try to convince myself, though I strain my eyes in the darkness to be sure. Ah, the head-

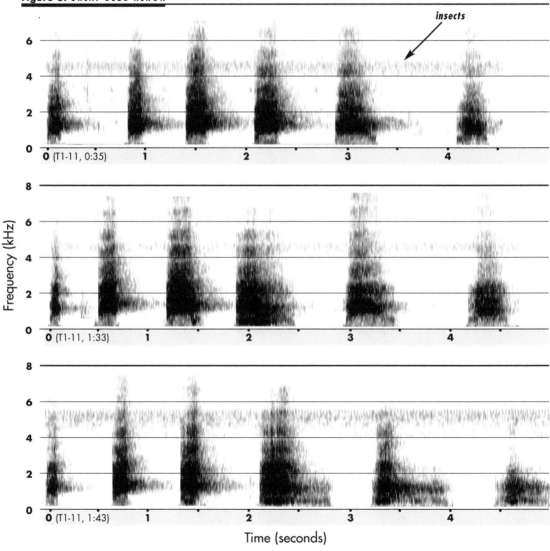

Figure 3: GREAT BLUE HERON

Birdsong by the Seasons

phones. Only once I slip them off can I be sure that the alligator bellows from down below. But what a roar it is (track 1-27), an alligator seeking love, if alligators do such, though for me it was a (fortunately brief) reminder of what it must be like to be a little lower on the food chain than where I'm comfortable.

I drift again, listening, 11:30 P.M. . . . And before I know it, nearly three hours have elapsed, the sounds in the headphones having taken me on countless journeys. I listen again, now fully conscious.

Great blues. Their outlandish declarations, *fraaahnk, fraaahnk, fraak, fra!* by far the loudest of sounds and often contagiously sweeping across the roost, have come to be my favorite sounds of the night (track 1-11).

Leopard frogs. More and more of them chuckle down below now.

The Unknowns. Some of these mystery sounds are low and heronlike, but some are high-pitched, like screeching bats or fighting raccoons. Who are these creatures of the night?

The roost . . . the rustling and fluttering, the occasional sneezing fits, the nearly continuous soft moans, the grunts, some crying out in the night — where have I heard this before? Yes, I remember, it was the 2003 Bike Across Kansas. Hundreds of cycling enthusiasts were headed east across the state, and my son and I were headed west across the country, our paths crossing at Tribune on the western edge of the state. Rather than pitch the tent outside in the threatening weather, we laid our sleeping bags on the floor along with all the others in the high-school gym. The nearly continuous rustling, coughing and sneezing, moaning and grunting, snoring, and some crying out in the night, the sounds from a roost of Kansas cyclists and Everglades birds not all that different.

A screech-owl visits again, down below, but how disagreeable this name for a bird with such a mellow whistled tune. Far in the distance, oh so faintly, *who-cooks-for-you,* a barred owl.

About 5:00. The night-herons return. A burst of *quarks* by who knows how many birds, a dozen or so perhaps, over 15 seconds. Almost all blackcrowns, I believe. A few have been here through the night, but the ones I hear

Figure 3. There's nothing "pretty" about the sonagram of a great blue heron giving its death-throes squawk, one might say. The sounds are atonal and harsh, spanning a broad frequency spectrum. But see the differences in rhythm and duration of notes among the three examples, and then listen to the differences in sound quality among the examples selected for the CD (track 1-11).

now seem to be flying in, returning to their day roost two hours before sunrise. And then they're silent again.

Gallinule, or moorhen? I've heard sharp *pip*s through the night, almost sure it was a purple gallinule, but now I hear a series of calls ending in more of a whine, suggesting it is a common moorhen. Are both species calling, or only one and I just don't know who is who? I wish I knew them better (track 1-13).

Pig frogs. Their guttural grunts surge now in the pond below, sounding so much like a herd of buoyant swine. There's another frog in there, too, rubbing its finger over a wet balloon, or so it sounds, *squeeek,* a Cuban tree frog, I believe.

6:00. Night-herons again, black-crowns, another caucus of quarkers, two just down in front of me, several others off to the left and right. Yes, birds of a feather, and frogs, too, they do stick together.

I hear my first yellowthroat song, checking my watch at 6:20, the first sure vocal sign of daylight approaching. The books say his song is a repeated *witch-i-ty,* but here in the Everglades it's more of a *witch-i-ty-ty-ty,* these southern birds adding an extra syllable or two.

The anhingas are winding up, too, crackling and rattling, the line playing out rapidly from a few spinning rods about the nesting colony. Whoever sits on the nest overnight, whether he or she, there's always some commotion about the upcoming exchange of incubation duties.

Now I hear night-herons, outbursts of *quark*s all around, it being light enough that I can see these birds returning. I'm hearing and seeing mostly black-crowns, only an occasional yellow-crown.

The transition from night to day. For some time now the eastern sky has been lightening, with just a hint of pink through the heavy clouds. Frogs and insects have quieted. Yellowthroats sing, a cardinal and Carolina wren now, too, as a distant crow caws. A few herons depart, tricolors and little blues and great blues mostly, typically one by one, each on its own schedule, it seems.

A great blue rises, squawking loudly on the wing, leaving the roost, flying off to the left (track 1-11).

Liftoff! With no obvious advance notice, just four minutes before 7:00, hundreds of miniature bleating white lambs take to the air, the white ibis streaming off in all directions, many past the tower where I now gawk (track 1-14) . . . And again, just minutes later, and again, and again, in four mass waves of white streaming over the landscape, all 2,500 or so birds departing in less than 10 minutes. Mentally I click frame after frame, my memory now on motor drive as I try to secure this scene forever. Into the distance they stream, though a dozen circle and land just below, soon actively foraging, with heads turned this way and that as they work the shallow waters.

What are those sounds I now hear from the roost (track 1-15)? With the white ibis gone, there's a freedom for others to be heard. But what, who? Like white ibis with an attitude, lower-pitched, hoarser, more pig- than lamblike, but all I see are the lingering great egrets in the roost. Liftoff again, but this time it's glossy ibis, so dark in the roost that I never saw them, 35 heading off to the west, 15 to the north. Yes, those were the glossy ibis I heard . . . birds of a feather yet again.

A wood stork. I have been eyeing this massive bird lingering out in the roost, all white except for those long dark legs, head, and drooping bill. Did he (or she?) spend the night? I think so. It now lifts off, flapping one, two, three, four beats a second, with each stroke the wings whistling through the air, legs soon dangling behind, head far out front, the black of its wings and tail now a stark contrast to the snow-white body. One, two, three beats a second now as it shifts into cruising speed (track 1-16). It flies directly at me, then veers to the right, just in front of me, then whistles north off into the distance, as if a majestic exclamation mark at the end of a long night.

I look around, listening, marveling at how night has yielded to day. A few night-herons linger atop the trees in the roost, but they'll soon drop down, preferring to roost by day in the cover of the trees. A number of great egrets linger, too, as if in no hurry, though one by one they drift off into the prairie. Now it's mainly the anhingas going about their business, and a few songbirds calling or singing.

Yes, what a night! Six miles into my return trip north to the Shark Valley entrance, I begin to encounter the day visitors walking south along the tram road. Such quizzical looks I get with my odd-looking bike and trailer in tow, and I stop to talk.

What was I up to? I try to explain that my listening devices are in the trailer and that I came out for the night, just to listen, just to be. I find that I can tell about the ibis or the snail kites or the bellowing alligator or the great blues in the night, but my explanations feel flat. The words just don't do. They don't add up to what swirls within, as the subplots could never capture the whole scene. You had to be there to appreciate it, I want to say, but the thought emerges only as a smile.

FEBRUARY

4

The Limpkins of Corkscrew Swamp

Groundhog Day, February 2
Naples, Florida

THE 4:00 A.M. ALARM comes all too quickly, and the heavy fog I can see in the streetlights outside the bedroom window makes it ever so tempting to cancel the outing. But this is to be my last day in Florida, my last chance to experience the limpkin, that oddest of birds in the Florida swamps. Eyes closed again, I can see them, big and brown, like groundhogs on stilts, and I hear him, noisy beyond belief, the old Latin name so appropriate to this beast, *Aramus vociferous vociferous.*

I force myself into the most difficult of moves for such a morning, simply sitting up in bed. From there it becomes easier, dressing deliberately, grabbing a banana and a glass of orange juice, picking up the recording gear, and heading out to the car. The drive from Naples to Corkscrew Swamp takes forever, so thick is the fog and so slow the going, but an hour later I pull into the parking lot, now facing the second most difficult task of the morning. My body, which has been cheated by so short a night, pleads with me to lower the seat back, to snooze ever so briefly. But *no,* I say, overruling the urge, pushing the car door open, and stepping outside.

It's muggy, everything dripping with moisture, the condensed fog raining on me from the pines overhead. But it's only ground fog, I can tell, because a lone star here and there peeks through. Gathering the gear from the back seat, I close the rear door and say a word of thanks to the director of Corkscrew, who has kindly granted me access to the boardwalk before the opening hour of 7:00 A.M. I walk through the parking lot, step over the low gate onto the boardwalk, and work my way past the visitors' center and out onto the main boardwalk. Here's where the adrenaline starts to flow. Will the limpkins be calling? Just a few days ago I sat here on a beautiful starlit night, a perfect night for singing I thought, but I waited and hoped for them through sunrise before giving up. Maybe this morning will be different. But so far, for the 10 minutes I've been out of the car, they've been silent.

The boardwalk forks, and I head to the right, taking the suggested sight-seeing route in reverse. It's the quickest way to the depths of the swamp, where the cypresses are the biggest and where I've heard a limpkin before. My head-lamp lights the way, the head-high strands of spider webs across the walkway so bright with moisture that I instinctively duck, lest the "ropes" strangle me. Through the pine flatwoods I walk, out through the prairie and into the heart of the cypress swamp. The trees are small here, so I press on. What? Gate closed? "Silence!" demands the sign, as the wood storks are nesting. How ironic, I muse, that the quietest of Corkscrew's birds, the adults being essentially mute, should detour me from the most vociferous. Okay, I know another route to my destination, I think, and take the walkway to the left, but soon I encounter another locked gate on my right. Is the entire boardwalk closed? Doesn't the boardwalk to the left take me right back to the parking lot?

Confused, frustrated, not sure where I am, I drop my gear on the bench nearby and sit down on my camp chair. What is plan B? I have none. For the 20 minutes I have listened since opening the car door, I have heard no limpkins, and I reason the morning is a limpkin bust anyway. "Just turn on the tape recorder," a small voice whispers to me, "and capture the sounds of Corkscrew awakening."

I unpack my minidisc recorder and my "shotgun" microphone, plug the cable into each, and secure it all to the railing with a strip of Velcro. Over the recorder and base of the microphone I tie a plastic bag to protect them from the water dripping from the leaves of the tree looming overhead. I aim the mike at a small island in the pond, only about 15 yards away. Done. I check my watch. It's 5:24 A.M.—sunrise is almost two hours away. Knowing the recorder will run for the next two hours and 40 minutes, I settle back onto the chair, adjusting legs and arms and head for the most comfortable position.

Everything but limpkins now creeps into my consciousness. What must be millions of crickets chirp everywhere, continuously, "crickets" the term that in my ignorance I apply to all of these chirping insects. I must learn more of who they are, I remind myself. Water drips from the trees, the moisture from the fog saturating every surface. Frogs croak and gulp, reveling in the wetness. *Zzzzzzzzz* buzzes a mosquito in my ear, and knowing it'll get worse, I dab a little repellent on my cap and head. Is that a heron shrieking in the distance? An anhinga purring? An ibis groaning? It is the unknowns that give this swamp such character in the dark.

Fully accepting plan B, I settle in for the Big Sit with eyes closed, head nodded forward, arms folded across my chest, feet flat on the deck. I will sit and hear the world awaken. In my mind I take in this entire scene. I know the boardwalk extends to the left and to the right, where the gate blocks my travel. Above me looms what looks like a strangler fig, which long ago snuffed the life out of the tree that once harbored it. The lettuce-covered pond extends out before me, perhaps 40 yards across. Cypress trees rise high above the pond to the left and right, but across the pond to the west, the trees are shorter, probably willow and red maple. And in the middle of the pond is the island, a shadowy mass of small trees and ground vegetation, my microphone on the railing just in front of me aiming there.

Crickets and frogs and . . . barred owls. Just up and to the left, so near. In my semiconscious state, I listen for the roles of male and female, and hear his *who who who who who who-all,* the simple *who-all* without a vibrato ending telling me it is he giving this legato call. She accompanies him with more of a whine than a hoot. Again he hoots, and again she whines. As the owls carry on, a limpkin shatters the night. *Kur-r-ee-ow kur-r-ee-ow kur-r-ee-ow kur-r-ee-ow kur-r-ee-ow kur-r-ee-ow kur-r-ee-ow kur-r-ee-ow.* That's him, but I hear her, too — off to the left his mate contributes to the racket, a simple *gon,* three times in there I believe.

A limpkin? A limpkin! I sit still, not stirring, trying to separate reality from dream. How could it be that I sit here, in frustration and confusion, yet aiming my microphone at the very point in this entire Corkscrew Swamp where the only limpkin is screaming? No, it's a dream. Sit, stay calm . . .

Reality or dream, I'm unsure which, resumes as I hear raindrops, frogs, crickets, a jet overhead, mosquitoes . . . a prop airplane. And what is that distant motor that starts up every few minutes and turns off after five or so seconds? How annoying. Heavy trucks on a distant road. Barred owls in the distance. Herons squawking, also in the distance. Ten minutes pass, maybe twenty. I feel myself floating, weightless, my spirit drifting over the pond and among the cypresses, visiting each calling creature in turn, consciousness slowly receding . . .

The motor registers faintly, *kur-r-ee-ow kur-r-ee-ow kur-r-ee-ow kur-r-ee-ow kur-r-ee-ow kur-r-ee-ow kur-r-ee-ow kur-r-ee-ow.* Instantly alert, I now know. The limpkin *is* real. He is very close, on the small island where my microphone is aimed. I savor this series from him, each *kur-r-ee-ow* lasting about two seconds, beginning with a brief stutter, a piercing scream rising and then falling, ending with a lower-pitched and softer stutter. It seems that this series is less intense than the one before, and she does not join in (figure 4).

And then it is raindrops and frogs and crickets, but I'm now digging into my backpack, eager to capture this limpkin with my parabola and higher-quality recorder, with headphones over my ears so I can hear every breath this limpkin takes.

Minutes later I'm ready, waiting for him, my parabola now also aimed at the small island, the headphones over my ears. The owls stir again, a distant *who-cooks-for-you, who-cooks-for-you-all,* three times before its mate calls nearby, *who-cooks-for-you, who-cooks-for-you-allllllllll.* Ah, it was the male in the distance, the female with the extended *you-allllllllll* nearby. For eight minutes the owls carry on, back and forth, then yielding to the crickets and frogs and . . .

Kur-r-ee-ow kur-r-ee-ow kur-r-ee-ow kur-r-ee-ow kur-r-ee-ow kur-r-ee-ow kur-r-ee-ow kur-r-ee-ow kur-r-ee-ow kur-r-ee-ow kur-r-ee-ow kur-r-ee-ow (track 1-17). Midway through the series, I turn down the headphone gain, lest I permanently damage my hearing. Spectacular beyond belief, but he *is there,* unseen on this small island, so close I feel I could almost reach out and touch him. I heard her, too, her simple *gon* uttered four times during his second, third, and fourth screams (in the preceding sequence, I underline roughly where she calls), but she's off to the left someplace, up in the trees it seems. I catch my breath. Twelve screams from him that time, four calls from her, over almost half a minute. So intense, though the last several *kur-r-ee-ow*s seemed to trail off, uttered a little more slowly and softly.

I'm ready now, the sight of the parabola trained at the exact spot where he must be sitting, low in the vegetation on the left side of the island.

It's only nine minutes until the next series, but this time he begins with several seconds of an odd clucking sound, and it's not the full *kur-r-ee-ow* this time, either, but a shorter version, a briefer and simpler *keoow,* without the stutter before and after, each *keoow* taking a little over a second: *kkkkkkkkkkkkk keoow keoow keoow keoow keoow keoow keoow keoow kkkkkk keoow keoow keoow keoow keoow keoow.* Three times I hear her simple *gon,* all during the first half of his calling bout (track 1-18).

A minute later he clucks for a few seconds from his secluded perch, and after another minute he does so again, then silence.

Kkkkkk keoow keoow keoow keoow keoow. Only five this time, and I

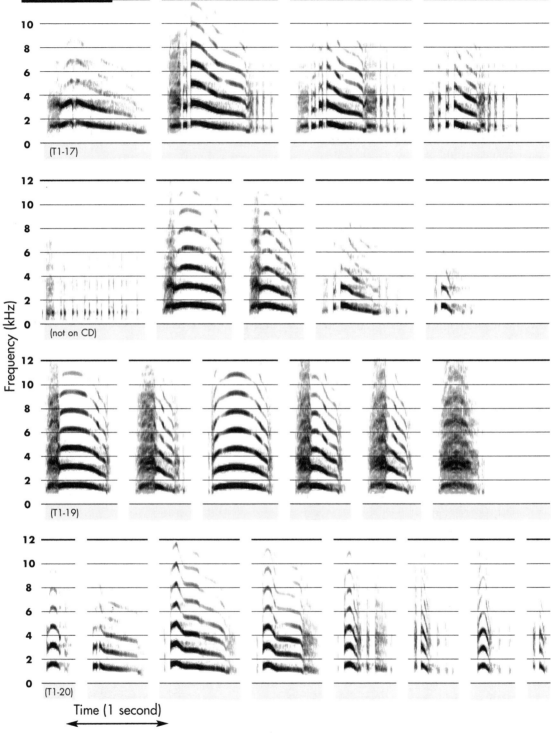

Frequency (kHz)

10 8 6 4 2 0 (T1-17)

12 10 8 6 4 2 0 (not on CD)

12 10 8 6 4 2 0 (T1-19)

12 10 8 6 4 2 0 (T1-20)

Time (1 second)

didn't hear her. Did he stop because she didn't join him, or did she not join him because she knew he was going to be brief, because she felt something less intense about this particular series?

I check my watch. It's 6:29 A.M. A little over 40 minutes before sunrise, and the songbirds are still quiet.

Two minutes later he's at it again: *kkkkkkkk keoow keoo<u>w</u> kkkk keoow keoow ke<u>o</u>ow_ kkkkeo<u>ow</u> keo<u>ow</u> keo<u>ow</u> keo<u>ow</u> keoow__keoow ke<u>o</u>ow keoo<u>w</u>_ keoo<u>w</u>_keoo<u>w</u>_ keoow keoow_kkkk<u>k</u>k_ keoo<u>w</u>_keoow ke<u>o</u>ow keoow keoow   kur-r-ee-ow* [six-second pause] *kkk keoow keoow keoow keoow kkkk keoow keoow keoow keoow kur-r-ee-ow kur-r-ee-ow kur-r-ee-ow kkkkk keoow keoow kkkk keoow keo<u>ow</u> keoow keoow keoow keoow keoow keoow keoow ke<u>o</u>ow keoow ke<u>o</u>ow keo<u>ow</u>_ keoow ke<u>o</u>ow keoo<u>w</u>_ kr-ee-ow kr-ee-ow kr-ee-ow.*

Wow. A minute and a half of ecstasy, a string of the simpler *keoow* calls punctuated occasionally by one to three of the longer *kur-r-ee-ow* calls, tapering to three halfhearted *kr-ee-ow*s at the end, her *gon* calls added where she

Figure 4. The male limpkin calls loud and long, and from four of his calling sessions I have selected sample calls to illustrate the variety in his effort.

Row 1. Track 1-17. Illustrated are 4 of the 13 *kur-r-ee-ow*s that he cries when I first train the parabolic reflector on him. See the delightful variation in the calls, as the component notes vary in composition and duration. See, too, the beautiful stacks of harmonics from which these calls are constructed; the fundamental (lowest) note in the stack of the second *kur-r-ee-ow* slides down from about 1,650 to 990 Hz, the better part of an octave, and, when slowed down to one-third or one-tenth of normal speed, sounds much like a trumpet or trombone (you can listen at slower speeds by importing this CD track into Raven Lite; see page xv).

Row 2. He calls again, this time stuttering at the outset; after the stutter come two relatively simple *keoow*s followed by a more complex but softer *kur-r-ee-ow*. Last is a short, soft phrase, trailing off in energy. (Not on CD.)

Row 3. Track 1-19. From this four-minute sequence of calling are illustrated six of his simpler *keoow* calls. See how the third illustrated call consists of only the tonal harmonics but how the others begin with hoarse, raspy segments; the last note lacks the tonal harmonics altogether and is hoarse throughout. Questions abound, such as whether he's a young bird and can't do any better, or whether he's fully capable of the pure notes but just doesn't care at the moment, or whether the harsh and tonal notes have special meaning.

Row 4. Track 1-20. He lifts off from his island perch, launching into the canopy of the nearby cypress trees, from where he calls his last for the morning. He begins softly but soon calls at full volume, only to taper off to a relative whimper at the end. Looking at the variety of calls illustrated in this figure alone and listening to the variety on the CD leave one with the inevitable conclusion that Mr. Limpkin has a delightful variety of ways in which he can express whatever is on his mind.

pleases. And where does she please? It's often toward the end or just after his *keoow,* and she's especially active during the first 30 seconds and then the last 10 seconds or so. Did she spur him on initially? And did he wait for her to chime in again before quitting? Does his choice of *keoow* or *kur-r-ee-ow* or something in between make a difference to her, or is it his tone of voice that she most cares about?

I strain to see him. I have read about how he contorts as he delivers this ear-shattering performance. The sounds are often likened to those of a peacock, though louder, or, as the famed ornithologist William Brewster put it, to those of a person being strangled. And the contortions! Yes, it's a person being strangled, but with the head shaking so violently that it is about to be dislocated, said Brewster. The violence no doubt somehow engages the special structures within his long neck that are designed just to amplify the sounds: a trachea (windpipe) that is especially long and folded into a double loop, and a large bronchial box, much like those found in cranes (see page 69), who are probably the closest living relatives of these limpkins. The female has no such sound-producing structure, her simple *gon* the product of the standard voice box and avian windpipe. Though I strain to see his shadow on the island and to catch him in the act, I fail.

Irrepressible now, he resumes a minute later (track 1-19): *kkkkkkkk keoow keo<u>ow</u> kkkk keo<u>ow</u> keoow kkkk keoow keoow kkkk keoow* . . . On and on he continues, cackling and *keoow*ing, she again chiming in where she chooses. For four full minutes they carry on, while I smile from ear to ear; this is no dream. This time he delivers several long series of *keoow* calls, about a hundred calls in all, each series separated by his stuttering, with a few silent periods up to 10 seconds' duration, punctuated by 12 *gon*s from her, all of this ending with two of his longer *kur-r-ee-ow* calls.

But something rather curious happens during the four-minute performance: His *keoow* calls seem to become more and more hoarse. It was especially noticeable the last two minutes. In a string of four or five *keoow* calls, the first two might be pure, the last two noticeably hoarse.

What gives? Does he intentionally modify these calls to convey some special significance to all those who listen? Or is he becoming fatigued, no longer able to produce the pure calls that he was capable of an hour ago or even at the beginning of those four intense minutes? I have read that a male gives a recognizable *kur-r-ee-ow* call when he's only nine weeks old, but without the fully developed trachea and bronchial box, his sounds are much hoarser than those of the adult males, and his calls remain hoarse throughout his first winter. It is only early February now, and perhaps this is a young male, one who has not yet reached peak performance levels.

Something else is puzzling. I listened more attentively there, and I definitely heard a second female in that last series. I heard what I thought was his usual duetting partner call *gon* four times in the first 20 seconds of his extended performance, all from high in the cypress trees at the left edge of the pond, but then she fell silent. Well over a minute later, a single loud, seemingly lower-frequency *gon* erupted from the island, as if beside the shrieking male, to which the female in the cypress tree immediately responded with five *gon* calls over the male's next eight *kreow* calls. About a minute elapsed before the female in the cypress gave one more *gon,* on what would be the male's third to last *kreow* call. Puzzling. There was no flight in and out of the island; I would have heard any movement in my headphones. There had to be a second female roosting beside the singing male. Why has she called only once during all of his performances?

Fascinating, but puzzling. Perhaps the male's mate is beside him and the female in the cypress is a young female from last year's breeding effort. Given the frequency difference between the calls, that might make sense, a younger bird having a higher-frequency call. Or maybe this male is paired to two females, one who roosts beside him and the other who roosts nearby, and their calls just differ. Again, no answers, just questions.

Five minutes after his last *kur-r-ee-ow,* at 6:44 A.M., almost half an hour before sunrise, I hear the male's lumbering liftoff (track 1-20) and see his shadow rising steeply to the left from low on the island. A long neck protrudes from the front of this dark mass, long legs dangle below, as up to the very top of the cypress he flies, in the direction from which the female has been calling. Just before he lands, she calls, *gon,* the first time that her call has preceded his. He calls, but it is neither the *kreow* nor the full *kur-r-ee-ow* that I now hear, but something in between, like a *kur-r-ee-ow* without the initial stutter. They are more intense than ever, it seems, she calling 12 times to his first 14 *kur-r-ee-ow*s. Six more times he then calls without her, each call successively softer and less forcefully given, the last just a whimper.

To the first songs of the morning from a local cardinal, as if the sounds of night and day now trade places, the male limpkin glides from the treetops to the railing along the boardwalk at the locked gate. From there he slips into the swamp, disappearing among the tangle of ferns.

I remain sitting, setting the parabola down, taking the headphones off, wondering what this was all about. Yes, now I remember reading how limp-

LIMPKIN

kins are more likely to call on cloudy nights than clear nights, and especially before rains. What a perfect night this has been, so foggy and dripping, but why, then, is he the only limpkin calling? I remember, too, that any loud noise can set them off, and the first series of calls seemed to be in response to the barred owls, another two to the motor that turned on and off periodically, another to loud shrieks by another bird in the distance. And perhaps it was my presence that disturbed him just enough to keep him going, as I heard no other limpkins in the swamp.

I swing my eyes from right to left, trying to take in this entire pre-sunrise scene, the tall cypress at pond's edge, the strangler fig overhead, the lettuce-choked pond, the island gradually emerging from the misty night, the likely perch of the limpkin low on the left side, the boardwalk extending to the left, *and there she is,* sitting on the railing, in plain view. It must be her, as he has just disappeared to the right. She's only 30 yards away, but it's too far. I slowly stand, binoculars in hand, and edge my way closer—25, 20 yards, pause and look. Fifteen, then 10, then 5 yards, and she seems undisturbed as she preens her feathers.

I raise the binoculars, studying her every feature; she is so large that she more than fills my field of view.

The bill is twice the length of the head, curved down slightly, with side grooves over half the length to the end. She turns to face me, and I see that the last inch or so of the bill is bent to the right, perfectly adapted to insert into the shells of apple snails and remove the meat from within.

Her eyes are huge, each with a beautiful brown iris and faintly yellow lid.

She's no longer simply brown. She's a greenish brown, a luscious dark olive brown, especially dark on the back, from the shoulders down to the tail. The main flight feathers (primaries) are dark, too, but the other large feathers have bold white triangular patches on them. Toward the neck, with its smaller feathers, the triangles become streaks, the lighter color of the feathers predominating and giving the neck and head a whitish cast.

Her legs. Oh, what beautiful long legs. And those toes, long enough to enable her to walk on water it seems, or at least on the flimsiest of vegetation on top of the water, and deft enough that she can be equally at home walking on tree branches. Three toes in front, one behind, and as she stands here on the railing, the toes are so long that her inner toes overlap, the rightmost toe of her left foot resting atop the leftmost toe of her right foot.

All the while she preens, her long bill working her body feathers, and she occasionally stops to glance my way. Now a wing stretch, first the right wing extended what must be a foot and a half toward me, every feather exposed, the wing outline broad and rounded, then the left wing to the far side. So close am I that I can hear the stiff flight feathers bristle against one another, each one beautifully asymmetrical along the vane, each feather a miniature airfoil.

Her stretching completed, she pauses and looks up at me with those big, beautiful brown eyes. One second, two, three . . . and then she turns, walking down the railing away from me, her head low, so that all I see is her long legs and the gentle swaying of her brownish rump from side to side, up and down. Such grace—there's nothing limping about the gait, nothing justifying the name limpkin. She's 10 yards away, 15, then 20, *gon . . . gon . . .* and she hops down to the boardwalk itself and then to the water, slowly moving off into the swamp.

5

Florida Scrub-Jay Families

Valentine's Day, February 14
Archbold Biological Station, Lake Placid, Florida

BY 5:30 A.M., more than an hour and a half before sunrise, I've parked the car in the station's lot, unloaded the recording gear, and am walking north on the access road with the railroad tracks to my left and the pine forest of the Lake Wales Ridge to my right. I try using my headlamp, but the reflections from the millions of tiny fog droplets floating by my face blind me. With the light off, I find the natural glow of the brilliant white sand in the road sufficient to guide my steps. I reflect on the sand—the Atlantic seashore lies 70 miles to the east and the Gulf of Mexico 70 miles to the west, but it is the sand of an ancient ocean and a relict seashore where I walk, the ridge to my right the only part of this Florida peninsula that rose above the ocean more than a million years ago.

North a few hundred yards, then left, across the railroad tracks, and the tall pine forest is soon behind me. Before me is a sea of scrubby oaks, four or five species, most no more than waist to shoulder high. Hugging the ground beneath the oaks are palmettos, and reaching high above the oaks are the scattered sand and slash pines; a few pines boast live needles, but most have burned and are lifeless skeletons reaching to the sky. It is the natural fire cycle of every 5 to 15 years that maintains the scrub community, and every so often the fires are so hot they destroy the older pines that have escaped earlier fires. Without the fires, there would be no scrub, and without the scrub there would be no scrub-jays, as the jays rely on the scrub oak community that the fires perpetuate.

A quarter mile into the scrub, I stand at the Crossroads, where two roads in the sand intersect, a big X marking the spot on my treasure map for today, for I am now at the heart of the territory owned by what has come to be known as the Crossroads Family. "Family," I muse, saying the word out loud. I know all about human families, of course, but the birds I have come to visit today are no less a family than my own.

This Crossroads Family is but one of 60 to 70 families at Archbold, where the jays have been marked and studied by my friend Glen Woolfenden since 1969. Each month a small army of ornithologists takes a census of the extensive scrub oak here, identifying every jay and with whom it is associated. During April, as the jays are raising their young, the territory boundaries are plotted, and the new jays are caught and banded. Making these studies easier is the fact that the jays have become so tame, not the least bit afraid of humans, even approaching them and landing on outstretched hands as the birds look for a handout of peanuts.

Glen has kindly kept me informed about the composition of the Crossroads Family that I can expect to see today. At the head is the adult male breeder, dominant to all in his family; I'll be able to identify him by his unique combination of leg bands, purple over aluminum on the left leg, green on the right (PA-G). His mate is second in command, aluminum left, blue over red right (A-BR). Third in the hierarchy is their daughter of two years ago, raised during 2002 (flesh over aluminum on the left, lime on the right; FA-L), but she's courting the widower on the territory just to the north and could move in there any time. Then there are the four kids, about eight months old, raised just last year during 2003; each has an aluminum band on the right leg and a lower purple band on the left; above the purple band, one of the boys has a red band (RP-A), the other a green (GP-A), one of the girls has a white band (WP-A), the other a yellow (YP-A). Simply put, it's four kids, their older sister, and Mom and Dad.

It's quite a simple family system these jays have, though the full story is now 38 years in the making, and counting. Among most songbirds, the young leave home to fend for themselves when only a month or so old. Not so with these jays. With a limited number of territories and breeding opportunities (in other words, all the good territories are occupied), young birds stay with their parents; they become older and wiser, and also help to defend the territory and raise their siblings, and raising siblings "counts" in evolutionary currency because siblings are close relatives. After their first year, during which yearlings are almost always "helpers," they come of age, seeking opportunities to breed on their own. Success can be achieved in a variety of ways, most often by dispersing and pairing with a widow or widower on another territory, but sometimes by taking over the natal territory or budding off an adjacent territory. Given the ubiquitous evolutionary processes that shape animal societies, it's clear that the relationships and power struggles within these scrub-jay families would be expected in families of any animal society, including our own.

That's the family. Given how much is known of these jays, words like "family," "mate," "daughter," "widower," "kids," "boys," and "girls" come easily, but they also gnaw at the edges of my scientific training. I must avoid being anthropomorphic, I have been taught, and these words flirt with danger. That adult male breeder—I really should call him "Purple Aluminum left, Green right," but what if I dared to give him a name, like Al? And his mate, is she "Aluminum left, Blue over Red right," or is she, say, Betty? Al and Betty have an older daughter, Cindy, and together they raised the four kids, Linda and Lily, Ron and Roy. I'm almost shocked that naming them was so easy, but I wouldn't have dared to name them before I retired from the academic world, as my peers would have frowned heavily on me, and peers, sometimes for better, sometimes for worse, police one another.

Right now, as I stand here in the sandy road at 6:25 A.M., I know they all are roosting in the dense patch of scrub oaks just to the west of me. I'm at the northern end of their territory, and yesterday, at 6:09 P.M., about 10 minutes before sunset, the last of them dropped silently into these oaks, disappearing for the night. The family was rather early to roost, I thought, as I heard the other common birds here carrying on for another half-hour: mockingbirds sang and growled, catbirds meowed, towhees sang and whistled their *sweee* calls, palm warblers chipped, mourning dove wings whistled by, yellowthroats sang a few *witchity* songs, all long after the jays had gone to roost.

So just what will this morning be like? How will they awaken and begin their day's business? That's what I'm here for, simply to commune with this family, and as sunrise approaches, I begin to take note.

6:28 A.M. First towhee whistle heard, a bold, rising *sweee*. It's the way they wake up, and soon it must be dozens of towhees calling. Then a few will no doubt offer a song or two, even though it's early in the year.

6:31 A.M. First song from a common yellowthroat. A killdeer calls *killdeer killdeer* in the shallow, muddy depression to the north. A palm warbler chips nearby.

6:34 A.M. Mourning dove coos. Mockingbird sings. Catbird meows.

6:37 A.M. Yellowlegs, *krill krill krill krill,* a greater yellowlegs, given the four calls.

6:53 A.M. A belted kingfisher rattles as it moves from one small pond to the next.

7:06 A.M. A flock of wintering robins moves through. Sandhill cranes bugle in the distance.

7:08 A.M. A red-winged blackbird sings from the trees above the pond to the north, *konk-la-ree.*

7:11 A.M. Ducks fly by. A red-bellied woodpecker awakens — as expected, about sunrise.

7:13 A.M. Finally! Up from the scrub bursts one jay, to perch above the oaks in the charred remains of a small pine; *weep weep,* it announces as it alights, bobbing and animatedly flipping its tail. It's Lily, I can see through my binoculars. Others in the family boil from the scrub, three, then six, and briefly I see all seven birds. From bird to bird, I scan the legs quickly with the binoculars, reading the bands that I can see, confirming not only Lily but also Al and Betty, Cindy, and Ron. The other two must have been Roy and Linda.

Two *weep*s is all? That's their awakening clarion? It's a rather unremarkable entry into the day; they know what they're doing, I'm sure, though I had hoped for a rousing chorus of jay sounds. Five jays are up now, all preening, fluffing their feathers, working the left side of the body, the right, the wings, the breast. One flies over to me at the road, landing in the branches of a dead oak. Another follows, and soon five are within 10 yards of me, two of them at my feet, Ron and Linda ready for any handouts. Stingy me, I hoard the peanuts that Glen had given me yesterday, thinking that for now I should try to observe, not influence these jays. No peanuts offered, Ron and Linda are soon up in the perches with the others. I watch and listen as jays drop into the scrub, come up with an acorn and hammer at it, or forage on the ground, swiping at the sand, seeking to uncover whatever might be edible.

Weep weep weep weep weep weep weep weep comes a rapid series from the north, most likely from the widowed male there. Almost immediately Cindy responds with the oddest of calls, sounding much like a rapid series of hiccups, her body vigorously pumping with each call, her bill pointed up at a 45-degree angle (track 1-21; figure 5). How beautiful, how touching, how . . . I catch myself, smiling, laughing, almost embarrassed that I am eavesdropping on their courtship. The "hiccup" is Cindy's response to the courting male; this call is used only by females and especially during courtship, as here. Cindy is "of age," too, having already helped her parents for one year; she's now about a year and a half old, and about half of all scrub-jays find mates by the time they are two, most often pairing with a widow or widower on an adjacent territory, just like here.

Curiously, the others in the family are silent during this exchange. Do they know what I know, that Cindy has been visiting this unpaired male to the north, courting him and the breeding opportunity there? In some sense, they almost certainly know, but I wonder if they have an opinion about this development, if they think about the prospects in any way. It's good for the family if Cindy is successful, as the currency of evolution is placing offspring into successful breeding situations. I regret that I have no way of knowing what they are all thinking, but I don't regret asking myself, as they are, after all, family.

By 7:35, it seems that all of the jays have flown down the road to the south, and I follow, only to stop dead in my tracks as I hear a lone jay calling behind me. I backtrack, listening carefully. It's a series of *weep* calls, one given every second or two (track 1-22; see also figure 6 for a variety of such calls). I listen, each call sounding pretty much like the others but with some wavering in the voice once in a while, a good 200 of them over about five minutes, until he abruptly switches to a subtly different *weep* call. Then he seems to switch back to the first, then he changes again. Remarkable. And who is this? Having

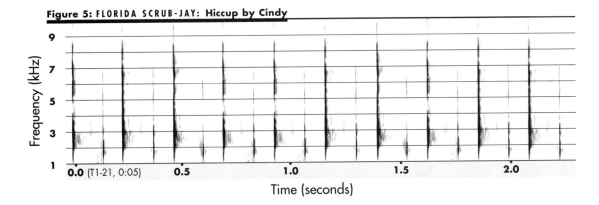

Figure 5: FLORIDA SCRUB-JAY: Hiccup by Cindy

Figure 5. The *hiccup* (track 1-21). With her bill pointed up at a 45-degree angle, the oldest daughter, Cindy, pumps her body with each of the eight *hiccups* illustrated here as she responds to the distant courting male on the territory to the north. The *hiccup* is used only by females, and often during courtship; most other loud calls are subtle variations of the *weep* call (see figure 6).

worked my way closer, I can see the left leg . . . green/purple. It's Ron, one of the kids, all alone on the northern end of the territory.

He's calling, and for what purpose? I've read about young birds doing this, as if they were "practicing" for some important role later in life. Or maybe the important role is now, as he simply practices getting the intonations correct for good jay-speak. "Tell me, Ron, what are you thinking? Why did you do that? Who was listening? Why two or three different *weep* calls? Why not just one type? Or why not more? That slight wavering once in a while —was that intentional, or are you working to gain full control of your voice? This doesn't have anything to do with Cindy's suitor just over the boundary from you, does it?" He answers with a flight to the south, far down the road, where he joins the rest of his family.

I follow along, watching, listening. Betty is now perched high, serving as a sentinel ready to alert the family to danger, which would come most likely in the form of a hawk. She calls, a raspy *weep* every three seconds or so, for one minute, almost two (track 1-23). Why does she call now? The others seem to pay no attention, so perhaps she's simply announcing that all's well, assuring them that she is watching. They flit about me on the road or hammer on acorns in the scrub. Occasionally one launches a few yards into the air, grabbing an insect at the apex of its flight, the jay then folding its wings and dropping back down to a perch. Betty drops from her perch, greeting another of the jays with soft, low-pitched, guttural *churr*s, then scratching her head with her right leg, my sensitive microphone picking up the jingle of the two metal bands there (track 1-24). Wings *churr*, too, as the jays make brief flights from branch to branch, or to the ground and back. I hadn't noticed before, but another sentinel has taken Betty's place—Lily.

7:51 A.M. I wonder exactly which jays are here, and I know how to find out. From my pocket I take a couple of the peanuts Glen gave me and break them into small pieces. The ever-observant jays soon appear in the branches near me, watching, waiting. Conspicuously lofting the pieces into the air and to the ground, I step back to get a good look at the legs of the jays now scrambling for the peanuts. Al screams a loud, sharp *weep*, once, twice, as he stuffs his bill, warding off the others (track 1-25). What a pig, I can't help but think, dominant to the others and showing it. Five jays are on the ground beside me, the adult female, Betty, the sentinel up in the tree again, all accounted for except Cindy, who is most likely visiting her suitor to the north.

Mom, Dad, and the four kids. I eye them, seeing them as part of a family; no, as part of a family dynasty, as this Crossroads Family has been especially successful over the years. Their success is thanks in part to the real estate they control, which seems to be of higher quality and somewhat larger than the average territory of about 9 hectares, or about 300 yards square; by chance, it has not all burned in any given year. Al himself has controlled this territory over 10 years, and when he lost his first wife, Betty joined him, thus keeping the territory under family control. The family real estate expanded when one of the sons from Al's first wife in 1994, after helping his parents raise his younger siblings in 1995, carved out an adjacent territory in 1996. About a third of sons acquire a territory in this way, budding off a portion of the parental territory and then attracting a mate from elsewhere. And partnering with a mate from elsewhere is crucial, as incest in family lines is strictly avoided.

All six jays are back in the scrub now, silent. They carry on, a minute, two, three, five. Then I hear one of the females, off to the west and separated from the group. She is gently hiccupping; then there are some soft musings and warbles and twitters, ever so softly and briefly. Who is that? Betty, Lily, or Linda? Or has Cindy returned to the group? Has to be one of them. I work closer, eyeing the leg bands in my binoculars: it's the young female Lily. "Why? Why do you hiccup now? Your brother Ron was off on a solo *weep* fest earlier, and now you're here hiccupping all alone? And what's the warble song all about? It's as if you practice singing, but there's no scrub-jay song to perfect." I chuckle at myself, wondering whether I'd be talking to her if she were "White over Purple left, Aluminum right" rather than Lily.

Ten minutes later she repeats her hiccups and her soft musings, and again she's off to the west, well separated from the other jays. I'm closer to her now, just a few yards away, and I focus my binoculars on her, getting a good look. The markings are subtle, not bold as on a blue jay. She's a study in shades of subtle blues and grayish whites: a dull purplish blue on the crown and sides and back of the neck; a pale blue on the forehead, wings, and tail; grayish white on the throat and breast, the throat set off by a blue-gray bib; and no crest, the very meaning of the Latin for the genus name *Aphelocoma*. And there's the ink black eye, the window on the mind of these intelligent creatures. The word "stunning" comes to mind. Lily and I study each other, contemplating . . . family.

I think of my roots, my name, my birth date, the little Michigan village where I was born along with my two brothers, and how and where we found mates and raised our own families. Our mom and dad had settled in that small Michigan village, she coming from a hundred or so miles to the north, he a mile from the south, where he perhaps could have inherited his father's farm but chose not to. Mom had two brothers and four sisters, as did Dad. I had lots of uncles and aunts, lots of cousins, and four grandparents scattered around western Michigan. I know these relatives and their relationships to me and to one another, remembering each by name. To know Lily by name is to see a bit of her history, too, to see her family in a broader context, to see her as part of an extended family and an intricate web of social relationships.

It's now about a quarter after 8:00, and Al flies to the west, giving a rapid series of *weep weep weep*s on the way, and lands in the oaks at the Crossroads. I lose track of who is where but soon see a flock of jays high in the dead pines to the south, a good 100 yards away. They move from right to left in undulating flight, making a loud, rapid series of *weep* calls, accompanied by an intensely loud *hiccup* call from a female. I count seven jays high in the dead pines—what a racket, and then there's another series of *weep* calls and a loud *hiccup*. Two jays are uninvolved, foraging nonchalantly at my feet: it's Ron and Linda, the two who seem most eager to hang out near me.

I work my way south along the road, out toward where the jays had flown down from the pine trees. There I find Al and Betty, and it was no doubt they who were part of that boundary ruckus with the neighboring flock.

I lose them momentarily, but by 8:40 a flock of jays is again calling loudly in the tall dead pines to the southwest. Rapid series of *weep* calls and loud *hiccup*s occur twice, three times, five times. Robins boil out of the pines, flying in all directions, as if fleeing a battlefield. There's silence for 20 seconds, and then a loud *hiccup* sets it all off again. The first flight is from right to left, and then part of the flock, perhaps members of the neighboring family, departs back to the right.

I look beside me to see two jays. Who? Lime over white on left? Light blue over white on left? Who are these jays? They must be the kids from the neighboring flock with which my family does battle.

By 9:00 A.M. it's all over, with Al and Betty and the four kids (but not Cindy) foraging quietly on the road just west of the Crossroads intersection. Betty is the sentinel, and Al flies up to her, offering her a morsel, not the last time that he will feed her during the coming season. The youngsters forage nearby.

Lily calls for 90 seconds, the same *weep* over and over, so consistently. A

FLORIDA
SCRUB-JAY

minute later, what sounds like the same *weep* call resumes, but this time it's Roy, over and over, for about two minutes. A minute later, the calls resume, the same *weep* call, but this time it's Linda. And is that Ron off to the west giving the identical call? I think so, as the other five birds are here. Remarkable! First Lily, then Roy, then Linda with most likely Ron in the background, the youngsters taking turns producing what sounds to me like the identical call (track 1-26; figure 6).

I find myself talking to them yet again, asking them what they're saying to one another. I hear the subtle nuances in their calls, how sometimes they respond with seemingly identical *weep*s and sometimes they switch from one type of *weep* to another. They've perfected this system of communication over countless generations, since the beginning of jay-time, and I'm confident they understand their "language" as well as I do mine. And although I want to simplify their code and identify different *weep* "types," it seems far more likely that there are no types at all but rather an endless variety of inflections that these

Figure 6: FLORIDA SCRUB-JAY CALLS

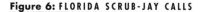

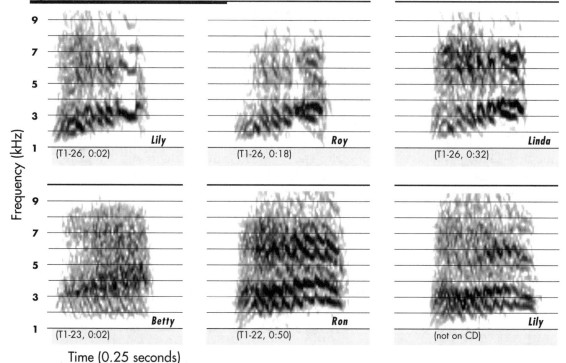

scrub-jays can give to their calls, each having some importance but all of it well beyond what I can hear or understand as I contemplate these creatures here in the scrub oaks of Archbold.

FEBRUARY 11, 2007. Three years later, I'm back, and Glen eagerly tells me the changes that have occurred in the Crossroads Family since I was last here.

After more than a decade in residence, Al disappeared in late summer 2006; surviving him on the territory are Betty, a son from 2005, and a son and a daughter from 2006, only four birds. Betty is unpaired, and right now it's a tossup as to whether she will retain control of the territory by accepting a new mate from outside the family or whether their remaining son from 2005 will take over and acquire his mate from outside the family. Who wins the territory will depend on several factors, says Glen, including which suitor the mother likes, which potential mate seems best capable of defending the territory, and which potential mate best dominates the aspiring son.

And Cindy? Yes! Back in the spring of 2004 she did pair with the male just to the north. She needed to wait to make her final move, though, until after my February visit, when insects and other food became more readily available; she stayed on her home territory through the food-scarce winter, enabling herself to take advantage of the acorns she had buried there. She continues on the territory to the north as the breeding female there.

Ron, one of the kids from 2003, is nearby. He helped Mom and Dad in 2004 and 2005, but then he budded off a territory to the north, breeding there in 2006 after attracting a mate from outside the Archbold tract. The family dynasty continues, with Ron, Cindy, Betty (or her 2005 son with Al), and Al's son from 1994 controlling four adjacent territories near the Crossroads.

And how about Roy, Lily, and Linda, the other kids I met three years ago? They're missing, either dead or having dispersed outside the study tract.

Figure 6. First row. Similarities in *weep* calls from different birds. Here is just one example of a *weep* call from each of three birds, the kids Lily, Roy, and Linda; over just a few minutes' time, these three youngsters give what sound like—and, in the sonagrams, look like—much the same call.

Second row. Differences in *weep* calls. Here are three different *weep* calls, the subtle differences evident both as seen in the sonagrams and as heard in the variety of *weep* calls on the CD.

We next visit the Crossroads in person. The birds fly to meet us as Glen offers them a few peanuts so that he can get a good look at who is here. In all, we see 11 birds, as jays from three different territories are present, though all the jays are part of the same extended family. Betty is here, and her son Ron is visiting from his territory to the north, just as Al's son from 1994 is visiting from the south. Betty wouldn't allow their mates to visit, Glen explained.

Back at the station, Glen asks if he may see the draft of what I had written after my 2004 visit. He's been the consummate professional all through our discussions, referring to all of the birds by their leg-band combinations, and I'm nervous about admitting to him how these jays have affected me, how it's hard to see them as "mere birds." In short, I fear he will disapprove.

He reads quickly, flipping the pages. I sit quietly but anxiously nearby. By now he sees I've given them names . . . and I'm talking to them . . . and I'm cheering the family dynasty at the Crossroads. He finishes, looks up at me, and with a broad grin on his beaming face says, "Everyone who works with the jays starts to think of them as people."*

---

* I offer a special thank-you and memory here for Glen Woolfenden. Sadly, Glen died in June 2007, four months after our February outing. He was a fine, no, a great ornithologist, who cared deeply about his birds, and the world is all the richer for the passion he brought to life. Thank you, Glen, for sharing your passion and your birds with me, too.

6

The Anhingas of Anhinga Trail, Everglades National Park

February 28, 5:00 A.M.

JUST A FEW FEET below me, a huge alligator bellows a deep, resonating growl that triggers every flight instinct in my body. I freeze, assuring myself that he is only a courting alligator, and even if he doesn't know that, he still can't get to me up here on the boardwalk. All around me are others, too, each in a slightly different key, the especially deep growls below verifying that he is among the biggest and presumably the most desirable to the females (track 1-27).

It's still nearly two hours before sunrise, and *I am here,* almost pinching myself to be certain. Yes, Anhinga Trail, Everglades National Park. It's the peak of the tourist season, but I'm almost certain to have the next two hours all to myself, because those who come here to look and especially to photograph will not arrive until there is "good light," leaving me alone to listen in the night.

And just listen to this symphony of life! The gators now seem to hum; they're more subdued, on idle, but they'll surge again soon. Now it's pig frogs, their grunts contagiously sweeping the pond, and splashes of unknown creatures in the water. A black-crowned night-heron *quarks* overhead, again, and again in the distance as he commutes to the south. Near the water's edge just behind me, a green heron offers a muted *skeow*. To the northeast, a great blue heron trumpets, catalyzing a frenzy of king rail duets rippling into the distance. Barred owls hoot an emphatic *who-who-who-who-who-alll*, both male and female, then some caterwauling, such expressive birds (track 1-28)— they're off to the east, among the cypresses that gracefully rise above the dark mangroves and pond apples, reaching into the orangish band that glows above the eastern horizon.

Cormorants. Oh, the cormorants—perhaps 50 of them roost in the island of pond apple trees just across the open water to the north. I can see their silhouettes against the northeastern horizon that glows with Miami's lights. There's movement, a wing stretched, a flutter here and there. I eye them through the binoculars, finding the persistent cougher, then searching for the bird with the sneezing fit. And what deep grunts, so guttural, some prolonged snarls or moans, others uttered in slow motion as series of deep, low notes (track 1-28). These double-crested cormorants are only visitors here, I believe, and will head north soon to breed.

Even the heavens sing, Venus brilliantly to the east, Jupiter overhead, the nearly full moon to the southwest. The soft, thin clouds dance in slow motion, offering glimpses of stars and then whole constellations, the clouds seemingly chased to the west by the breaking day. Moving about the eastern sky are brilliant planet-mimics, headed no doubt for the Miami airport.

Just to my left I feel a warm presence, a being standing beside me. I turn to face a shadow as tall as I, eyeball to eyeball until I kneel to see him better against the sky. A great blue heron, standing on the railing. How long has he been there? Wouldn't I have heard him if he had arrived after I did, now more than an hour ago? Or perhaps he walked down the railing to meet me? "Good morning, Mr. Heron." I try my most cordial voice. He's unmoved. I retreat, yielding.

Ten minutes later he's aloft, the *swoosh* of giant wingbeats flying past me, and he lands at the base of the pond apple just south of the boardwalk, just beneath the anhinga nest where the male still incubates and the female has

Figure 7, Row 1. The *chitter-chitter-chitter-chee-cheer-chitter-chitter-chitter* of male and female anhinga as they greet each other. See the pulsating nature of the call and how each of the notes spans a broad frequency, making it an atonal and rather "noisy" call (track 1-29).

Row 2. A young anhinga nestling lets it be known, early and often, that he is hungry, or at least that he is eager for a feeding. About once a second he makes his case, punctuating his chatter with a brief down-slurred note, and then he repeats himself, over and over and over. See how the rhythm of the youngster's call is much like that of the adult's *chitter* call (track 1-30).

Row 3. When a parent approaches with possible food and there's reason to get excited, the youngster calls more frantically. The chatters are now a little longer and emphatically higher-pitched, as are the down-slurred notes, the overall effect designed to make the youngster sound even more hungry and helpless and desperate to the caring parent (track 1-31).

been sleeping in the branches just above him. Now clearly awake, she stretches a wing to the side, then works her way down to the nest. He's awake, too, his long neck rising to meet her, the two of them erupting simultaneously into a clicking and chattering *chitter-chitter-chitter-chee-cheer-chitter-chitter-chitter,* rising and falling, undulating and repeated, their necks arched back, bills open, heads swaying like two dancing snakes (track 1-29; figure 7). It is the

Figure 7: ANHINGA

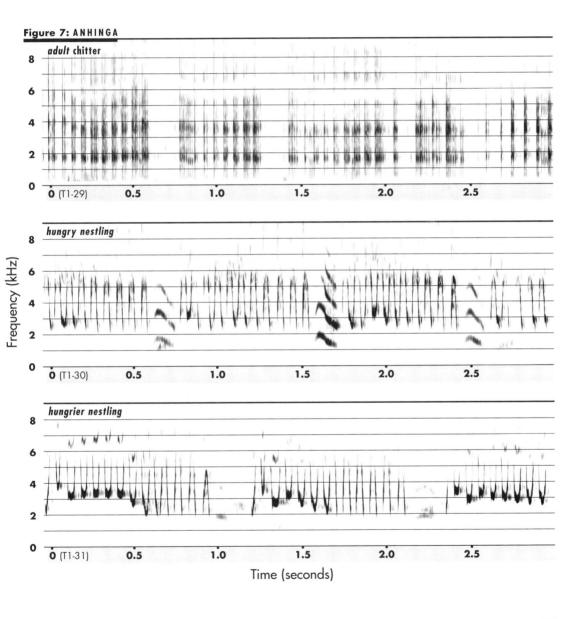

sound I'll hear around me throughout the day whenever mates greet each other at their nests; often they'll trade places, too, swapping incubating duties, but this time the male decides it is too early to yield, and he sits, the female standing nearby.

They're incubating, just as they were when I was last here, 12 days ago. That's not surprising, as it takes up to 30 days to hatch an anhinga egg, but I had so hoped to see and hear the babies today, almost within arm's reach of the boardwalk—what a treat that would have been. And *he* incubated overnight again, just as he did last time, just as males do most of the time.

What a handsome pair, the two of them together. The bills are black daggers, the necks long and snakelike, the two together no match for the sunfish and other flattened fish that these anhingas thrive on in the shallow waters. The heads seem tiny, the tails huge in comparison, fanlike, turkeylike even, and the feathers are stiff, superb underwater rudders. He's black with silvery white streaks on the back and upper wing; she much like him except buffy on the head, neck, and breast. Last time I was here, the fleshy colors about their eyes were gorgeous, his a brilliant turquoise, hers more greenish blue, but now they're a drab brown. Chameleons, I can't help but think—in just 12 days they've changed from their flashy courting plumage to dress that's more appropriate for the routine duties of parenthood.

Yes, it has already been 12 days since I was here last, on February 16, and I'm eager to see how things have changed. Back then, as I stood on the boardwalk looking to the south, it was as if I were in a small amphitheater, the life story of anhingas being told all around me.

February 16

NEST 1. To my left, just off the boardwalk, were the two incubating anhingas, at Nest 1 as I numbered it. He incubated overnight, until about 20 minutes after sunrise, when she silently approached and sat beside him. He slipped off as she slipped on. It was her turn now, and while she incubated their eggs for the next three and a half hours, he was usually nearby, preening, sunning himself spread-winged with back to the sun, or just hanging out. About an hour into her watch, he flew off, soon returning with a single shiny red leaf, all to much clicking and chattering and neck weaving. She seemed eager to take the leaf, he reluctant to yield, and in the frenzy they fumbled it, the leaf falling to the water below. Their long necks arched downward, frozen momentarily, silently watching as their treasure fell, but he soon sprang into action, tugging loose a small branch from nearby, offering that to her instead; she accepted, tucking the gift into the nest. Seven more times in the next two and a half hours he would deliver her leaves or small branches, all with much fanfare, and on the seventh time, she yielded and he began his turn on the nest.

Nest 2. In the next nest out from the boardwalk were the youngest babies, all three still in the nest, perhaps 15 days old. And what gorgeous babies they were! Their eyes and daggerlike bills were black, the heads pinkish, and the entire bodies were wrapped in white fleece with a grayish cast on the necks, grading into a buffy white on the lower necks and with buffy fore edges to the white wings. Starkly contrasting with this fluff of immaculate down were the emerging black stubs that would eventually be the magnificent wing and tail feathers. And those throat pouches, how odd, extending not only down but out to the sides, too, as the bony supports for the tongues pressed outward, giving the gular pouches an oddly angular appearance.

How these youngsters bobbed and weaved, those long necks snaking about, the heads in constant motion, the gular pouches fluttering, altogether almost comical, like hyperanimated wind-up toys, and all this motion was accompanied by an incessant, frantic begging (tracks 1-30, 1-31, 1-32; figure 7). Catch just one youngster alone in his act and it's clear how he's calling, a rapid chatter followed by a down-slurred tonal note, as if he breathes out on his chatter and in on his tonal note, this pattern repeated nonstop every second, a metronome, so steady, each cycle just like the next. But hear him when he's more frantic, and he modulates the pitch, sounding all the more urgent that he be the next one to receive some food. Then add a tree full of such calling babies, and the effect is sublime.

For each baby, though, there's nothing sublime about it. This is a matter of who gets fed and who doesn't, a matter of life and death, and the youngster that shows how healthily and energetically he can beg is likely to get the food. If adults can't find enough food, the younger or weaker nestlings may starve. In some species, especially among herons, parents will even stand idly by as an older, stronger nestling kills a younger, weaker sibling; from the parents' perspective, having one or two stronger offspring is better than having three weaklings, as only the stronger offspring are likely to survive and compete successfully in the next generation.

Both parents attended Nest 2 overnight, but she left just before sunrise. Over the next two hours, I couldn't help but sense some exasperation on his part, and he offered what he had to the hungry kids, opening his bill and allowing first one, then another of the babies to thrust its entire head and half its neck violently down his throat, all in search of some regurgitated, half-digested morsels. Perhaps they got a little, but not much, because the frenetic begging quickly resumed and their necks were lean, nothing like the distended neck of a contented baby who has accepted a huge regurgitated load from a parent who has just returned from fishing. Two hours after sunrise she returned and he departed, and just an hour later they traded places again, each arriving adult offering a load to frantic babies, who seemed only partially satisfied.

NEST 3. The next nest on this semicircle of anhingas also contained three youngsters, but they were standing beside the nest, not in it, as they were at least a week older than those in Nest 2. The brilliant white down had given way to an overall buffy appearance, from cinnamon on the necks and breasts to a dusky tinge on the backs. And how those wing and tail feathers had grown! And those feet, with webbing all around, looking as if big beige mit-

ANHINGAS

tens had been pulled up over the toes and the birds were doing their best to hold on to the branches.

Both adults attended the nest overnight, but both departed at sunrise, leaving the youngsters unattended. While alone, they were fairly quiet for the most part, knowing no doubt that their time would come, which it did about 9:30 A.M., when the male returned to feed them. He left almost immediately, and the female returned about 10:30, the male again at 10:35. With each visit, the first baby who plunged its head and neck into that of the adult came away with a good meal, the lower portion of its neck bulging from the intake.

"NESTS" 4. In the next group of pond apple trees, to the south-southeast, were a lot of young anhingas. I counted 11, their tail and wing feathers almost adult length, their appearance approaching that of the female. Perhaps they were four weeks old, and they were throughout the trees and no longer in their nests. Just how many nests did they represent? One clue was the number of adult females who flew from the trees near sunrise: six. Males left, too, and with the adults gone, the youngsters were quiet, mostly preening or sleeping with their long necks tucked down along their backs. But what a sight when they were active, the trees full of fleece-covered bodies beneath long, waving necks.

The sibling groups became apparent only when an adult came in to feed them. At 9:10 A.M., a male returned, and five of the babies began their frantic begging. The other six seemed largely uninterested, several yielding ground before the approaching male. Five babies were all waving their necks and bobbing their heads and calling frantically in the face of the male, who when he opened his mouth found not one but two young birds diving in, though one far deeper than the other. The other three youngsters then turned their attention on one another, the only remaining faces, as if they might have food. The first baby to feed was no sooner shaken from the adult than a second plunged in, and eventually a third, though only the gullet of the first baby was fully extended. The youngsters continued to beg wildly until the adult flew off, and instantly they were quiet, as were all the others in the tree. Other adults came and went, exciting first two youngsters, then three, then only one. I watched that lone bird, somewhat off to the upper left of the others, and it was visited once by an adult male and once by an adult female—a loner, I concluded, the only survivor from that nest.

"NESTS" 5. Directly across the small pond, I counted 12 young anhingas, but they were the oldest of all, perhaps five weeks, the age at which they begin to fly, and at 25 yards difficult to distinguish from an adult female. I could see four nests, though none of these birds remained in those nests. Adults came and went, with sibling groups of two, three, three, and four identifying themselves, the members of each family unit clearly recognizing one another as easily as I recognize members of my own family.

NEST 6. To my far right were an adult male and female with no young. They had a nest, and they took turns sitting on it, but a photographer told me he'd been watching these birds for a month and they seemed to be just going through the motions. There were no eggs as yet, but at one point I saw a mating, he gripping her neck in his bill as he held his position atop her, so perhaps there was hope.

February 28

So all that was 12 days ago. What changes have occurred since then in these six centers of anhinga activity?

With the sun just peeking over the horizon, I now scan to the right of the incubating pair at Nest 1. At Nest 2 and Nest 3 there are still three young anhingas, but no adults are attending. That makes sense, as the young in these nests are roughly 25 and 35 days old, respectively; nestlings are typically unattended after 12 days, and adults return to the nest area only to feed their young once they are over 16 days of age.

In the trees at location 4, where there had been 11 youngsters, I now count 17, and maybe more! Directly across the pond, at location 5, where there had been 12, I count only 4. They left the nest long ago and are now moving about from tree to tree, as many of the babies are over six weeks of age, the age at which they begin to fly. To my right, in Nest 6, there apparently are still no eggs, as the male and female stand near the nest, not on it.

"Morning." I greet the first of the day visitors at 7:20. These people look too much and listen too little, I note and chuckle to myself, and I've been looking forward to having a little fun with those who walk by me today.

I strike up a conversation with one of the photographers, soon inviting him to slip the headphones on and listen. The parabola is aimed at Nest 2, where the youngsters are calling rather continuously, and the recorder is running, too, not only recording but also amplifying the sounds in his ears: "sensational . . . it's binocular sound . . . I'm going to get one of these for my grandkids, and for me . . . you've changed my life . . ." Tony, who I learned was from back home in New England, was amazed at what he had been missing as he eyed the world for a good picture. Truly listening to these birds can change lives, I know.

An adult male anhinga lands beside us on the railing, and he is soon joined by a young bird whose head and upper neck quickly disappear into the mouth of the adult. Wow, that was fast. How do they find and recognize each other? What clues do they use? They do recognize each other, as is obvious when an adult flies into a tree full of babies and only a few respond, and here the father is almost certainly feeding one of his offspring. Perhaps they use voice, as there's ample evidence in other species of many other parents and their offspring recognizing one another's voices. Or perhaps it's in their looks. Or perhaps both.

"What is this?" I explain to the inquisitive woman the parabola, and what I'm listening to, and invite her to listen. "Oh, listen! It's fabulous . . . That is fabulous. That is fabulous. Ohhhhhh . . . Oh, my . . . This would be something our grandchildren would love to hear." Another victim.

Below me are three young anhingas, sitting on the roots of a pond apple at the water's edge. One peers into the water, its head submerged. Another picks up small twigs and bits of vegetation, manipulating them in its bill. The third pecks at the second, while the first dips into the water for a brief swim, only to be chased underwater by a cormorant and quickly climb back out, soon spreading its wings in the sun as a good anhinga should. Kids. Practicing, learning the ropes. Soon they'll be swimming gracefully underwater, stalking and spearing sunfish and the like, then surfacing and throwing the fish into the air and swallowing them headfirst.

I invite more passersby to listen: "Unbelievable!" says one woman, soon followed by another. "Oh my goodness. That's fantastic." A boy in his early teens: "Oh, wow, that's cool." Another young fellow, "Cool."

Meanwhile, I've been watching the anhingas in the trees about me. Just like 12 days ago, the female at Nest 1 came and relieved the male a little after sunrise. Over the next three and a half hours, he delivered treats that were added to the nesting material, and a little after 11:00 A.M. he took over incubating duties again.

Activity in the other trees was much the same, but deep in the same tree with Nest 1 are two courting couples. I've been watching the males especially. One of them erects the feathers on his head and neck, then waves his wings slowly, at first together and then alternately, his perch shaking with him. He bows and arches his neck deeply so that his bill points down; he then raises his tail over the back and waves his body slowly back and forth, his feathers slightly quivering. With all this going on, he calls, a sweet, low, rolling warble (track 1-33). Suddenly the head and neck are extended up, and then he bows in reverse, his head resting on his back, then bows forward again. From all of his advances, it's clear he thinks it is not too late to begin a nest now, in late February.

A group of schoolchildren is about to pass, second graders from St. Thomas Episcopal Parish School near Miami, I soon learn. I know the adults won't appreciate my disrupting their march around the boardwalk, but I can't resist, picking off child after child and slipping the headphones over their ears: "Whooooaa, that's cool . . ." "I'm after you, Ben . . ." "Cool . . ." "That's so cool . . ." "That's cool . . ." "Listen to that . . ." "That's awesome . . ." "Thank you . . ." "Thank you . . ." *"Come on, people"* [adult leader weighing in, without addressing me directly, as if I didn't exist]. "Cool . . . Awesome . . ." *"We need to move on . . ."* "Thank you very much . . ." *"Okay, we need to catch up . . ."* "Cool . . ." "Neat . . ." "So cool . . ." "I'm after Olivia." "No, I'm after Olivia . . ." "It's loud . . ." *"Time to move on . . ."* "It's so beautiful . . ." "It's pretty but loud . . ." "Thank you . . ." And from the more shy ones, there are simply big smiles. Yes, I'm smiling, too, wondering where a brief listening adventure can take a young child who is not yet so hurried and harried.

I hear a foreign language from the next four approaching visitors, all adults. "That's great . . ." "It's beautiful . . ." "Noisy children! . . ." I'm disappointed that they spoke English for me, so I inquire about their accent: it's Dutch, the language of my ancestors. I ask for a translation: *fantastisch, schitterend!*

Just a little before noon, two large tour groups approach, one from the left and one from the right, and as the masses converge on this very spot, I realize that my time here is up for the day. I've had my fun, my two hours of communing before the first photographer and five hours of sharing the fun with others after that. But there's an opportunity for one last casualty, a woman approaching with binoculars and camera, middle-aged and by herself: "Oooooohhhhhh, thank you, that was so much fun."

MARCH

7

Sandhill Cranes on the Platte River

March 31, 5:00 P.M., two hours before sunset in the parking lot of the Platte River Crane Trust, Wood River, Nebraska

IT IS THE BEST of omens, I sense, as here is Paul Johnsgard, a living legend, biologist and author, scientist and humanist, passionate about sandhill cranes since he first met them in 1962, some 40 years ago. Yes, Paul Johnsgard, here in the parking lot with me, heading out to the north blind to take in the same spectacle that I will witness from the south blind. Over the past two days here, I have sensed that I could never tire of these cranes, and here is living proof of the lifelong spell these birds cast on those who come. It will be a good evening, we agree.

Just 48 hours ago I stood here, too, ready to walk out across the fields for an evening at the same south blind overlooking the river. Or at least I thought I was ready, but I soon realized that all of the firsthand accounts of cranes coming in to roost could not have prepared me for what I was to see and hear. I found it impossible to leave that night and instead threw a pad and sleeping bag down behind the barrier of hay bales that formed part of the blind. I dozed some, but mostly listened through the night to the conversations of cranes and geese and ducks on the river just yards away. Up and into the blind well before sunrise, I listened and gawked as tens of thousands of cranes departed for their feeding grounds.

Yesterday afternoon I drove about watching cranes feeding and dancing in the cornfields, fattening for their trip north. By late afternoon I was at another blind, this one farther upstream and to the west, though I was only slightly better prepared. I couldn't leave that night either. Despite threatening storms, I took a chance with pad and sleeping bag just 50 yards back from the river, with a parka to huddle under in case of rain. The skies cleared by 10:00 P.M., when the two pointer stars of the Big Dipper pointed directly north to the North Star. Six hours later, the Big Dipper had swung to the west, the pointer stars now aiming east. As meteors burned their trails in the sky and the heavens rotated above me, I dozed and dreamed and gazed and listened, at times chuckling, at other times talking to myself, as if all this needed to be shared with someone, if only with myself. And as I watched at dawn just this morning, thousands upon thousands of cranes lifted off for their daytime routines, their mass departure deafening (track 1-37).

Today I visited National Audubon's Rowe Sanctuary, then checked out the cranes at Mormon Island, but I was just killing time, I realized, until I could return to see the spectacle on the river at sunset one more time. And here I am, Johnsgard and I having parted ways. We each head to our respective blinds.

By 5:30 P.M., I'm across the open fields and into the blind, an enclosed wooden structure with metal roof and burlap on the west side that offers fine views of the Platte River through the portholes. I quickly ready the recording gear, then scan the river. It's perhaps 150 yards wide, and shallow. With small gravel islands scattered about, the river here is perfect for the roosting cranes, as they choose to roost in ankle-deep water, apparently so they can hear and see any coyotes or other predators that might approach them in the night. The current flows toward me from the west; the bridge at South Alda Road is about a mile and a half away. A few ducks swim on the river. Surveying this scene, I find it hard to believe that anything special could happen over the coming hours on what appears to be a rather ordinary stretch of river.

Oh, geese! How many thousands of snow geese I wouldn't dare to estimate, but in a raucous launch from a quarter mile upstream they are off, up, swirling, rising higher and higher, heading off to the west . . . and then the south . . . and 15 minutes later, when I think they are long gone, I look high overhead and there they are, heading east. A monstrous serpent snakes through the sky, easily more than a mile long, multiple strands breaking and weaving and re-forming, a mass of geese accumulating at the front, then thinning out again, the ranks merging and splitting, undulating, surging and heaving, thousands upon thousands of geese, gradually becoming smaller and smaller specks in the sky. And by 6:00 they are gone.

I see no cranes in the river, but I've heard a few bugles, and now I see five birds approaching from the south, just above the horizon, five sandhill cranes in single file, all of them dropping below the horizon and out of sight into the upland staging area just beyond the river. There and in a similar area on this side of the river to my right is where they'll accumulate, and at some moment, the group decision will be made for the mass flight to the river. At least that's what happened two nights ago.

I scan the horizon with my binoculars now, swinging from the south around to the west, and everywhere there are cranes. There are single lines, some of just a few birds, some of a hundred or more, some multiple lines flying side by side, some V-shaped formations, some low on the horizon, those cranes nearer appearing higher and larger, some lines crossing each other, the head of one line now tacking on to the tail of the one in front, merging, cranes everywhere. Through the binoculars, I look to the west, planning to swing the binoculars from the bridge to the south and count the cranes on the horizon, but counting by tens I quickly fall behind, the cranes filling the field of view faster than I can count.

To the left of the setting sun, a dark cloud forms on the western horizon where there was none just minutes ago, and incredulous, yes, I confirm through the binoculars that they are all cranes. Ever so slowly, the cloud grows as they approach, a mass of large grayish birds. When I swing the binoculars toward the south again, it is cranes cranes cranes, long lines and masses of them approaching, flying just above the rolling hills, over the farmhouses and trees, wave after wave streaming my way, and closer by they drop into the two staging areas in the fields to the north and south of the river, often dropping in as smaller groups, of two, three, or five.

For half an hour now I have watched this spectacle unfold, all the while muttering to myself "unbelievable . . . incredible . . . man, oh, man . . . they just keep coming and coming and coming . . . holy smokes . . . no one would believe this . . . what a sight . . . the sky is black with them . . . billions and billions . . . I don't believe this," repeating myself, over and over, at a loss for words that could capture what is unfolding before me. I've watched flocks of birds before, perhaps 30,000 robins in the winter roost back home (page 12), but there are at least as many cranes here, and a crane is 60 times the mass of a robin, and these cranes are *bugling*. And there were a few thousand wading birds in the Everglades (page 23), lots of moaning and bleating, but nothing like this. Together, the cranes and geese here tonight will number perhaps 100,000 birds, and what a racket!

There, checking my watch, 6:33, I see the first few cranes are in the river, perhaps a quarter mile to the west. Within minutes, hundreds follow these pioneers, a mass of seething gray now beginning to fill the river far upstream. Birds are flying directly to the river now, too, skipping the stopover at the staging area. I aggressively scan the horizon, estimating by hundreds this time: 1,000 . . . 2,000 . . . 3,000 . . . 4,000 birds in the air, their numbers undiminished.

Small squadrons of ducks dart among the larger cranes. I've seen pintails, wigeons, gadwalls, mallards, and teal. The geese are long gone.

The clamor of the cranes upstream grows, flanked by the clamor from the staging areas on the banks to the left and to the right. Do they trumpet or bugle? Both, I decide. Surely they don't croak or rattle, as some have said. No, it's far more magnificent than that. It's a rich, explosive sound, pulsating, rising from deep within the lungs, bursts of air hurled through the voice box and into the extralong windpipe that coils into the breastbone itself; there the resonating sound is amplified and enriched with harmonics, and with beak open, the bugling hurtles into the air. One bird close by is deafening, the bugling of thousands upon thousands of them unimaginable until there they are.

A pair, male and female, flies by, his bugling noticeably deeper and richer than hers, she calling immediately after him as if they were one. And they are one, paired for life, till death do them part, and they may live up to 20 years. Many of the cranes I've been watching these last few days are clearly paired, a male and female flying about or foraging together, often calling as one. There are trios, too, the third bird often giving itself away as a "colt," a one-year-old without the rich bugling but instead with a tentative, high-pitched whistle or trilled whistle, a "poor little helpless me, take care of me" kind of call that it uses as it stays with Mom and Dad through its first winter up until this spring (track 1-36).

And what fun listening to those colts. Get two of them calling together, and I can hear each colt's distinctive voice. Some calls are high, thin whistles, others more trilled, some liquid, some more raspy. Curiously, the trill in the whistle seems to have the same rhythm as the adult's bugle, and, just listening to these colts, I would bet that, as the windpipes elongate in the chests of these youngsters, the whistles gradually become more trilled and eventually deepen to rich adult bugles. Now almost a year old, each of these youngsters will soon be on its own, eventually finding a mate, renewing the cycle. A few of these colts will pair next year, when they are two years old, but some not until they are five or even six years old.

Just before 7:00, the sun hangs on the western horizon, the flights of cranes across the fireball and against the pinkish blue sky to the south holding steady. Flocks now stream past the blind, too, landing directly in the water, the

SANDHILL
CRANES

mass of cranes in the river growing toward me. In the windless calm of this evening, the cranes arrive and land from any direction, so graceful and in such controlled flight, so different from their approach of two nights ago. Then, with a strong south wind, I watched as birds came in high from the south, flying beyond the river and then circling, lower, approaching the landing into the wind, sideslipping, plummeting, necks and legs askew as they made last-minute adjustments for touchdown.

Now, with a great racket, the staging area to the right erupts into flight, thousands of cranes taking the short flight to the river. Strong wingbeats launch each effortlessly into the air, the neck soon outstretched and legs trailing, the neck then rising and legs dropping just before landing, so graceful yet in some ways so prehistoric-looking, with those long legs and neck and six-foot wingspans.

Twenty minutes past sunset I scan the horizon again, and in the orangish band on the horizon and the shades of orangish blue to orangish gray to bluish gray above, the numbers of cranes are no fewer than before. By 7:30 there is an enormous clamor again; this time the south staging area is lifting off, thousands upon thousands of cranes shuttling to the river. I have been watching the meter on my recorder as an objective measure of how loud these cranes are; until now the meter has been dancing safely among the green LEDs at the lower end of the scale, occasionally venturing into the orange, but with that liftoff, the red LEDs warned of too intense a sound for my recorder's settings.

And minutes later the geese, oh, the geese, wow. It's as if the flock of untold thousands that departed about two hours ago has returned, but in the gathering darkness I can no longer see clearly what is going on out there. I glimpse white forms, surely the snow geese flying about, many seeming to land upstream and swimming down, soon appearing in the water before me among the towering gray cranes. I slip the headphones for my recorder on, the sounds now amplified in my ears: cranes and geese, geese and cranes, my, oh, my.

In the dark I listen, focusing on the cranes, trying to grasp how the river has filled before me (track 1-34). Half a million cranes have swept north from their wintering areas to the south, mostly in New Mexico, Texas, and northern Mexico, just as their ancestors have migrated throughout North America for the last several million years. They stand in the waters of the Platte River, which have flowed east across the plains from the snowfields and glaciers of the Rockies of Colorado and Wyoming. In their perhaps month-long stay here, their bodies fatten for the flight north as they gauge the whimsical winter winds that just last week blanketed this area with a foot of snow. And at some moment, any day now, when they decide that spring has the upper hand, they'll be off, heading north, spreading out to breed over the vast Arctic expanse of Canada and Alaska, far into the islands of the Arctic Ocean.

Half a million, I try to comprehend, half a million sandhill cranes now standing somewhere in Nebraska's Platte River, either upstream or downstream of me, most of them in the 50 miles between Kearney and Grand Island. At almost eight pounds apiece, that's about 2,000 tons of cranes, 4 million pounds. Stand them head to toe on top of one another, and their collective four-foot statures would tower 400 miles overhead; stand them wingtip to wingtip with their six-foot spans and they'd stretch from here across eastern Nebraska, across Iowa, across Illinois, and halfway into Indiana, or they'd stretch west across western Nebraska and all of Colorado into Utah. And just how many of those half million cranes are roosting here before me? Tens of thousands, beyond a doubt. Thirty, forty thousand? Fifty thousand would not surprise me.

And many of them now are so close, just tens of yards away. The first cranes landed so far upstream I was disappointed, but two nights ago I learned patience, and as their numbers grew tonight, they spilled over the islands and shallow channels up there, the graying mass growing toward me. Two brave souls then advanced well beyond the front and landed on a small island 100 yards directly out in front of me; soon tens and then hundreds followed, other nearby gravel islands also becoming crane islands, each growing until it merged with the others, cranes soon landing near me. Still others landed upstream and walked downstream past me as if in search of better footing for the night.

As the cranes settle for the night, their general clamor yields to individual voices. Now, an hour and a half after sunset, the new moon perhaps two hours above the western horizon, I slip the headphones on, close my eyes, and listen. I can focus better this way, with nothing in sight, nothing to distract my ears. I hold steady, focusing on individual cranes, listening to where and when and how they call, listening for vocal evidence of the social ties that bind pairs and families. I pick out individual birds straight in front, to the right, everywhere before me.

Nearby off to the left, a crane calls loudly, repeatedly, a beautiful rolling bugle, the first half low-pitched, the second half higher, so striking (track 1-35). No, wait, one crane can't do that! That's a pair, the male calling first, followed immediately by the female, *as if they were one.* Again and again they call, and I try to hear their individual efforts; yes, I hear them, male first, female second, sometimes overlapping, sometimes she lagging just a bit behind him. How I wish I could slow those voices down now, maybe to quarter speed, because I know I'd hear the individual voices even better then. I'll be sure to do that on my computer when I return home.

For what must be half an hour, I amuse myself by listening for their individual voices. I hear such variety in their calls, and especially those of the colts, from plaintive whistles to trilled whistles so liquid or raspy, but no calls of the colts seem synchronized with those of adults. An adult male to the left now duets repeatedly with a female to the right, separated by perhaps 50 yards. How fascinating. Are they paired and just temporarily separated, I wonder, old hands at calling to and finding their partners of many years in the masses? Or could they be younger birds seeking mates for the first time? What is clear to me is that they know who they are, and they can no doubt identify each other by their voices as well as I can identify family and countless friends and acquaintances by voice alone.

From the left I now hear the roar of approaching cranes in flight, only adults bugling at first and then youngsters bleating; they fly across to the right just in front of me and then circle back, their bugling soon fading (track 1-36). I will never tire of their sounds. Were they newly arriving birds or spooked cranes resettling in the roost? In the dark I cannot know, but how wonderful to hear the youngsters. I replay those few minutes in my mind and gradually realize that the calls of the youngsters were not coming from the flock overhead. No, the bleating colts were standing in the water before me, and they continued to call after the flock left.

So why were the colts calling? It wouldn't surprise me if they were yearlings recently separated from their parents, given that this is the time when the colts and parents typically part for life. I try to imagine myself as a yearling standing there in the river. I'm now heading north on my first spring migration, and, although thousands upon thousands of other cranes mill about me, how could I not feel downright alone and abandoned by my parents, who have always been there for me? How could I not call out when the flock passes, hoping that Mom and Dad might be among them and come to me? I recall a feeling like this just recently when, as a lone cyclist without immediate friends in a crowd of 2,000, I had never felt so lonely.

And it is fairly quiet again. I listen . . . as a colt calls loudly off to the right, repeatedly, for perhaps two minutes . . . to the babble of ducks and geese as the clamor of the cranes dies . . . to a beautiful rolling trumpet call on the right, gradually rising and falling, followed by just a few isolated notes, and again, again, how playful, I think . . . to just a few individuals, wondering how deafening it would be if they all were calling . . . and to mystery sounds in the night, the sources of which I do not know. Out on the river, I sense gray shapes standing in the water, some movement, the lighter snow geese swimming about.

Ten o'clock looms, the time I had promised myself I would depart to ensure a smooth journey home. Orion and Big Dog are just above the western horizon, the new moon having ducked into the ground haze, and the cranes have quieted, settling in for the night. Yes, I must go. I pack up, oh so reluctantly, and sneak out of the blind to the open field away from the river, there pausing for one last listen. Behind me is the babble of the roost, before me the incessant traffic noise of Interstate 80 and the world to which I must return. I'm torn, my mind racing through all that has overwhelmed me in the past two and a half days. I stand there 10, 15 minutes, listening one last time to the distant cranes, increasingly knowing that I'll be back.

APRIL

8

A Tropical Pilgrimage

April 19–30
Nicaragua and Costa Rica

AT LEAST ONCE a year I try to make a pilgrimage to the New World Tropics, the ancestral home for so many of the birds I know in North America. Many of these northern breeders also return home annually, as they take advantage of the long summer days to raise their families at northern latitudes and then avoid the northern winter by coming back to the Neotropics. Other species, of course, have grown accustomed to our northern land and stay year-round. Whether migratory or resident in North America, many of these species are members of large species groups with close relatives who have chosen to remain year-round in the Neotropics. The flycatchers, for example, have maybe a dozen species in North America but about 400 throughout the Neotropics; among wrens, about 9 species occur in North America, but 60 to 70 remarkable songsters are found in the Neotropics; and hummingbirds have fewer than 20 species in North America but close to 300 in the Neotropics.

On this pilgrimage, I sometimes have a focused agenda and am obsessed with a particular species (returning with a "trip list" of 10 or so species, much to the consternation of my birding friends), but other times I go with an open mind, ready to listen to any bird that will speak to me. Such was the case when my son invited me to join him on the Managua to San José leg of his extended bicycle journey from San Francisco to the tip of Argentina (see www.ridefor climate.com). In mid-April 2006, I packed my folding Bike Friday in its suitcase, flew to Managua, Nicaragua, and met David at the airport; there we reassembled my bike, attached wheels to the suitcase (thereby converting it to a trailer), hooked this trailer to my bike, filled the trailer with sleeping bag and tent and other gear, and away we rode, ready for any listening adventure that came our way.

As we biked, I heard countless tales directly from the beaks of parrots and doves and hummingbirds and trogons and toucans and so many more, but it was my encounters as I lingered, off the bike, that stood out. I relate four of my favorites here.

Great Kiskadee—A Flycatcher

APRIL 19, 4:30 A.M., AN HOUR BEFORE SUNRISE. Behind me, waves lap the shore of Isla de Ometepe as I stand on the beach in the Charco Verde wildlife reserve on the south shore of this island in the middle of Lake Nicaragua. In front of me across this narrow beach is Laguna Verde, the Green Lagoon, and to the right an extended forest. We took the ferry to this island just yesterday, and during a quick walk to the reserve I realized that where I now stand would be a fine place to listen to the world awaken. Specifically, I liked the kiskadees here, one of the most common and recognizable birds throughout the Neotropics, one of the very first vocalists of the morning, and as a tribute to the 400 or so flycatchers throughout the New World, I hoped to commune with the kiskadees at dawn.

I stand, motionless, facing the lagoon, hearing the gentle waves on the beach behind me, the *quark*s of commuting night-herons and the deep rumble of the giant marine toads all around. A crowing rooster to the far left, perhaps tonight's dinner back at our residence, howler monkeys sounding off to the right, answered by another group to the left. The sounds of night and day meet now, such variety, low moans, chuckles, screeches, all seemingly distant, all muted, but so rich. Who are they? Of what lives do these sounds tell?

At 4:54, yes! there's a muffled, half-second *weeer* directly overhead, an almost immediate response to sounds of another kiskadee to the distant left. Then it's *weeeer,* slightly longer, more exaggerated, also rising and falling in frequency and so rich in harmonics, as I know from having looked at sonagrams of these calls. And in an unbroken sequence, he follows with *weeer, weee-eep* (a two-part emphatic note ending high), then *zikikikikikikik* (a raucous chatter), *weee-eep zikikikikikik, weee-eep weee-eep zikikikikikik,* and after a slight pause *weee-eep weee-eep,* a seven-second burst of exactly what I have read kiskadees do at dawn! And all right above me, as I stand motionless here in the sand and take it all in (track 1-38; figure 8).

Over the next minute he calls more simply, with 11 single *weeer* notes, each seemingly in response to the kiskadee to the distant left, who utters all variety of sounds, some of them the *kiskadee* namesake.

In the next minute I count nine *weeer* notes, followed in rapid succession by *weeer weee-eep zikikikikikik weee-eep* and then *weeer weee-eep weee-eep zikikikikikik*. Wow, such a variety of sounds, such a variety of expressions. It's hard not to ascribe some higher intelligence to this variety; yet, if these fly-catchers are like the flycatchers I've studied in North America, they don't learn their songs. Rather, their songs are somehow encoded in the genetic material. But that doesn't preclude some level of intelligence, I remind myself, as I check my bias in thinking that a songbird is likely to be more intelligent because it learns its songs the way I learn to speak.

Then seven *weeer* notes, *weee-eep weee-eep zikikikikik,* and four more *weeer* notes.

I chuckle at my primitive attempt to capture these kiskadee sounds in my notes. They may make sense to no one but me. Next are four more notes that sound something like my pronunciation of *weeer,* but he plays with the frequency of those notes, one lower, the next higher, then a *chick-weeer,* the *weeer* intermediate in frequency. Then *chick-weeer weee-eep weeeer zikikikikikik weee-eep,* another *weeer,* followed soon after by *weeeer weee-eep zikikikikikik* . . .

Figure 8: GREAT KISKADEE

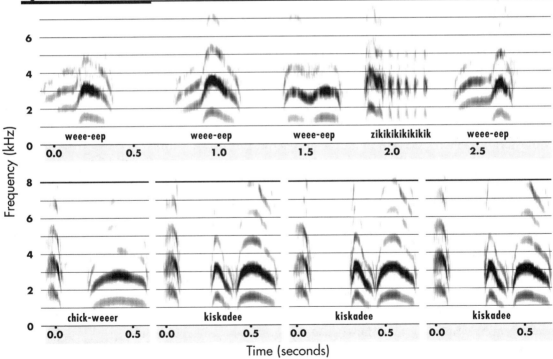

weeer... chick-weeer... weeer weee-eep zikikikikikik weeer. But no two of those *weeer* notes sound alike now, as they vary in pitch and inflection and loudness and duration and who knows what else.

Another minute begins with *chick-weeer* and then, yes, a solid *kis-ka-dee!* Finally, there is absolutely no doubt who calls overhead. It *is* a kiskadee, a great kiskadee, no less. I cannot know whether it is he or she, I remind myself, as both males and females are believed to call like this. But he or she continues with *kis-ka-dee, kis-ka-dee,* 10 in all over the next minute, two other kiskadees audible in the distance, all three birds now increasingly insistent on shouting *kis-ka-dee! kis-ka-dee!*

Then a pause, an extended pause, and I hear a boisterous round of *kis-ka-dees* by several birds off in the distance, suggesting that the bird above me has moved on with its day and joined others of its kind. For six minutes it called above me, ending almost exactly at 5:00 A.M., a half-hour before sunrise.

My feet firmly planted in the sand, I still stand motionless, eyes closed, just listening, just absorbing it all. The kiskadees continue in the distance, as I hear them over the sounds of boat-tailed grackles and other creatures increasingly noisy nearby. Every few minutes the kiskadees burst into a round of calling, then fall silent. To the distant right, beyond the lagoon and in the forest, I hear banded wrens, special birds that will no doubt lure me back here tomorrow.

"Buenos días." I am jarred from my trance by a workman with a machete, walking the fence line to my right. Yes, I respond, *buenos días,* a very good morning indeed.

I try to grasp what has happened over the past 45 minutes. Dawn. A

Figure 8. Sounds of the great kiskadee. Though kiskadees are flycatchers and almost certainly do not learn their songs like songbirds do, these kiskadees nevertheless have a varied repertoire of calls and songs. As this kiskadee greets the dawn, just look at (and listen to, track 1-38) the variety of sounds he makes. See especially how the *wee-eep* calls differ from one to the next.

Sonagrams here are made from recordings in the archive of the Macaulay Library of Natural Sounds at the Cornell Laboratory of Ornithology (MLNS 105553 and 7879 by Geoff Keller and Paul Schwartz, respectively); though recorded in Texas and Venezuela, these nonlearned sounds vary little geographically and therefore match well the sounds of the bird that I listened to in Nicaragua. Because of the microphone I used—two small mikes clipped to my eyeglasses—my recordings contained too much echo and reverberation to obtain a sufficiently clean sonagram, though they did capture accurately the way that I heard the birds in nature.

Nicaraguan dawn, with the sounds of howler monkeys and so much more, including the all-consuming sounds of a kiskadee awakening overhead as the sun's first rays swept toward us from the east. And such a variety of sounds, so expressive are these kiskadees, the simple *weeer* alone varied in pitch, duration, loudness, and inflection, all of the variation signifying, well, what? And the meanings of the conversations with other kiskadees awakening in their roosting places? I don't know what it all means, nor does anyone else. But it must signify something, expressing some inner feelings or "thoughts" that the bird has.

All of this kiskadee's singing feels vaguely familiar. My mind drifts north, to those few flycatcher species who will soon migrate and breed in North America. Many of them—kingbirds, pewees, phoebes, the *Myiarchus* and *Empidonax* complexes—also greet the dawn in special ways. How nice to see the roots of their dawn singing behaviors among their close relatives in their ancestral home.

Yes, *buenos días* indeed!

Banded Wren

APRIL 20, I'm back. It's now 5:00 A.M., and I've hiked beyond the calling kiskadee, farther down the beach to where I expect to find the banded wrens singing. It's classic dry forest here, and it *is* dry, the brown leaf litter crunching beneath my feet because the rainy season has not yet begun. There, up ahead, a wren sings.

I work my way closer, marveling at song after song (track 1-39; figure 9). What a rich variety! He is a superb songster, one of the finest, each song consisting of several phrases with loud, clear whistles and melodious trills, and from my readings I know that each male has about 20 different songs. Now, during the dawn chorus, his singing is at its finest, successive songs almost always different, each strikingly different from the song just before and the song to come.

The beauty of his songs would be enough to draw me to him, just to hear him run through his dawn routine, but I have come for something extra. I need to hear what I have read about how males interact with one another, as these banded wrens seem to differ from all other birds I know. In my familiar song sparrow, for example, a male has perhaps 10 different songs at his command, but he sings one of them over and over before switching to another; the switches come much faster, however, when two territorial males engage in a heated discussion. It's the same with North American wrens; get two rock wrens or marsh wrens or sedge wrens or Bewick's wrens or Carolina wrens or house wrens or winter wrens engaged in a dispute, and they pull out all the stops, using a much greater variety of songs than when each male sings by himself. Not so with these banded wrens. During routine singing, successive songs are likely to be different, but engage two males in a dispute and they seem to lock horns, hurling the same song back and forth until the dispute is resolved. Yes, I need to hear that, as these banded wrens are different, and reading about it is not enough.

I concentrate, trying to memorize each song, but it is tough. I give the

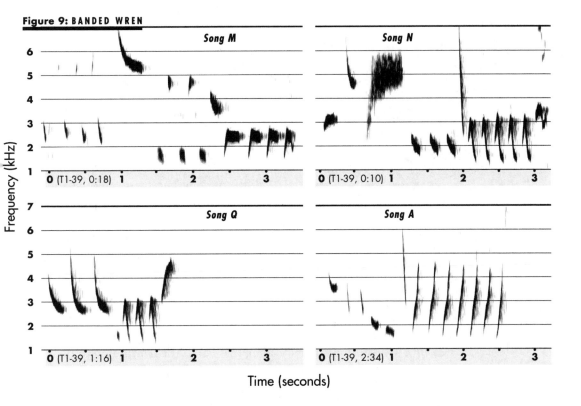

Figure 9: BANDED WREN

Time (seconds)

Figure 9. What fine songs the banded wren sings, as they consist of multiple parts, many phrases with clear whistles slurred either up or down. Illustrated here are four songs, labeled M, N, Q, and A, with A being the song that was used repeatedly as two neighboring males escalated their interaction. Keep an ear out for these particular songs as you listen to the three minutes of singing on the CD (track 1-39).

next song the letter A, and the next different one B, and my best concentration can get me to C, three different songs in mind, and then I lose it and have to start over. I hear A, B, A, B, A, B, C, as he alternates two different songs and then moves on. I yearn for my computer and Raven software to make the sonagrams, as his different songs are so distinctive that I know I could recognize each if I simply had the sonagrams in front of me.

And he's gorgeous. He sings nearby in the bushes now, such a beautiful cinnamon brown above with black bars in wings and tail, snow-white beneath with bold black bars on the sides and flanks. I can see a bit of the Carolina wren in him, can see why these two wrens are both placed in the genus *Thryothorus*.

I resume the lettering game, as it helps me focus. A, B, A, B, he alternates two songs now . . . C, C, C, three of one kind in a row, and in the distance I hear a faint echo, another male seeming to respond with the identical song. The near bird then moves on to a different song and then some incomplete songs, as if he stutters on the introductory notes. Then three renditions of yet another song, back to back.

WREN

He sings on, and I begin to lose track, only to hear a definite echo, what sounds like emphatic back-to-back songs from the neighboring male, who has come close enough for me to hear him. Wow. I've not heard that particular song before. It's so distinctive, ending in a beautiful trill with six or seven rising whistles, *sweet-sweet-sweet-sweet-sweet-sweet*. I start over with my lettering scheme, calling that Song A. The near bird responds in kind, with A, the neighbor with AA, near bird A, neighbor again AA! Back and forth, matching song after song, the near bird even singing a triple A song in there. And just as quickly as it had begun, it is over, the birds now moving apart, the singing more distant.

I'm breathless, screaming for an instant replay, and I have it, sort of, in the relatively poor recording that I am making with my short shotgun microphone and minidisc recorder. I slip the headphones on and rewind to the beginning of the exchange, listening and rewinding again and again, trying to capture in my notes what I had heard. I'm finally satisfied: over 80 seconds, these two males sang this particular A song more than 20 times, in an exchange I code as follows:

Near bird	A	B		A		A		A	B		AA		AAA		A		A	Y	
Neighbor			AA		AA		AA			A		AA		AA		AA			Z

I look at my scribbles and see how insistent the neighbor was, staying on message and singing the A song 13 times in this exchange, with six double songs. The near bird seemed less insistent, uttering single A songs at first, seemingly trying to escape this exchange with a different song (denoted as B), then singing a double A and even a triple A song before again seeming to disengage with a different song (Y), the neighbor then also moving on with a different song (Z).

Astounding! In the routine singing during the dawn chorus before this exchange, I heard no song matching and recall no double or triple songs, but here, during this most intense interaction, is where they slow down and repeat the same song over and over. How different this wren is from the other birds I know, as other birds during intense interactions sing more rapidly and are less likely to repeat a song. Here is a striking exception to what I thought was a general rule among songbirds about how songs are used in escalated interactions.

How befuddling, yet how enlightening. In either system, males can readily convey exactly how they feel. When a male banded wren is excited, he slows down and repeats a song; when other birds are excited, they speed up and repeat themselves less. As long as the rules of engagement are understood by all participants, and they are, of course, either system can work.

The Tropics, I think. Leave it to the Tropics to teach us a few lessons about what we thought we knew based on North Temperate Zone birds.

Three-wattled Bellbird

APRIL 24. "RESERVA BOSQUE NUBOSO. SANTA ELENA, MONTEVERDE." David and I stand beneath the sign over the entry path, smiling, expectant, capturing this moment on camera. In this cloud forest reserve is so much life, and thanks to my conservation-minded friends at Monteverde, Costa Rica, places like this are secure. Secure, at least, until climate change modifies these mountaintops and makes life inhospitable for many of these creatures, such as the already extinct golden toad. That's primarily David's interest here, to see where climate change is already having an effect and to talk to local biologists about the problem. I'm concerned, too, but for the moment one thought overshadows all others: I have been promised singing bellbirds here.

Bellbirds, as in three-wattled bellbirds, the birds that enticed me to retire from a university professorship. That's the way I think of them, and thank them, too, birds so exciting and charismatic and revolutionary that I dropped other research projects and wrote two grant proposals to the National Science Foundation in search of funding to try to understand them better. These bellbirds are close relatives of flycatchers, yet the songs of flycatchers are inborn, encoded in the genes. Not so with the bellbirds; they learn their songs, and the evidence is undeniable. As these bellbirds evolved from their flycatcher-like ancestors, something happened that caused this learning, just as something happened as we evolved from our apelike ancestors and learned to speak as we do. It was that "something" that I needed to know more about, why learning evolved in some groups but not others, and I needed help funding the research. But the response of my peers who reviewed for the National Science Foundation was a simple no. Evidence of song learning that I know to be undeniable was rejected out of hand. I soon realized that I thought more of the bellbirds than I did of those peers, and kept only the bellbirds in my life.

They're an hour or so away, we're told, so we're led by our guide Tona from one trail to the next, I all the time straining my ears to hear the first bellbird BONK or whistle in the distance. "Bellbird," I soon exclaim, the loud whistle carrying. He calls again and I hear it more clearly, realizing now that my bellbird is "only" a black-faced solitaire. False alarm. But what remarkable songs. The field guide describes them so perfectly: "high, thin, clear whistles, drawn-out and leisurely, with fluty transitions and liquid undulations, occasional metallic notes with overtones, sounding exquisitely beautiful in its natural surroundings." I relax my bellbird sensors and now hear other birds, too, nightingale-thrushes, wood-wrens, barbets, wood-quails, hummingbirds, a quetzal.

We turn next onto Sendero Encantado. I ask Tona for a translation. "Path of the beautiful, the amazing," he says, and at that instant, in the distance, I hear an unmistakable bellbird. First it is the loud whistle, then a BONK. In a hushed tone appropriate to where we stand in this vast cloud forest cathedral, I point out to David the sounds that have so obsessed me the past 10 years.

Closer and closer we hike, until we hear three of them call, all birds of the Monteverde dialect, each with its ear-shattering BONK and whistle songs.

Now for the moment of truth. The last time I visited Monteverde was in 2002, four years ago. I know that, from 1974 to 2002, the loud whistle in their songs had plummeted from 5,600 to 3,610 hertz. Why males lower their whistle over time is a mystery, but the only way they can all stay in tune is by listening to and learning from one another—it's one of the unequivocal pieces of evidence for song learning. So what has happened to their songs since 2002? If I had perfect pitch, I'd be able to listen and know, or if I had my laptop computer with me, I could record directly to the computer and then use my Raven software to determine today's frequency precisely.

No, what I do have are my ears and a recording of the bellbirds in 2002. If I listen to a live singing bellbird and the 2002 recording back to back, I will know what has happened. On my recorder, I cue up the song with four whistles in it and wait . . . The bellbird sings, the tape plays. Wow. Did I hear right? I wait for another song . . . Bellbird sings, tape plays. Yes, the whistles in this bellbird's songs are much lower than the whistles of 2002. I play the same game with the other two bellbirds down the trail. They are all on message, all singing much lower whistles than just four years ago (track 1-40), having dropped about as much as I would have expected.

So they're still at it. I hardly believed it several years ago, when I first documented this annual change in the songs, because few if any other bird species are known to learn and continually relearn their songs this way throughout the year. Humpback whales, yes, but birds, no. The bellbirds' songs change in other ways, too, but it has been the whistle that was easiest to track and measure. There's a physical limit to how low the whistle can go, of course, and at some point that limit will be reached. For now, though, it seems that they're still going down the scale. And it's still a mystery, too, why they change their tunes and who leads the way.

"He's banded!" Tona exclaims. Finally, one of the bellbirds has landed in the open, high in the tree right over the trail, and Tona is quick to get his spotting scope focused on the bird. "Azul . . . oro . . . plata." He reads off the colors on the bands, halting, uncertain. It's so tough to read the colors, as green leaves reflected in a silver band make it look green. One by one, Tona, David, and I study the bird in the scope until we agree: azul/oro, oro/plata, which is blue over gold on the left leg, gold over silver on the right.

Here is a bird with a known history, one who was caught by the bellbird research team some time ago and banded so that we could get to know these birds better. I check the little cheat sheet of bellbird histories I keep in my notebook, finding that A/O O/P was caught and banded on August 10, 1994. At that time, the bird had just a few green feathers in an otherwise adult plumage, and by knowing how plumages change as the males age, we can know that he was about 7 years old at that time. He was hatched about 1987, which makes him 19 years old this year (2006), and when he learned his first whistles, they were about 4,600 hertz. In his lifetime, to keep pace with other bellbirds around him, he has lowered the frequency in his own whistle about 1,200 hertz, from about 4,600 to 3,400.

Oh, wow, he just exudes charisma. Up close in my binoculars, I see the snow-white head, the cinnamon body, the three black wattles hanging from the base of his black bill . . . and how he jumps into the air from his perch, landing to face in the opposite direction, and from the cavernous gape explodes a loud BONK, then whistles and soft swishing sounds, and he bounces and dances some more. It's as if he needed to remind me that there's so much more to him than his song, and in a dramatic departure, he's off, disappearing over the treetops.

THREE-WATTLED BELLBIRD

I glance over at David, as I am warmly amused at how intensely he's been using the spotting scope as a telephoto lens to try to capture this bellbird on his digital camera. It's wonderfully clear that my son now understands just a little better what has so captivated me these past years. The bird itself is stunning, but its glamour goes far beyond looks. One of the biggest questions among those of us who study birds is why some species learn to sing and others don't. Songbirds learn, but their closest relatives, the flycatchers, don't. These song-learning bellbirds (and their cotinga relatives) evolved fairly recently in evolutionary time from the nonlearning flycatchers, and I believe that, by studying the bellbirds and other cotingas, we'll find an answer to why learning has evolved among them. Someone, someday, will tackle this big question.

Clay-colored Robin

APRIL 30, SUNDAY MORNING. Here I am, packing my bicycle back into its case in the courtyard at a friend's house in San José, and who should be singing so insistently above me but the national bird of Costa Rica, the clay-colored robin. No, not the quetzal, not the bellbird, or a toucan, or any of the other absolutely stunning birds of Costa Rica, but rather it is the clay-colored robin that has such recognition.

What a familiar sound, so much like the robin I know back home. There's no mistaking the invitation from this robin in the courtyard, so I settle in and listen. Sweet carols, I think, one caroled phrase after another, 14 in that first series, then a pause for a few seconds, then 10 phrases, pause, now 27. Yes, so much like the American robin back home. I hear two phrases that are recognizably different from the others, too. One of them sweeps smoothly from an especially high to a low frequency, *phew*. The other rapidly falls and then rises, *chu-wi*. None of the others jump out at me, so I listen for those two to recur, and sure enough, they're consistently there, as the robin sings one of them roughly every five seconds (track 1-41).

I should get on with my packing and leave it at that, just enjoying each caroled phrase, enjoying how those two recognizable phrases recur, but he's too inviting, and I have the time. I pick up my notebook and scribble in a line each series of caroled phrases there, designating the *phew* with the letter A, the *chu-wi* with B, and any of the other caroled phrases with simple dashes:

```
- - - - B A - - - - - - - - - - - B - - - - - - B
- - A - A - B - - - - - - - - B A -
- - A - - - - - - - - - (and he stops when a loud table saw buzzes at a
     construction site over the fence)
- - - - (he resumes when the saw is quiet and again stops immediately
     when the saw resumes)
- - - - - - - - - - - - - - - -
```

There's a minute already. He sings on — can I really stop my note taking? I don't think so.

```
- - - - - - - B - - - - - -
- - A - B - - A - -
- - - - - - - - - - - - - - - - - B A - - -
- - - - - A - B - B - A - - - - - A - - - - - - -
```

And there's another minute . . . Oh, just one more, I tell myself . . .

```
- - - - - - - A -
- - - - -
- - A - - -
```

```
- - - - - - A -
- - - -
- - - - A
- - A - - -
- - - - A - - - - -
- - - A -
```

And there's a third minute. But he pauses now, allowing me to pause, too. I count how many caroled phrases occur in each string: 26, 18, 12, 4, 17, 14, 10, 23, 25, 9, 5, 6, 8, 4, 5, 6, 10, 5. In just three minutes of his life, he has sung 206 phrases. Of those 206 phrases, 28 were either A or B, an average of 14 times for each. I divide, 206 ÷14, getting about 15, letting me conclude that this robin has about 15 different phrases that he is using.

That's nice. I like that. In just a couple of minutes I am already inside this robin's head.

He resumes, and I sit back, enjoy, simply tallying how many caroled phrases he sings and how many are of the two that I can recognize. For four more minutes he sings, then pauses for a minute, then sings for two more minutes before flying off.

I tally the results. For the nine minutes I listened, he sang 509 caroled phrases, 42 of which were A phrases, 29 B phrases. He seems to favor his A phrases over his B phrases, at least he did during these nine minutes. A little math lets me estimate roughly how many different phrases he used during these nine minutes: 509 ÷ (42 + 29) × 2, or about 14 different phrases, about the same estimate I got after only three minutes.

If I were home, I'd be tempted to enter all these sequences into my computer and then play with the numbers, studying how he uses the A and B phrases, but it's nice to listen here more simply. He soon returns to the tree overhead, and I breathe with Mr. Robin, listening to him sing, listening to the fine Costa Rican national carols roll off his bill . . . Yes, this is good. Life is good. I resume packing my bike, still listening. I can go home now, as the trip feels complete.

MAY

9

Two Virginia Mimics: Brown Thrasher, White-eyed Vireo

First weekend in May, Grundy, Virginia

"IT'S A BIRDY PLACE" is Friday's consensus as members of the Virginia Society for Ornithology return from the backyard of Lynda and Roger Mayhorn, two of the hosts for the annual meeting being held the first weekend in May in far western Virginia. That's good enough for me, I decide, site unheard, for my free morning during the weekend. I'll go there tomorrow, to hear what I can hear.

SATURDAY, MAY 6, 6:00 A.M. Roger has guided me over the hour's drive through the winding roads of Buchanan County, and now, half an hour before sunrise, I'm here, standing beside the car, listening, recording gear ready. Oh, where to begin!

The brown thrasher is most insistent, singing continuously from the very top of the tree just 30 or so yards away on the other side of the garage. Long tail drooping, back slightly hunched, he sings in couplets, *I'm here I'm here, listen up listen up, record me record me.* The invitation accepted, I slip the headphones over my ears, aim the parabola, and start the recorder. Wow, song after song, more song than silence, continuously, never ending. Greedy for more, I work my way closer, knowing that if I can halve the distance between us, his songs will be four times louder in my ears. Slowly, smoothly, quietly, I slip across the lawn and around the garage until I am *beneath him,* with a clear shot up.

Every little morsel he offers to the world is now sharp and crisp in my ears, the parabola so effective at reaching out and seizing the songs directly from his bill. What variety, song after song, on and on, every second and a half a new one, each so different from the one before and the one to follow. How does he do this, coming up with such variety, with what I know can be thousands of different songs? He has a vast memory, I know, but he probably makes many of his songs up as he sings, too, improvising on the spot. "Thank you, lady thrasher," I find myself saying. "Without you, who knows what dull tune he might sing. But why? Why have you designed him so? Why have you and your female ancestors chosen males who sing this way?" Oh, if I could only rattle around inside the mind of a female thrasher for a day, to hear what she hears, to know consciously what she is listening for.

I listen, taking in what I can (track 1-42). The phrases are paired, sort of, though rarely perfectly, as the second one often isn't complete, and sometimes there are singles, sometimes triples and more. He's mesmerizing, the whole performance hypnotic. What was that, a hint of eastern meadowlark song? . . . was that starling? . . . red-bellied woodpecker? . . . purple martin? Before I can secure a thought, he's on to another song, and another, while I race to keep up.

Carolina chickadee! There, finally. It's a perfectly unmistakable imitation, well, a perfect fragment, a high-low-high whistle, as the chickadee would normally add another low note to complete the four-phrase pattern (figure 10). Wow, he's good, a better mimic than many other thrashers I've listened to. My confidence boosted, I'm now on high alert for other imitations, concentrating . . . flicker song, I'm sure of it, but just three notes, *wick wick wick* . . . goldfinch song, two phrases . . . meadowlark rattle call . . . flicker again? . . . *chick-a-dee* calls, also unmistakable! He does like the chickadee . . . meadowlark song? . . . bluebird song? . . . robin *tut* notes? . . . a female red-winged blackbird call, unmistakable . . . flicker again? . . . a cardinal whistle, I'm sure of it . . . the chickadee high-low-high whistle again! Yes, he's repeated himself . . . flicker again? . . . red-bellied woodpecker calls? . . . *killdeer* . . . goldfinch song . . .

He *is* good. He repeated himself in that brief sequence, too, with about two minutes between the two renditions of that distinctive chickadee high-low-high song fragment. How nice, too, that he slipped the *chick-a-dee-dee* call in between, showing he's mastered the two main chickadee sounds. It could be another hour or two before he sings those particular sounds again, as the brown thrasher needs a long time to tell all that is on his mind. I wonder what his "return time" would be. I could camp here, listening, timing, counting how many other songs he sings before I hear the chickadee sounds again. I could listen for that female red-winged blackbird call again, too, another distinctive sound, and for other sounds I pick up along the way. How satisfying it would be to sit here, to get to know him better . . .

But another voice argues, "Move on—there's so much more to hear." I'm torn, but the second voice wins and I reluctantly move on, listening briefly in turn to the chatter of a female cowbird, then the songs of a scarlet tanager, an American redstart, a northern cardinal, a white-eyed vireo, and the rapid *chick-a-dee-dee-dee* calls of a Carolina chickadee, perhaps the very bird the thrasher has mimicked.

"Wood thrush/white-eyed vireo," both sensors fire at once, and instantly I realize what I am hearing. Near the beginning of the white-eyed vireo's song are four sharp *whit whit whit whit* call notes of the wood thrush, the notes with which the thrush awakens at dawn and goes to roost at dusk, the notes he uses when seemingly disturbed. With the vireo's blatant mimicry of the thrush, I now remember how a friend showed almost 30 years ago that many of the notes in the songs of white-eyed vireos are calls pilfered from other species (track 1-43; figure 11). *Calls,* I emphasize. How fascinating, as he mimics not songs, only calls.

Figure 10: BROWN THRASHER MIMICS CAROLINA CHICKADEE

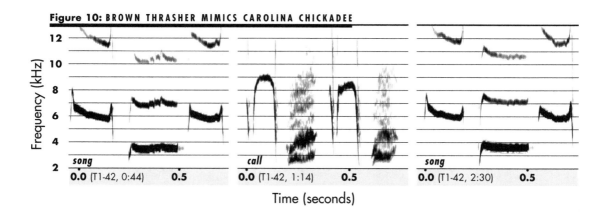

Figure 10. This particular brown thrasher is an excellent mimic and, in the brief span of about three minutes, shows that he knows the sounds of many of his neighbors, including song sparrows, northern flickers, red-winged blackbirds, and, as illustrated here, the Carolina chickadee (track 1-42). Furthermore, he knows not only the chickadee song (far left and right) but also the *chick-a-dee* call (middle). And, to my great satisfaction, he proves that, in spite of being able to sing 2,000 or so different songs in a few hours' performance, he also has an excellent memory, for he can recall and sing the same chickadee song from time to time, as he does here two minutes apart. In the chickadee song, hear the high-low-high pattern, but in the sonagram see the stack of harmonics that occurs above each of the three fundamental tones (see page xiv in the Introduction for a discussion of harmonics).

"Okay, you got my attention"—I find myself chuckling to the vireo—"now show me some more." I listen more carefully: the *whit* notes of the thrush are easy, as they're repeated, making up a good third of the song, but what are those other little bits in the rest of the song? There are at least five or six parts, but he's too quick for me, the brief notes flying by too fast for them to register. "Could you please slow down and give me just one note at a time?" Foolish to ask it of him, I know, but not of myself, as back in my motel room awaits my computer, and my Raven software will do just what I ask, isolating each sound so that I can at my leisure contemplate its source.

For now, I listen to his performance as song after song is collected by my parabola and reflected to the microphone, the sounds there converted to electrical impulses that are then broadcast into my headphones while they are captured permanently by my recorder. The "four-*whit* song" soon gives way to another, one beginning with a nasal *chew* note, but I'm stumped as to who the vireo is mimicking here. Over and over he sings this "*chew* song," 32 times in all, as if trying to impress me with how little I know. The next song begins with what sounds like a sharp *piiik* note of an American robin, but the rest eludes me. After 34 times, he's on to another song, and in the middle of each I hear the *whit whit* of the wood thrush, but this time just two notes—the "two-*whit* song." The next series has the downward-slurred *klear* note of a northern flicker, the next the unmistakable *chewink* of the eastern towhee. Then it's a series of the "four-*whit* song" again; how nice to have him return to a song that I already know. Next are songs with a longish *nyeeh* note near the end, almost certainly the call of a red-eyed vireo. Songs in the following series begin with another robin note, but it's more of a *tut,* not the emphatic, sharp *piiik* note of before—58 times he sings the *tut* song. Blue jay! The next song has a subtle *jay* in it, unmistakable though muted, nothing the audacious jay would be that proud of—and 59 times he sings this song.

Below the vireo, a Carolina wren now sings, and how cooperatively they seem to share the airwaves, each singing in turn, neither ever interfering with the song of the other. The wren stops and an eastern towhee begins, now the vireo and the towhee taking turns: *vireo, towhee, vireo, towhee, vireo, towhee.* And when the wren resumes, it is the vireo up above, the towhee and wren down below: *wren, vireo, wren, towhee, wren, vireo, wren, towhee, vireo, wren, vireo, towhee, v/wren, vireo, towhee, wren, vireo,* those 23 songs in the first minute alone.

Throw 20-some songs at random into 60 seconds' time, and by chance alone multiple songs would overlap and interfere with one another; but there's

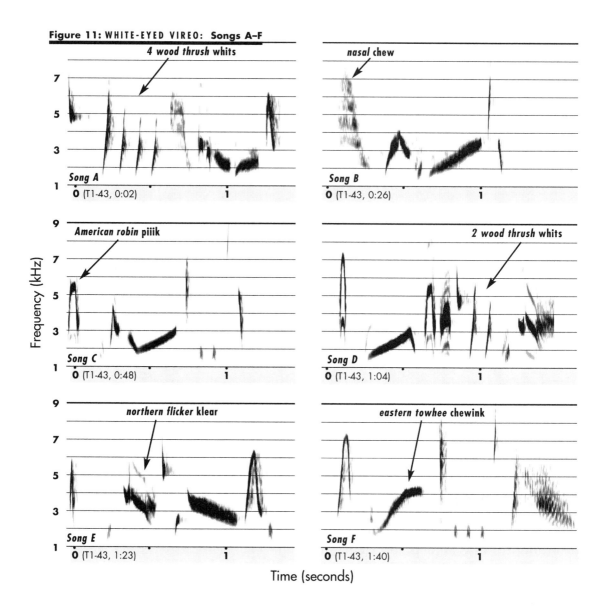

Figure 11: WHITE-EYED VIREO: Songs A–F

4 wood thrush whits

Song A
0 (T1-43, 0:02)

nasal chew

Song B
0 (T1-43, 0:26)

American robin piiik

Song C
0 (T1-43, 0:48)

2 wood thrush whits

Song D
0 (T1-43, 1:04)

northern flicker klear

Song E
0 (T1-43, 1:23)

eastern towhee chewink

Song F
0 (T1-43, 1:40)

Frequency (kHz)

Time (seconds)

no interference here. These three singing birds seem to tiptoe around one another's songs, each taking his turn singing, not really caring about the others, of course, but each presumably making sure that his song is heard. It is no doubt the saucy wren who sets the pace, though, with the vireo and the towhee making sure their songs aren't blocked by his especially loud songs. At one point, where I heard *v/wren, vireo,* the vireo actually uttered the first note of his song and then stopped short when the wren interrupted; after the wren

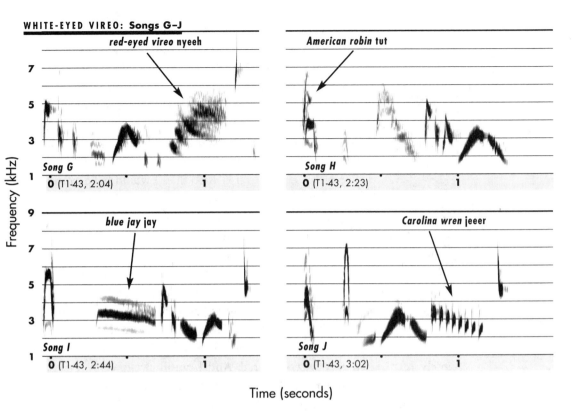

Figure 11. The 10 different songs (A–J) that I heard from the white-eyed vireo who spoke to me on May 6, 2006, in far western Virginia (track 1-43). Most of the songs are recognizable by a note that has been mimicked from another species.

completed his song, the vireo started over, only then delivering a complete song (track 1-44).

As the vireo switches to his next song, I can almost hear him thinking, but I quickly distance myself in disbelief. *"No way,"* I say, yet there it is—he switches back to his *chewink* song again, the song that contains an unmistakable call of the towhee. Does this vireo know what he has done? Does he know that the *chewink* is the call of this very bird with which he now shares airtime? I puzzle as he sings all 58 renditions, flabbergasted when he switches next to a song that has the Carolina wren's *jeeer* note at the end! In all, the vireo sings his *jeeer* song 50 times, though the wren now fades into the distance after nearly 10 minutes of *wren/vireo/towhee* singing.

How fascinating. Does this vireo know the relevance of those two songs?

Did he choose his *chewink* and *jeeer* songs just for the towhee and wren, even though the towhee and wren were singing and not using their calls at the time? Just how well does he know his neighbors and the sources of his imitations? In my head I do a little math, concluding that it is highly unlikely that those two songs would have been chosen by chance alone (about a 1 in 45 probability), suggesting to me that there's more to this vireo than I would have expected.

He continues. Next is the song that begins with the robin's *piiik* note—48 renditions. And there's the red-eyed vireo's *nyeeh* at the end of the songs in the next series, all 56 of them. The *chew* song again. And the Carolina wren's *jeeer* song again. He forages as he sings now, and so close that I can see the whites of his eyes, his irises as white as the irises of the closely related red-eyed vireo are red. And beautiful yellow spectacles, the white throat, the whitish breast and belly with yellowish flanks, the two yellowish white bars on the grayish brown wings, the soft olive green above. Immaculate.

VIREO

I have now followed him for roughly two hours as he has worked his way through his song repertoire, singing from the apple tree across to the high dead tree on the corner of the lot to low in the underbrush, where he forages as he sings, a circular area perhaps only 50 yards across. But now I see him fly off into the distance, and he's soon singing beyond the neighbor's house. I should follow him, but the terrain is tough and the neighbor's permission not granted. Maybe he'll return soon. I spread my rain poncho on the ground and sit, adding water to my cereal and powdered milk mixture and eating my breakfast, trying to quiet my growling stomach, which has increasingly competed with the birds for the microphone, but half an hour later he's still on the far end of his territory. Okay, that's his move, I decide, as he seems to be encouraging me to head back and get to work on dissecting his songs on my computer.

On my drive back, in my mind I run through the 10 different songs I've learned to identify from him, each easily distinguished from others based largely on the mimicry (see page 288).

A repertoire of 10 songs is not atypical, as I recall that the average Virginia male has about 13. If I had stayed with him longer, I probably would have heard additional songs from him.

A good hour later, back in my motel room, I download the recordings to my laptop and then use my Raven software to study sonagrams of each of his songs in turn. I listen first to the entire song, but then to each song note by note, quickly realizing that I'm rusty on these call notes. Although the vireo clearly knows the intimate lives of Virginia birds far better than I, I am astonished at what I can hear. Besides the blatantly mimicked calls I heard as I listened in the field, I now hear the subtle *yank* of a nuthatch, a single harsh *chat* of a mockingbird, the *pituk* note of the summer tanager, the *weep* of a great crested flycatcher, and more. I list my new finds with the others, coming up with 16 species whose calls are known by both this male white-eyed vireo and me.

SPECIES	SOUND IMITATED
downy or hairy woodpecker	sharp *peek* notes
northern flicker	*klear* note
great crested flycatcher	*weep* call
red-eyed vireo	*nyeeh* call
blue jay	*jay* call
white-breasted nuthatch	*yank* call
Carolina wren	*jeeer* call
wood thrush	*whit whit* notes; also soft *bup* notes that precede song
veery	a variety of low *veer*-type notes, thrushlike; or perhaps they are from a yellow-throated vireo?
American robin	*piiik* and *tut* notes, of different intensities
northern mockingbird	harsh *chat* note
yellow warbler	"chip" note, typical of a variety of warblers
eastern towhee	*chewink* call
summer tanager	*pituk* note
northern cardinal	hard *tik* note
house sparrow	husky *chirrup* call

I'm sure I sell him short. Someone who knows Virginia bird calls better than I would surely pick out more mimicry (and maybe I misidentified a couple of the more subtle calls, too). I've read that up to 75 percent of these vireo song components are mimicked, making this vireo more of a mocker than the famed mockingbird itself, which borrows perhaps only 15 percent of its songs from other species. It's just that the vireo's mimicry is so subtle, and few of us know calls well enough to identify their sources. The vireo (unintentionally, I'm sure) makes it more difficult for human ears by how he puts those mimicked calls together, too, in such snappy little packages with so much spunk. Brief, pilfered notes follow each other quickly, the resulting song a striking performance, such as *CHICK'-a-per-weeoo-CHICK'*, with strong emphasis on the sharp, brief first and last notes, the *weeoo* lazily slurred up and then down.

Why he mimics in this way is largely a mystery, but perhaps what white-eyes do with their mimicry in another context provides a clue. When small birds mob a predator such as an owl, they use their own species' sharp "alarm notes," and such calling then often alerts individuals of the same and other species. When a white-eye confronts an owl, he disassembles his songs and uses all of these mimicked notes, sounding as if he alone were a flock of different birds mobbing the owl. Perhaps the owl feels more harassed by this ploy, but the vireo's diverse repertoire no doubt helps to recruit individuals of the mimicked species to help with the mobbing task, too. The vireo is no dummy, as he knows that, to be effective in this task, he must mimic the call notes of all these other species, not their songs.

What a remarkable creature, this mimic with one of the best-kept singing secrets of all North American birds. Because his song is so distinctive, he's easily identified without careful listening as a white-eyed vireo, but the good fun comes in the listening. The blatant mimicry is relatively easy, such as the *whit whit* of a wood thrush, the *chewink* of a towhee, the *klear* of a flicker, but the real challenge is to hear who he's mimicking in those ultrabrief notes throughout the song.

It has been the best of days. It began as do the best of all spring days, with a promise to myself to get out early. And today, once I was up and out at the appointed place, the only plan was to let it happen. As it turned out, the thrasher and the vireo spoke to me, and I chose to listen, and how fascinating, two mimics that differ from each other so much in how they sing and no doubt why they mimic. If they had been silent, I wonder where my listening would have taken me. To the cowbirds? To the redstart, cardinal, or chickadee? Or to any of the other birds I heard, each one a possibility, as each has its own story that can be heard if I'm there at dawn to listen.

10

Baltimore Oriole—She Sings, Too

May 28, 3:55 A.M.
Norwottuck Rail Trail, Amherst, Massachusetts

IT RAINED OVERNIGHT AGAIN, and the water is still dripping from the trees, but I couldn't wait another day, as the perfect morning might never come. No, I'll take my chances this morning, perching here at my favorite place on the Norwottuck Rail Trail, the paved bike and recreation path from South Amherst to Northampton.

My perch is near the one-mile post, where the railroad crossed high above Hop Brook. The trail has taken over the railroad bed, the beavers the brook below; it is now more of a lake, the wetlands extending below me to the west and to the east. I had stopped here just a few days ago to record a male Baltimore oriole and was soon confused about a second loud bird in my head-phones. I searched all around me for this second bird and only then recalled what a birding friend had told me, that there was a nest above the bridge. Looking just over my head, I saw it, about 10 feet up, the typical pensile, gourd-shaped nest hanging from near the end of an elm branch. And I could see the nest fidgeting. Stepping back, I aimed the parabola at the nest and was astounded at what I heard. It sang, and beautifully, a song I savored more than what I was hearing from the male.

Hearing her on the nest and him in the nearby trees, I knew I would return to spend a morning listening to these two orioles converse. In the meantime, back home, I searched some of my literature but found little about female song. One paper in the journal *Condor* over 20 years ago told of occasional "duets" between male and female, but only 12 songs were heard during 15 hours of listening. How different from my experience, as my female sang every few minutes. Then I found a clue, that all of the listening in that report was from *before* incubation! I was listening *during* incubation, as the female sat and sang for long hours on the nest while her mate sang in the trees nearby.

So I have returned this morning, ready for a good listen. I'm sure she's in the nest; I tucked her in last night just before sunset. She had foraged frantically during her brief periods off the nest while he accompanied her, but at 7:48 P.M. she returned to the nest, and at 8:09 they exchanged their last songs, the sun setting just seven minutes later. Other birds—a rose-breasted grosbeak, catbirds, yellow warblers, red-winged blackbirds, cardinals—continued to sing, and a kingbird circled overhead. With his sharp *whit whit* calls, the wood thrush announced he was going to roost, the robin likewise with his *qui qui qui* and *tut tut tut*. A willow flycatcher offered his evening serenade in the calm, cooling air. As the intense aroma of the evening's honeysuckle engulfed me, the songbirds faded and the green frogs took over—a woodcock circled overhead, whistling with his wings, then chattering with his voice. It was 8:46 P.M., half an hour after sunset, when I called it an evening, promising an early return in the morning.

Standing on the bridge now, well before sunrise, I feel the bike path disappearing into the darkness to the north and south, the path a tunnel through shadows of bushes and overhanging trees. To the east and west, I see fresh swamp and marshland, the beavers' handiwork. And all about me, I feel the energy of the dawn. An hour and a quarter before sunrise, it is the frogs' turn to fade, and in the distance a willow flycatcher blurts out a *whit-bew*. There's an isolated song from a swamp sparrow . . . a song sparrow, followed immediately by his neighbor . . . a yellowthroat . . . a yellow warbler . . . a robin warms to the dawn, *qui qui qui qui qui qui* . . . a cardinal. So far just calls or a single

BALTIMORE
ORIOLE

song, the singer poised for the intense singing competition that will soon follow.

At 4:14, a kingbird launches into the air, and one by one, the others soon join the frenzy, so that by 4:30 all are flaunting themselves: cardinals, phoebes, willow flycatchers, yellow warblers, red-winged blackbirds, yellowthroats, catbirds, tree swallows, song and swamp sparrows, robins, wood thrushes, mourning doves, and a distant rooster on Mad Woman Farm. In the swamp I continue to hear an American bittern, a sora, and lots of wood ducks and mallards, but no orioles.

4:35 . . . 4:40 . . . 4:45. What extraordinary energy, each singer now in peak form, the yellow warblers chipping frenetically between songs, the swallows singing on the wing, the kingbird circling, on and on they sing, but without the orioles. I'm distracted by the catbird imitating the descending whinny of the sora, and I keep track on my watch of how long it takes him to return to sing the sora again: 2 minutes and 10 seconds, then 50 seconds later. As the catbird plays out his mind, he offers me an easy handle on how to listen: Determine how much time between the whinnies and I have an idea of how long it takes for this catbird to tell me most of what he knows, or count the number of other sounds between sora whinnies and I have a rough idea of how many different sounds he can sing. But I also know there's a sora down in the marsh to the west, because I heard it well before the catbird awoke. Or could the catbird have been teasing me, singing from his roost, blurting out a few loud sora whinnies now and then? I wonder. I didn't actually see the sora, I remind myself.

It's 4:55 A.M., and I sense that the peak of the dawn chorus is already past. It's quieter, the singing not as intense, and 22 minutes until sunrise. Still, nothing from the orioles, but she is in the nest, I know, as I have seen it move. Now and then she squirms, no doubt a little restless after a night of sitting.

As I am wondering if it will be a silent day, the orioles never to sing, the hickory tree just north of the bridge bursts into oriole song, and she immediately sings, too. Ah, I know those songs well, because they are so distinctive, so different from the songs of the other orioles I have heard on the bike path. I think of his full song as being two low notes followed by two higher ones, about a second long, to my ears a *tew tew twe twe* (track 1-45; figure 12). Her song is a bubbling cascade of notes, about as long as his but with twice as many notes, and with a wonderful rhythm, *we-chew-dle-wee-dle-wee-dle-weet*. They no doubt know each other's songs, too; she responds immediately to his first song of the morning just as she did to his last song almost nine hours ago.

He continues to sing, 18 more times over the next five minutes, all to the north of the nest. His next song is from a different location, in the oak to the south of the nest, and she responds immediately, but still she sits on her eggs.

It seems he was just checking in, as he now flies a considerable distance to the north, singing there, his songs fading. The catbird whinnies the sora . . . and whinnies again three and a half minutes later . . . but the male oriole is silent, as is she. At 5:10 I hear him in the distance again, returning from somewhere, and a minute later he sings from the nearby hickory, she again bursting into song immediately after him.

So far, she's responded to him three times. The first time was when he burst on the scene nine hours after departing for the night. Five minutes later the position of his song had abruptly changed, and she responded again. Eleven minutes later, he returned from a distant foray, singing near the nest, and she sang in response. All this time she has been deep in her hanging nest, presumably unable to see his whereabouts.

By 5:25, eight minutes *after* official sunrise, he sings from the hickory just north of the nest, and I am to the south. Here's a chance to hear them both better, I realize. I move so that the nest is in line with him, then aim my parabola at the nest in the foreground, with him beyond. She is perhaps 15 yards from me, he 30. The headphones over my ears, I now hear them both clearly (track 1-45).

His pattern of singing seems different now. During the first 10 minutes of his singing this morning, his four-part song predominated. Now, however,

Figure 12

Row 1. Here are two exchanges between the male Baltimore oriole who sings near the nest and the female who sings on the nest while incubating. For both exchanges, his song is the four-note complete *tew tew twe twe*, with two low notes and two notes that sound distinctly higher. In the first exchange, she responds immediately with a full *we-chew-dle-wee-dle-wee-dle-weet*, in the second with a slightly delayed, incomplete *we-chew-dle-wee-dle*.

Row 2. Sometimes the male and female of a pair have nearly identical songs. This male song begins with two chatter notes, followed by a complete song. The female's song is similar to the first part of his song (notes a a b c), and often he sang only that part while interacting with the female.

Row 3. More commonly, it seems, the male's song is more complex than that of the female. In this example, the male's song is longer and far more complex than the six simple notes of the female.

most of the time he utters only a single *tew*. As I listen, I count the number of notes in his song and mark when the female sings: 1, 4, 4, 1, 1, 4 and female responds, 1, 1, 1, 1, 1, 1, 1, 1, 1, 1, 1, 1, 1, 1, 1, 1, 1, 1, 1, 4 + female, 1, 1, 1, 1, 3 + female, 1, 1, 1, 1, 1, 1, 1, 1, 4, 1, 1, 1, 4, 1, 4 + female. In these seven minutes, the female sang four times, responding not to the single *tew* notes but rather only to his more complete songs.

Figure 12: BALTIMORE ORIOLE

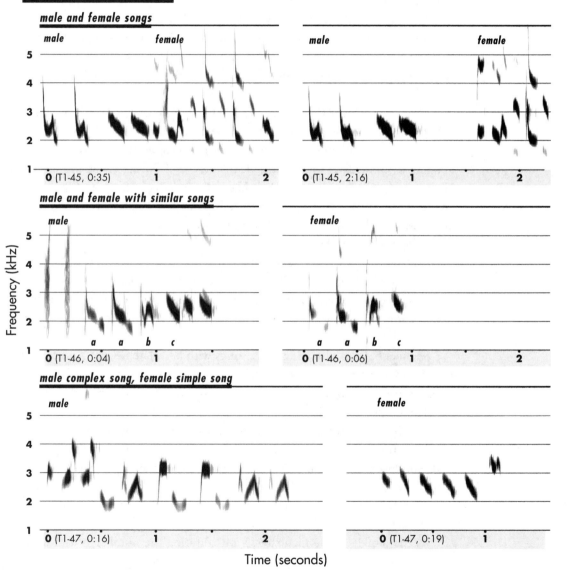

Frequency (kHz)

Time (seconds)

For the next 25 minutes, until 5:50 A.M., the male hangs out in the hickory, as if awaiting the female's departure, and for 25 minutes I stand down the bike path to the south and listen intently. When she chooses to sing, she typically responds within a second after the male's song, though sometimes she doesn't wait for him to finish, and occasionally she takes two or even three seconds to respond. Many of her responses are the full song, but some are abbreviated, some even consisting of a single note, a muted *we,* as if the situation didn't demand the full effort.

The male flies far to the north again, and after a three-minute silence he returns, singing just south of the nest; she then sings, too. The pattern continues. She preferentially responds to full songs, and she is especially likely to respond when he changes positions or when he returns from an absence of a few minutes.

At 6:29 — I repeat that to myself, *6:29,* over an hour *past* sunrise — she is still sitting on the nest, and he has been silent for five minutes. She sings without him, as if impatient or querying his absence. I soon hear him to the north, and half a minute later he sings beside the nest, as if she has called him home. He's now nearer the nest than he's been all morning and utters three loud chatter notes there. She sings immediately, hops to a branch above the nest, and together they fly off to the north, with more chattering and a series of twittering notes from her.

It's been 11 hours since she settled into that nest, and she must be famished and now searching madly for food. Only seven minutes later, though, she's back, accompanied by the male and arriving with great fanfare, including a chatter, then male and female song, and within seconds she settles in again.

She incubates, exchanging more songs with her mate nearby. And at 6:48 the first biker passes, heading south. Joggers and walkers soon follow, sometimes with others, sometimes alone. I catch bits of conversation as they pass.

Two cyclists: . . . built his way up to a nicer bike . . .

Two (female) walkers: . . . blondes seem kind of boring now . . .

Two runners, after passing me: . . . wonder if he knows anything about that woodpecker . . . (This is May 2005, just after the "rediscovery" of the ivory-billed woodpecker was announced.)

Cyclist: Passing on your left.

Walker to his inquisitive dog: Let's go . . . Hey!

As the female oriole incubates, I am counting the number of times she sings during each 10 minutes: 6, 9, 8, 2, 4, 6, 8, 9, 6, roughly a song every $1^1/_2$

to 2 minutes, and almost always in immediate response to one of his songs. And after 91 minutes, the male sings a complete *tew tew twe twe* especially near the nest; she then sings immediately and hops out of the nest, chattering and twittering as she flies off with him.

She again allows herself only seven minutes to replenish her reserves, and she's back on the nest. My birding friend Deedee Minear arrives by bicycle; this is her favorite place to come and linger. She's full of wisdom about what has happened here this year and in the past, the yellow-throated vireo and waxwing nests last year, for example, the two marsh wrens this year, the robin nest just below, and the bittern. "There's a sora out there," she tells me, pointing to the west, and I chuckle and tell her of my trickster catbird. "Yes, most likely a sora," I agree, "but not as many soras as the catbird would have us believe."

Another birding friend, Jim Marcum, soon arrives, having learned from Deedee that the best way to bird the bike path is, not surprisingly, by bike. We enthuse about retired life, find a chickadee nest in a hollow stump down below, and enthuse some more about retired life. Jim was a dean at the university; now he is proving the tale he posted 24/7 on his door, "Gone birding."

Lone walker, on cell phone: I'm out walking today. . . . I did the bike trail. It's very lovely. . . . There's nothing out here."

Two walkers: Yes, this is the bridge. . . . And there's the nest, right there!

Through all of this, to the whir of knobby mountain bike tires, the hum of smooth road tires, the rhythmic *sjweer-sjweer* of in-line skates, the *clip-clop* of runners, the shuffling of walkers, the heavy breathing of those in a hurry, and the cheery voices of those just meandering down the path and taking it all in, some headed north, some south, and me just standing in place, yes, through all of this the orioles go about their business. They continue their singing exchanges, she alternating periods on and off the nest. Beginning at 8:16, she sat for 27 minutes, foraged for 3, sat for 16, foraged for 14, sat for 48, foraged for 12, then returned to the nest at 10:16 A.M.

For over six hours I have been here, these two orioles active for the last five. And nearly all of that time he has been near the nest, every 5 to 10 seconds offering a single *tew* or a more complete song, *tew tew twe twe*, perhaps 2,000 songs or song fragments in all, she responding every minute or two with a song of her own, about 200 overall.

What does all this mean? I've seen behavior not unlike this in expectant human parents. There's a buzz about the upcoming family, true excitement, a renewed commitment to each other, and more frequent expressions of love.

But these are avian beings I'm listening to. What do they know? What do they feel? Whatever it all means, I feel a togetherness, that they are two, working together on this parenting. The eggs are their mutual investment in the future, with both male and female determined to give those eggs the best chance of surviving. Their parents, grandparents, and, indeed, every generation of their ancestors was successful, all the way back to the beginning of time, and here is the next attempt at preserving that unbroken lineage.

My mind wanders to the other orioles I've been hearing up and down this bike path. I realize that I need to visit them to learn more of what these orioles can teach me.

So I return over the following days, biking up and down the path, stopping to listen and record the orioles I encounter there. What I find thoroughly intrigues me. There seems to be no such thing as a "typical oriole pair." Just north of the bridge is another oriole nest, high up in a cottonwood tree. The male and female sing only occasionally, but when they do, they respond to each other with what sound like identical, fairly complex songs (track 1-46; figure 12). In a pair to the south, the male's song is beautifully complex but hers especially simple (track 1-47; figure 12). And in another pair, the female's song is again simple, but the male's song is identical to that of his neighbor. All females that I encounter sing from the nest, though none as often as the female of my favorite pair at the bridge.

What do I make of all this? Perhaps the particular song a male uses is easiest to explain. Each male tends to have a unique song, but every once in a while two neighbors have identical repertoires. I've seen that pattern once before, among chipping sparrows, and my friend Wan-chun Liu showed that such pairs typically consist of a yearling and an older bird, the yearling having learned his song from the older bird.

The singing by the females is more difficult to explain, as far less is known about female song in general. Within pairs, the songs of the male and female are usually strikingly different, but, again, every once in a while mates have identical songs. Could they be older birds, I wonder, perhaps paired together for a second year, therefore having had more time to learn from each other? Did she copy him or he copy her, or did both copy a third bird; or did they learn from each other and in that way converge on a common tune? And why? Do they have some advantage now in communicating that other pairs don't have?

And why are some females so much more vocal than others? Could the females' behavior vary with age, as for some species it is known that older females sing more? The female of the pair at the bridge was older, I believe; her plumage was dazzling, almost indistinguishable from that of her brilliant male. The two females with the simpler songs were drab, probably yearlings.

All I really know for sure from my time with the orioles is that I will never listen to them the same way again. For that I have especially the pair at the bridge to thank. But I yearn to know more, too. I'd love to record each of the birds as they arrive from migration and then follow them through the summer. I think I could distinguish most of the birds by their unique plumages, so I'd know them as individuals. Who pairs with whom? How similar are their songs initially? Do the songs change over the season? Can any evidence be found of male and female modifying their songs during a season, to become more alike, or even more different? When neighboring males have identical songs, do they sing them upon first arrival, or does one of the birds learn the song of the other during the first few weeks? And how does all of the singing change over the season? Yes, there's so much more to learn, and routine visits to the orioles during the spring and summer would yield many answers.

11

A Prairie Dawn on Our Pawnee National Grassland

Memorial Day Weekend
Pawnee Grassland of Colorado

MAY 27, 3:45 A.M. Exactly three miles north out of Briggsdale, Colorado, I turn left opposite the big white gate, right where my Colorado birding friends had promised it would be. Murphy's Pasture—I smile—hailed as some of the finest birding in this arid, short-grass prairie of northeastern Colorado, the "other Colorado" that so few people know. Yes, it's a *national* grassland, government-owned, just as it was before Lincoln's Homestead Act of 1862 gave free land to all comers and just as it is now again after the government bought back the land from the bankrupt farmers during the dust bowl years of the 1930s.

I drive west into the prairie on a narrow dirt road, over an occasional cattle guard, four miles to the intersection of county roads 96 and 69. This is as good a place as any, I reason, so I pull over and park the car. As I open the door, I remind myself that whatever happens will be good, as I have no planned agenda other than to lock onto some prairie bird and listen to my heart's content.

Calm, dead calm. No airplanes, no traffic noise. And dark—no streetlights, no lights visible on the horizon. And stars, so intense, the Milky Way a bright ribbon stretching from horizon to horizon. My friends the Eagle and the Swan are overhead. Jupiter lies just above the western horizon, a couple of its moons visible in my binoculars.

Horned Larks

The larks are everywhere, already singing in all directions, though there's only a wee hint of the sun that will rise in an hour and a half. That's it, I decide quickly, this morning's menu is larks, one of the prairie birds on my hit list and first cousin to the famed sky lark of Europe and Asia. I laugh aloud as I remember how some of the science-minded students in my ornithology classes have rolled their eyes as I've read poetry to them, my all-time favorite being Shelley's "To a Sky-Lark," who sings "a flood of rapture so divine." With the larks as my audience now, I replay the first verse:

> Hail to thee, blithe Spirit!
> Bird thou never wert—
> That from Heaven, or near it,
> Pourest thy full heart
> In profuse strains of unpremeditated art.

I know that these horned larks can also sing from the heavens, as high as 200 yards up for eight minutes at a time. I could hope for such a performance.

I step across the road to the west and into the prairie; with headphones over the ears and recorder turned on, I start in the north and slowly swing the parabola around, listening in all directions. Larks! They're everywhere, dozens within earshot, but none close by. Some sing short songs and others sing continuously, but none close. I walk, slowly, trying to approach one, but he goes silent, no doubt flying off and resuming his song elsewhere. I walk again, spooking another, but then choose to stand and wait, hoping that one will come to me.

By 4:30, an hour before sunrise, I'm distracted by a nighthawk *pzeeent*ing and booming overhead, by the two Brewer's sparrows to the northwest, by a lone lark bunting to the west. Then, just to my right, a horned lark arrives, and I slowly swing my parabola around, past the bird and back, then up and down, finding the sweet spot where the bird is the loudest, the sweet spot where the parabola is aimed directly at this phantom bird who sings in the dark, so near yet so invisible (track 1-48; figure 13).

And how he now sings! Continuously, four to five reedy notes every second, each different from the others, a stream that in the distance from untold larks sounds like a thousand tinkling bells, and then unexpectedly he punctuates it all with a flourish, a flurry of notes that to my ears are all slurred together, rising in pitch, and then he resumes, 10, 20, 30 seconds and then another flourish, and again, and again, and again he repeats this pattern.

I imagine launching him into the air, higher and higher, 100 yards up, 200 yards up, now singing high overhead, hovering over his territory in the small breeze that must blow up there, yes, a "Spirit . . . from Heaven, or near it, . . . profuse strains of unpremeditated art." Unmoved, he continues from the ground for a good five minutes but then in a flutter is gone—I have heard his wingbeats but seen nothing.

Yes, there was Shelley's "harmonious madness." For any lark who chooses to listen, I offer Shelley's last verse:

> Teach me half the gladness,
> That thy brain must know,
> Such harmonious madness
> From my lips would flow,
> The world should listen then—as I am listening now.

Five minutes of bliss, enough to make a morning. I try for more with other larks, with the Brewer's sparrows, with the lone lark bunting, with a western meadowlark, but nothing compares. By 5:20 I'm struck by how quiet it is, 10 minutes before sunrise and the larks are now uttering far simpler, isolated songs, nothing continuous like before. On the rise to the east, I see cattle silhouetted against the sky, the national grassland grazed by the national herd. And at 5:30, the moment of sunrise, brown-headed cowbirds whistle

Figure 13: HORNED LARK

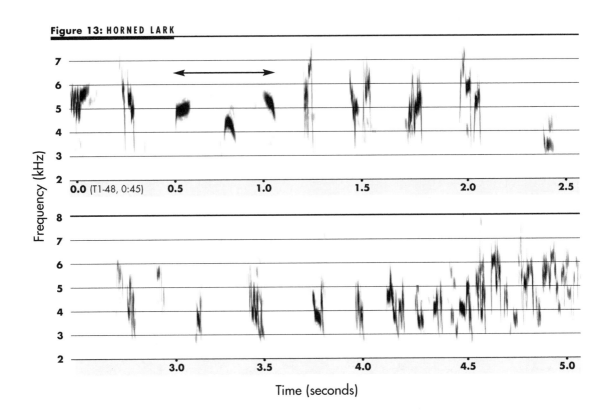

Time (seconds)

Birdsong by the Seasons

and rattle just to the south. Startled by my presence, four antelope snort at me for a minute, two minutes, then bound off, as if to signal that the morning is over. I drive north through the prairie for four miles, marking the spot where I hear a Cassin's sparrow, and then return to the motel where I am staying in Sterling, about a two-hour drive to the east.

"Unpremeditated art," I muse. I wonder. In those five minutes of "rapture so divine," what has he told me about himself? I sense no pattern as he sings, but just how organized and premeditated are his songs? I listen again to those minutes, then transfer the recordings from the hard drive on my recorder to the hard drive on my computer. Now I can peer into the mind of this songster, looking at the sonagrams and seeing details in the songs that only the lark knows are there.

The flourishes. Why not start there? They are the exclamation points after long series of tinkling notes, so I ask how often they occur. I listen to the five minutes again, and then again, identifying 15 flourishes in the 330 seconds, about one every 22 seconds, but once he sang nonstop for 50 seconds between flourishes.

And are all flourishes the same, or is each a unique, on-the-spot, unpremeditated creation? One by one, I compare sonagrams of each of the 15 flourishes with the others. Ah, the 1st and 10th flourishes are identical, as are the 2nd and 7th and 11th. I give each unique flourish a letter and note the sequence: A B C D E F B G H A B B C D F. Look at that. Eight different flourishes, the last 6 all repeats. He has a set repertoire of flourishes, 10 or so different ones, I conclude.

And what about all of that continuous rambling between flourishes? What's he doing there? I pick a particular phrase that is distinctive and on my laptop monitor scan the 330 seconds of sonagrams for that phrase, finding it eight times. The two phrases before it are the same all eight times, too, this little half-second trio of phrases always occurring together. I pick another

Figure 13. At a clip of four to five brief phrases each second, the male horned lark sings continuously from the ground, eventually punctuating a long series of such phrases with a flourish, a hastened, rising series of jumbled notes. The three bold notes marked with an arrow occurred together like this eight times in five minutes, suggesting that they are a small "package" of elements that the lark bundles together when he sings. A quick survey of this male's songs suggested he has about 200 of these brief phrases that he rearranges to create an endless variety of songs (track 1-48).

distinctive phrase; this one also occurs eight times, but the phrases before and after are not always the same. A third distinctive phrase occurs four times, always as part of a trio.

What has he told me in this simple exercise? The numbers indicate roughly how many different phrases he knows. Suppose he sings 4 to 5 phrases (average, 4.5) each second for each of those 330 seconds, for a total of $330 \times 4.5 = 1,485$ phrases. The 3 unique phrases I searched for occurred an average of $(8 + 8 + 4) \div 3 = 6.7$ times apiece. Dividing 1,485 by 6.7 gives 222 phrases, a rough estimate of how many different phrases this horned lark sings. The lark has also told me how he arranges these roughly 200 phrases in his continuous singing. He has favored sequences, and often 2 or 3 phrases can reliably be found together, but he must have an infinite number of ways that he can arrange all these phrases from one flourish to the next.

So each of his 10 or so flourishes is premeditated, each one having been carefully rehearsed until he knows the routine precisely. Each of those less-hurried notes between the flourishes is also premeditated, as he has also practiced and perfected a limited number of them, about 200. What is unpremeditated is how all of those sounds play out, as he probably doesn't know for sure from one phrase to the next which will be offered to the world.

Gladness, harmonious madness. I cannot know what the lark feels, but how wonderfully satisfying I find it to know now just a bit more of what is on this lark's mind as he sings.

Cassin's Sparrows

MAY 28, 3:00 A.M., MURPHY'S PASTURE. A day later I'm back; this short-grass prairie is growing on me. My plan for the morning is Cassin's sparrows, so I return to the spot where I heard one yesterday. And there he is, off to the east, singing already! Or still, I cannot know which — perhaps he sings through the night.

I gather the gear and hustle out as near to him as I dare without spooking him, perhaps still 50 yards away. There I set up my stereo microphone on a tripod and then run the 125-foot cable back to the west, well away from him. Settling into my camp chair, I connect the microphone cable and headphones to the recorder, punch Power and then Record, and slip the headphones over my ears. Silence. I turn up the gain, the amplifier now hissing at me, straining to find some sound to boost, and seconds later, in the dead of the night's silence, there rises the sweetest of songs (track 1-49; figure 14). Wow, I know this feeling. Eyes closed, I imagine myself in the pines and palmettos of south Florida, listening to his cousin the Bachman's sparrow. But eyes open, I sit half a continent away in the dark here in the short-grass prairie, listening to a Cassin's sparrow.

Eyes closed again, I prepare for the next song. Fifteen seconds later, he begins with a pure, high whistle, perhaps half a second, followed by a trilled whistle on the same pitch, about a second long, then a brief whistle a good octave lower, and a final note lower still. Is it the song itself or his solo performance in the dead of night that is so striking? I await the next, and it is the same as the first. I memorize the pattern, drawing a stick figure in my mind for what I imagine the sonagram would look like. Ah, but this time I hear something a little extra, two especially high notes just before those last two lower notes. "Song A," I say to myself, as I prepare to identify what I expect will be only three different songs in his repertoire.

And the next . . . different, Song B. Seconds later he sings it again, a brief whistle followed by four tiny notes on the same pitch, both lower than the beginning of Song A, then a lower trill, the song's end again dominated by two low notes, but now the last note is higher, just the opposite of Song A. Again just barely detectable to my ears are those tiny high notes paired with the two low notes on the end.

The next song is different still. The initial whistle is the lowest yet, yielding to a slurred trill that slows at the end, then the two bold notes, the first higher than the last, just like Song A. And ever so faintly I again hear the high, thin note just before each of those two bold lower ones. Song C.

Concentrating, I listen for the next, expecting another C, but, no, he's back to A. In my mind I see the high whistle and the high, steady trill, relish the descending pattern in the two bold lower notes. The next is A also, and the next, three times in a row.

Just listen to him sing, four to five songs a minute, and on so silent a stage still *two hours before sunrise*. I smile, looking about, trying to take in this entire scene. The stars overhead are silent but intense. Jupiter is about an hour above the horizon to the west. Give Venus half an hour to show in the east. No moon. In the still, calm air, a distant horned lark sings, more sputtering than singing, and a distant lark bunting blurts an occasional song into the night, too. There's one song from a western meadowlark, and then he rests. Another Cassin's sparrow sings in the distance to the east, just one. A moth flutters about the microphone, the amplifier creating an elephant-size flying beast in my headphones.

I settle in, listening to the sparrow sing, concentrating on him alone, wondering how he uses his songs at this time of the night. In roughly five-minute strings, I note what his sparrow mind offers to the world:

A A B B B B C A A A A B A C A A A B B B
C A A A B B C A B B B A A A C C B B B A A A A B
C B B B A A A A C C B B B A A A C C B B B
A A A C B C B C A A A A B B C C A A A B B A A C C
B B B A A A A B C C B B A A A B B C A A B B C A A
B B A C A A B B C C A A B B A C A A B

In that half-hour are well over 100 songs, 4 to 5 a minute. He favors Song A, singing it mostly in strings of three and four. B is next, in strings of one to three. C is least favored, never more than two at a time, most often occurring as just a single song before he returns to A or B. I see now that it isn't only the quality of his songs that reminds me of the Bachman's sparrow, it's also his style of singing, offering one of his songs only a couple of times before moving to the next. The Cassin's song repertoire is much smaller, though, its 3 only a tenth that of a Bachman's 30 or more.

An hour before sunrise, I listen to the sparrow's world awaken. All about me now are lark buntings, horned larks, western meadowlarks, and mourning doves; a nighthawk booms overhead, and still the sparrow sings, all from the same perch. I've been waiting for him to move on to another perch, waiting eagerly for him to begin "skylarking" about this territory. Yes, "skylarking," defined by a dictionary as "frolicking," but for birds it is a style of singing in flight, so named after the Old World sky lark, of course.

There, 10 minutes before 5:00, he sounds more distant. He's definitely moved. The next song is even more distant, but the next is closer, the one after that even closer! I stand, listening in the headphones and scanning the eastern horizon, and there he is, a tiny mite of a bird launching into the air, singing, and fluttering back down.

Figure 14. The three songs of the male Cassin's sparrow. See how distinctive each song is and how easily each could be memorized; especially noticeable is whether the two low notes at the end rise or fall in frequency (see arrows). By knowing the songs of a given male, one can stand in the prairie and listen to all that he has to say—noting how many times he sings a particular song, when he switches to a new one—and perhaps understand better why he moves through his song repertoire the way he does (track 1-49).

Against the glowing eastern sky, I watch him in the binoculars. He sits atop the tallest bit of vegetation, now launches to the left into the air at about a 45-degree angle, maybe 5 yards up, begins his song just before the peak, sets his wings, and glides down as he sings, landing perhaps 20 yards from where he launched. Beautiful. Ten seconds later he's up again, now coming toward me, beginning the song just before the peak and then gliding, singing, but

Figure 14: CASSIN'S SPARROW

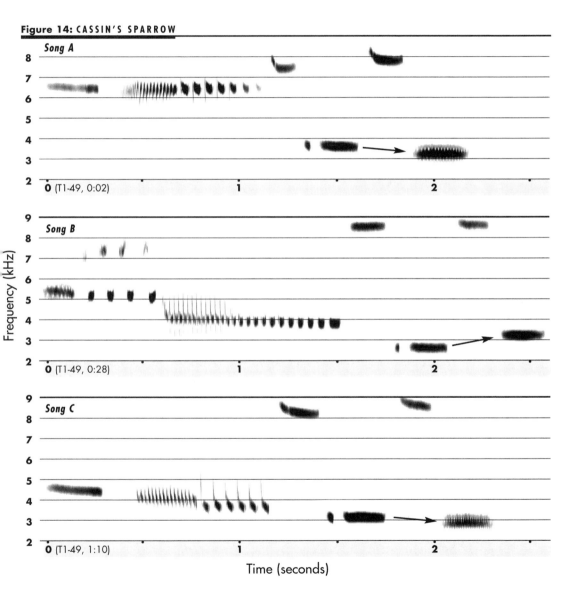

Time (seconds)

after the song he flaps his wings and covers another 10 yards before landing. He's up again, singing, coming closer. Now he launches to the right, sings and glides, then flies with the gentle breeze, 25, 50 yards to the south, rising into the air to sing once more there before landing. Another 10 seconds and he's into the air again, this time into the breeze, rising, singing, and then gliding back to the perch he just left.

I watch and listen until sunrise as he skylarks about his territory. Then, for a more intimate experience, I collect my parabola from the car and return, now walking with him, the parabola lifting the songs from his bill and delivering them directly to my ears. I hear his wingbeats as he launches, then the delicate details of Song A as he glides to earth. Three times for Song A, two for B, one for C before he returns to A, the dainty high notes paired with the low ending notes now much clearer in each of his songs.

For another half-hour I hang with him, listening, enjoying, feasting, and at 6:00, as his skylarking wanes, I choose to call it a morning, too. I pack the gear into the car, take one last, sweeping look at the prairie expanses and one last soulful listen, then say my good-byes, until tomorrow.

Lark Bunting

EVENING, MAY 29, MURPHY'S PASTURE. I'm back for an all-nighter, as I cannot get enough of this short-grass prairie. Dusk gives way to darkness, and with the pad and sleeping bag on the ground, I crawl in . . . listening to the coyotes, watching the play of lightning in distant thunderstorms on the horizon, dozing on and off throughout the night, and awakening around 4:00, not knowing for sure what was real and what was dreamed.

A *pzeeent* call overhead announces a common nighthawk; he soon follows with a boom, his display dive that is heard as a loud, freight-train *hoooov*, the sound of a mighty rushing wind through his wing feathers at the bottom of his dive (audible in the background of track 1-48). In the stillness, I count the booms of distant nighthawks, about 10 to every 1 from the bird overhead. The deep, booming *hoooov* travels well in the night, perhaps half a mile or more, the displays of nearly a dozen competing males all audible, though the higher-frequency *pzeeent*s of all but the closest are lost.

As the day breaks, I wallow in the sounds of nighthawks and horned larks and Cassin's sparrows and lark buntings and all that the prairie has to offer . . . and there, at 5:00, a latecomer to the chorus, is the first song of the McCown's longspur.

By 6:00, I feel that the morning is slipping away, so I grab the parabola and, with headphones over my ears, aim the sight on the parabola directly at the lark bunting who perches perhaps 30 yards away. As he sings, I quickly lower the gain on the recorder —I had not realized he was so loud. It was only a brief song, not the full performance that he'll sing on the wing, but how sweet the beginning, with rich whistled notes slurred down the scale, about 10 of them over two seconds, and then a high buzz, such a contrast between the two phrases. Again he sings from his perch, just the two phrases, a little over two seconds long (track 1-50; figure 15).

LARK BUNTING

Then he takes flight, toward me, rising perhaps 15 feet into the air. I hear every wingbeat in my headphones, the normal wingbeats of flight soon becoming deeper and slower, as if he's rowing more slowly through the air to show off his huge snow-white patches on pitch-black wings; his tail is now spread wide, with white tips showing there, too. He sings the sweet notes of the opening phrase followed by the high buzz that I had heard as he perched, but he continues now, a different sweet phrase followed by a high, buzzy phrase, then another slow and sweet, then fast and low, then slow and sweet, and as he glides to a landing perhaps 20 yards beyond me, a final high, buzzy phrase. I keep the sight of my trusty parabola aimed at him, waiting, and up he flies again, to my left, rising and now rowing, singing, dropping and swinging around to my left, finally landing, twisting me in a knot as I try to follow him with the parabola.

He offers a brief song from his perch again. Then he's up, flying away, rising, rowing, singing, this song beginning the same as all of the others I've heard from him, but the second phrase is now fast and low, not buzzy and high. On he sings, through another 10-second song, successive phrases contrasting sharply with one another as the song fades and he lands in the distance.

For another hour I watch and listen from the center of his territory, swinging the parabola with him as he flies, twisting to the left, then the right. They're such fine, bold songs, those on the wing always longer than those given when perched. Each song begins with the same phrase, the second phrase then either the high buzz or the fast and low trill, the entire song always sounding so familiar yet so different, as if the songs consist of the same limited set of phrases rearranged for added variety. The neighbor, I hear, always begins differently, the two birds easily recognized by their songs.

I lose him briefly, but to the south I hear a great ruckus and instinctively swing the parabola that way, catching three male lark buntings in a mad song flight, heading to the east (track 1-51). They seem to tie knots about one another as they fly and sing together, 10 seconds, 20, and at half a minute their

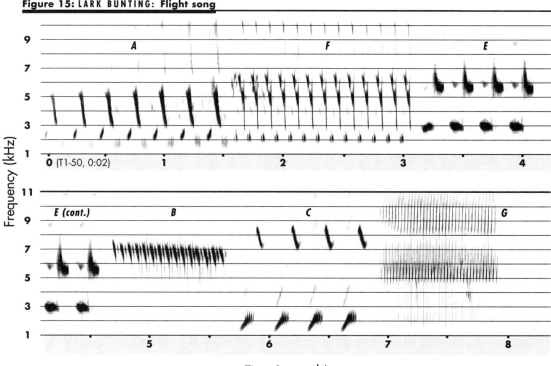

Figure 15: LARK BUNTING: **Flight song**

Time (seconds)

Figure 15. One clear, bold song from a lark bunting. While perched, he may sing an abbreviated song, typically just the first two phrases (A B, for example), but when he takes flight, he flashes the white in his wings as he rows with steady wingbeats into a full song, such as illustrated here. The six different phrases in this song, A F E B C G, are rearranged and combined with another phrase (D) to produce a considerable variety of songs, so that one never knows exactly what is coming next (track 1-50).

songs fade into the distance. Impressive! I've read about these group flights, how each male eventually circles back to his own territory, but what's it all about? Who starts it, and why? It must be some kind of a challenge among males, a show or test of strength; perhaps the females take note.

McCown's Longspur

Just to the north, a longspur beckons with his song from high in the air (track 1-52; figure 16). Walking the 50 yards or so to the center of his territory, I soon spot him on the ground, walking about in the sparse vegetation. Now he's up, the parabola so far-reaching that I hear each of his wingbeats. Up he goes, steeply, in five or six seconds reaching perhaps 50 feet into the air, and with bill open he offers a tinkling introductory note, then another. With his wings now outstretched and back, the undersides glow white; the tail is spread wide and low, showing the outer white feathers and the striking inverted black T; the back and rump are hunched and fluffed. And all the while, the tinkling, tumbling song continues as he floats back to earth. Oh, Emily, you said it so well: "I hope you love birds too. It is economical. It saves going to heaven."

Again and again he takes flight, and I follow along, flying and singing with him. A gentle breeze arises from the south, and I find myself edging to the southern end of this territory; he favors gliding into the wind, thus prolonging his flight and his song, and I position myself so that he sings directly to me. After landing near me, he flies with the wind and rises as he doubles back, gliding effortlessly and singing into the wind while he floats toward earth, then rising again on outstretched wings and singing again as he glides down to a landing.

Eager to learn more of the buntings and the longspurs, I return to Sterling, soon scanning sonagrams of the lark bunting's songs on my laptop computer. Yes, he does always begin his songs with the same sweet phrase. After that it's either a particular low, fast phrase or a high, buzzy phrase. If I letter the phrases, his first 10-second song has eight: A B C D E F C G. Next he sings A F, then A F E B, then A F C D E, then A B C G E, and a variety of other songs that rearrange the seven phrases in his repertoire into different sequences. Never boring, always exciting was the way I heard him. He achieved this effect by delivering boldly contrasting phrases back to back, arranged and rearranged so that I never knew what was coming next. And, just for kicks, I count his wingbeats as he launches from his perch—20 to 25 during the 1.5 to 1.7 seconds from liftoff to when he begins singing. Very nice.

The tempo of the longspur's songs is far faster, and was far more difficult for me to track as I listened with the parabola. Now I see in the sonagrams that the first note is almost always the same, as are the first one to two seconds. Then the songs get more complicated, and I cannot know where he's going once he is under way. His songs are organized a little like those of the horned lark, it seems, and consist of favored brief sequences of notes pieced together in unpredictable ways to generate an endless variety of songs. And from liftoff

Figure 16: McCOWN'S LONGSPUR: Flight song

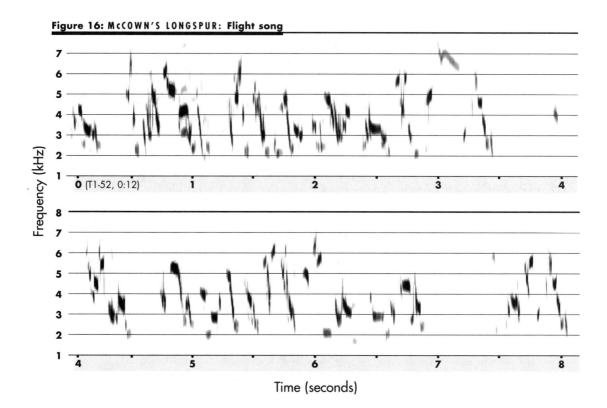

Time (seconds)

Figure 16. From his perch on the ground, the McCown's longspur launches skyward, up and up and up, steeply, to a good 50 feet, and with wings outstretched and back, flaunting all of his good looks, he parachutes back to earth, his song tinkling and tumbling as he glides down. In this double song, see how he begins with a single note, the way all of his songs begin, and then bubbles through a diverse series of phrases, ending a good eight seconds after he began (track 1-52).

to when he begins singing, I count 60 wingbeats in four seconds, then 68 wingbeats in six seconds for the next. Yes, very nice.

Sights and sounds of my Pawnee grassland linger on the drive to the airport: The intense predawn singing of horned larks from the ground, and how I would have loved to launch them skyward. Cassin's sparrows singing in the dark of night, then skylarking near dawn. Lark buntings in low, rowing flight, white in wing and tail fully showing, such a bold, strong song. Longspurs launching 50 to 100 feet in the air, extending wings and tails for maximum surface area, gliding down on tinkling voices. Nighthawks never seen but overheard, the boom of their dives carrying such distances. Chorusing coyotes, snorting antelope, thunderheads and lightning on the nighttime horizon. Darkness . . . silence . . . solitude . . . stars . . . Jupiter setting, Venus rising . . . the glowing eastern horizon, the rising sun . . .

What wonderful variety in these five flight singers, the four songbirds and the nighthawk. Each has taken to the air to tell its message in its own way in the treeless expanse of the short-grass prairies. Nice. Very nice.

JUNE

12

Belted Kingfishers on the Connecticut River

Saturday, June 10, 7:55 A.M.
Hatfield, Massachusetts

I STEP OUT of the car at the Hatfield boat ramp on the Connecticut River, and a cloud of mosquitoes instantly descends on me. I dance about, flailing, whirling, and in one not-so-graceful move slip under the mosquito netting that I carry for just this kind of occasion. Now safe beneath the head-to-knees netting, I listen calmly to the whining swarm, each blood-sucking wannabe telling of the rains that have wreaked havoc with my kingfishers over the past few months. One more time I've come here to sit and listen to the kingfishers, hoping that this will be the morning when I'll once again hear their lusty rattles over the river. If yes, I'll celebrate, returning again and again; if no, I'll call it a year, as the kingfishers will have, too.

On the bank of the river just above the nest of a month ago, I drop my camp chair to the ground and sit down, tucking the netting in all around. Where am I? The river looks so different from how I remember it. Yes, the river still flows to the right, and the grand sweep of the landscape is the same, but all the familiar landmarks along the shore have been rearranged or swept away by the raging water. One old friend remains about 20 feet out in the water, the aged, upright trunk that tells how the riverbank has moved in recent years. At the waterline on that trunk, I make a mental mark, wondering what the river will do in the next few hours.

And I listen: robin, cardinal, redstart, warbling vireo, flicker, cowbird, red-eyed vireo. On the river I see an inner tube, a buoy, a log, an entire tree, so much debris swept down from who knows where in the vast watershed extending far to the north, in Vermont and New Hampshire. Behind me, red-bellied woodpecker, waxwing, jay, oriole, two catbirds. And all about me the incessant hum of mosquitoes—I enjoy their higher-pitched comings and especially their lower-pitched goings; even at their slow flying speed, the Doppler effect is audible. A single cormorant to the west at the bend of the river where it turns south again.

March

I sense that the river is still a kingfisher desert, but it wasn't always so. In late March, I began what was to be a yearlong vigil. On the 22nd, I stopped by to check out the area that Dan, a former graduate student, had identified as one of the best kingfisher spots, the half mile upstream from the Hatfield boat ramp. The river hadn't frozen over during the winter, so a male would almost certainly be there, as he would have stayed on this fine territory all winter long. And, yes, a male was there, and with him was a female, recently returned from wherever she spent the winter to the south.

Early the next day I came back with the canoe and paddled upstream in a moderate current. For late March, the river was especially low, I remember thinking. Spring flooding normally occurs during late March and April, the water level then dropping by early May, when the kingfishers can be reasonably assured that the lower level will help concentrate the fish and not drown a nest.

On that Thursday I watched from a distance as a male and a female took turns flying from dead branches overhanging the water to the sandbank where their nest would be, in exactly the place Dan predicted. It's just a perfect spot, Dan had explained, the only vertical sandbank of sufficient height for a good distance in any direction, and with each trip to the bank, the pair signified its approval that this would be the place. I watched, seeing them mate twice, and I listened, enjoying their banter, he seeming to rattle at a lower pitch than she in this exchange.

Hooked on these birds, I was back the next day, again watching and listening from a distance. Too distant, I soon concluded, as I wanted to be there beside them, listening as if on the same perch. I canoed to the nest area, studied it, and hatched a plan.

For the fourth day in a row I returned, this time well before sunrise, and by land rather than by river. I worked my way through the woodland to the bank above the nest and used a rope to drop myself down to the river's edge; there, on the sandy shoreline about 10 yards upstream, I hid my parabolic microphone and aimed it directly at the perch where the two kingfishers would almost certainly land. From there I uncoiled my 125-foot microphone cable upstream to where I could sit well hidden behind a mound of sand at what is locally known as the Hatfield beach. Comfortably settled in my camp chair, I could listen up close to their banter in the headphones and, with a camouflage shirt draped over my head, peek out with binoculars to see the birds.

About 6:00, 15 minutes after sunrise, across the river and about 100 yards away, I heard the first rattle of the morning. Scanning the bank, looking for a patch of white against the dark background, I saw him, the single gray band across his breast distinctive. He muttered a soft rattle every 10 seconds or so, the quality of each so consistent, but I heard no answers from her. On the river between us were wood ducks, mergansers, and buffleheads, all in immaculate spring dress. A beaver swam by, spotted me, and alerted the world with a slap of its tail (track 1-53).

BELTED
KINGFISHERS

I remember glancing upward, staring in disbelief at the debris in the trees above me. Bits of straw and stems had accumulated on maple branches a good 10 to 15 feet overhead. Could the river really have been that high? I could think of no other explanation and shuddered at the thought of sitting here with so much water flowing above me.

In another 15 minutes, both male and female appeared near the nest site. After a flurry of activity and rattling, they perched quietly, just hanging out. She sat directly in focus with the parabola, he a little higher, farther out over the water and 10 yards downstream. She scratched herself, fluttered a little, her diminutive tail bobbing up and down. Facing me, she yawned, her beautiful chestnut bands extending up from the flanks and narrowly meeting across her breast. She yawned again, raised her tail, and shot a powerful white stream from her behind. What a huge head for a bird her size, I remember thinking, appearing so top-heavy, the long bill and the ragged double crest so out of balance with the short tail and the tiny feet.

The couple then rattled softly, back and forth, their banter having resumed. I watched her head bobbing up and down as she called, her bill barely open. She preened, under her left wing, then the wing itself, calling again, her head bobbing up and body extending upward, the tail rising slightly as if pumping the rattle out.

And what banter it was, so expressive (track 1-56; figure 17). The books describe this sound almost dismissively as a "loud, dry rattle," about 20 notes a second, but with my parabola aimed directly at her from just a few yards away, I heard so much more in their exchange. Most noticeable was how much higher-pitched her calls sounded than his, the loudest frequency in a series of her calls later measured on my computer at about 3,400 hertz, the loudest in his about 1,900. But that could change in an instant, too, as each of the pulses in the rattle consists of a series of harmonics, and the kingfishers could choose which portion of the harmonic range would be emphasized from rattle to rattle or even within a rattle. Rattles varied from a split second to several seconds in duration, too, and from delicately soft to ear-shatteringly loud.

And how intriguing the "attack," the beginning of the rattle. Initially, the notes are delivered more rapidly, perhaps at the rate of 30 per second, and then, over the course of the rattle, the rate gradually tapers off, perhaps to 15 a second at the end. This attack could vary not only in note rate but also in either intensity or frequency relative to the rest of the rattle.

I loved listening for the rhythm of each rattle, too. Most often the notes were evenly spaced, gradually tapering off in rate, but sometimes they were clearly paired or even in triplets, and sometimes the rhythm was highly irregular, with no clear pattern at all. Yes, how expressive their back-and-forth banter, how meaningful must be all of the nuances, though how naïve I am at listening to this foreign tongue, and how sadly simplified is the "loud, dry rattle" description of my field guides.

April

For the next two weeks the kingfishers and I carried on our separate lives, but I needed to return, as I needed to find the nest entrance itself. On April 8, canoeing slowly along the bank, I studied the tangles of exposed tree roots in the vertical sandy bank, and there it was, well hidden, perhaps two feet from the top of the bank, eight feet above the water, a four-inch-diameter hole leading back probably three to six feet into the bank among the tree roots.

A day later, I was back, again well before sunrise. This time I tucked my

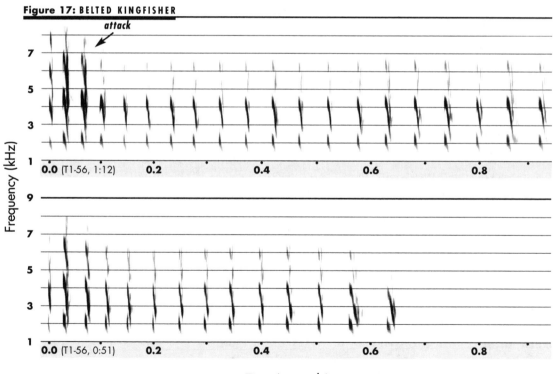

Figure 17: BELTED KINGFISHER

Time (seconds)

stereo microphone into the bank just below the nest entrance; I yearned to hear the male and female rattling as they approached and departed their nest cavity. The long cable led back to where I could again sit in comfort just beyond the beach. Heaven, I remember thinking, yes, this is what heaven must be like: a calm, clear early-spring day sitting on the river from well before sunrise to late morning, listening and watching the world go by.

Two wood ducks cavorted on the river and courted in the trees overhead. How vocal she was, how silent and beautiful he was, and how surprised I was to hear so much from a duck, from the female no less. She swam slowly upstream past me, calling loudly five or six notes a second; he followed closely behind, a barely audible *ji-ib ji-ib* emerging from his bill (track 1-54). Then off they flew, only to return to the trees overhead — yes, the *trees*. How odd up *there*, and how continuously she called, a simple call perhaps up to 10 times a second early in each series, slowing gradually and building to a crescendo of a squeal every 10 to 20 seconds, each squeal a hint of her loud *oo-eek* alarm call, which is the only sound I had ever associated with wood ducks before this. After each squeal, she immediately resumed the series, calling more rapidly, gradually slowing, building to a squeal, only to resume again (track 1-55). How extraordinarily expressive, just like the kingfishers, if only I took the time to listen.

As I awaited the kingfishers, the local resident birds had greeted the day: cardinals, song sparrows, robins, mourning doves, white-breasted nuthatches, chickadees, Carolina wrens, phoebes, titmice, crows, jays. A woodcock's wings whistled high overhead, and unseen whistling wings of other species commuted up and down the river. After sunrise, a cowbird called overhead, woodpeckers were out and about, including red-bellied and hairy and downy, and a flicker, too. How different were their drums, the rhythm of each species distinctive but the quality so dependent on the characteristics of the particular tree on which each individual chose to drum.

Figure 17. The "loud, dry rattle" of a belted kingfisher. See how successive elements are essentially the same, consisting of a fundamental note at about 2,000 Hz and then the harmonics above that centered on 4,000, 6,000, and 8,000 Hz. See how "the attack" (the first few tenths of a second) is more intense, the elements there louder (darker on the sonagram) and delivered more rapidly. This seemingly simple rattle can vary in so many ways, such as in overall loudness, emphasized frequency, and the grouping of individual elements; these features can change, too, throughout the brief rattle.

Where are the kingfishers and what are they up to? Based on their recent behavior, my best guess was that all excavating for the nest burrow and its terminal nesting cavity had been completed; the birds might be taking turns lingering in the nest cavity, as if trying to get used to the idea of all that was to come. The river was low, almost a month ahead of schedule, and all signals from the river declared that nesting should begin. I could be sure the eggs had not yet been laid, however, because neither kingfisher was in the burrow overnight.

Then, at 7:36 A.M., an hour and a quarter after sunrise, he arrived, landing perhaps 10 yards downstream, rattling every 5 to 10 seconds; three minutes later he flew to near the nest cavity, and half a minute later, with an explosive burst, he rattled into the nest burrow itself (track 1-57). With my microphones well placed, I felt as if I were welcoming him at the nest cavity myself.

And then silence, until a little over half an hour had elapsed, when, at 8:16, she showed up. She rattled softly every 5 to 10 seconds from the dead branches outside the burrow (track 1-58), but after four minutes was silent. Did she know he was in there? Was he rattling in response to her and I just couldn't hear it? Probably.

The female wood duck continued calling in the tree overhead. A hot-air balloon to the south announced itself with the blast from its burner. Two goldfinches blurted out their butchered songs, songs that didn't need to be perfected for a couple of months for their late-summer breeding. Woodpeckers drummed. And after six minutes the female kingfisher resumed calling, seemingly more insistent, flying into the nest burrow four minutes later, just as he did with an intense rattle.

And silence again . . . until the male's explosive rattle (track 1-57) announced his departure from the burrow 2 minutes later. He flew downstream about 10 yards and landed on a favored perch over the water. For 50 minutes, the last 2 with her, he was in the nesting burrow, and now it was her turn to, well, to do what? They must have been close to egg laying, though it seemed so early in the season.

And what was he doing there just downstream? He flew from the perch and launched a kamikaze attack on the river below, as if attacking his own shadow, plunging into the water and then flying directly back to his perch. It wasn't the calculated trajectory of a fishing bird but more of a mad dash. Twice more he did that. And then he preened his rump, under and over both wings, the back, the belly, finally ruffling the entire body, as if to say everything now felt just right. Then off he flew, downstream and up and over the trees, no doubt on his way to the prime fishing grounds of Great Pond, just to the northwest.

Over an hour later, just before 10:00, she departed the nest just as he had, rattling explosively and flying downstream to the very perch where he had sat (track 1-58). She, too, preened, though she skipped the attacks on the river, and after 18 minutes, she also flew downstream and over the trees, perhaps to join the male at the pond. I waited another hour, savoring the morning, but they did not return.

May

A full month later, on Friday, May 12, I returned for another morning vigil. Rain was in the forecast, but I hoped the morning would be dry. And just where were the kingfishers in their nesting cycle? I calculated: 7 days for her to lay up to seven eggs and 22 days to incubate, for a total of about 29 days. If she had begun laying eggs by April 14, they could have hatched by now. April 14 wasn't unreasonable, because during 1995, a year in which spring flooding was also absent, eggs were laid as early as April 20. And when I had stopped here briefly yesterday, I could have sworn that he had a tiny fish in his bill when he went to the nesting burrow, suggesting that he had little nestlings to feed. By 4:30 I had the microphones in place and I was sitting pretty, eager for the morning to break, but at 6:34 I felt the first drop, on my nose. I quickly gathered the recording gear before the rains hit.

Back home, on the USGS website for the Connecticut River (http://water data.usgs.gov/ma/nwis/uv?01170500), hour by hour I watched the gauges tell of the rising water. By midnight Friday the river was up 4 feet, midnight Saturday up 7 feet, and by midnight Sunday the river had risen 16 feet. Throughout New England, rivers rampaged in the worst flooding since the Great Hurricane of 1938 (figure 18).

On Monday, May 15, a friend and I returned to view what I had most feared. The river flowed at a dizzying pace and height; the nest burrow was well below water and the kingfishers nowhere to be heard. Any life in the nest had been drowned, and in these swollen, muddy waters, a kingfisher could find no fish to eat.

Over the next four days, the river began to recede, only to surge again on May 20 and 21 to a foot higher than it had been at its May 15 peak. If the river had settled down then, I knew there would still have been time for the kingfishers to renest, and, watching the receding river on the website, I had hope.

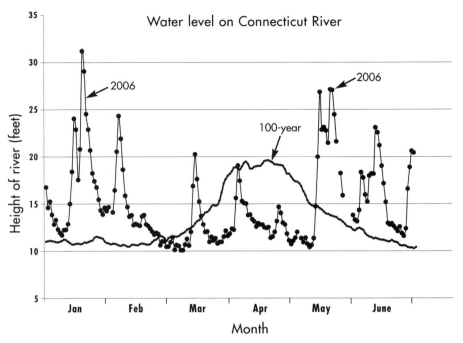

Figure 18. Water levels on the Connecticut River from January through June 2006, compared to the 100-year average. For the 100-year average, see how the water level is typically higher during the spring runoff in April; the river level then drops, enabling the kingfishers to find fish in the river and to nest in the banks. The year 2006 was anything but average. The river level dropped significantly during April, inviting the kingfishers to begin nesting earlier than usual. But the rains in mid-May and then again in June dashed any hopes of their being successful on the river during that season.

June

That hope has brought me to the river today, June 10, to listen again for the kingfishers. It's now 11:00, and in the three hours I have been here I've heard nothing. My friend standing in the river has offered a bad omen, too; the water has risen two feet on his trunk over the last three hours.

The answer to my question when I first sat here this morning is a clear no; the kingfishers are done for the season, washed out. There'll be no babies here this year. Maybe the kingfishers will have better luck elsewhere, fishing some of the local ponds, where floodwaters recede more quickly, and nesting in high sandbanks well away from flooded waters, such as in the local gravel pit. Maybe. As for my river watch, I'm washed out, and I'm torn between accepting what has happened this year and knowing what could have been. Next year. Yes, there's always next year. The kingfishers will be back, as will I, eager to resume my watching and listening.

13

Listening with Dave: A June Dawn in Hatfield Cemetery

June 6, 4:00 A.M.
Hatfield, Massachusetts

"NO MOSS GROWS ON DAVE." Yes, those were your words, and it was so you.

You've been a good friend since the day we met 25 years ago at Plum Island, on the best birding day ever, the warblers and other spring migrants dripping from the trees. You showed me western Massachusetts, especially the flycatcher haunts in the Berkshires. We stood side by side on the flanks of Volcan Barva in Costa Rica, our parabolas aimed at our first bellbird, enthralled by what we heard in our headphones. Just this last December, we owled through the night, taking the route you've taken for twenty-some years on the local Christmas Bird Count. And in January, on a crisp winter morning, we spent our last minutes in the field together, gawking at the sight and sound of, oh, how many did we dare estimate? Thirty thousand? Yes, 30,000 robins emerging at dawn from their night roost just a few miles from your home. And now, the cancer having run its course, your ashes lie here beneath this tall birch in the cemetery just across the field from your home.

I've come to listen with you once again, to hear what you hear as dawn unfolds on this June morning. Cemeteries are birdy places, we know, and yours is no exception. I especially like those dead branches at the top of the birch towering overhead; good birds will surely come calling there.

Pretty quiet still, a little after 4:00. Sunrise is still about an hour away. And it is calm, not a rustle in the leaves, your definition of a good morning, so that every birdy movement and sound can be detected. A few peepers make their presence known in the woods to the northwest. There's the *chug* of a green frog, too. The highway to the west is pretty noisy already, or still. So far, no birds stirring.

Ah, robins, of course, by the streetlights to the east, along Main Street.

Reminds me of one of my favorite hymns, in which a "blackbird" is the first bird to "speak" in the morning. I don't know the author, but it has to be a song from England, where their "blackbird" is actually a black robin. You know it well from your life in Scotland. It's nice to know that robins are robins everywhere, almost always first off the roost. How many robins by the lights? At least three, maybe four or five. And none elsewhere, only by the lights. It would be nice if one came closer, so that we could hear his high-pitched *hissel-ly* notes and follow whatever pattern there is in his low carols.

4:25. And now chipping sparrows, three of them together, also to the east, all down low, sputtering their songs to one another among the gravestones. I love their dawn huddles, how they gather at a territory boundary and sing in a small cluster from the ground or from low perches, rattling off as many as 60 split-second songs a minute. Hear how different their songs are from one another, each of the three males easily recognizable. With two sparrows they might take turns singing, but with three it's mayhem, two or all three sometimes singing at the same time. Which one owns this birch? Give them 30 minutes to finish their dawn business and we'll know, as eventually one of them will come to sing here.

4:28. Nice, a bluebird (track 1-59). Let me get the parabola on him. I am a sucker for bluebirds. I can see him in the hydrangea just 10 yards to the south, though there's nothing blue about him in this light. Listen to him chatter, then sing, chatter, then sing—he's pretty excited. Hear the cuckoo in the background? I've got the parabola focused on the bluebird, but I can't make out any pattern in what he is singing, all the songs sounding different to me. If he were a little less animated, we'd hear him play with perhaps only three of his songs for a few minutes, then move on to others, but there seems like an endless variety now. Had we the ears and mind of a bluebird, though, we'd know exactly which of his 60 or so different songs he's singing.

4:34. Oh, I'm torn. The bluebird continues, but now there's a cardinal, in the very top of our birch. Bluebird or redbird, which will it be? I'm unable to move the microphone off such a fine singer, but the ears now listen overhead to the cardinal. His songs are just a series of short whistles delivered rapidly, each seeming to rise briefly in frequency—not his finest song, to be sure. He sings it again, and again, so unlike the impatient bluebird, who races through his repertoire. There, the cardinal switches to another song, also a series of rising whistles, but slower and sweeter . . . again . . . and again, now ending with a series of falling *chew* notes. *Sweet sweet sweet sweet sweet sweet sweet sweet sweet sweet sweet sweet sweet chew chew chew chew.*

I do like that. Seven more times over the next minute he sings his *sweet-*

chew song, but I can take it no more and swing the parabola from the bluebird to the cardinal (track 1-60). Now it is the cardinal and he alone that I hear, the songs seeming to get longer and longer with more and more *chews* added to the end, until songs are 8, then 10 seconds long, and to some he adds that curious red squirrel–like chatter on the end. Abruptly he switches to yet another song, each song now just a few deliberate whistles, each magnificently sliding down the scale.

I stop counting, just savoring over and over this simple yet remarkable song. I try to imagine the two voice boxes at work on each whistle, the right syrinx singing the top of the whistle, the seamless transition to the lower part of the whistle produced by the left syrinx. And he switches songs again, the now up-slurred whistles delivered in a great rush, a whole new memorized routine of neurons firing to adjust tensions in his two voice boxes, to breathe precisely, with the left voice box leading, the right following. And he switches to still another song in his repertoire, and I know there are half a dozen more that I've not yet heard.

To the north, in the trees across the open field, there's another cardinal, the two perfectly matching each other's songs, back and forth. Our bird switches to another song, as does the neighbor. And another switch, and another, the two birds dueling back and forth with identical songs, until our bird departs the birch overhead at 4:45, a good 10 minutes after he arrived.

I swing the parabola toward the other cardinal and now hear to the north all that we have been missing while focused on the cardinal overhead. There are two tufted titmice, *peter peter, peter peter,* each also matching the other's exact song, the titmice playing the same matching game as the cardinals; they'll switch to a new song far less often, though, perhaps every 15 minutes, not every minute or 2 like the cardinals. There's a chickadee, too, *hey-sweetie, hey-sweetie;* at the rate he's singing, he'll drop or rise to a new pitch soon. There's an eastern phoebe, no, two. I aim the parabola first to the left — *fee-bee . . . fee-bee . . . fee-b-be-bee,* hearing the two songs that he and all good phoebes sing — then to the right — *fee-bee . . . fee-b-be-bee.* A yellow warbler races through his dawn repertoire of a dozen or so songs; what wonderful variety, but before sunrise, right on schedule with whatever internal clock he uses, he'll switch to his one daytime song, which he'll repeat over and over, *sweet sweet sweeter than sweet.*

Our chippy has arrived, the one who owns this part of the cemetery (track 2-1). He's left the dawn huddle and now sings behind us from the juniper. I train the parabola on him, capturing his rapid, liquid song, knowing that later, at home on my computer, I'll try to match his particular version of the chipping sparrow song with one of the three that we heard earlier. A crow flies in from beyond the chipping sparrow (track 2-1 continued), and I aim the parabola to follow its flight. Oh, how nice those sharp *ca ca* bursts on the wing, only 3 at first, then 4, then 11, and he flies directly overhead, his wingbeats swooshing in my ears.

And he lands in the top of the birch! Glory be. There's nothing like a good conversation among these most intelligent of creatures. Just listen to him! He sounds frantic with sharp bursts of *ca ca ca ca,* not the hoarse, throaty calls that one expects from a crow. He continues, and a minute after arriving bursts into a cacophonous blast of *ca*s extending over half a minute. As if responding, a second crow soon arrives, and in silence they bob and eye each other in the top of the birch, no doubt listening to the other crows in the distance. Except for the shuffling of their feet and wings, which I hear in my headphones, they are silent for 10, 20, 30 seconds, and then there's a 2-second burst of, what, did you hear that? I saw and heard each speak four times, the second bird a nice series of hoarse *caaw caaw caaw caaw,* but the first crow changed midstream to match the throaty quality of his friend's *caaw,* beginning with two sharp *ca-ca*s and then changing to *caw caw!*

CROWS

Were you standing beside me with your parabola also aimed at them and your headphones over your ears, too, we'd glance at each other, smiling, nodding with that knowing look that we'd heard something truly special. But we'd be greedy for more, too, saving our talk for later, after the crows had finished theirs.

Parabolas still raised, we eavesdrop on their conversation. I hear *caw*s from the first bird, but the *caaw*s of the second bird are noticeably longer. As I listen to the next exchange, a smile creeps over my face, because both birds now *caw* in unison, the second bird having changed his longer *caaw* to match the shorter *caw* of the first. And then they diverge again, the second bird changing back to his longer *caaw.* This pattern plays out several more times over the next few minutes, the second bird briefly matching the shorter *caw* from the first bird before the two settle into their *caw* and *caaw* routine again (track 2-2; figure 19).

How extraordinary! Wow, I do love crows. What was said in this exchange? Were those crows calling in the distance friend or foe? And who were these two? Were they siblings, part of a larger crow family in the neighborhood? Or an adult pair, male and female? And just what were these birds thinking? I hear you chiding me, reminding me that I shouldn't be so anthropomorphic, that it's preferable to ask simply "What do they know?" I like both questions. Mine reminds me of a mental process that must be physiologically identical in both crows and humans, and I come to wonder how different we really are. Yours helps me focus on the social life of these crows, what they know about each other and how they interact. At any rate, these crows have raised more questions in these few minutes than will ever be answered.

It's 5:00 already! Listen to all that's going on beyond the cemetery, in the trees to the east and south. I aim the parabola in that direction, swinging it left and right, and it's still robins everywhere. Why have none come closer, to sing here, where we could better read their minds? There's the *yank yank* of a white-breasted nuthatch. What a puzzling bird. Why does he sing his heart out during late winter and then utter only these simple calls during spring and summer? I'll come back in March to hear them in full voice. And a house finch in the hemlocks, sputtering, stuttering. He gives a note or two of his song again and again. What's with him? What's on his mind? Okay, what does he know?

Swinging the parabola to the southeast, I catch two house wrens, gurgling and burbling away . . . a chickadee, *hey-sweetie* . . . two titmice, each singing *clear clear, clear clear.* Oh, hear how the chickadee just shifted his *hey-sweetie* to a lower pitch? He continues on the low pitch now . . . a blue jay, just one, sadly, as it takes at least two for a good conversation . . . the mournful *who-a-who-who-who* of a mourning dove . . . a catbird, squawking and squeaking and meowing, a master improviser and imitator, a few hundred different sounds to his credit. Wish he were closer.

Hey, the house finch (track 2-3; figure 20). Listen! He's found the end of his stutter and now sings nonstop songs back to back, with a high-pitched note or two in between. Wow, I've never before heard a house finch sing with such exuberance, nor have I ever heard that high note before. That can't be the performance of a lone finch. No, there must be a female in there with him, deep in the cover of the hemlocks. On and on he sings, one, two minutes, and now he stutters again, not getting beyond the first note or two of his songs.

It's 5:10, just a few minutes to sunrise, and it seems quieter now. I listen all around — north, east, south, west. I hear the familiar voices, but the dawn burst of singing is already over.

Overhead, a chimney swift twitters, the twittering cigar on wings, the illusion of a bird flying on alternating wingbeats, though physics and slow-motion video show that it just ain't so. And a goldfinch in bounding flight commuting to who knows where, *per-chick-o-ree, per-chick-o-ree.* Or is it *po-ta-to-chip, po-ta-to-chip?* We could argue that one.

Ah, a cowbird in your birch, in the very top. A sharp, high whistle, and another, the local dialect of his flight whistle. And the rattle of a female a little lower in the tree. We never got around to talking about cowbirds, but I know you must love them. You loved this world and all the forces that make it what it is, and what better story than the making of a cowbird, how it relies on all the savvy accumulated over eons of time to foist its child-rearing duties on other birds? A villain to some, but you knew otherwise. And the cowbirds are displaced by two grackles, *check, check,* simple calls, then a song, *krshee, krshee,* and they're off to the north . . . where a woodpecker drums, so rapidly I can't count the beats, so it must be the hairy. Has to be about sunrise now that the cowbirds are about and woodpeckers have emerged from their roosting cavities.

Figure 19. Selected calls from the crow conversation in the top of the birch tree. All examples can be heard in real time on track 2-1 and at half speed on track 2-2 (and it is the half speed that best reveals what these crows are doing).

A. As the first crow arrives in the birch overhead, it calls at a moderate pace, as illustrated by this series of six fairly sharp notes, *ca-ca-ca-ca-ca-ca.*

B. Shortly after landing, this crow calls far more frantically, almost doubling the pace, but the duration and quality of each *ca* stays pretty much the same.

C. In this two-second burst, the second crow (2) to arrive in the tree utters a throaty *caaw-caaw-caaw-caaw*, four in all. Simultaneously, the first bird utters two sharp *ca* notes and then switches to a more throaty *caw*, matching the quality of the second bird's slightly longer *caaw* (compare especially the last two notes, a *caaw* by Bird 2 followed by a *caw* from Bird 1).

D. The two crows now call back to back, the first bird uttering his relatively brief, throaty *caw-caw-caw*, the second bird his slightly longer *caaw-caaw-caaw*.

E. As the two crows call from the top of the tree, their voices are usually distinctively different, Bird 2 with a longer call (*caaw*) than Bird 1 (*caw*). But look how in this example Bird 2 *caaw*s 3 times to start the sequence; Bird 1 then calls 7 times, *caw-caw-caw-caw-caw-caw-caw*, followed immediately by Bird 2 matching Bird 1 and adding 3 *caws* on the end, *caw-caw-caw*, the entire sequence of 10 *caws* looking (and sounding) as if it is one bird. (Because those last 3 *caws* of Bird 2 are more softly recorded, they are lighter in the sonagram, without all of the harmonics that would be seen if they were louder.)

And a starling! Up above, yes, in those dead branches atop the birch (track 2-4). Cowbirds, starlings, yes, what fine birds. *Good* birds, often my answer to birders who ask if I've seen any good birds. The starling, a close relative of the mockingbird and so underappreciated as a fine singer, so soft and subtle is his effort. He whistles now, a low, throaty whistle, *weeeeooooo,* rising and falling over two seconds, then two low whistles, and he's off, *phit phit phit phit phit*

Figure 19: AMERICAN CROW

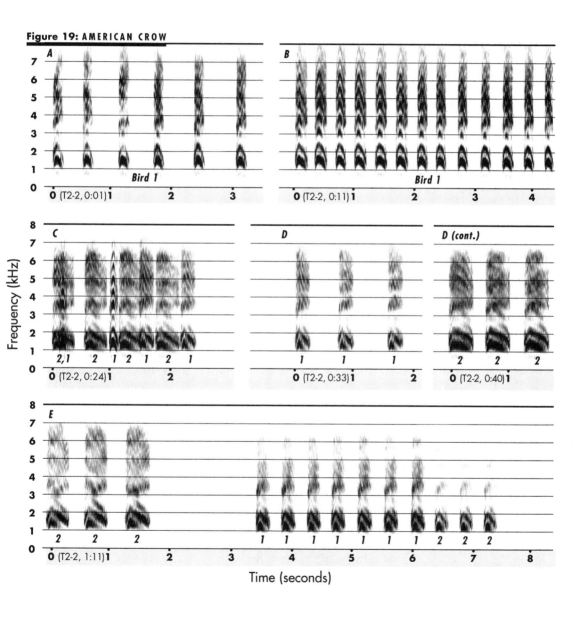

Time (seconds)

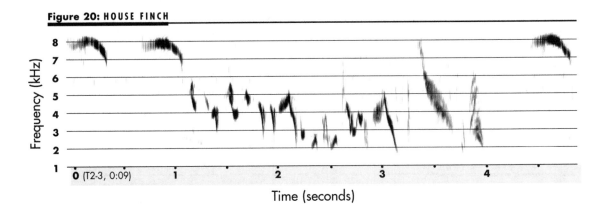

Time (seconds)

Figure 20. A courting male house finch sandwiches his typical song between one or two high courtship calls.

shree phit phit shree phit phit pit pit pit pit pit, and there's no way to keep up. He sings so quickly and now uses both voice boxes to sound as if he's a flock of, oh, what all do I hear there? A soft but beautiful sequence of *jay jay caw jay jay caw jay jay caw,* mimicking crows and jays to be sure and others I'm not fast enough to identify, on and on "they" sing, and now he clicks and rattles with one voice box while he *ckeck*s and screeches with the other, now waving his wings frantically and screaming, and *finally* they have all finished. How long was it, 40, 45 seconds? What a wonder he is, a multitongued maestro, sounding as if he's many rather than just one. He begins another song—the throaty whistles, the crow mimicry—then stops short, and another, more like the first, but only half a minute long, stopping again before the frantic wing waving and screaming on the end. What a bird! And he flies, too, also to the north.

There's an indigo bunting singing to the west, in the tree along the drainage ditch.

A song sparrow. We've heard them in the distance all morning, but now one has come to sing here, in one of the small junipers just to the south. Wonderful, such a measured tempo, every six seconds. And two others sing off to the south. Hear each repeat his particular song over and over, feel the rhythm of all three. Who will switch first to another song in his repertoire? Ah, the near bird, now switching from his song with the nice whistled introductory notes to one with far more dissonant notes. He's the master of perhaps 8 to

10 different song sparrow songs, most of them rather different from those of his neighbors, as that is the nature of our eastern song sparrows.

And a savannah sparrow, in the hydrangea just to the west, so close (track 2-5; figure 21). Where's he been all morning? Off in the fields, I guess. *Tsit-tsit-tsit-tssit-tssit-tssit-tssit-tsseeeeeeeeeee-tssayyyyyyy.* Three seconds of fine, high buzzes dropping down the scale, a raspy song, though pleasing in its own way. He sits facing us, as if he has not a care in the world. *Take take take take-it eeeeeeeaaaaa-sssssyyyyyyyyyy,* he seems to sing. What is it about this song that is so striking? Perhaps it is his relaxed pace, a song every 10 seconds or so. Perhaps it is the simplicity of his message, as this is his only song, the one he will sing forever, so unlike the robin and bluebird and cardinal and catbird and starling and song sparrow and titmouse and phoebe and warbler and, well, all but the chipping sparrow, the grackle, and the indigo bunting, the only other birds we've listened to this morning with just a single song; even the chickadee varies the pitch of his simple *hey-sweetie* song, keeping listeners on their toes. Or perhaps it is the relative silence of the other birds now, almost an hour after sunrise, or how close he sings, how fearlessly he comes calling, as if he does so often.

I back away from the savannah, giving him space, and, closing my eyes, I listen once more, as I have from 4:00 A.M. on, through the silence and then the

Figure 21: SAVANNAH SPARROW

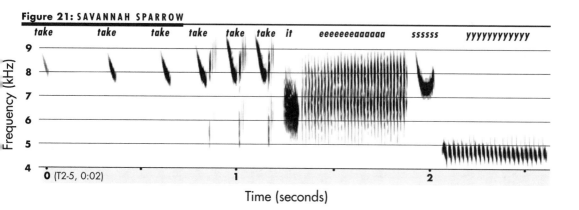

Figure 21. The song of a savannah sparrow, with the stuttered notes at the beginning and two prolonged buzzy notes at the end, a cascade of stutters and buzzy notes dropping down the scale; *take take take take-it eeeeeeeaaaaa-sssssyyyyyyyyyy,* he seems to sing.

early robins and chippys, the bluebird, the cardinal overhead, the crows and cowbirds and starling up there, too. Titmice, chickadees, goldfinches, swifts, a finch, catbirds, wrens, a bunting, song sparrows, the savannah, and more. Some still sing in the distance, but it is mostly quiet now, the sun well above the trees to the east.

I think we'd agree on the best of the morning. Had to be the crow conversation; I've never heard them speak so clearly before, so eloquently of what has so captivated us about birds all these years. The starling was nice, too. A good cowbird show would have rated higher, but there wasn't quite enough. The bluebird and cardinal weren't too shabby either. That house finch was special. And the savannah, to close the performance. Quite a supporting cast, too, mostly in the distance.

And how do I now leave? In life you were so sharp and witty and impassioned and, well, the model of how a life should be lived. For you, at first it was the magic of watching birds, especially owls and those tropical flycatchers and antbirds and their relatives, but then it was the songs that so moved you. You loved your solitaires, for the beauty of their songs and for the evolutionary puzzles they presented, the wonderful opportunities to travel a bonus. And now this. It's not fair, I catch myself saying, and then remember what you said to your kids once, that if life were fair they'd be sitting under a tree in Africa, starving. So I'll go now, but I'll be back, and we can listen together some more then.

14

Blackburnian Warblers of Mount Greylock

June 9–27
Western Massachusetts

ON A CLEAR DAY, about 40 crow-flight miles to the west across the Connecticut River Valley, Mount Greylock beckons. Through the binoculars, I can see the large rock slide on its eastern flanks and the stone tower atop this lord of the Berkshires. I have biked up this mountain with my friends on silent full-moon nights in autumn, but I have never heard this mountain sing in spring. I must go, to listen, to somehow capture Mount Greylock in my mind's ear so that, when I gaze to the west from my home, I will both see and hear this mountain.

During early June, I try biking up the mountain at sunset and sunrise, hiking its trails, and standing at an overlook as the dawn wave sweeps by. It's all magical, but not quite right. What is missing, I realize, is that intimate connection with just a few of Greylock's birds as they go about their lives.

BLACKBURNIAN
WARBLER

On those brief scouting visits to Greylock, I had stayed in the campground and then raced about the mountain. Slow down, I now tell myself, and just walk the campground. Listen to all that is here. Warblers of all kinds, a pair of purple finches, both the male and female singing, sapsuckers, winter wrens, blue-headed and red-eyed vireos, and warblers: an occasional late June song from black-throated greens and blues, ovenbirds, redstarts, yellow-rumps, magnolias, but just listen to those Blackburnians singing so lustily from the spruce spires high above the hardwood canopy. Through the binoculars, I confirm their markings, the brilliant orange and striking black unmistakable. Walking along the main road (figure 22), I linger in the territories of half a dozen singing males. Straining my neck to look upward, I use my parabolic microphone to pluck the songs from the tops of the spruces and amplify them in my headphones. It's the next best thing to being up there, high atop these spruces, as I get acquainted with each of these birds in turn.

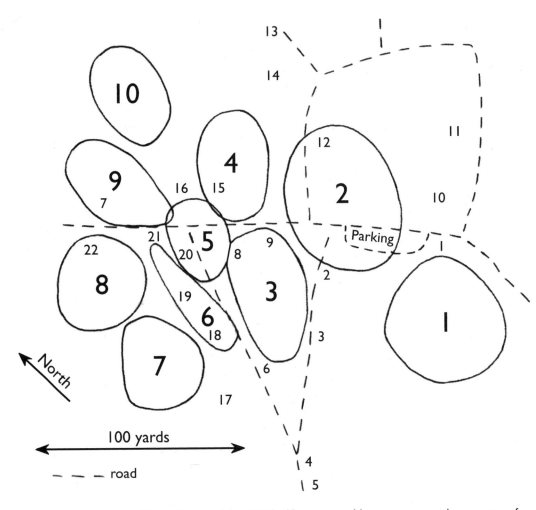

Figure 22. The territories of the 10 Blackburnian warblers superimposed on a map of the campground at Mount Greylock. On June 24, at about 4:00 A.M., I parked the car in the lot beneath the nest of Bird 2 and then, until noon, walked a circuit from one territory to the next, getting to know each bird in turn. (Smaller numbers designate campsites.)

So little is known about Blackburnian warblers, and it's no surprise given how high in the canopy they live. It is known that each male can sing two types of songs, and in that sense, they're like many other warblers, with one song used aggressively and especially at dawn, the other primarily in courting females and during the day (for shorthand, I will use "dawn" and "day" to represent the aggressive and courting contexts respectively). I've been obsessed with warblers over the years, eager to learn more about these specialized "dawn" and "day" songs, but I've never had the opportunity to learn about these Blackburnians. Does each male really have only two songs, one dawn and one day song, or does he have several songs in each category? What do the details of the songs look like? Do the local males have similar songs, indicating that they learn them from one another? Are there dialects in the two songs, so that they vary from place to place? I know the answers to these questions for many other warblers, and the variety of singing styles among the different species is intriguing. Just how do these Blackburnian warblers fit into the larger warbler picture?

Yes, these warblers will be my Greylock experience. It has been swirling about my tent as I have been off searching elsewhere. My Big Day on Greylock will be a morning with the Blackburnians.

Friday, June 24, 2:00 A.M.

The car loaded with recording gear, I'm out of the driveway of my Amherst home, starting the two-hour trip to the Greylock campground. I am hoping for one last chance this summer, as this is the Friday before a busy weekend that will be the beginning of a busy summer. It's the last day this year that I can hope the campsites will be sufficiently empty for me to be able to walk freely among the singing warblers.

3:50 A.M. Creeping slowly into the campground, I park the car in the easternmost lot, soon checking for campers as I walk as softly as I can down the gravel road. All clear in Sites 12, 2, 9, 13, 14, 8, 15, 16, 19, 20 . . . A dog! From Site 21, where I was camped just a few days ago, it barks loudly, the campers soon barking loudly at the dog, the fracas shattering the silence of the night. I retreat, reassessing. I can linger among the five territories to the east without disturbing these campers, I reason, and wait to visit the warblers around Site 21 later in the morning.

Back at the car, I load up with my gear: binoculars, stereo parabolic microphone, headphones, and recorder. In my pack are enough supplies for a marathon session, as I plan to visit with these warblers from their first awakening until noon, eight hours from now. I stand at the car, waiting for their day to begin.

It is sooooo quiet. I hear a tent zipper in some distant campsite . . . a truck two miles to the west on Route 7 . . . a brief flare-up argument of exasperated voices from Site 21. At 4:15, a robin sings softly and slowly nearby . . . a barred owl in the distance . . . winter wren . . . chipping sparrow . . . the flight song of an ovenbird. By 4:30, the robins are deafening.

And at 4:31 I hear my first Blackburnian song. It is from the male I had numbered 2 here at the parking lot, his nest in the spruce high above my parked car. His dawn song is the oddest of the campground, a cascade of notes with none of the typical high notes at the end of the song. I'd know him anywhere. He now sings from one of the tall spruce trees just south of Site 9 (tracks 2-8, 2-9; figure 23).

To the west, perhaps only 10 yards from Bird 2, Bird 3 now sings; he's also high in a spruce spire, directly above Site 9. His is the sweetest song I've heard in the campground, usually beginning with six rising whistles over a second and a half, followed by a brief high chatter and then the high whistle at the end, starting up around 9,000 hertz. Birds 2 and 3 chip frantically, pausing every 10 to 15 seconds to deliver their distinctive songs.

Beyond Bird 3 and just to the northwest, I hear Bird 4 where I expect him, opposite Site 8. His song is much like Bird 3's, except that he's more hurried, those whistles in the opening phrase delivered noticeably faster. He, too, calls frenetically between songs.

Three singing Blackburnian warblers. I linger, gaining my bearings in the dark, the headphones now off as I listen to them, each one so distinctive (track 2-9). Birds 2, 3, 4, each filling the time between songs with chipping, each singing from one of the spruces he has claimed, and still another warbler now

Figure 23. Four dawn songs of individual Blackburnian warblers, illustrating the features that I heard as I listened on my Big Day on Mount Greylock and a later day at Quabbin Park (track 2-9). See (and hear) the cascade of notes in the unique dawn song of Greylock's Bird 2. Songs of Birds 3 and 5 from Greylock are more typical; each begins with an introductory phrase unique to that individual, then proceeds to a brief chatter and a high-frequency note or two on the end. The Quabbin dialect in the dawn song is evident in this song's unique ending, those two notes just after 2.0 seconds never occurring among the Greylock males.

beckons from just west of Site 8. I know his song, too, that opening phrase sounding as if he's juggling pebbles in his throat—Bird 5 owns the intersection bounded by Sites 8, 16, and 20. I tiptoe the best I can beneath him to hear him better.

Beyond him is yet another familiar bird, above Site 16, opposite Site 21. I swing the parabola his way, catching just a couple of distant songs, just documenting his presence; I'll follow him more closely when the campers in Site 21 are more approachable. Yes, he's the same bird who was there a few days ago; the opening phrase of his song sounds especially harsh—I called him Bird 9.

I work my way back to the south, toward the car. Bird 5 sings above me, and I record another brief sample from him. Walking again through the territories of Birds 4, 3, and 2, I record a few more songs from each; each chips frantically and, to my ears, delivers his own unique song. I don't trust my ears, though, so I record, knowing that I'll inspect all of these songs later on my

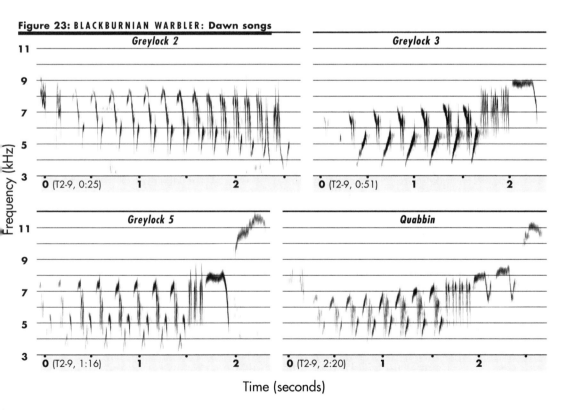

Figure 23: BLACKBURNIAN WARBLER: Dawn songs

Time (seconds)

home computer. I want to see the details in these songs that the birds themselves no doubt hear, so I sample as I pass, and by noon today I hope to have over a hundred such brief recording sessions to inspect. It is those samples that will help answer my questions about how these warblers sing.

There, off to the far southeast, is Bird 1. He's back in the woods now, so I work my way under him, thankful for vacant campsites, finding just the right window in the canopy so that I have a direct aim at the top of the spruce where he sings. His song sounds most like those of Birds 3 and 4, but the whistles in the opening phrase of his song seem to slur down, not up.

The distinctive dawn songs of six birds now play in my head, and I review each in turn, listening to the images I see there: Birds 1, 2, 3, 4, 5, and Bird 9 in the distance above Site 16. Each has a unique beginning phrase, followed by a brief chatter and then a high, thin note or two on the end.

I walk the circuit two more times, listening to each in turn again. Yes, they are all in their places, each male chipping between songs, each singing his own distinctive song.

It is from Bird 2 that I first hear the day song, at 5:33 A.M., an hour and 2 minutes after the dawn singing had begun and 20 minutes after sunrise. The chipping between dawn songs had slowed, and now he has abruptly switched to that high, thin *wee-see-wee-see-wee-see-wee-see-weeeeee* so reminiscent of a black-and-white warbler song. He's left the border of his territory, where he seemed to battle Bird 3, and he now sings above the car, nearer to his nest: *wee-see-wee-see-wee-see-wee-see-weeeeee,* ending on an especially high note (tracks 2-10, 2-11; figure 24).

It's contagious, as if the war-weary dawn singers are ready for a truce. Bird 3 now indulges in the day song, as he has retreated into the forest to the south. Like Bird 2, he sings midlevel in one of the deciduous trees and forages between songs. Bird 4 sings his day song, too; he's deep in the forest away from the road. What different birds these Blackburnians are now, singing more slowly, well below their lofty dawn posts and away from the territory boundary, and with none of the frantic chipping between songs. Yes, they are different birds, with entirely different mindsets. And the nearby American redstart concurs, having switched from singing a series of different dawn songs to repeating his one "day song" over and over.

Just beyond and southwest of Bird 5, who persists with his pebble-juggling dawn song, I hear another day song. That's odd—that male wasn't there just a few days ago, and I didn't hear a dawn song there this morning either. The campers in Site 21 are up and about, so I tread a little closer, recording this male's day songs and wondering where he was at dawn. He becomes Bird 6.

Into the woods beyond Bird 6, I hear two others, just where I heard them several days ago. Birds 7 and 8. I head into the woods, tracking them down, recording their dawn songs from the same spruce trees where I had heard them singing four days ago.

Across the road, I pause at the picnic table in Site 16, but I have not heard this bird since early this morning. Where is he, my phantom Bird 9? In the woods beyond him, another male (Bird 10) sings, just where I expect him, from the same small cluster of spruce and birch where he had been four days ago.

Figure 24: BLACKBURNIAN WARBLER: Day songs

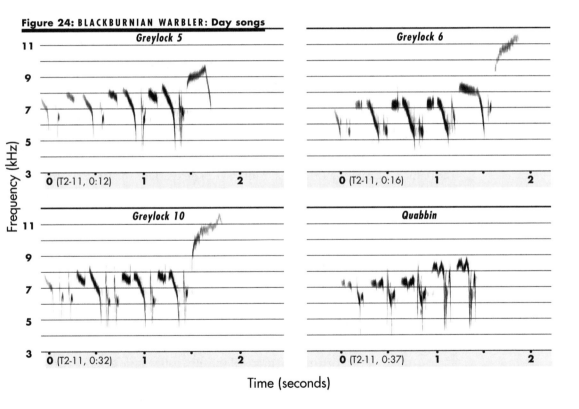

Time (seconds)

Figure 24. Four day songs of Blackburnian warblers. See (and hear, track 2-11) how the introductory phrases are almost identical among the three Greylock birds and how the one at Quabbin Park differs.

Ten birds, 10 Blackburnian warbler males, each singing on his own territory, except for Bird 9, who has been silent. I swing east again, sampling Birds 8, 6, 5, 3, and 1, as the others are temporarily silent. Some sing their day songs, some their dawn songs, as if unsure what the proper message is at this time.

I linger at the car with Bird 2, curious about his nest. He sings a *wee-see* day song, then switches to his unique descending dawn song. But what's that? From the open bill of the same bird I now hear a dawn song much like that of his neighbor, Bird 4! Again he sings it. And again, an opening series of whistled notes, a brief chatter, and the high notes on the end. Here is a second dawn song from him, and if I hadn't actually seen him switch songs, I might have concluded that another bird was singing here.

Oh, I like that. Here is the first hint that a male might have more than one dawn song. All this time he's been hiding this song that is more typical of those from other males in the campground. And this rarely used dawn song is, at least to my ears, indistinguishable from the commonly used song of a near neighbor. Thinking back to what my fellow warbler fanatic Bruce Byers has found for the closely related chestnut-sided warblers, I'm not surprised. Each male chestnut-side has a small repertoire of dawn songs that he shares with his neighbors, but the favorite song of each male is different from those of his neighbors. Very nice. Yes, a small piece of the bigger Blackburnian picture is revealed.

I continue. Back to Bird 1, whom I record as I stand in the parking lot, the parabola gathering his songs from the top of a distant spruce. Back to Bird 2, then 3, then 4, then 5, and into the woods, looping through the territories of 6, 7, 8, crossing the road and listening in vain for Bird 9, then into the woods for Bird 10 again. It's the routine for the rest of the morning, a brief break here and there as needed to sustain the body. At noon I reluctantly call it a day, as increasing numbers of campers are arriving to claim my sites for their weekend.

On the ride home, I reflect on the morning. I'm sorry about disturbing the dog in Site 21. From the sounds of the two human voices there, it was his dog and she wasn't happy about it. They all left early, before 7:00 A.M., before most campers were stirring. I'm grateful the other sites were open. The robins sang intensely for a while, then quieted down. In fact, overall it was so quiet this morning. By late June, it seems that most of the birds are largely done breeding for the year. I saw juncos but heard only one song all morning, and I heard no intense dawn chorus from the other warblers. I enjoyed the occasional sounds of other birds: the cedar waxwings, purple finches, a phoebe, two vireos (red-eyed and blue-headed), the drums of a sapsucker and a pileated woodpecker, and especially the songs of a winter wren in the swamp to the southwest. But how wonderfully the Blackburnians sang all morning! Their nesting season must lag behind that of the other species, as there is no other explanation for why males would be singing so intensely.

I relive the hourlong dawn extravaganza, then puzzle over some of the birds. Who was Bird 6? Where did he come from? He wasn't here just four days ago. I wonder if he has another territory with a female somewhere nearby, and when there he acts as if he is a good family man, but here, away from "home," he sings his day song continuously as if he has no mate. Other birds, such as chipping sparrows and American redstarts, are known to do that. Yes, that's my best guess.

Bird 9. Why did he disappear after sunrise? Does he have a second territory, too, spending dawn here and much of his day elsewhere as he tries to attract a second female? Perhaps he and Bird 6 have the same game going.

It is the best of mornings. This is what retirement is all about, I think with a chuckle, the freedom to be among the birds, getting to know them, breathing their air and singing their songs. For a few brief hours, I have come as close as I can to being a Blackburnian warbler, flitting from one spruce spire to another, visiting with each bird in turn, they in turn sharing some of their secrets with me. Yes, it is the best of mornings.

Back home, I contemplate the full four hours of recordings I now have. Over the coming days, I must buckle down at the computer, studying each song that I have collected from these birds. In the end, I know that what I find will enhance my memories of Mount Greylock. Blackburnian songs soon flit across my computer screen, the printed sonagrams accumulating in 10 stacks on my desk, one for each bird. Notes on the contents of the recordings pile up, too. A few days later I finish, the details of that Berkshire morning now scattered about my desk, largely confirming what I had heard that morning on the mountain.

From most birds, despite repeated sampling, I recorded a single dawn song (Birds 1, 4, 5, 7, 8, 9, 10; see track 2-9). From two birds (2, 3), I recorded two different dawn songs, one of which was used far more frequently than the other; and from the bird who didn't show up until after the dawn chorus (Bird 6), I recorded no dawn song.

The details of those dawn songs intrigue me. I see in the sonagrams that the first phrase in each male's song is unique to him, so each is readily recognizable, especially if one listens with the ears of a warbler. In contrast, all of the songs end in the same way, with a high, thin whistle between 8,000 and 9,000 hertz that then drops off abruptly in frequency (some songs also have an even higher whistle on the end, one that rises from roughly 10,000 to 12,000 hertz). Between the opening phrase and the high, thin whistles on the end, I find three types of chatters: one type shared by Birds 1, 3, 5, and 10; one by Birds 2, 4, and 9; and a third by Birds 3, 7, and 8. That's interesting, as from the beginning to the end of these dawn songs, the songs of these 10 birds seem to become increasingly similar.

I look again at that rarely used dawn song of Bird 2. It is almost identical to the commonly used dawn song of neighboring Bird 4. Could these birds carry other dawn songs about in their heads that they are slow to reveal? I wonder. I'd need far more time among the warblers to know, and then I'm sure I'd still have only a partial picture.

For the day songs, most males used only a single type in my samples (track 2-11; Birds 1, 2, 3, 4, 5, 10). Three birds (Birds 6, 8, 9) used two different day songs, and from one bird (7) I recorded no day song at all.

I am struck by how similar these day songs all are. Each bird conforms to one or two general patterns. The pattern of sharing day songs among birds contrasts sharply with how distinctive their dawn songs are, just as is the case with the closely related chestnut-sided warblers.

All of these details are put into perspective during a brief trip to Quabbin Park, about 50 miles east of Mount Greylock (tracks 2-9, 2-11). The Blackburnian songs at the Quabbin are distinctly different from those at Greylock! I hear the difference readily in the dawn songs, as these Quabbin birds end their songs with one or two wavering high-frequency notes, the second higher than the first. In the sonagrams, I see how both the Quabbin dawn and day songs differ from those in the Berkshires.

Intriguing. These Blackburnian warblers have dialects in both dawn and day songs. In a simple-minded way, I had hoped that the Blackburnians would be like two of my favorite warblers, the chestnut-sided and the blue-winged, which have dialects in dawn songs but not in day songs. But no, the Blackburnians are different, with dialects in each. Why? It's a Big Question, and a stab at the Big Answer would require an extensive survey of the entire warbler family. We'd need to know not only how songs vary within each species but also a host of other features of their natural history. Someday, I hope we can.

Greylock looks different these days. Sure, there's the familiar silhouette off to the west with the rock slide and the stone tower, but it feels different. There's something more. It looks bigger, feels closer. Closing my eyes, I am there, walking among the Blackburnian warblers in the predawn darkness, savoring their dawn songs, anticipating the switch to their day songs, all to the accompanying songs of winter wrens, chipping sparrows, purple finches, and so many more of my favorite songbirds. Greylock now sings! Yes, it was the best of mornings.

JULY

15

The Dawn and Day Songs of Scarlet Tanagers

July 5, 3:50 A.M., an hour and a half before sunrise
Quabbin Park, Massachusetts

IN THE DARKNESS, I stand on the road at Gate 52 in Quabbin Park, in the heart of a vast "accidental wilderness," the watershed of the Swift River, which was usurped from the locals in the 1920s so that their stream could be dammed to create the vast reservoir that now serves as the water supply for much of Greater Boston. Protecting the water meant protecting the land, and numbered gates around the reservoir now limit access to the extensive forests that once again cover the land.

I was here yesterday, too, scouting for where the scarlet tanagers sing at dawn. By 4:00 A.M. I had parked the car 2 miles to the south, just inside Gate 51. At the first songbird peep, roughly 4:30, I began cycling to the north, past Goodnough Dike, past Gates 52 and 54, looping to the west and then south around Quabbin Hill, and roughly 5 miles later coming to Winsor Dam, the monumental earthen wall holding back the reservoir, which stretches nearly 20 miles to the north. Then backtracking to Gate 51, I listened again, confirming where the singers were, finally returning to Gate 52, to listen some more.

Yes, it is here at Gate 52 where I best heard them. One sang directly above the road in the top of the ash tree that now looms overhead, rising well above the canopy of oak and pine. Another male sang just downslope to the east, with two more up the hill to the northwest. It's as if these tanagers gather here at dawn, perhaps to match wits, to try to outperform one another. So here I stand, waiting, wondering why these scarlet tanagers sing as they do at dawn, eager to record a single male during and after his dawn singing and then hurry home to dissect his performance on my computer.

I concentrate on the sounds of the night: occasional *chug*s of a green frog; the wail of a loon far to the north; water from recent rains trickling down the hill, beginning a journey through viaducts and pipes that extend far to the east; a distant whip-poor-will, calling nonstop, most likely at Gate 54, where I heard him yesterday.

There, the first songbird, a *wee-ooo* of an eastern wood-pewee. Just one song. Lighting my wristwatch, I read 4:20 A.M. About a minute later he utters a second *wee-ooo,* and a tanager begins up the hill to the west, soon followed by another down the hill to the east. I start the recorder, slip the headphones over my ears, and then swing the parabola from one tanager to the other, listening to each in turn. But where is the one I had expected overhead? Is he singing elsewhere, or still to arouse? Should I pick another bird to follow this morning, or should I wait, hoping for the one overhead in the ash tree? Headphones removed, I choose to wait and listen; for a complete morning, I reason, I must be with a male scarlet tanager as he awakens, not joining a male who is already singing.

Is that him? Ever so faintly I hear a tanager, somewhere overhead, his songs weak, ventriloquial in effect. I swing the parabola upward, aiming at the top of the ash; I turn up the gain on the recorder, and there he is, his amplified songs now booming into my ears! But in 10 seconds he's silent. Has he flown? I keep the sight on my parabola aimed at the top of the ash, and 30 seconds later I hear four more phrases. Ten seconds of silence, then two more phrases. A good minute passes before he resumes, now in greater earnest, though still muted.

In his singing I hear so clearly what has puzzled me since I first heard these tanagers sing at dawn. I know well the daytime song, consisting of four or five burry phrases, 2 to 3 seconds of what sounds like "a robin with a sore throat," as Peterson described. The tanager then pauses for 3 to 5 seconds and sings again, as if needing time to regroup or listen for a distant response (track 2-12; figure 25).

How differently he now sings at dawn. Instead of singing a bundle of phrases in rapid succession, he picks a phrase and utters it, pauses what seems an eternity (though in reality it is only a half second or so), picks another phrase, pauses, another, pauses, continuing until he's delivered 4 to 10 phrases; the pauses are uneven, the effect halting and deliberate, yet uncertain. Then he pauses a little longer and gives that distinctive *chip-burr* call, the note that he typically uses in circumstances throughout the day when he seems disturbed about something. He then pauses another second or two, and then repeats the pattern. Though he sings continuously, he sounds so much less energetic than during the day.

How odd. Most birds I know sing with the greatest energy at dawn. A long list comes to mind: robins and bluebirds and thrushes and chickadees and sparrows and towhees and warblers and wrens and flycatchers and . . . well, take that eastern wood-pewee now in full dawn song just to the east. He's singing at a clip of about 25 songs a minute, a nonstop barrage of *pee-ah-wee*,

Figure 25: SCARLET TANAGER

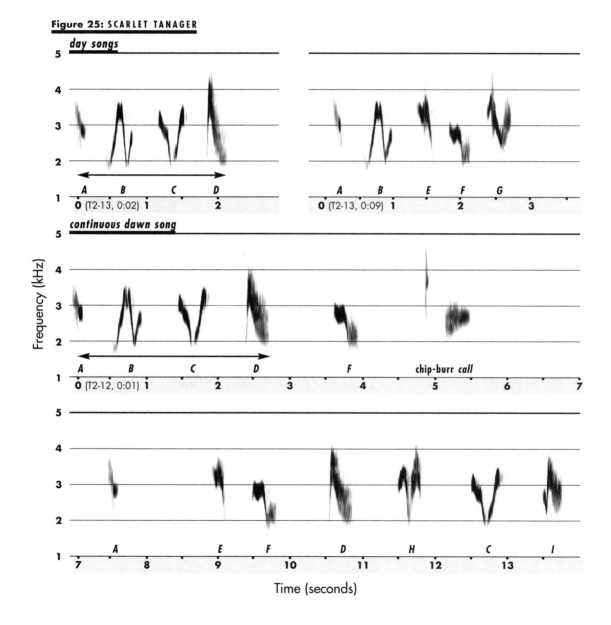

Time (seconds)

Birdsong by the Seasons

wee-ooo, and *ah-di-dee* songs, the *ah-di-dee* a special song used mostly at dawn; later in the day he'll sing far more slowly, only three to five songs a minute, a leisurely delivery of *pee-ah-wee* and *wee-ooo* songs.

Beginning at 4:30, I count, starting with the first call: *chip-burr,* then 4 burry phrases, *chip-burr,* 7 phrases, *chip-burr,* 9 phrases, *chip-burr,* 4 phrases, *chip-burr,* 8 phrases, *chip-burr,* 10 phrases, all in 64 seconds.

At 4:32, eight minutes after I first heard him, he falls silent, but he soon resumes across the road in the top of a large oak. I walk about, up and down the road, moving in and away, trying to get a good aim at him, a direct line of sight so that the songs will be crisply recorded with a minimum of reverberation caused by the dense foliage between him and me.

He continues, this tropical jewel in my temperate forest. In my mind's eye, I see him up there, his scarlet body with ink black wings and tail. From watching him during the day, I know that, in the tiniest fraction of a second, his throat swells and a *chip* explodes from the sharply opened and then closed bill; the throat again swells, and the bill is opened wide, more slowly now, closing after the much longer *burr.* The tail seems to pump both sounds from the bill, dropping sharply for the *chip* and then snapping back to position, only to be lowered more slowly for the *burr,* again snapping back to position when he's finished. But how does he deliver each burry song phrase up there in the dark? Is he in full battle gear, his aggressive posture, I wonder, his wings dropping slightly away from his body, the tips of the wings below the slightly raised tail? Or is he more relaxed?

With my headphones off, I now hear four other tanagers in the area, two up the hill to the northwest, two below the road to the east. Other than the pewee, I hear only an occasional song of a chipping sparrow and a common yellowthroat, an occasional call (but no song) of a veery—how quiet it is in

Figure 25. During the day, a male scarlet tanager sings a concise song of two to three seconds, each song with four to six phrases, and then he pauses several seconds before singing again. Illustrated here are two such consecutive songs, with each of the component phrases labeled. At dawn, the silent interval between phrases is 70 percent longer, and even the phrases themselves are 8 percent longer, the entire performance more drawn out; see how much longer it takes this male to deliver the phrases A B C D at dawn than during the daytime (indicated by arrows). Every so often, too, the song phrases at dawn are punctuated with a *chip-burr* call.

the woods already in early July, and how easily my ears can reach into the distance to pull out the tanagers.

On and on he sings from the dense foliage atop the oak. And at 4:47, after 15 minutes in the oak, he pauses, the songs resuming just seconds later high in the ash on the other side of the road. I sense he's a little more restless now; he seems to be moving about more within each tree, too, as I need to adjust the aim of my parabola every few minutes to get better reception.

At 4:54, I hear a somewhat different pattern of singing from him, and the change feels rather abrupt. The burry phrases seem to occur in distinct groupings of three or four, sometimes two or five, more like his daytime singing, and the *chip-burr* calls are less frequent. By 4:56, he sings more softly, just one or two burry phrases at a time followed by 5 to 10 seconds of silence, and then he's silent, fading out of his dawn performance just as he faded in a little over half an hour ago. It's 4:57 A.M., 22 minutes before sunrise.

Within a minute, a blue-gray gnatcatcher begins his wheezy singing from where the tanager was last heard, as if the gnatcatcher had been waiting his turn in the ash. I swing the parabola to the east, listening in turn to two tanagers who sing there—I don't think either is my bird, as both of them have been singing there for some time and their particular combination of burry phrases sounds different from the ones still playing over and over in my head. At 5:03 I hear my first red-eyed vireo, at 5:05 the first American crow, at 5:07 a muted veery call and song, and at 5:09 a drumming yellow-bellied sapsucker, 10 minutes before sunrise. The gnatcatcher continues in the ash, but all the tanagers are now silent.

Where is he? I need a sample of his daytime singing for comparison. At 5:28, perhaps 250 to 300 yards south along the road from his ash tree, I hear him. At least I think it's him; his phrases sound so familiar, and I know that I can verify whether it is him by trying to match his daytime phrases to his

SCARLET
TANAGER

dawn phrases when I get back home to my computer. He sings from a pine, in daytime mode, four or five burry phrases in a nice package, a long pause, then another package of phrases with four to five seconds between songs (track 2-13; figure 25). He takes his turn singing, it seems, with a Blackburnian warbler who also sings his daytime songs from the same pine. The tanager continues for nearly 10 minutes, delivering about eight songs a minute before I next hear him well off the road to the south.

I let him go, amused now when I realize I have yet to see him. Although he flew from tree to tree, I was so focused on the listening that I never bothered to look. It must be that way among male tanagers, too, I rationalize, because once the boundaries are settled in early spring and the leaves come out, they rarely see one another either.

All that really matters to me is that we connected this morning. From my scouting mission yesterday, I learned where he might arise this morning, and I was there waiting for him. He obliged, showering me with his dawn songs and *chip-burr*s for over half an hour, as I heard his first and last soft, dawn phrases from the towering ash. I felt the rhythm of his dawn effort, the slow, measured delivery of the burry phrases punctuated with the sharp *chip-burr;* I felt the contrast with his daytime singing, the rapid delivery of four or five burry phrases separated by long pauses, without any *chip-burr*s. Yes, he spoke and I listened—I was there, with him, and that's all that really matters.

I could leave well enough alone, I reason, as nothing beats a good hour or two in the field. But there are some burning questions that I need to answer. So, back home, I turn to my computer, the sounds of this tanager soon dancing across the screen.

I start with the daytime songs, all 72 that I recorded. Most (48) consist of four phrases, many (21) are five phrases, and only a few (3) are two or three phrases. Here is how most songbirds sing, delivering a nice package of phrases, then pausing at least as long as the song itself, then singing again.

Searching through the burry phrases, I discover 10 different ones, a typical repertoire size for a scarlet tanager, and I label them A, B, C, D, E, F, G, H, I, and J. Phrase D is that emphatic burry phrase that I thought distinguished my tanager from the others. This particular combination of 10 phrases is a tanager voiceprint, enabling me to distinguish this tanager from others that I might record.

He uses these 10 burry phrases in several favorite sequences. Of the 72 songs, 70 begin with Phrases A and B. Half of his songs (36) are the 4 phrases ABCD. Another 11 songs are ABEFG, and another 17 phrase sequences were infrequent, found only one to three times. A longer recording would no doubt have revealed an even greater variety of phrase sequences but probably no additional phrases.

And his dawn singing? Ah, yes, the same 10 burry phrases, the same bird —I can be certain. But with such continuous singing, I cannot identify "a song." What I can do is count the burry phrases between successive *chip-burr*s, and for 10 different minutes spread out over the 30-minute dawn period, I get averages of 5, 8, 8, 6, 7, 15, 6, 6, 5, and 5 phrases. I can detect nothing special about that minute in which he sang an average of 15 burry phrases before uttering another *chip-burr*.

Are his favorite daytime phrase sequences also evident at dawn? I study two of his long sequences of song phrases at dawn, where I have used X to denote a *chip-burr* and spacing to reflect the relative duration of pauses in his delivery:

X A D F D <u>A B C</u> I F <u>A B</u> E G D <u>A B C D</u> <u>E F G</u> <u>A B C D</u> X
X A <u>A B</u> D <u>A B C D</u> <u>F G</u> A B <u>A B</u> <u>E F</u> D H <u>A B</u> D A <u>E F</u> <u>A B</u> D H B <u>E F G</u> X

I do see some of his favorite sequences, which I've underlined, but they're patched together with sequences he doesn't routinely sing during the day. The singing is more random, it seems, the next phrase more unpredictable than during the daytime.

It's my impression that he sings more slowly at dawn and with less energy, but what do the numbers tell me? During those daytime minutes, he delivered seven to nine songs a minute, with an average total of 34 phrases a minute. For his dawn singing, I calculate an average of 52 phrases a minute, including that *chip-burr* call. I am surprised at what I see. I recheck the numbers, making sure. Yes, at dawn, he delivers 50 percent *more* song phrases than during the daytime. I had been fooled by his style of delivery, which sounded more leisurely at dawn. On top of that, the dawn message is reinforced with the aggressive *chip-burr* call.

So what exactly am I hearing that makes the dawn and daytime efforts sound so different? Back to the computer I go, to collect more numbers. First I measure from the beginning of a daytime song to the beginning of the fourth phrase in the song, repeating the process for 20 songs and obtaining an average: 1.9 seconds. I do the same for the first four phrases after a *chip-burr* at dawn: 2.5 seconds. At dawn, he delivers his phrases about 30 percent more slowly.

Does he also draw out each phrase more at dawn than during the rapid daytime singing? I measure samples of Phrases C and D during both dawn and daytime singing. Yes, each phrase is about 8 percent longer at dawn than during the day!

I next study the pauses between the phrases. Here is what is so noticeably different about his dawn singing. The pauses are almost twice as long (about 70 percent longer) during the dawn performance than during the daytime.

Very nice. I'm satisfied for now, as I understand a little more of this tanager's world than when I began. He has 10 different burry phrases that he uses both during the day and at dawn, and I can recognize him based on the particular phrases he sings. During the day, he sings, as do most songbirds, well-formed songs with long pauses between them. At dawn, he delivers his phrases more slowly and more haltingly than during the daytime, but he fills more of a minute with this halting performance.

I had been fooled. I thought that these tanagers sang less intensely at dawn, unlike all other songbirds that I know. I was wrong: This tanager actually delivers 50 percent more song in each dawn minute than in each daytime minute. Now I know that this supposed exception supports the rule: Male songbirds do sing more, and more energetically, at dawn than during the daytime. For the scarlet tanager, the *chip-burr* adds a distinctive touch to the dawn singing, too, as if here is a bird possessed, or "disturbed," singing as birds of so many species do at dawn.

Am I really satisfied? Well, I think there's just one more thing. I need to go back to the tanagers tomorrow morning, to record a few minutes of dawn song from those other four tanagers that I heard. Then, using their voiceprints, I'll return next year to Gate 52, just to see how many of the five will have made the successful flight to their ancestral home in South America and back.

"Ancestral home." The words roll off the tongue easily, but there's so much to them. For years I have loved to think of the remarkable journey that has brought us this small slice of tropical splendor. I have imagined the journey beginning a few million years ago somewhere down in tropical South America, well before North and South America were connected by the Panamanian land bridge. I could go there in my time machine, I reasoned, to see the one songbird species that could lay claim to being the ancestor of all these tropical tanagers. Was it inconspicuous and plain, or was it already a multicolored extravaganza?

And I would gawk at the tanagers in the Neotropical field guides, the hundreds of descendants from that one, the variety of colors bedazzling. They are named for their extravagances, ours in the Northeast being the scarlet one, chosen from a palette that describes other tanagers as red, crimson, ruby, rose, cherry, vermilion, rust, rufous, chestnut, cinnamon, ochre, orange, fulvous, brassy, buff, and fawn, not to mention the multiple shades of blues and greens and golds and every other color imaginable. The oh-so-descriptive names tell where the color is found, too, and it's not just on the head, but more specifically on the crest or the crown. Or on the cap, brow, goggles, spectacles, whiskers, nape, ear, throat, cheek, lore, bill (or beak, take your pick), scarf, or hood. Or check out the shoulder, or breast, or back, belly, wings, flanks, or rump. Or the bird is such an extravagance that a single color and place descriptor won't do, as perhaps he's seven-colored, or multicolored, or the paradise tanager, such redundancy in these names.

In my heart I still see my scarlet tanager among all of its tropical cousins, but my head now tells me otherwise. It seems that the scarlet tanager is not a tanager at all, but instead a cardinal in disguise. The genes tell us so, and the genes don't seem to lie. The same goes for the summer tanager in the South, the western tanager in the West, and the hepatic tanager in the Southwest. Perhaps it is no surprise, as they are, after all, far better singers than the tropical tanagers I know.

All of my dreams haven't been dashed, though, as it is still possible that our North American tanagers are tropical in origin and that they do return to their ancestral home each year. So I'll continue to imagine some tropical grandeur from which just a few species broke ranks. For a short season, only a few months of the year, they found that food was abundant to the north, where they could quickly raise their families before retreating from the northern winter to their home in the Tropics, the success they had in raising their families offsetting the increased risks of the journey. Gradually the distance between the Tropics and their breeding home lengthened, and with full retreat of the glaciers, these tanager renegades covered much of the North American continent.

Well, okay, for now I'm content, but I don't think I'll ever be completely satisfied by what I know of these tanagers. I love their characteristic calls, the scarlet's *chip-burr,* the summer's *pit-i-tuck,* the western's *pit-ick,* the hepatic's sharp, incisive *tchuk;* I need to visit these other North American tanagers at dawn, too, to hear how they use their songs and calls then. And, whatever the blood relationships of these North American tanagers, the Tropics will always beckon.

16

Yearling Indigo Buntings Learn the Local Microdialect

Enfield Lookout, Quabbin Park

JULY 18, 4:00 A.M. I've nestled into my camp chair, sitting comfortably on the stone wall above the overlook just a half an hour's drive from my home. One last time for the summer I choose to perch here to welcome a new dawn, to listen to the world awaken, to reflect on all that has happened here during the last two months. By the light of the half-moon I can see the shrubby clearing below me, a clearing carved from the forest so that visitors could gaze out upon the wilderness that was created here the better part of a century ago so that Boston could be assured of its water supply. To my right, the east arm of the reservoir itself stretches nearly 20 miles to the north, disappearing in the distance behind the islands that were once hills in the meandering valley of the Swift River.

INDIGO
BUNTING

Already it is 73 degrees, the promise of a hot day to come, and a gentle breeze blows. An occasional green frog chugs in a small pool behind me, but all else is quiet, the sweep of forest and water before me uninterrupted. Overhead, the brightest stars shine through the moonlight, and I pick out the swan flying south-southwest. How quiet, I realize, with the earthly woodcock and whip-poor-will as silent as the swan overhead, both having finished their seasons some weeks ago. By mid-July there's little for the males of most species to sing about, as females have already made their choices and the fathers of the next generation have been decided. Not so for the buntings, though, as females, who raise two to three families during the summer, are still listening and choosing at least through July.

At 4:29, exactly an hour before sunrise, a chipping sparrow sputters a single, longish song from the ground behind me. And three minutes later Ol' Blue sounds off, just one song, but oh, how familiar. I'm sure he doesn't remember, but we first met exactly two months ago, on the 18th of May, when I dubbed him Ol' Blue because the sheer radiance of his indigo plumage declared that he was at least two years old. He still sings the same four-second song, a sequence of eight different phrases, most of them paired; invariably, I sing along, rather crudely I admit, just by counting out the phrases and feeling the rhythm, 2 2 *buzz* 2 3 2 2 *buzz*, a unique song punctuated by a buzzy phrase uttered only once in the third and the last position (track 2-14; figure 26). I've tried a mnemonic, such as *fire fire where where heeerre my my run run run faster faster safe safe pheewww.* I've tried to use letters, too: A A B B C D D E E E F F G G H, one letter for each phrase sung, the eight letters signifying the eight different phrases, but the simple counting still works best for me to hear him: 2 2 *buzz* 2 3 2 2 *buzz.*

It's 12 minutes before he delivers another two songs, then another 5 minutes for two more, and by 4:50 A.M. he's steady, singing roughly a song every 10 seconds. The songs are all the same, though sometimes he stops short, omitting just the last buzzy phrase. Among all the buntings I've been listening to this summer, I'd know him anywhere, thanks mainly to those two buzzy phrases.

Figure 26. Songs of two indigo buntings at the Enfield Lookout, Quabbin Park, illustrating how a yearling comes to match the song of his adult neighbor.

Row 1. A typical song from Ol' Blue, the older adult at the lookout, with Phrases A B C D E F G H; this is the song used by this male throughout the season, from first arrival on May 18 until departure in late summer.

Row 2. The June 17 song of Li'l Brown, the yearling who settled next to Ol' Blue. See how this yearling includes six of the older bird's song phrases (A B D E F G) but omits two (C, H) and adds two of his own (I, J); by this date, he has finalized the song that he will sing for the rest of his life.

Rows 3 and 4. Two weeks earlier, on June 5, the form of this yearling's songs was still uncertain. These preliminary songs contained phrases—K, L, M, and N—that would eventually be dropped from the song; Phrases A and B would need to be modified to match those of the older bird; and Phrase D was absent on June 5 and would be learned during the following two weeks.

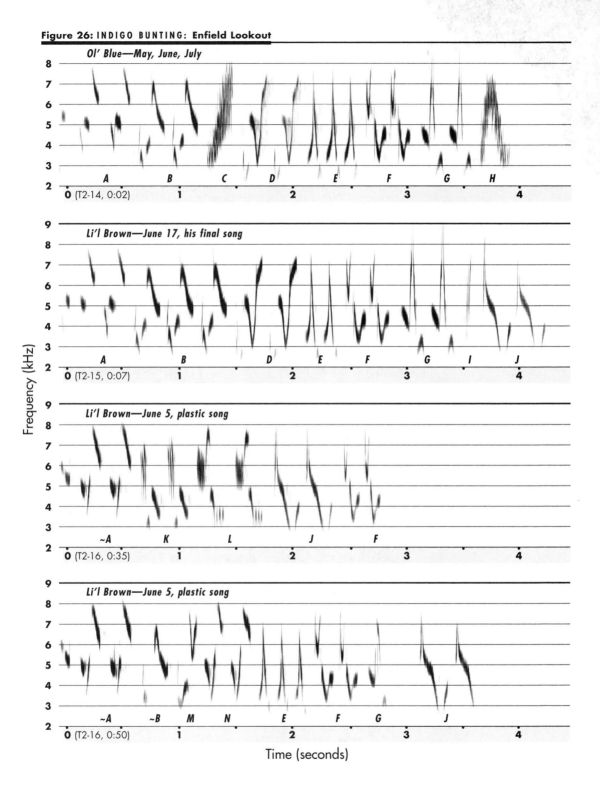

Ol' Blue—May, June, July

A B C D E F G H

0 (T2-14, 0:02) 1 2 3 4

Li'l Brown—June 17, his final song

A B D E F G I J

0 (T2-15, 0:07) 1 2 3 4

Li'l Brown—June 5, plastic song

~A K L J F

0 (T2-16, 0:35) 1 2 3 4

Li'l Brown—June 5, plastic song

~A ~B M N E F G J

0 (T2-16, 0:50) 1 2 3 4

Frequency (kHz)

Time (seconds)

ompared with just a few weeks ago, so few other birds are singing. A solo an carols halfheartedly in the trees to my left, singing none of the flutey *hisselly* phrases that mark his more intense dawn singing. Two chipping sparrows sputter their broken songs on the ground behind me, but any day now they could quit their dawn battles for the season. And a single towhee warms up down below, alternating his *chewink* call with bits of songs.

Beyond the towhee, where the clearing extends into the forest to the southwest, I now hear the bunting I have come to know as Li'l Brown. Easing out of my chair, I walk the narrow footpath down the left side of the clearing, working my way closer, eager to stand on the territory boundary between these two buntings and listen once again. Ol' Blue soon obliges, as he has been making the rounds, and he now comes to sing nearby, from his favorite perch in the tall maple. As I listen to these two birds, I smile, marveling at what I hear. From the very top of his favorite birch tree sings Li'l Brown; with splotches of brown in his less than radiant blue plumage, he is almost certainly a first-year bird, and, except for a few quirks, he has come to match much of Ol' Blue's song. Ol' Blue sings Phrases A B C D E F G H, Li'l Brown A B D E F G I J, omitting the two buzzy phrases (C, H) of Ol' Blue and adding two unique phrases of his own (I, J; track 2-15; figure 26).

Thank you, I find myself saying to these buntings, for letting me in on your lives this summer, for giving me a glimpse of what it means to be an indigo bunting. I had known roughly what to expect, based on my readings, but merely reading was not enough. I needed to experience you firsthand, to be among you week after week, to see and hear your singing life for myself.

My bunting quest actually began on the 17th of May. It had been raining for days, and I was desperate to get out and search for some buntings. I laugh now, remembering how I left home in the middle of the first rainless night, at 2:00 A.M., searching for just the right place where I thought buntings might reveal themselves at dawn. I tried Mount Holyoke at Skinner State Park— surely buntings would be here, and what a sweeping view of the Connecticut River Valley, but the traffic noise from Interstate 91 down below was deafening. Eventually, I retreated to my favorite wilderness, eagerly bicycling the Quabbin Reservation at dawn, finding some buntings about a half mile to the south of here (near the tower on Quabbin Hill) but none here at the Enfield Lookout itself.

On May 18, just one day later, three buntings had arrived here, one older adult and two yearlings. Ol' Blue was identifiable both by his brilliant plumage and his unique song. One yearling had a lot of brown in his mostly blue plumage, with a beautiful striped brownish patch in the middle of his back (hence his name, Patches). The third bird I hardly recognized as an indigo bunting, as the plumage was splotched not only with blue and brown but also with white.

Ol' Blue and Patches contested the area sharply, Ol' Blue chasing the yearling about the clearing, both of them singing repeatedly. The songs of Ol' Blue were already stable, I could tell, with all phrases sharp and crisp and their sequence in the song consistent. Not so with young Patches. I could hear the uncertainty in his song, as he was still refining each phrase and where it would fall. I never heard the whitish yearling sing; perhaps he didn't yet have a song worth singing, or perhaps he knew not to bother in the presence of these other two.

At one point the two yearlings had landed in a small dead tree together, with Patches chipping softly, as if lording it over this clear underdog. As I watched, Ol' Blue completely circled the tree once about 10 yards out and then landed to the upper left of the other two. Three ornaments now decorated the branches of this small, leafless tree, each so different from the others, yet each a male indigo bunting. Minute after minute they sat there, frozen, silent, my parabolic microphone trained on them, I listening with headphones for any peep that might be uttered. After 10 minutes, I heard the faintest of songs, recognizable as Ol' Blue's. Twenty seconds later there was another, and then another, and three more over the next minute, each seemingly a little louder and bolder than the one before, until Ol' Blue made his move, chasing Patches from the tree and resuming the pursuit. The whitish yearling was presumably less of a threat.

And then there was only one. How quickly it happened, I don't know, but when I returned three days later, on May 21, Ol' Blue ruled the clearing, uncontested. The two yearlings had moved on, no doubt in search of more friendly real estate, where they'd have a better chance of settling in.

I checked back every few days and heard only Ol' Blue until June 5, when far to the southwest, in the most distant part of the clearing, a second bird sang. I was quickly there, scoping him out, seeing that, though he was brownish, he was not Patches but instead another first-year bird, whom I would later dub Li'l Brown. His songs sounded uncertain and were delivered haltingly, yet somehow I sensed his effort to match the songs of Ol' Blue (track 2-16; figure 26).

Back home, I studied his songs on my computer, and I could see that he was already singing five of Ol' Blue's eight phrases—A, B, E, F, and G— though A and B still needed some work to match those of Ol' Blue. He also sang five other phrases, which were used by other buntings within half a mile but not by Ol' Blue (J, K, L, M, N, underlined here). I started writing out the sequences of different phrases in his songs, ABAEFGAB, AKLJFGABA, AKLJFG, ABMNEFGH, AKLJF, ABNEF. Just where will he go with all this? I wondered. I wanted to post a sign on his territory, "Singing Mind at Work. Listen!"

By June 17, two weeks later, I had my answer, as Li'l Brown had made his final changes. His song had stabilized, consisting of the phrases A B D E F G I J, and that would be his song for life. In those two weeks, Li'l Brown had perfected Phrases A and B, added Phrases D and I to his repertoire, abandoned Phrases K, L, M, and N, and arranged his phrases so that his song was now strikingly similar to that of Ol' Blue, his more mature neighbor.

Now, a month later, on July 18, I can listen and know how these songs came to be here at the Enfield Lookout. Patches and his whitish companion had tried their luck here on May 18, but in the face of stiff competition from Ol' Blue, they'd moved on, just as Li'l Brown had no doubt first tried his luck elsewhere, eventually settling here in early June, when he realized that this corner of this particular clearing was probably as good as it was going to get for him. As hatchlings last year, these young birds were quick learners, memorizing far more song phrases from adults than they would eventually need; now, as yearlings, they would select and modify and add phrases as needed when they settled on their first territory and worked to match the song of a neighbor who would most likely be an older, radiantly blue bird. Given the rich variety of song phrases that buntings can sing (well over 100) and the immense number of sequences in which these phrases could be sung, the song of Li'l Brown is probably now more like that of Ol' Blue than that of any other bunting on the planet, just as the song of Patches is no doubt like that of some adult neighbor where he eventually settled.

How satisfying to have been here the day the buntings arrived and to have followed them through the summer. By sharing a small part of their lives, they have taught me to listen in new ways. Instinctively I now compare successive songs of any bunting, just to hear how stable they are. I compare the songs of neighbors, too, wondering what their relationship is or has been. Yes, very satisfying, just to hear and to know.

Quabbin Hill, Quabbin Park

How satisfying, too, to have caught glimpses of this same process among other buntings that I have been following this summer. Just a half mile away, below the stone tower on Quabbin Hill, the bunting battles have been equally intense, the outcomes just as predictable. On May 17, two all-blue birds sang there, well separated on their own territories. Blue-1, in the territory just below the tower, sang Phrases P K L J Q R S. Blue-2, far to the southeast, sang A K T U H F V (tracks 2-17, 2-18; figure 27). Most likely two years or older, these two adults would stick to their guns all summer long, singing essentially the same song throughout the season.

In these simple song formulas, one begins to see the essence of how indigo bunting songs vary from place to place. Phrases K L J of Blue-1 were also sung a half mile away in the same sequence by Li'l Brown at the Enfield Lookout, but Li'l Brown abandoned K and L to conform to the song of Ol' Blue there; the other four phrases of Blue-1 (P Q R S) were not encountered at the lookout. Blue-2 shared A K H F with other birds, but not T U V. These phrases and at least 100 more occur throughout the geographic range of the indigo buntings, each bird seemingly capable of singing any one of the phrases, the particular phrases and the phrase sequence that a young bird settles on being determined largely by the adult next to whom the yearling settles.

And, oh, what battles I witnessed for the territory of Blue-1. On May 17, one yearling (identifiable by his brownish plumage and his "plastic," rambling songs) battled endlessly with Blue-1, singing nonstop (track 2-20; figure 28). The sequence of phrases in one of his 16-second songs was L J Q̲ R̲ d W V H S̲ R̲ K X K̲ L̲ J̲ Q̲ R̲ S̲ H Y Z K̲ X C J̲ Q̲ R̲ S̲ H J a b J̲ Q̲ R̲ L̲ J̲, a total of 16 different phrases. Six of those phrases (underlined) already matched phrases in the song of Blue-1 (who sang P K̲ L̲ J̲ Q̲ R̲ S̲), and already this young bird tended to use the shared phrases in the same sequence as Blue-1 (continuously underlined letters); only Phrase P was missing.

By the next day, that yearling had moved on, and two other young birds battled for this territory. One seemed to have the upper hand, defending the core of the territory, and he sang all seven phrases of Blue-1 and a host of others as well. The songs of the other brownish male were less refined and highly variable, and he made repeated assaults from the trees to the south. Repulsed, he'd fly back to the trees, sing some more, only to attack again a minute or so later, and after a flurry of buntings swirling about the scrubby oaks and maples, he'd retreat again to the trees. Curiously, on this day Blue-1 was nowhere to be found, as if he were letting the two young ones tire themselves out. Three days later he was back, in sole control of the territory.

And then there were just Blue-1 and Blue-2, all the yearlings having been repulsed. I returned to these tower territories often over the following weeks, mostly to listen, but partly to admire the view these buntings had from

Quabbin Hill. It wasn't until June 14, over three weeks later, that I realized I had been duped. On that day I listened in the usual way and heard the songs of what had to be Blue-1 and Blue-2 in their usual places, but then I heard Blue-1's song simultaneously from the center and from the far western edge of his territory. Wow, here was a newcomer that I had missed, a third bird that had moved into the area and copied the songs of Blue-1. A glance through the

Figure 27: INDIGO BUNTING: Quabbin Hill

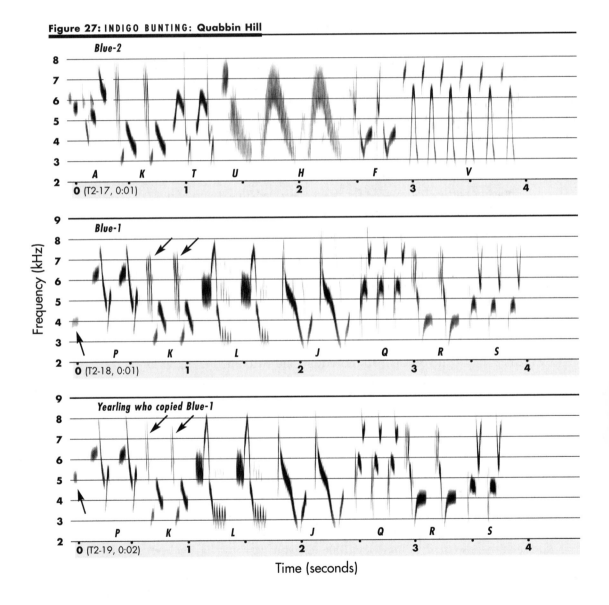

Time (seconds)

spotting scope revealed that he was indeed rather brownish, a first-year bird but with a different plumage pattern than the others I had seen here in May. And, yes, how remarkably similar his song was to that of Blue-1, with Phrases P K L J Q R S, all in the right order, all impeccably revealed later that morning on my computer monitor (track 2-19; figure 27).

Bunting Life

When I return to the Quabbin next year, who will be there and which songs will I hear? These are two different questions, of course, but interrelated. About half of the male buntings return to their territories in the following year, so the probabilities can be calculated. Each individual male has a 50/50 chance of returning, but because yearlings have copied the songs of Ol' Blue and Blue-1, these songs are twice as likely to survive to next year as is the song of Blue-2.

How and where a young bunting acquires his song seems fairly clear, but the *why* is far more mysterious. It's possible that learning a song in this manner is simply a sure way of acquiring a functional song, not necessarily one that is better than any other, but I think there's more to it, as perhaps there's some advantage to sharing a song with at least one neighbor. One early idea was that a young bird who has copied an adult's song could quickly step in and take over the territory of the adult should he disappear, thus deceiving other birds into thinking there was no change in ownership. I don't like that idea, though, because it gives the birds no credit for knowing who is who in their neighborhood, and I'm convinced they can easily recognize one another even if their songs appear essentially identical to us.

Figure 27. Songs of three indigo buntings at Quabbin Hill, showing how different the songs of two adult neighbors can be and how a yearling came to match perfectly the song of one of those adults.

Row 1. Song of the adult male Blue-2, with those three distinctive buzzy phrases in the middle (one U phrase and two H phrases).

Row 2. Song of the adult male Blue-1. Notice how the songs of these adults contain Phrases K and L, two phrases that were in the early repertoire but then discarded by the yearling Li'l Brown a half mile away at the Enfield Lookout (figure 26).

Row 3. The song of this yearling matches almost perfectly the song of his adult neighbor Blue-1. One has to strain to find differences, such as the different frequency of that tiny opening note, or the slight difference in the K phrase, with three strokes in the high note for the adult, only two for the yearling (see arrows).

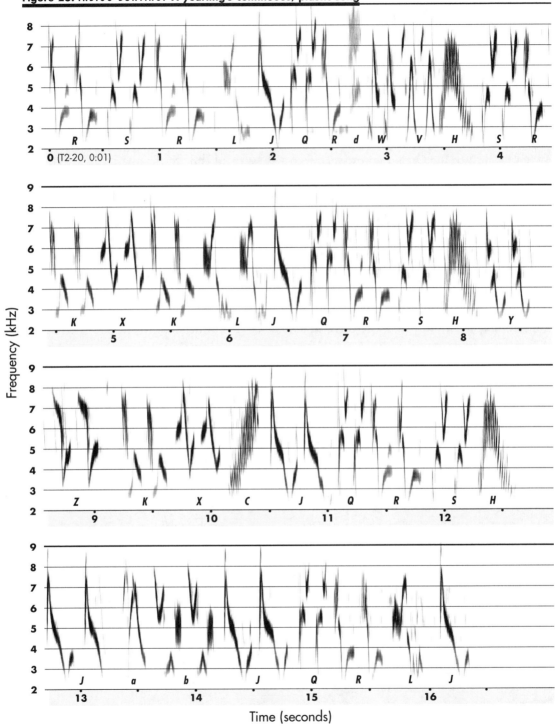

Frequency (kHz)

Time (seconds)

No, I think rather that it must have to do with the dynamics of the relationship between the adult and the imitating youngster. Buntings tend to be socially monogamous, with a male and female pairing to raise offspring, and perhaps it is relevant that a third or more of the baby buntings are fathered not by the male attending the nest but rather by a neighboring male. So it can matter greatly who one's neighbor is. It seems, for example, that an older male would prefer a dull yearling for a neighbor rather than a brightly colored yearling, because the older male's relative attractiveness to the females in the neighborhood would be greater with dull neighbors and he'd father more offspring as a result.

Perhaps song also plays a role in this mating game, and by copying the song of an adult nearby, the youngster somehow gains an advantage in the eyes of a female. When the young bird matches the song of an adult neighbor, the female can know, for example, a small bit of his history, that he has committed himself and chosen to settle here; maybe she likes that stability in his life, as it might suggest that he's less likely to desert her if she settles with him. Or maybe the youngster gains favor with the neighboring adult, who will be less aggressive and allow him to stay, because the young bird with an identical song is somehow less of a threat to the adult's success. In return for being allowed to settle on a good territory, the yearling may raise a nestling or two that has been sired by his neighbor but gain a foothold on a territory that might serve him well for a year or two to come, especially if the older bird dies. Maybe. Perhaps. The ways and whys of bunting lives remain largely a mystery.

I've retreated to my camp chair on the rock wall above the Enfield Lookout again. Now a half-hour past sunrise, at 6:00, Li'l Brown and Ol' Blue continue to sing. Perhaps each has a female who will raise another brood, or perhaps there's only one female still active, but neither male will give up singing until

Figure 28. This 16-second rambling song of a yearling just back from migration shows the great potential already in his singing mind. In these few seconds, this young male sings 16 different song phrases (C, H, J, K, L, Q, R, S, V, W, X, Y, Z, a, b, d); in finalizing his song, he'll choose to retain those phrases that best match the song of a nearby adult, learn additional phrases as needed, and then arrange the phrases in the correct order. With this approach, a yearling male can come to match the song of most any adult male bunting where he might settle throughout the range of the species.

all mating opportunities in the neighborhood are exhausted for the summer. Joining them has been a persistent yellowthroat, the same bird with the same *witchity* song that I have heard here since mid-May, and the towhee continues as well. The red-eyed vireos chimed in shortly after 5:00 A.M., too; they are always late to the dawn chorus and busy singers into late summer.

As I often do in the minutes before leaving a favorite place, I consciously engage each sense, one at a time. With eyes closed, I breathe deeply, smelling, the scent of the ferns, the fresh air. I feel, the gentle breeze, the warming air. I hear, a trickle of water behind me, the two buntings, a goldfinch's *per-chick-o-ree* overhead, the yellowthroat, the towhee, the distant vireos, now a sapsucker drumming, the quaking of the aspen leaves. Eyes now open, I scan, from the clearing before me to the horizon, following the sweep of forest and water off to the north, wilderness as far as I can see. A few minutes is all it takes and I'm then ready to leave, knowing that anytime, anywhere, and under any circumstances, I can close my eyes and return here, breathing, feeling, listening, and seeing as if I'd never left.

Epilogue

A year later, on July 19, I returned to search for indigo buntings at both the Enfield Lookout and Quabbin Hill. I heard only two buntings, but I recognized them immediately as Ol' Blue at the lookout and Blue-2 up on the hill. The recordings I made that day and the sonagrams I studied later at home confirmed the identities.

I cannot know why only two buntings held territories this year where five had lived the year before. What is clear is that these two buntings migrated south and then returned for another year, as did their songs, these particular oral traditions secure for one more generation. Blue-1 and his song were no doubt lost, as buntings typically return to the same territory year after year if they are alive.

AUGUST

17

The Cedar Waxwing: A Songbird Without a Song?

"No song." That's the simple message that I remember from Jim's doctoral thesis at the University of Michigan. For over 30 years the photocopy of my friend's graduate work has been yellowing on the shelf, and all those years a small voice has been whispering to me: "Get to know those waxwings better." Other voices have been louder, however, attracting me to study some of the finest songsters on the planet, wrens and mockingbirds and thrashers and sparrows and thrushes and so many more. But over the past year that small voice has reached me.

"No song." That's Jim's opinion, and he's recorded and analyzed more waxwing sounds than anyone else, so he should know. Another waxwing enthusiast, without the benefit of recordings and sonagrams, concluded the same 55 years ago. More recently, in 2006, Pete Dunne echoed "No song." Waxwings "call," say the Golden Guide and the National Geographic Guide; Kaufman and Peterson in their field guides are more noncommittal, referring only to the waxwing's "voice." Sibley adds some confusion: "Song simply a series of high *sreee* notes in irregular rhythm. Call a very high, thin, clear or slightly trilled *sreee*."

So what *is* the difference between a song and a call? I've heard that question so many times, and I still don't have a good answer. "Well, a song, you see, well, you'll know it when you hear it. It's typically the male who rises to the top of a tree and sings, ah, utters, something rather complex and loud and prolonged. And if he's unpaired, he utters this utterance in a regular fashion all day long. When he pairs, he utters far less, but if he loses his mate he'll, well, *sing* all day long again. For songbirds, the song is learned, too, while most calls are inborn. And song is a breeding-season sound, having to do mostly with males impressing females and defending a territory. A call is typically simpler and shorter, not so loud, routinely used by both male and female, and in a great variety of contexts, such as feeding, flocking, warning of predators. For most species it's obvious which sounds we'd think of as the song and which the calls, except for birds like . . . waxwings."

No song. That's a brief but huge statement, as losing a song for a songbird is a rare evolutionary reversal. Waxwings are *songbirds* and belong to that special taxonomic group of about 4,600 species with all of the specialized songbird brain and syrinx anatomy for learning and singing. Close relatives of waxwings, including the phainopepla, clearly *sing*. Over evolutionary time, perhaps during the last few hundred thousand years, the lineage to waxwings simply lost what we would think of as a song.

CEDAR
WAXWING

Although I'd love to know why these birds have lost their songs, my goal for this past year has been more modest, as I simply wanted to understand better what cedar waxwings do have to say. My journey has taken me many places throughout my home state of Massachusetts at all times of the year, and what I have learned is best told as a series of defining moments in my relationship with waxwings. I begin with *the* defining moment, listening to hungry young birds begging for food during early August, and then reflect back on other events during the year.

Secrets Revealed by a Young Bird's Begging Calls

AUGUST 6. It's 5:30 A.M., a few minutes before sunrise at the entrance to Plum Island, birding mecca on the coast of Massachusetts. Surely there would be babies out of the nest and flying about by early August, I reasoned, and what better place to listen to them than where all the trees are below average height, forcing the birds to mingle with me near the ground, where I can hear them best. And after fasting all night, they'd be hungry and all the noisier at dawn rather than later in the day.

For me, a big piece of the waxwing's evolutionary puzzle is learning what sounds a baby waxwing knows as it enters the world. A hungry, begging baby is going to be loud and frantic, and whatever sound it uses will be innate, because it needs to communicate with its parents the moment it emerges from the egg. That's the way it is with all songbirds, and at about two weeks of age the youngster of a typical songbird species begins to memorize sounds from adults that it will later use as a learned song; maybe by three or four weeks the young bird ever so softly starts to practice those future songs. My goal for the morning, then, was to find hungry baby waxwings and record them so that I could identify innate sounds in the waxwing vocabulary. Sounds that I did not hear from these young birds would be candidates for the evolutionarily lost "songs," vocalizations that might at least to some extent be learned but are now used more simply and disguised as "mere calls."

Driving south with the windows open, I heard their frantic calling on the left side of the road just before Hellcat Swamp. I parked the car at the swamp lot, gathered the gear, and quickly walked back the quarter mile to where they were still calling, yes, still calling and chasing the adults about, wing-waving and begging loudly. They were hungry all right. Recorder turned on, headphones slipped down over the ears, parabola aimed and following the youngsters about, I listened, savoring every trill, every beautiful, intense, rapidly trilled *bzeee* (track 2-21; figure 29A). Yes, that's what they were using, innate trills, somehow deeply encoded in the DNA, and from these young birds I heard none of the tonal *see* notes that make up the other sounds in the waxwing's vocal repertoire. Very nice.

Within an hour the youngsters were fed and far quieter, but they had told me much. Their innate trilled begging notes are no doubt the basis for the trills that adult waxwings use in a variety of situations. The tonal *see* notes will come later; perhaps the *see* notes are homologous with songs of other songbirds, and perhaps they are more learned, like typical songbird songs. Maybe. It's just a guess at this point.

Adult Females Beg Like Fledglings

JULY 1, EARLY MORNING ON QUABBIN HILL. In the fruiting tree above me, the waxwings came and went. They were mostly in pairs, a male and female foraging together, as this was the beginning of the nesting season for them. There was the usual conversational dialogue between them, but this morning I was fascinated by her sounds of frantic food begging (track 2-22; figure 29B). At least to me it seemed like begging, so much like a young bird pleading for another morsel from its parents, but perhaps I misinterpreted, in part because I'm a male; a female ornithologist friend kindly pointed out that it's not begging at all but rather a test of the male's ability to provide for her. She's demanding, and if he doesn't produce, he may be history.

As this bird demanded, she called frantically and waved her wings, sounding ever so much like a frenetic young waxwing begging for food from its parents. I remember thinking initially that these sounds were all wrong, that I shouldn't hear babies for at least another month.

Sitting at my computer in August now, I can compare the sonagrams that I've prepared for the "begging" youngster and the "demanding" female. How similar they are. Both the fledgling and the adult female use the same high, thin trill, 50 to 60 brief notes each second, the notes alternating slightly in frequency. Based on the small sample of recordings I have, I'm tempted to suggest that the youngster's call is a little higher and a little thinner, spanning a narrower frequency range, but there's so much variability from one example to the next that I can't be sure. What does seem clear is that this female's call is based on the innate call she herself used as a youngster.

Conversational Banter by Paired Birds

JUNE 14, SUNRISE AGAIN ON QUABBIN HILL, clearly a favorite place of mine to hear and see the world awaken. It was two weeks before the frantic courtship exchanges, and pairs of birds foraged together far more quietly, male and female whispering affectionate-sounding messages to each other. Were it not for the large parabolic microphone trained on them, I would have missed so much of what they had to say. With the parabola, though, I could hear everything!

Two pairs I especially remember. With the first, the banter was all trills (track 2-23; figure 29C). They began side by side, and I couldn't tell if one or both birds were calling, but then they separated and I could hear each bird's role in the conversation. I now look at the sonagrams and see the same structure that I saw in the begging of the youngster and the demanding of the adult female. But the tone of this banter is so different, as these split-second bits of trilled conversation were offered so softly, so gently, so rapidly. And, I suspect, tenderly.

The conversation of the second pair was more complex. In addition to the brief trills, some only $1/10$ of a second long, some calls began with a tonal

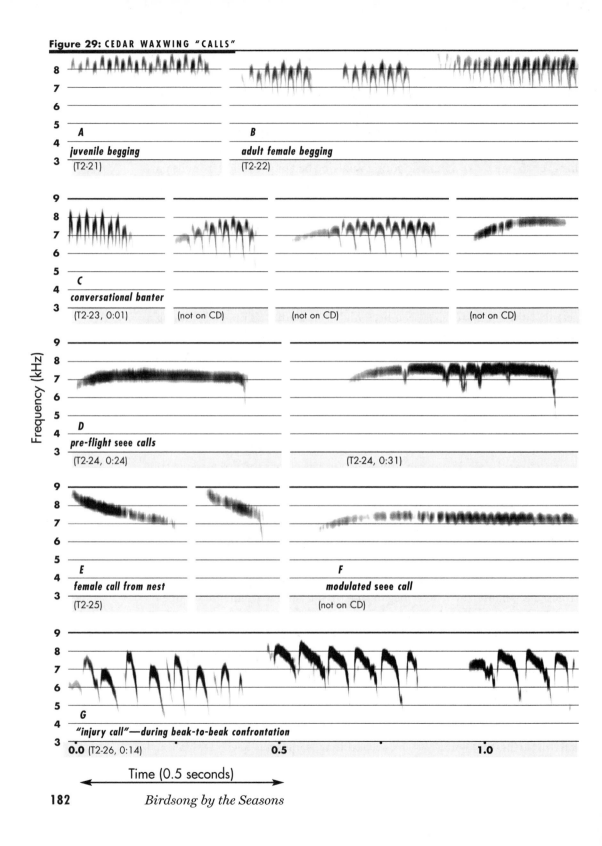

Frequency (kHz)

A
juvenile begging
(T2-21)

B
adult female begging
(T2-22)

C
conversational banter
(T2-23, 0:01)   (not on CD)   (not on CD)   (not on CD)

D
pre-flight seee calls
(T2-24, 0:24)   (T2-24, 0:31)

E
female call from nest
(T2-25)

F
modulated seee call
(not on CD)

G
"injury call"—during beak-to-beak confrontation
0.0 (T2-26, 0:14)   **0.5**   **1.0**

Time (0.5 seconds)

seee and ended with a trilled *bzeee,* and still others were brief tonal notes alone.

Touching, I remember thinking when I first heard this conversational banter, and my thought is the same now. Here were Mom and Dad dining at sunrise, probably soon heading back to their nest to add the finishing touches before they shortly raise a family of young waxwings together. Why wouldn't they have a lot to say to each other?

Flight Intentions and the Tonal Seee

In the *Birds of North America* account for the waxwing, the authors recognized two types of sounds, the trilled *bzeee* and a more tonal call, a thin, ethereal *seee.* And in all of my outings with the waxwings, I have heard what others have also pointed out, that the waxwings often use the tonal *seee* when they are about to fly, the shift from *bzeee* to *seee* notes signaling that a pair or a larger flock is readying to depart (track 2-24; figure 29D). Perhaps the mood shift begins with a suggestion by just one bird, and as more birds agree, they also *seee,* and more loudly, too, until they're off.

Yes, I have heard that repeatedly, but I cannot think of this *seee* as a song. This sound is used to coordinate the flock's departure, typical of the context in which a "call," not a song, would be used. This *seee* is not about defending a territory or impressing a female, so I must still think of it as a call, not a song.

Figure 29. Examples of the wide variety of *bzeee* and *seee* calls by cedar waxwings.

A. *Bzeee* calls from a frantic youngster just out of the nest as it begs for food from its parents. See how its call consists of a series of alternating higher- and lower-frequency notes. Compare those calls with **B.**, the *bzeee* calls of an adult female demanding (or begging for) food from her mate. Sometimes the notes alternate in frequency, and sometimes not.

C. A sampling of brief notes used in conversational banter by a male and female as they forage together before the nesting season. Calls used in this context are the raspy *bzeee,* the high, thin *seee,* and calls that contain both the thin whistle of the *seee* and the raspy elements of the *bzeee.*

D. Intense, tonal *seee* calls, with some broken modulations, that were used by a flock of waxwings just before flying off.

E. Brief, down-slurred whistles used by the female as she incubated her eggs.

F. A *seee* call nicely modulated in frequency.

G. "Injury calls," intense *bzeee* calls used by a bird who is physically confronted or attacked by another bird. Note especially the broad frequencies that these notes span.

A Special Tonal Call—Female on the Nest

JULY 3, BUFFAM ROAD CEMETERY, PELHAM. Headphones over my ears, parabola mounted on a tripod and aimed at the nest high overhead in the oak tree, I punched the Record button at 5:17 A.M., a minute before official sunrise. I would sit here among the gravestones for a few hours, just listening to the activity at the nest.

The first hint that she was sitting there came just 10 minutes later, a wee-thin *peep*, then another, and another, 11 in all over the next 2 minutes (track 2-25; figure 29E). Then silence, then a few more *peep*s, silence. It was on and off like that until 6:07, when she trilled several times before departing and joining the male in the pines nearby, where she burst into a frenzy of intense "demand" trilling, then returned to the nest only a minute later.

That cycle repeated itself several times over the next few hours, more *peep*s from the nest, a few trills immediately before departing the nest, the male feeding her, and she returning to the nest. Once he came to the nest and fed her there; her subdued yet rapid trilling told of the food delivery.

How fascinating these tonal but brief and down-slurred notes, not rising slightly as do most other tonal notes. In his thesis, Jim called this a "disturbance call," saying it was "eerie, unlocatable," often given by members of a flock that seemed anxious because of some disturbance. He likened it to the ventriloquial call that songbirds often give when they sight a hawk. Yet here it is given by the female on the nest, perhaps signaling a restlessness and increasing hunger, perhaps a message to the male that it would be in their best interests if he delivered some food so that she could continue incubating their eggs.

An Extreme Bzeee Call?

NOVEMBER 15, NEAR THE BIKE PATH OFF STATION ROAD, AMHERST. Midmorning, I stood on the railroad tracks beneath a flock of about 60 birds, watching them mill about in the treetops, a continuous stream of birds dropping down to the bittersweet to feed and then rising back to the treetops. They called softly, using both *seee* and *bzeee* calls.

Four times I watched a brief squabble in the treetops, and four times in the headphones I heard what I was certain my friend Jim in his thesis had labeled an "injury call" (track 2-26; figure 29G). Such a call was "intense" and covered a "wide range of frequencies," Jim wrote. He heard it from agitated adults when he was disturbing a nest or from the adult when he caught the bird and held it in his hands.

At home, I studied the sonagrams, confirming that they looked the same as Jim had described. It's amazing, I thought, how the waxwing varies its simple trill to accomplish such a variety of calls.

Bzeee *and* Seee: *Two Calls or One?*

The human mind instinctively classifies events and experiences, as the world would be unmanageable without our imposed structure. I classify bird sounds for the same reason, and for the waxwings I yearn to put each call into its proper bin. My two bins are the trilled *bzeee* and the tonal *seee* calls, but I now see all too well that my bins bleed into each other. Yes, there are the two extremes, the trilled *bzeee* with up to 60 or so tiny little notes each second and the pure, thin *seee* with no detectable modulations. But I now look at all that happens in between these extremes (track 2-27; figure 29). Some *seee* notes waver beautifully, and some are seriously fragmented, just a hint of all that these waxwings can do. Other calls begin with a *seee* and end with a *bzeee*, some begin and end with *seee* but have a *bzeee* in the middle, the *seee* and the *bzeee* all mixed up together.

I go back to Jim's thesis, to the section that I had marked on page 4: "waxwings' vocalizations consist of a series of calls all of which can probably be considered variations of a single basic type." Wow. A single type. I can see how Jim came to that conclusion, though he waffled a little with that word "probably." Perhaps I'd put it a little differently: there seem to be two extremes and all kinds of intermediates in between, a continuum of variations between the tonal *seee* and the trilled *bzeee.*

And in the thousands upon thousands of waxwing calls I have recorded and looked at on my computer monitor, there's one in particular that I return to time and again. I enlarge it, too, so that it fills the entire field of view, as I enjoy simply gazing at this sound (figure 30A). That call begins with a tonal *seee,* though slightly wavering, but by the end it has morphed into a trilled *bzeee* with the typical upper and lower elements.

It is how the *seee* transforms into a *bzeee* that is so enlightening (please follow along in figure 30A). I start on the left of the sonagram, following the tonal *seee* across to the right, gradually rising with it, dipping down (at a) and up, down (b) and up, then down (c), and there's a break, after which I imagine the *seee* continuing as two isolated, lower elements of the *bzeee* call. I then look back to where the *seee* dips for the first time and see the upper element of the *bzeee* note forming there (at a). That upper element of the *bzeee* occurs simultaneously with the lower tonal *seee*, as does the second upper element of the *bzeee* (at b), revealing that the waxwing is using both of his voice boxes at the same time here.

At that I am smiling from ear to ear, almost giddy, because I believe this one call among thousands tells so much about how the waxwing uses its two voice boxes to produce its fascinating repertoire of varied calls. Because most songbirds use the left voice box to produce lower-frequency sounds, I bet that

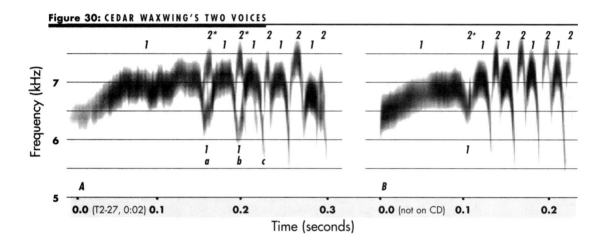

Figure 30: CEDAR WAXWING'S TWO VOICES

Figure 30. My absolute favorite calls of all the thousands that I looked at on my computer monitor (enlarged so that the details are more easily seen).

A. See how the call on the left begins with the tonal *seee* but then morphs into the buzzy *bzeee;* in the transition from one type of call to another, this waxwing shows how it uses one voice box (probably the left, labeled 1) for the *seee* and for the lower note in the *bzeee,* and the other voice box (right, 2) for the upper note of the *bzeee.* See that the first two notes from the second voice box (2*) are given simultaneously with the sounds from the first voice box, thus revealing the contributions of the two voice boxes. Usually the sound emitted by a waxwing comes from either one voice box or the other, not the two simultaneously, but it seems that the bird producing this particular call was a little sloppy, thereby revealing the two sound sources (see text for a more detailed description).

B. The call on the right shows just a hint of the same phenomenon, with the small spike at 2+ indicating how this bird is bringing in the sound of the second voice box as he phases out the sound of the first.

Birdsong by the Seasons

the tonal *seee* is produced on the left but the trilled *bzeee* uses both left and right, the left for the lower *bzeee* element, the right for the upper *bzeee* element. In producing the *seee*, the waxwing breathes continuously out of the left voice box, vibrating the membrane there; to change the *seee* to a *bzeee*, all it needs to do is engage the right voice box, too, now perfectly alternating between the two voice boxes to produce a highly coordinated series of 60 elements per second, the roughly 30 notes from the left voice box usually slightly lower in frequency than the 30 from the right. This one call (figure 30A), perhaps somewhat sloppily produced by a young bird, has told me so much about the inner workings of the waxwing's brain and voice boxes.

Yes, that must be it. I don't see how it could be any other way. Jim was right. He'd be pleased that I've come to agree so enthusiastically with him after all these years; next time I'm near Yellow Springs, Ohio, I'll stop in at the bird blind erected in his memory and tell him so. There *is* just one "basic call," Jim, and I can now see how the waxwing does it. I see the bird breathing out the left voice box, producing a perfect *seee;* as the air is then gated to the right box, alternating left to right and back again at 30 cycles a second, I hear a *bzeee.* Intermediates between these two extremes are easily generated by playing with tensions of membranes and how often air is gated from right to left and back again. How elegantly simple!

No Song

I concur. There is no special sound used by males (or by females) during the breeding season that is anything like a song. During the prenesting season, in fact, the time when males of most species sing intensely, both male and female waxwings are remarkably quiet. Instead, waxwings communicate with *bzeee* and *seee* notes and all manner of intermediates, and oh, how I would love to know what each little twist and turn of these notes means to the birds.

Two questions linger in my mind: *Why* no song? And why the waxy tips on the wing feathers? I sometimes wonder if these two questions aren't related and if my tendency to type "waxsing" on my keyboard isn't part of the answer. The birds do not defend territories, so no loud territorial proclamation is necessary, and perhaps the wax is used to impress potential mates at close range. Older birds have more waxy tips on their wings than do younger birds, and older birds are more successful breeders. Perhaps, just perhaps, the wax on the tips of the wing feathers does function as a "song," and birds inspecting each other's wax learn about the age and health of a prospective partner.

Once again I'm reminded of a fellow student in my ornithology class over 40 years ago. She had decided she was going to study frogs or lizards, I forget which, because everything was already known about birds. She scared me, as I thought that perhaps there was no future in birds. Now I chuckle, realizing how little we know about our most common birds, realizing, too, what a joy it is to step outdoors and begin asking questions about the intimate lives of the everyday birds all around us.

18

Young of the Year Practice Their Songs

August 8, 4:35 A.M., 75 minutes before the sun rises at 5:50
Norwottuck Rail Trail, Amherst, Massachusetts

I FEEL THAT I'm late this morning, but I'm just following the sun, as it is already half an hour later rising today than when I was here in late May, "here" being the special place on the bike path near my home where I enjoyed the duetting orioles (see page 99).

I face the east, awaiting the dawn. The oriole nest, long empty, hangs just above and behind me over the bridge, and between me and the active railroad tracks a quarter mile to the east is one of my favorite wetlands. At the moment, the wetland is a chorus of chugging green frogs, and from the bushes and trees lining the bike path sings a symphony of insects, including katydids. I turn my recorder on and swing the parabola around, stopping to listen when it focuses on an individual singer. Some are smooth singers, but some sputter—same species, I wonder, just different individuals? I know so little about these insects other than that they make good August sounds.

The energy I feel is so different from what I felt just 72 days ago, when I was listening to the orioles here. Back then, there was an urgency in the air, and in the darkness male songbirds blurted out isolated songs as if eager for the dawn frenzy, anxious for the do-or-die singing competition that would no doubt determine who would succeed and who would fail in fathering the next generation. By 45 to 50 minutes before sunrise, the singing was intense, each male strutting all that he had, robins and flycatchers and phoebes and sparrows and warblers and cardinals and swallows and catbirds and thrashers and thrushes and more.

Today is different. Now 45 minutes before sunrise, I hear a lone cardinal singing far to the southeast. Other than the insects and the green frogs, it is eerily quiet. A few wood ducks and mallards call and splash about in the marsh, but the songbirds are largely silent. Minutes later, a wood thrush awakens just to the north, calling sharply, *whit whit whit;* he spits out a few strained song fragments before the next *whit* series, but within a minute he mellows, calling softly, *bup bup, bup bup bup,* then fades to silence. Catbirds! Every bush around me now seems to *meow,* but there is no song. Down in the marsh, a song sparrow sings halfheartedly, his songs soft and wavering, the season for them nearly over.

Yes, today is different. In the gathering light, I look down the bike path to the south and see them hopping about; the nearby bushes, too, are crawling with birds. They're *everywhere!* If every pair of May adults has produced three to four offspring, there are now two to three times as many birds as before.

On this early August day, it is their energy that I feel, much like the energy of my year-old grandson, Benjamin, who is now into everything. A phenomenal number of neuronal connections form in his brain every few minutes, and it is the same with these young birds, as they are learning their way in the world, and, like Ben, they are also listening. Within a few months my grandson will be babbling away, practicing saying what he has heard, and today it is the babbling of the young birds that I have come to hear. I've heard none of them yet, but it's still early. They seem to fill their stomachs first and practice their tunes later, unlike the singing adults, who sing first and eat later.

I already hear some evidence of the next generation (track 2-28). Across the marsh to the east, probably beyond the railroad tracks in the woods, a young great horned owl screeches. A couple of great blue herons squawk bloody murder, one to the left, one to the right; they've been here all summer, not attending a breeding colony, so most likely they're youngsters, perhaps only one or two years old. And a good mile to the north, a young human (male, most likely) struts his stuff in these early-morning hours with what must be the noisiest muffler he can find.

To find the young, babbling songbirds, I'll ride my bike slowly back and forth on the mile of bike path between here and Station Road to the south. I'll listen for the soft, scratchy sounds in the bushes, or for loud, blurted blurbs of nonsense, for anything out of the ordinary that might suggest a future maestro in the making.

I set out to the south, headphones atop my head, recorder over the shoulder, the parabola dangling at my side. Young wood ducks soon scurry from near the bike path ahead of me, swimming to the safety of cover, their rising squeals already much like the thin, whistled adult squeals that I associate with wood ducks. A flock of cedar waxwings, mostly young birds it seems, catches insects by sallying out from the tops of the dead trees drowned by the beavers; I train the parabola at them, listening through the headphones, hearing their trilled *bzeee* notes and the high, thin, whistled *seee.*

Just a few hundred yards south of the bridge, near where the marked KC foot trail leads off to the west, I pause, listening to a calling song sparrow (track 2-29). It sounds suspicious to me, like an invigorated, curious youngster; I don't think that an adult would have so much to complain about at this time of the year. So I dismount, waiting, wondering who he or she is. It calls from the alder bushes about 15 yards away on the other side of a small pond, and I note the yellowthroat calling *djerp djerp djerp* from a small patch of cattails over to the left. Then silence. I see the sparrow foraging, hopping about in the bushes. It disappears, but I follow it by the shaking branches, an occasional call, 5 minutes, 10, and . . . yes! Listen to *him,* as now I know it's a male. It's a soft, scratchy bit of song, amorphous and so faint that I would not have noticed it if I hadn't half expected it. I train the parabola on him, turning up the gain to hear him better. After half a dozen feeble attempts over half a minute, he's silenced by a jogger on the path nearby.

Wonderful! He's the first catch of the day, the first young male songbird I hear practicing his songs. I check my watch: 6:20 A.M., half an hour after sunrise. By his performance, I never would have known he was a song sparrow if I hadn't watched him sing. How old is he? At most about 70 days, I would think, if he hatched in the first wave of song sparrow babies, during late May. But his singing is so weak that I bet he's younger, closer to 50 days, probably a June baby.

I wait, hoping for more. A house wren chatters at me, again rather suspiciously, but nothing more. Ten minutes, 20, the insects continue, the late-summer flowers abound, the cattails are full and robust. I had noted the small chickadee flock around me, but now I detect one of them whispering faintly. Training the parabola on the bird, I hear the distinct *chick-a-dee-dee-dee* calls, but there's more. A young chickadee faces a daunting task, as it must learn not only the song (the whistled *hey-sweetie*) but also two kinds of calls. One is the *chick-a-dee-dee-dee* call, the other the "gargle calls" that are used in aggressive contexts. This young bird now practices all three kinds of sounds, first a series of *chick-a-dee-dee-dee* calls, then gargles, then back to the *chick-a-dee-dee-dee,* then a faint whistle, this one a *hey-sweet,* tentative and incomplete (track 2-30). It could be either a young male or a young female, I realize, as both sexes call and practice-sing, though females rarely sing as adults. Time—about 6:40.

While I listened to the chickadee, something had blurted out a loud, low-pitched attempt at a song near me over the bike path. I now search but see nothing. Again, I plead. Give me a hint as to who you are. Stay, I remind myself. Listen. Linger. . . . There it is again, now perhaps 100 yards to the west, across the pond and field and high up in the towering oaks. I train the parabola on the general area and turn up the gain on the recorder, hearing one more, then another attempt at a song. But who is he? A robin? How about a thrasher? It's something largish, given the low pitch. Something rather melodious. And by chance the parabola is aimed directly at him when he blurts out his next attempt, an oriole chatter now embedded in the attempt at the song (track 2-31)! The chatter call is a dead giveaway. It's a Baltimore oriole, maybe one of the babies from the many nests that I was watching during May along the bike path. I hope for more, but that's it from him for now. The time—a little after 7:00 A.M.

Minutes later, the yellowthroat is calling again (track 2-32; figure 31). I train the parabola that way, finding the source of the sounds down in the cattails. He or she is perhaps only 15 yards away, but the call is soft, and I leave the recording gain high. *Djerp . . . djerp . . . djerp.* It's perfectly recognizable as

Figure 31. For all three species illustrated here, the adult song consists of a particular phrase repeated boldly and emphatically several times; songs are crisp and sharp, the male confident in his delivery of a well-rehearsed song. How different are the practice songs of these young birds (though the sound quality unmistakably identifies these individuals' species).

The yellowthroat's song will eventually become a repeated *witchity-witchity-witchity*, and this young bird clearly has the right idea, as he's working on elements A and B, which might eventually crystallize in some form into his adult song. He sings softly from the cattails, too, barely audible over the din of the insects calling loudly on this August morning.

It's much the same with the young Carolina wren, though the repeated elements in his songs are more evident. As an adult, he'll sing 30 to 40 distinct, precisely delivered songs, and the repeated phrases of 5 future songs (A, B, C, D, and E) seem evident in the three brief excerpts here. See how the pitch wavers within a song and how no two efforts at the same phrase are the same (compare successive D phrases, for example); also, as in the first and second song here, he practices what will eventually be 2 different songs in the same outburst.

The same uncertainty is revealed in these songs of a young tufted titmouse. When he is an adult, all three to five phrases in each song will be identical, but this youngster clearly doesn't yet have it down.

the call of a yellowthroat, the call that most likely isn't learned but is encoded somehow directly into the DNA. Male or female? If male, show me what you're learning for a song. And within a minute I hear his uncertain, boyish voice, a clear attempt at a *witchity* song, recognizable as a yellowthroat anywhere but far from perfected. Three attempts are all he gives in a 10-second span, and then he's back to his calls, then silence.

Figure 31: BABY SINGERS

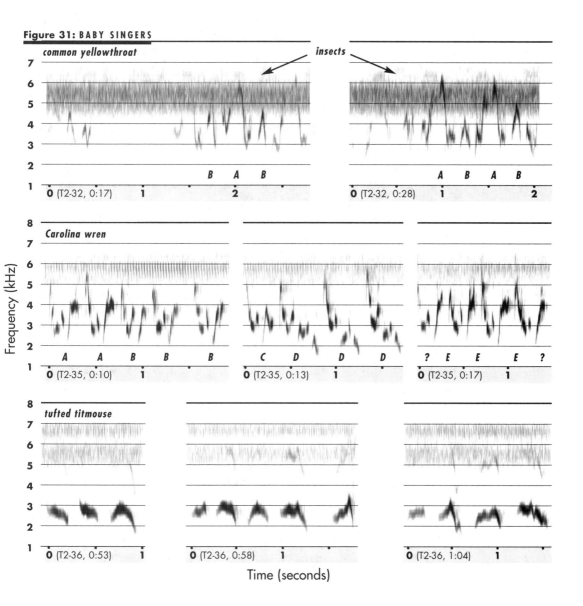

Time (seconds)

I take another look around. I've barely moved my feet, and I've heard the young song sparrow in the alder bushes across the small pond, the yellowthroat across to the left in the cattails, the young chickadee in the passing flock, and the young oriole as he passed by to the west. Four young birds, all practicing, all babbling, all working at finding their voices. The house wren still calls sassily, and there's nothing sassier than a young male wren. I could wait here longer, but I'm eager to return to the bridge. I'll be back.

At the bridge I find Deedee Minear, a friend who often perches here to watch and listen. She tells me of the bittern she's been watching and of the two singing marsh wrens. There's a kingbird nest down below, she points out, and on a nearby dead branch are two babies who have just left the nest. And sometimes, she tells me, there's a Carolina wren who never seems to repeat himself. A young male! Deedee is observant, knowing that an adult wren repeats himself over and over, eventually switching to a new song, but here was a different kettle of wren.

I'm distracted by faint songs in the alders along the brook to the south. Excusing myself, I walk to the bridge and climb up on the rails, aiming the parabola and listening more closely. Oh, so faint, just above the din of singing insects and the chirps from bushes that seem to swarm with birds, I swear it's a young warbling vireo. Same tempo and rhythm as an adult, rising and falling, about the right length, but so ill-formed, and perhaps I'm only imagining.

I return to the kingbirds. Through the binoculars, Deedee and I watch the two young birds opening and closing their bills, but we hear nothing. Aiming the parabola at them, however, tells a different story (track 2-33). Each calls sharply, over and over, ever hungry, ever demanding attention from the adults nearby. I find myself listening and watching, asking Deedee where the adults are, making sure I'm recording only the young birds, because their repeated *tzeet* calls already sound so much like those of the adults. String those *tzeet* calls together excitedly and you get the adults' *t't'tzeer, t't'tzeer, t'tzeetzeetzee* song.

What I've already heard this morning is the tale of two roads taken. Some 60 to 80 million years ago, a special lineage of birds split into two, one to become the songbirds, the other to become the flycatchers and their suboscine relatives (woodcreepers, antbirds, and their relatives of the New World Tropics). The songbirds, like the sparrow, chickadee, oriole, and yellowthroat, must learn their songs, and the youngsters memorize the adult songs and then babble to match their singing to their memories. But the kingbird is a flycatcher, and its songs are not learned but rather encoded in the genetic material.

When a young flycatcher leaves the nest, it already uses sounds that are much like the adult calls and songs. Yes, I'm hearing history, two highly successful lineages but with different approaches to acquiring their adult calls and songs.

I'm distracted again. It *is* a young warbling vireo, and he's now just behind me, in the elm tree over the bridge. I walk beneath him, headphones on, parabola aimed at him, and I quickly turn down the recording gain. Wow. Overhead, almost within arm's reach and the parabola almost overkill, is a wonderful warbling vireo in the making, the youngster's version of the familiar *If I sees you I will seize you and I'll squeeze you till you squirt* (track 2-34; figure 32). There are a lot of false starts, partial songs, and uncertainties, but every once in a while he squeezes out a wavering rendition of the entire song. I raise the binoculars, overkill again, just to bring him closer, greedily studying his immaculateness, watching him sing. . . . The wren! In the headphones, I now hear Deedee's young Carolina wren nearby.

Low in the bushes beside the bike path, he blunders through the songs he is practicing. A few wavering attempts at one, then another, then mixing the two, then on to another, all evidence of the 30 or so different songs he is practicing. He's loud and audacious, with nothing apologetic about his uncertainty, and he throws in a loud *jeer* call on occasion for good measure (track 2-35; figure 31). He works his way to the south and then retreats into the dense woodland to the west.

Deedee has lingered, and we begin to enthuse about the young wren when I'm distracted again, this time by a tufted titmouse in an isolated tree perhaps 70 yards to the west. I turn up the recording gain and listen as he sings a few phrases of one song, then a few of another, then another, and another (track 2-36; figure 31). Every few seconds he seems to switch to another song that he's practicing. How many was it, five different songs in half a minute? How interesting that the wren and the titmouse both practice like this, too, just a stab or two at a given song before rushing on to the next, even though the adult sings each song many times before switching. The Bewick's wren is like that also, I know. Wouldn't it be easier to practice the same song many times before trying another? That's the way I learn complex tasks, one at a time. But then, when baby humans babble, they ramble on like this as well, uttering all the practice sounds in a nonsensical sequence.

A little closer, another young song sparrow practices his songs. He perches atop a dead tree about 10 yards off the ground, surveying the world as he sputters. Behind me, to the east beyond the kingbirds, I hear the faint, unformed *witchity* attempts by another young yellowthroat, too.

On the bike path I head back south, escorted by a young titmouse. He's younger than the one I just recorded; his songs are far more unsteady and poorly formed, with interspersed call notes (track 2-36; figure 31).

I ride the mile south to Station Road, lingering, savoring, amused by a chickadee that comes to life as a train rumbles by on the tracks just to the east.

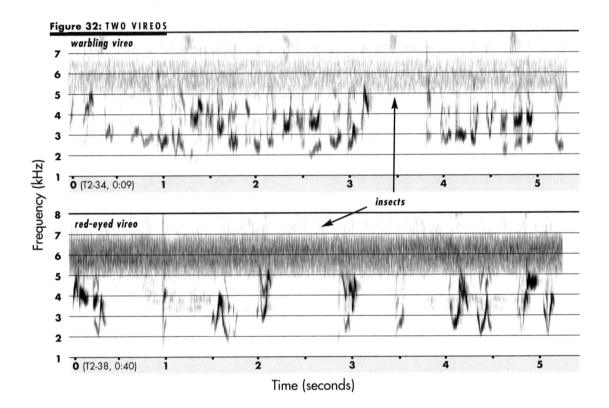

Figure 32: TWO VIREOS

Figure 32. The songs of these two young birds are already unmistakably those of the warbling and red-eyed vireos, as the overall rhythm and quality are distinctive (tracks 2-34, 2-38). The warbling vireo's song swings from high (at 1.4, 2.3 seconds) to low (at 1.8, 2.6 seconds) and ends on the characteristic high note, just like a good warbling vireo should; and the red-eye delivers each of his phrases and pauses before offering the next, just like a good red-eye should. For each bird, though, see how the cadence is all wrong; the young warbling vireo pauses less than a second between songs, and the young red-eye similarly blurts out a series of phrases far more rapidly than an adult would (between Seconds 4 and 5).

A little later, a loud airplane circles overhead, and another chickadee begins its babbling routine, too, running through ill-formed gargles and *chick-a-dee* calls and whistled notes for the song. I'm reminded of how we often induced birds to sing in our research laboratory by turning on a vacuum cleaner, as the white noise seemed best to stimulate them.

Thanks to the beavers, the wetlands along this mile of the bike path are special, but I'm drawn again to the north, back to the two spots just a few hundred yards apart where I've already heard so many young birds. Near the small pond by the KC trail, I stop and listen. Nothing. No yellowthroat. No chickadee. No oriole. No song sparrow. No, wait, faintly I hear what must be the murmurs and warblings of a sparrow in the alder bushes. The parabola aimed at the bush, headphones over my ears, I hear him more clearly (track 2-37). A harsh call, too, but is that the sparrow? He contin-

HOUSE WREN

ues, rising, I sense, perhaps to show himself. And, yes, there he is, brownish, flitting about, tail cocked, a house wren! No, *the* house wren, the wren who no doubt was sassing at me earlier. He's a beginner, a neophyte, his scratchy songs sounding no different to me than those of the young song sparrow who must lurk nearby. A jogger silences him, but he resumes a minute later. Yes, a house wren. Then silence. I want to hear more from him but choose to move on.

Back to the bridge. I hear the young song sparrow to the left again, the adult kingbirds to the right, so the young kingbirds must be there, too. Above the bridge is the vireo. No, wait, he's changed. Could that be a red-eyed vireo? There's a phrase every second or so, sometimes several blurted out quickly, sometimes the pauses longer, the timing all off (track 2-38; figure 32). *Myaah!* Yes, there's the call of the red-eye mingling with his song phrases. I find him in the binoculars, too, the dark line through the eye, the white line above it unmistakable, giving him that meanish red-eyed vireo look. I hear a bill snapping, and then he adopts an aggressive posture with bill wide open, and with a flurry of feathers he's gone. Was that the warbling vireo chasing the red-eye? I think so. The tree is not big enough for the both of them?

With the time nearing 10:00 A.M., I bike south toward the parking lot on

Station Road, ready to call it a day. About halfway there, just past the impressive beaver dam on the left, I come to a stop. What is that in the treetops? Goldfinches? Yes, they have to be, as I hear that unique, wiry ascending note, as if they ask a question, *twweeeeee?* But there are other voices, like *tew, tew tew,* lower, steady, less varied. Are there two kinds of birds up there, or one kind with two voices? I work to see them, struggling to find just one in the dense foliage. Glimpses are what I get, and, yes, they seem to be American goldfinches, youngish birds, pale versions of the adults. But how many?

I work up and down the bike path, craning my neck upward, hoping to find one young bird isolated from the others, as I want to hear just one at a time to know better what each is doing. Finally, a little lower, over to the side

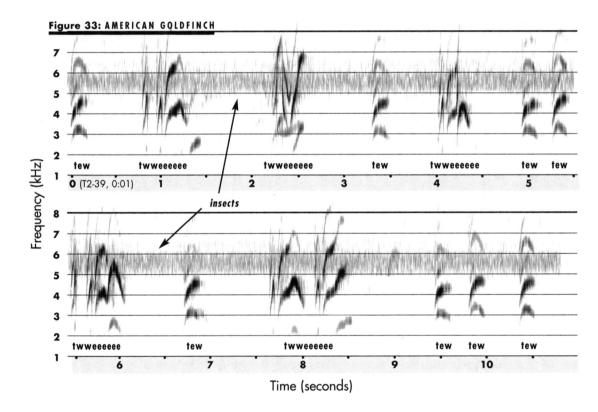

Figure 33: AMERICAN GOLDFINCH

Figure 33. A young American goldfinch calls repeatedly from the treetops, alternating a series of simple *tew* notes with a higher-pitched, wiry, ascending *twweeeeee* (track 2-39).

on a dead branch, one calls—*tew, tew tew twweeeeee tew tew tweweee tew, tew tew* (track 2-39; figure 33)—I've never heard anything like it. The one constant in his stream of sounds is the simple *tew,* one to five at a time, punctuated every few seconds by some version of his wiry, ascending *twweeeeee,* but no two of them sound alike. It is one bird with two types of sounds, a young goldfinch calling and already working on his querying *twweeeeee* phrases, which will be so distinctive in his adult life. With one bird sounding like two, the family group together sounds like a flock at least twice its size.

Laying the recording gear next to my bike beside the path, I look about, breathe deeply, and recount where I have heard birds this morning: a titmouse in the tree to the west, a song sparrow just below, the two vireos in the tree over the bridge, the yellowthroat and kingbirds down in the swamp to the east. And earlier this morning the young great horned owl far to the east, along with a couple of subadult great blue herons. Another titmouse accompanied me down the bike path to the pond at the start of the KC trail, where I listened to a young song sparrow, yellowthroat, oriole, chickadee, and house wren. There were other chickadees, too, and cedar waxwings, and wood ducks. And, just now, the goldfinches.

I am astounded at what I have heard this August morning. I never go birding in August, as the singing season is all but over, and I live to hear birds sing. The dawn chorus this morning was nothing, but what a treat to hear future dawn choruses in the making. What a treat to listen to these young minds at work as they find their voices. August for me will never be the same. I have extended my listening season, and I must return here next week, too. I wonder if I'll find the same birds in the same places, their songs having improved.

SEPTEMBER

19

A Wood Thrush Goes to Roost

September 3, 7:22 P.M., Amherst, Massachusetts

IT IS THE OFFICIAL INSTANT of sunset according to the Farmer's Almanac website, but deep in the woods here, how could I know? It is already so dark, the sun having disappeared long ago, and it is so quiet, except for the countless insects of late summer that chirp and click and buzz all around. I hear a distant dog, voices of children playing at a house across the shallow ravine, distant traffic . . . but no thrush, at least not yet. For some time now I have been standing beside the chimney of my house, standing and waiting for the thrushes to go to roost; I wait for the sound of transition from summer to fall, as for me it is the wood thrush's evening routine that so nicely signals the changing of the seasons. This spring and summer I have enjoyed a wonderful symphony of evening songs and calls, but by early September I expect a different routine.

WOOD THRUSH

Two minutes later I hear a thrush off to the left, about 20 yards into the forest, a soft *tut-tut-tut-tut-tut*, only a half-second call but a dead giveaway (track 2-41; figure 34). Yes, they're still here, not having left yet for somewhere in Central America. I begin marking the time and the events of each minute, starting at 7:24 P.M.

- Just one soft series of *tut* calls, off to the left, beyond the hemlock, still about 20 yards away.

- Twice the same thrush sounds off, a series of five and then a series of six *tut*s, so thrushlike, reminding me so much of the robin's mild alarm. But that's all.
- The pace picks up in the next minute. It's the same brief series of *tut*s, but there are more of them, soon every three to four seconds, and a second bird calls now, too, more distant and off to the right, *tut-tut*, back and forth between the two. How I would love to know who they are. They're here on the same territory, near enough that I think they'd be clashing if they were not family. A male and his mate? A parent and one of the summer's offspring? Perhaps it's father and son, or father and daughter, or perhaps mother and either son or daughter?
- The bird to my left continues to *tut*, but the bird to the right now calls sharply, *whit-whit-whit-whit*, first four, then six, then seven sharp *whit*s, a half-second burst every three to four seconds, sounding so much like how the male has gone to roost here all summer. During the summer, though, he'd intersperse bits of song with these *whit* calls. Here is my first hint as to who is who, that the bird calling *whit whit* is the male who has owned this territory all summer. And the other bird? Perhaps his mate or a young bird. I can't know for sure, but as a first guess, I'll go with "he"

Figure 34: WOOD THRUSH GOING TO ROOST

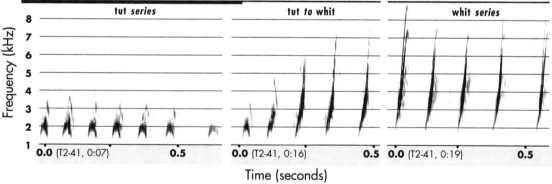

Time (seconds)

Figure 34. When going to roost, wood thrushes use soft, low *tut* notes and sharper *whit* notes, but every once in a while the thrush reveals that these two calls are merely ends of a continuum. These three sonagrams show first a series of soft *tut* notes down low, around two kHz, and last a series of sharp *whit* notes that span two to nine kHz; in the middle is a five-note call in which the first note is clearly a low *tut*, the last two sharp *whit*s, the second and third intermediate in form.

and "she" to identify them here, though I need to keep an open mind about this first guess.

- As his *whit*s intensify to the right, she pauses, still off to the left, 10, 20 seconds before resuming her soft *tut*s, the two birds now taking turns, it seems, his *whit*s and her *tut*s alternating in the growing darkness. He pauses, the rhythm broken, and then resumes calling nearby, as he's flown to within 10 yards of me.
- She continues, but he's mostly silent now, and when he does call, he uses his soft *tut* call, not the loud *whit* notes.
- 7:30 P.M. More of the same, she calling with her *tut*s, he occasionally offering a soft *tut* series as well. Ah, there's an intriguing call from him, something intermediate between a *tut* and a *whit*. I had a hunch he might do that. I can almost hear the conflict within him: Do I *whit* sharply now or *tut* a more mellow tone? The answer is something in between. And then he reverts to more *tut*s.
- She calls softly, a spring peeper joining in, but he shifts his mood in a half-second burst of five notes, the first note a *tut*, the fifth a perfect *whit*, the others intermediate (figure 34). In half a second he declares that the *tut* and *whit* are not discrete calls but rather the ends of a continuum. Very nice. He continues now with his *whit* calls, shattering the growing silence of the evening. *Whit-whit-whit-whit-whit* he calls nearby to the right, *tut-tut-tut-tut-tut* she calls off to the left, back and forth, the two birds alternating, almost never overlapping and each calling every three to four seconds.
- He dominates the scene now, one series of ear-shattering *whit*s after another, 30 in all, with her slipping in a brief *tut-tut* only twice in the entire minute. The cardinal who has been chipping the last several minutes is now silent.
- Out of curiosity, during this minute I keep track of his *whit*s, doing my best to write down how many *whit* notes occur in each burst: 3, 4, 3, 5, 4, 7, 3, 8, 4, 4, 7, 4, 4, 8, 4, 4, 7, 4, 6, 3, 6, 5, 11, 5, 4, 2, 12, 11, 4, 4, 7, 2, 2, 3, 3, 5, 2, 4. He fills almost all available time with his nearly 200 *whit*s, while she chimes in ever so softly on only five occasions.
- His pace continues, but by the end of the minute he's clearly slowing, calling just twice in the last 15 seconds, a *whit-whit-whit* and then a *whit-whit*. She is heard only twice.
- 7:35 P.M. In a single burst of six notes, his *whit*s morph into *tut*s, now softer and less intense, the two birds again trading series of *tut* calls, she

more vocal now than he. But soon he reverts to his sharp *whit* notes, though they seem softer, more mellow.

- More *whit*s from him, more *tut*s from her, but I hear how his voice has mellowed, the sharp *whit-whit-whit* of before now softer, then a *whit-whut-tut,* in three notes making the transition from one end of the spectrum to the other. She continues, but he is now silent. A catbird meows, just once.
- Softly now, a series of *tut* calls every three to four seconds, all from her, I believe, ever so softly, fading into the night.
- She continues, but now he chimes in, too, the two of them calling softly as they go to roost, *tut-tut-tut, tut-tut-tut,* rapid but soft exchanges. She is still well off to the left, he nearby on the right.
- Yes, very nice, back and forth, trading *tut-tut-tut,* so softly, but then 20 seconds into the minute I hear a *tut-whut-whit-whit-whit,* followed by more of his sharp *whit-whit-whit* notes again. What brought that on? She now *tut*s and he *whit*s, back and forth at least 10 times until the end of the minute, when he reverts once again to *tut-tut-tut-tut-tut.*
- 7:40 P.M. Within a second, she responds in kind, calling again eight seconds later, and then ever so softly after another five seconds. Then silence. I listen, waiting for more, but they have finished.

Just 16 minutes after I first heard them and just 18 minutes after sunset, they apparently have settled into their night roosts. My guess is that they are not roosting in the same tree, though they're close enough that they can hear each other. They're no doubt restless on their roost, perhaps fidgeting all night long, because maybe tonight, maybe tomorrow night, but for certain some night soon they will take flight, their silence at sunset then being the best clue that they will have joined millions upon millions of other migrants and returned to their ancestral home in the Tropics. It will then be another eight months before I can expect to hear their gentle *tut*s, sharp *whit*s, and flutey songs again.

Leaning against the chimney of the house, I smile, reflecting on a rather special time of the day. For me, birds are most fascinating as they greet the new day and as they close the day. In going to roost, these two wood thrushes clearly conversed with each other, one using soft *tut* notes, the other using *tut* and *whit* notes as well as several intermediate calls. Almost certainly they were family, as I heard no hostilities between them. And just what did they say to each other?

Being a bit greedy, I had hoped for more, though I couldn't reasonably have expected more at this time of the year, after the nesting season and just before migration. One of the most remarkable series of bird sounds I have ever heard has been from a male wood thrush at dusk. He seemed supremely agitated, apparently arguing with the neighboring male, and what emerged from his bill was a continuous stream of calls and song fragments. I yearned to hear it again, to capture it in a recording and then study it to know how he dissected his songs to produce such a dazzling performance. That's okay, I reason. Greed will bring me out here again next season, as these wood thrushes have more to share.

20

The Flight Calls of Nocturnal Migrants

IT ALL BEGAN back on August 8, a Monday, a good hour before sunrise. I was standing on the Norwottuck Rail Trail near my home and listening to young great horned owls and great blue herons (track 2-28). It was then that I first heard them, faint calls seemingly coming from nowhere and from everywhere.

AUGUST 19. It isn't until the following Friday that I realize what I'll be doing much of September. Having returned to the bike path, I step out of the car in the parking lot and hear them again—brief low-pitched calls, but from where? I cock my head, turning this way and that, trying to determine if they are coming from the trees around me or from the patch of open sky overhead. Unsure, I quickly assemble my highly directional parabolic microphone, aim it at the sky, and slip the headphones on, now hearing an occasional loud, crisp call from *above,* the calls of songbirds flying south by cover of night.

I had read about these calls. Back in 1993, in Ithaca, New York, I met Bill Evans, a man obsessed with identifying the peeps and squeaks of each of these night migrants. What a powerful conservation tool it could be, he reasoned, one that would enable him to estimate the number of individuals of each species moving about the planet by simply recording and decoding the sounds of the night.

The task was enormous. There was no field guide to all of these night calls, so he set out to match the calls with the species. It took painstaking effort and perseverance, recording birds by day and by night and matching each little squeak to the right species. In 2002, I cheered Bill and his friend Michael O'Brien when I noted their publication of a CD, *Flight Calls of Migratory Birds: Eastern North American Landbirds,* the culmination of years and years of work. In this reference CD were the flight calls of 211 migratory species! It contained audio recordings, sonagrams of the calls, and lots of information on the behavior of the calling birds.

Returning from the bike path outing, I now pull out that CD and go straight to the thrushes, as I'm fairly sure that the birds I heard were veeries. What Bill and Michael say about the veery is right on: "*Flight call description. Highly variable. Typically a low, burry, descending 'vheeu.' Sometimes a two-syllabled 'veer-y' or a more monotone 'vhee'. Burriness becomes more pronounced toward the end of the call.*" My sonagrams match those beautifully. Yes! Veeries confirmed.

AUGUST 22. Three days later, eager to listen some more, I'm up at 3:00 A.M., this time driving the 20 minutes east to Quabbin Hill. I'm miles from highway traffic noise here, and I'm now perched a little over a thousand feet above sea level, hoping to be closer to these calling migrants and to hear them better. I set out my stereo microphone system, then sit in my lawn chair, listening over the headphones because the microphones together with my amplifier hear more than I can with my unaided ears. I relish the sounds of the night: the owls, including the barred, great horned, and screech; the loons wailing on the Quabbin reservoir below; spring peepers still giving it a go; strong wingbeats of birds occasionally flying by in the night; what sounds like a hummingbird buzzing the microphones, though it must be a big moth. But only one *tseet,* the kind of call expected from a night migrant. Only one call! I had hoped for more on this calm, clear night in late August.

AUGUST 25. I set out the parabolic microphone on the roof of my house, aiming it up at the sky through the opening between the trees. At 10:00 P.M. I start my eight-hour recording, which finishes just before sunrise. Listening to the recording the next day, I learn only how loud the katydids are all night long, how loud the traffic is on nearby roads, and how unpleasant it is to listen over this noise for the faint calls of migrants.

SEPTEMBER 2. I try Quabbin Hill again. It's dark, with no moon, and the stars are intense; a gentle northwest wind blows. It rained the last two nights, and the wind was strong from the south last night, both the rain and the headwind probably keeping birds from flying. Surely the birds will be flying and calling tonight. Microphones are out by 3:50 A.M., and I listen, taking notes. At 3:53, I hear a jet overhead, a train whistle in the distance . . . a screech-owl . . . an occasional faint *tsp* or *tzeet,* evidence of some distant migrants . . . a barred owl . . . a single peeper . . . a large moth fluttering about the microphones . . . a whip-poor-will sings! . . . a loon wails . . . and there are more faint calls of what must be migrants, but they are soooo distant. The stars fade as the eastern horizon brightens; night sounds give way to day sounds, to a local wood thrush calling *whit whit* sharply as it awakens (see page 202), to the raucous calls of crows and jays, to the *per-chick-o-ree* of a goldfinch flying by, but I have not heard the great flight I had come for. Here is another recording that will go straight to the shelf, perhaps never to be listened to again.

SEPTEMBER 5. I need a change of scene. Birds must migrate above the Connecticut River, I reason, using this north-south landmark to navigate, and if I listen near the river in Hadley, surely I'll hear some good migrants. I aim my parabola at the sky, string the cables back to the car, and at 4:12 A.M. I recline in the car seat, headphones on, the recorder now capturing . . . the heavy traffic noise of Interstate 91 just a half mile to the west. But wait, high above that low-frequency racket I hear them, the ultrabrief chirps and buzzes and peeps and squeaks of the migrants I have been seeking! There are low ones that must be veeries, but the high-pitched calls are impossible to know. How many different types are there, how many different species?

It is a good veery night (track 2-42; figure 35). There's another loud *veeer,* a single call that wavers and drops in pitch, beginning as a pure tone and becoming burry at the end, a single bird moving past the parabola's beam at 4:42 A.M., as I check my watch. I hear veeries faintly every minute off in the distance. There's a loud veery again, at 4:57, this time more tonal but slightly burry at the beginning, and another, another, a whole series of them. It takes almost two minutes for these louder calls to pass and fade to the south. Then another loud call at 5:20, and above the traffic noise I hear others in the distance, off to the left and right, some far, some close by, some individuals no doubt heard several times as they approached and then disappeared into the distance; this flock takes about three minutes to pass.

Back home, I return to my computer, importing the morning's recording into my Raven software, now aghast at the variety of calls that I can see in the sonagrams (track 2-43; figure 36). Most are about $1/10$ of a second long, and I see all kinds. Some are V-shaped; some are sine waves of various amplitudes and periods, some rising in frequency, some falling; some are double bands rising, some of them pure tones, some modulated; and there are more complex notes of all types, too. Not a minute goes by that something isn't calling, some phantom in the sky, some angel on its way south. I'm overwhelmed at the diversity, but I buckle down, printing and then trying to sort sonagrams of these calls into categories. The veery pile grows, as does the pile of V-shaped notes, and others, too.

I next go to the Evans and O'Brien CD and try to find all of these tiny signatures. I feel reasonably confident about those veeries but am uncertain about the others. How much do the calls of a given individual or species vary?

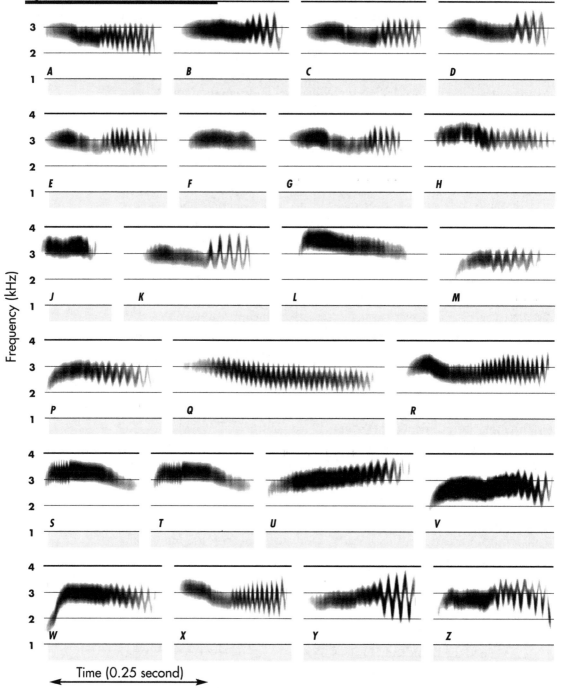

Frequency (kHz)

Time (0.25 second)

Can the sources of all of these calls really be identified? The printouts are pushed to the back of the desk as I contemplate the difficulties.

SEPTEMBER 9. The best cure for any frustration is to head back to the field, so armed with every recorder and microphone I own, I leave home in the late afternoon for Quabbin Hill. From sunset to sunrise, I will listen and record, capturing the entire night's events. The weather website has promised a gentle north wind of two to three miles an hour, with clear skies and a low of about 50°F. The moon will set by 9:45 P.M. Low clouds would be better, I have read, because they would cause the birds to fly lower and perhaps call more. But the north wind is good; the birds know it gives them a free ride.

By sunset, at 7:10 P.M., one set of stereo microphones points to the north, capturing the sounds of the night much as I'd hear them with my unaided ear. Half an hour later, I aim my three-foot parabolic microphone directly upward, hoping to capture calls of especially high-flying migrants in a second recording. Yes! In the headphones I soon hear a few birds calling high overhead, but with unaided ear I hear nothing. Then, because night migrants seem to be especially vocal in the hours just before midnight, I deploy a third recording system by 10:15. This system also has a parabola, and as I listen over the headphones, I am astounded at the variety of calls that I hear from these high-flying migrants. As each recording system fills its recording disc, I replace the full disc with an empty one, continuing to record the night away.

By 1:30 A.M., I am fading. It would be okay to get out my pad and sleeping bag, I reason. With my stereo parabolic microphone aimed upward, I run the microphone cables 75 feet back to the amplifier by my side. Knowing that the recorder will capture the next five hours, until sunrise at 6:30 A.M., I slip the headphones on and crawl into the sleeping bag, listening, smiling, knowing that there's no place in the universe I'd rather be.

I hear the calls now as if I am up there myself, flying with these birds, navigating over this landscape. Behind me, I can see the fingers of the Quabbin reservoir extending far to the north, and in all directions I see the wooded hills; the stars are a canopy overhead; and in my mind I can see my final destination thousands of miles to the south.

Figure 35. Examples of a variety of my favorite night flight calls, all believed to be from veeries. Most calls begin with a pure tonal note and end in a buzzy vibrato, the overall effect down-slurred, but other calls are more tonal, without the buzzy effect on the end (calls A–L are on track 2-42; M–Z are not on the CD).

I have read that I can direct my dreams by such a thought process as I go to sleep, but I am only partly successful. In the first dream I remember, I am in a swimming pool, but by concentrating, I become weightless, rising out of the pool and up into the air, only to hit the roof over the natatorium. In another dream, I am soaring over a large lake but only a few feet above the sur-

Figure 36: CALLS FROM NIGHT MIGRANTS: Warblers

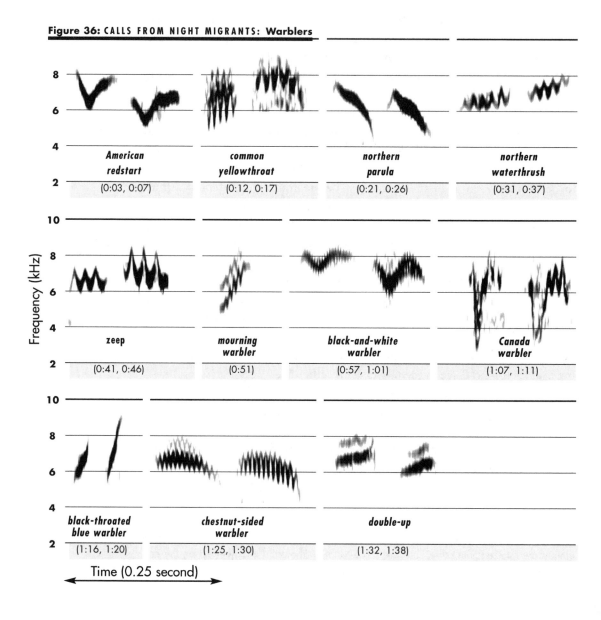

American redstart (0:03, 0:07)

common yellowthroat (0:12, 0:17)

northern parula (0:21, 0:26)

northern waterthrush (0:31, 0:37)

zeep (0:41, 0:46)

mourning warbler (0:51)

black-and-white warbler (0:57, 1:01)

Canada warbler (1:07, 1:11)

black-throated blue warbler (1:16, 1:20)

chestnut-sided warbler (1:25, 1:30)

double-up (1:32, 1:38)

Frequency (kHz)

Time (0.25 second)

face; wings outspread, I glide to a standstill, now poised a few feet over the water, my only escape simply lowering my feet and walking out of what proves to be a shallow lake. In a third dream, I soar with great skill down a steep, wooded canyon, banking left and right, taking the turns magnificently, only to exit the canyon in a strip mall of fast-food restaurants. Between dreams, I rouse, listening some more and gawking at the richest part of the winter sky, the area of the Great Hexagon, and one by one I check off those stars at the hexagon's corners: Sirius in Big Dog, Procyon in Little Dog, Pollux and Castor in the Twins, Capella in the Charioteer, Aldebaran in the Bull, Rigel in Orion.

I drift in and out of consciousness, listening, looking, dozing, flying . . . and by 6:00 A.M., less than half an hour to sunrise, I'm fully awake, realizing that the birds have quit flying. I gather the gear and stash it in the car, but before leaving I climb the enclosed stone tower atop the hill. I take one last look, to the east, where the sun will soon rise; to the west, out into the valley of the Connecticut River; to the north, from where they have come; and to the south, where they are all headed.

Back home, I study the sounds, first graphing the calls in the hour from 4:40 to 5:40 A.M. What a rich variety of sounds I see, many of them the same mysterious shapes that I recorded just a few days before along the Connecticut River. There are the veeries, and I'm convinced one of those thrushlike sounds is a gray-cheeked thrush, as I know that distinctive burry, arch-shaped signature on the sonagram. But there are so many others. I search back through the recordings, working my way into the wee hours of the morning, scanning quickly in my Raven software and pausing at the loudest and best of the recordings, when the bird was directly in the beam of the parabolic microphone. My sonagram printouts pile up, each sonagram a bird in flight on its way south, each sonagram a bit of magic from a winged marvel going about its business, moving unseen about the globe.

SEPTEMBER 11. Two days later, I'm back, 3:43 A.M. on Quabbin Hill, the recording under way. Although the weather website had promised a gentle north wind, it's blowing steadily, gusting; I have my parabola anchored to keep

Figure 36. It's a delightful variety of call signatures that rains down from the sky on an autumn evening. Illustrated here are one or two examples each of what are believed to be 11 different warbler species or groups of warbler species (*zeeps* are produced by any of about 8 warbler species and double-ups by a similar variety of species—see text; track 2-43).

it upright. I listen in the headphones and hear nothing but wind. If they are flying tonight, they are flying high or quietly, or both, the northerly winds a gift that perhaps can't be refused. Ah, but when was the last time I have seen the northern lights like this? An east-west arc of yellowish light extends across the pole, a halo through which shoot pillars of light from the horizon high into the sky. The pillars, sometimes broad, sometimes narrow, dance on the left of the arc, then the far right, then the middle, then seemingly everywhere. Smaller eyebrow arcs form above the main halo, then disappear; the entire northern sky is alive. A little before 5:00 A.M., still an hour and a half until sunrise, the lights begin to fade, giving way to the growing sunlight in the east.

SEPTEMBER 16. I'm back. The weather the last few days has been warm and rainy with a south wind. Tonight the wind pattern is to shift, calm by midnight but with a gentle north wind after that. Surely the birds will be moving. By 3:50 A.M., the recorder is running, but it is soooo quiet. I hear almost nothing calling, except for the chorus of insects in the trees surrounding the hill. It is, after all, 68°F; the late-summer insects are having a fleeting fling on a warm mid-September night. I nap on and off in the car — another set of recordings to the shelf.

SEPTEMBER 19–22. On a canoe outing to the Adirondacks of upstate New

LISTENING,
SMILING,
DOZING,
FLYING

York, I deploy the microphones at night, listening from the tent. On the first night, the full moon sweeps across the sky, but I hear nothing, though I do awaken at dawn to the ground covered with spectacular multicolored birds of all kinds, though only in a dream. The ducks and loons on the lake nearby generate their share of sounds, but the skies are silent, no doubt because of the strong south and west winds these days.

SEPTEMBER 24. Quabbin Hill. I'm back again, but it is so windy that I seek the shelter of trees lower on the hill. I begin the recording at 3:51 A.M., capturing mostly the sound of wind blowing in the trees. There are a few low-pitched, thrushlike sounds, and as the wind dies down in the hour before sunrise, I hear a few high-pitched squeaks, warblers most likely.

Back home, I make the graphs, recognizing again some of my favorite signatures. There's a definite gray-cheeked thrush, I conclude, but I see a new species, too. I'll figure all of this out eventually, I'm sure.

OCTOBER 1. Just one more time, I tell myself. It's Quabbin Hill again, and the forecast calls for a light south wind, only 1 mile per hour. I deploy two recording systems, but the south wind picks up until it is blowing steadily, perhaps 10 miles an hour, and over the two hours I detect perhaps one or two notes, but they could have easily been from a bird on the ground, not one flying by. No bird in its right mind would buck this wind.

September, the month when multitudes of migrants depart the North and head south, has come and gone. It's time, I tell myself, to try to make sense of all this. Who are these birds I've been listening to? To whom do these sonagram signatures belong? I spread out on my desk the printed sonagrams for my three best outings: 4:00 to 6:00 A.M. on September 5 along the Connecticut River in Hadley, the all-nighter of September 9 and 10 on Quabbin Hill, and the 4:00 to 6:00 A.M. period on September 24 on Quabbin Hill.

In the September 5 file on my computer, I focus on the hour from 4:12 to 5:12 A.M., electronically sorting and resorting the 392 sonagrams. That's 6.5 calls a minute, or about one every nine seconds. Wow! All overhead, all unseen, all these birds presumably heading south to avoid our northern winter.

I finish sorting with a group of 48 V-shaped calls, then 199 low-pitched, veery-type calls, but what a remarkable variety of them, as Bill warned on his *Flight Calls* CD (figure 35). That leaves me with 145 calls of a bewildering variety (figure 36). I try to locate them on the CD but find myself discouraged though amused. I yearn for a pictorial guide laid out much like a field guide, with little arrows pointing to the distinguishing features of each sonagram and calls of similar species grouped together.

At this point, early on the morning of October 1, I can't help but share my feelings with Bill and tell him of my admiration for all he has learned. Hoping for a little help but also knowing he'd enjoy seeing them, I include in the e-mail a sample of the sonagrams I've been sorting.

In just a few hours, I get back a lengthy reply, so encouraging and informative. He says he's working on some guides that will make sorting tasks easier for people like me. "In the meantime you've done a good job sorting the various shapes." Hooray! Those V-shaped notes? Likely all American redstarts, he says, though he advises that some rare redstart calls are somewhat like those of the ovenbird. And, yes, those low calls are veeries, "one of my favorites," confides Bill.

What Bill then does with my bewildering variety of 145 other calls astounds me. One by one he clicks off the warblers that he sees calling from these sonagrams: Cape May, common yellowthroat, northern waterthrush, northern parula, mourning, black-and-white, Canada. Then there's the *zeep* complex, consisting of nicely modulated, high-pitched calls that could be blackpoll, Connecticut, yellow, cerulean, Blackburnian, worm-eating, magnolia, *or* bay-breasted! He offers educated guesses about a couple of the calls, based in part on their shapes but also on which birds would be expected during early September (more likely yellow than blackpoll, for example, as blackpoll is a later migrant). And there's one more warbler complex, the "double-up," describing the sonagrams that consist of double rising whistles about a kilohertz apart; my samples could be from Tennessee, Nashville, orange-crowned, or black-throated green warblers. Oh, there's also a white-throated sparrow, but it's probably a call from a bird on the ground, as they aren't really migrating in early September, Bill says.

And don't quit listening yet, Bill encourages; the big sparrow flights are still to come! They "come between now and mid-Oct on light northerly wind nights, so you have a few more weeks of good opportunity."

My confidence now soaring, one by one I check off the sonagrams from that hour along the Connecticut River early on September 5. About 200 are veery calls, and lots are from warblers: 50 from redstarts, 30 yellowthroats, 7 Cape Mays, 7 parulas, 6 northern waterthrushes, 3 black-and-whites, 2 Canadas, and 1 mourning. In the two complexes are about 20 *zeep*s and 5 double-ups, warblers of some kind. There are also a number of single-ups, what Bill calls "single-banded upsweeps" on his website (www.oldbird.org); given my location in western Massachusetts and my date in early September, they're most likely blue-winged or yellow-rumped warblers, or ovenbirds (less likely golden-winged, prothonotary, or Swainson's warblers or white-crowned or clay-colored sparrows). And many of the calls are too faintly recorded for me to be sure what they are.

Next I go to my all-nighter from September 9 and 10, studying in detail the sonagrams in the hour from 4:40 to 5:40 A.M. There's the one, classic, high-arched gray-cheeked thrush call, starting below two kilohertz, rising to just above four kilohertz, then trailing down to about three kilohertz, especially burry toward the end. It's not a Bicknell's, as a Bicknell's would be much higher. There's another, fainter gray-cheek call about 10 seconds later, perhaps the same bird in the distance. For the other 32 thrush calls, I announce "veery" but then have my doubts. Many do not descend as the veery usually does, and some of them look identical to the calls of the rising, nonburry Swainson's thrush calls that Bill displays on his *Flight Calls* CD. Bill warns that the calls of these two species may be indistinguishable at times, and I conclude that I have some unknown mix of gray-cheeks, Swainson's, and veeries in this morning's flight. They're all wonderful sounds, low and slow enough that I can savor them with my unaided ear.

Another 175 sonagrams to go, all much higher-pitched than those of the thrushes. I see redstarts, though far fewer tonight than just five days ago, parulas, black-and-whites, mournings, yellowthroats, Canadas, ovenbirds, what look like Cape Mays and bay-breasts to me, *zeeps* and double-ups and single-ups, all now familiar. But there are some new ones, too, signatures that I don't immediately recognize. One is a gorgeously modulated sound, dropping overall in pitch, about 14 swings of the voice every $\frac{1}{10}$ second giving it a buzzy sound; I scan the library for small songbird sonagrams on Bill's website, homing in on the chestnut-sided warbler. I double-check the CD, measuring on one example 14 swings of the voice each $\frac{1}{10}$ second, and reading that nocturnal flight calls typically sweep downward. There's no doubt. Five times a chestnut-sided warbler called within the range of my microphones; at least three different birds are involved, as two pairs of calls were close enough in time that the same bird could have called twice in passing.

Another call is high-pitched and ultrabrief, only one-fiftieth of a second, rising abruptly, occurring 14 times during the hour. Twice either the same bird calls in rapid succession, less than half a second apart, or two traveling companions call back to back. And there it is in Bill's website library, a black-throated blue warbler: "A short, abruptly rising 'stip.'

Nocturnal migrants often give a double call with the notes about a half-second apart." How satisfying.

And what new might I find in the September 24 recording? Above the noise of the wind in the trees, I extract only 28 sonagrams. I see more thrush sounds, eight in all. There's another classic gray-cheek, but the rest look like Swainson's, as they rise and the end is either burry or not; none descend, which must mean the veery is absent. I see white-throated sparrows (five in all), though I cannot be sure if a bird calls from the trees nearby or from the air. I see two new calls. There are eight double-banded downsweeps, as Bill calls them, only $1/20$ second—savannah sparrows, I conclude. Another single call is beautifully modulated 15 times in $1/10$ second, and high-pitched, too. In my obsession with the warblers, I've never seen anything like this—must be a sparrow. I can't find it on Bill's website, so I search the CD. Sparrow after sparrow is rejected until there, near the end, is the call of the Lincoln's sparrow. It's a perfect match, though after checking the rest of the sparrows, I realize that the calls of the Lincoln's and swamp sparrows are probably indistinguishable. Although some warblers still pass on this date, including a few yellowthroats and a single warbler *zeep*, the big news is that a few more sparrows are showing up.

I do need a good sparrow night. The season will not be complete without it.

OCTOBER 1, SUNDAY, 4:00–6:00 A.M. QUABBIN HILL. In an increasingly strong south wind, I hear practically nothing.

OCTOBER 6, FRIDAY MORNING. It's still a south wind that's predicted, though slight—maybe they'll be moving. Between 3:00 and 4:00 A.M., I deploy my microphones in the fog along the Connecticut River, but I hear nothing other than a few thrushes, mostly Swainson's, a gray-cheek, too. Lots of savannah sparrows call from the ground at dawn—they're not moving, at least not yet.

OCTOBER 7. Okay. I'll record sparrows on the ground. To Quabbin cemetery I go, amusing myself by recording the *tsees* calls of chipping sparrows sitting on gravestones and flying to and fro. Success! I get a taste of how Bill Evans and Michael O'Brien have had to match night and day calls of all these species, one by one.

OCTOBER 8. I've never seen so much rain.

OCTOBER 9. I'm desperate. Tomorrow morning I must leave for the airport at 3:30 A.M., and I'll be gone a week. Bad planning, as I need the sparrows.

Watching the weather website, I see that the forecast is adjusted occasionally, eventually to, *yes,* a gentle northeast wind, and perhaps there will be a few hours without rain in the night.

By 9:00 P.M. I'm on Quabbin Hill, the car packed and ready to head directly to the airport. Rain. I listen but hear nothing. By 10:00 it's only misting. I step out of the car, and there they are! They're flying *and* calling. Out in the grass, I set up the stereo parabolic microphone on the tripod, run cables back through the car window to the amplifier on the seat, connect batteries and recorder, and slip the headphones over my ears. Among the lower calls of Swainson's thrushes and a variety of what must be the brief calls of warblers are the high, thin sparrow calls. There aren't a lot of them, perhaps one call every one or two minutes, but they're certainly there. As I listen, I drift in and out of consciousness, smiling ear to ear, wondering what my catch will be tonight.

By 12:30 A.M., it's quieted significantly. I'd love to stay, but discretion wins out. I pack up the gear, drive home, sleep for two hours, and head for the airport.

OCTOBER 18, MY FIRST DAY HOME. I download the two-hour recording of October 9 into the computer and soon view the calls in my Raven software, calling out each sonagram as I see it: common yellowthroat, white-throated sparrow, Swainson's thrush, savannah sparrow . . . I continue, but how confident can I be? How far have I come in the two months since I started listening to these night migrants? I pick up the phone and call Bill Evans. "Hello . . ." Yes, he's there, working on his migration data! Of course he'd be willing to look at my sonagrams, eager even. I e-mail the information and soon have my answer.

"You definitely get a passing grade!" cheers Bill. Yes, the sparrows predominate, with 37 white-throated sparrows and three savannah sparrows (figure 37). Next most common are the Swainson's thrushes, 18 of them—no veeries so late in the season. I counted 12 yellowthroats; 13 of those beautifully modulated *zeep*s, most of them probably blackpoll warblers given how late in migration it is; 11 single-ups, many of them perhaps yellow-rumped warblers, as I'm seeing a lot of them these days; two indigo buntings; one, maybe two, black-throated blue warblers; one black-and-white warbler; one single downsweep, a "descending *seep*" that I narrowed down to a field sparrow, pine warbler, or northern parula—most likely a parula, says Bill. I had made a couple of mistakes: I thought one call might have been a gray-cheeked thrush and another a swamp or Lincoln's sparrow; no, probably Swainson's thrush and white-throated sparrow, suggests Bill.

He offers one caveat, too: do your best to identify the calls, he encourages, but keep the word "presumed" in the back of your mind, as there remains so

Figure 37: CALLS FROM NIGHT MIGRANTS: Sparrows and thrushes

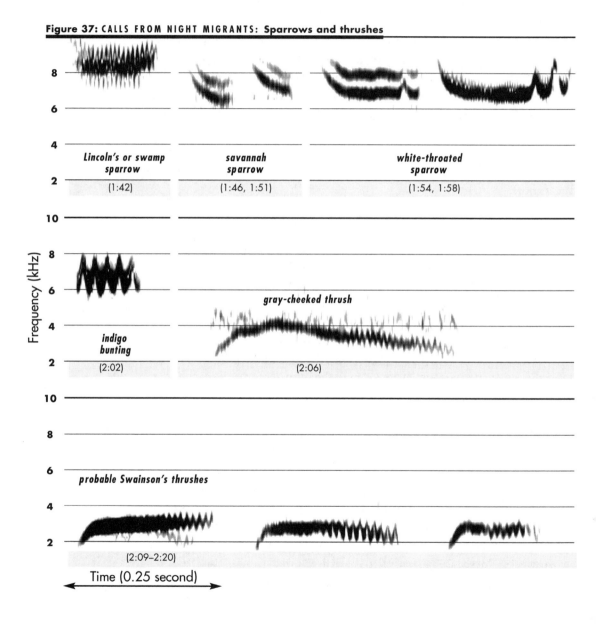

Time (0.25 second)

much we don't know about the calls of many species. It's a "presumed red-start," a "presumed yellowthroat," and so on, because we cannot be 100 percent sure of anything. Check.

I seek closure to this two-month obsession, but Bill offers another thought: "The distinctive night flight call of the tree sparrow should be evident on light north wind nights in the first week of November." Bill will be out listening, and so will I, I know. I'll be watching the weather until the snow flies, hoping for gentle north winds.

Figure 37. Calls from sparrows and thrushes later in the migration season. Note the similarity of calls from Swainson's thrushes here and veeries in figure 35; the calls of these two thrushes may not be separable, and the identity of the caller is sometimes best distinguished by the time of the season (veeries early, Swainson's thrushes later; track 2-43).

OCTOBER

21

The Autumnal Drumming of a Ruffed Grouse

Wednesday, October 11
Quabbin's Prescott Peninsula, Massachusetts

WITH THE HEADPHONES slipped over my ears, I settle back in my lawn chair and run through my mental checklist. I'm comfortable, multiple layers everywhere, gloves, stocking hat, extra coat on the floor beside me. The blind's viewing window is open, mosquito netting clipped over the window so he won't be able to see me. Binoculars around my neck. Spotting scope on tripod to the left, video camera on tripod to the right, both slipped under openings in the netting and ready to go. Digital camera, ready for digiscoping. Two microphones well hidden in a pine bough just below his drumming perch, 75-foot cable carrying sounds to recorder, all the right LEDs on the recorder now lit, sounds in my ears. Or are there? It is so quiet. I reach down and crank up the gain on the recorder, just to be sure, and yes, there are the sounds of the night, in stereo.

The night. I check my watch, 5:38 A.M., and laugh aloud, my laugh picked up by the ultrasensitive microphones and echoing back a split second later in my ears. Sunrise is about 7:00, and the very earliest he could be expected to arrive is over an hour from now. Ah, but "take no chances" was the motto of the day. Get out here plenty early and get settled—don't risk spooking him in the dawn's gathering light. For six days Mr. Grouse and I have been playing games, and just once I caught a glimpse of him, but today we meet, or at least I meet him, as I hope that in my camouflaged blind I will go undetected.

Yes, six days it's already been, with me out here every day well before sunrise.

Thursday, October 5

Day 1. Last Thursday I scouted by bicycle, confirming a drummer just where my friend Tom had told me he'd heard one, a half mile inside the gate, just before the first open field on the left and the second pond on the right. I listened for other drummers as I biked a dozen miles on the forested back roads of the Quabbin Reservation that morning, but heard none.

Friday, October 6

On Friday, the October quest to find a drumming log resumed. Another birding friend, Harvey, joined me, and we sat comfortably in chairs on the road, listening for our drummer. The barred owls and great horned owls were soon silent, sunrise came and went, but we heard no grouse. So we stretched our legs, checking out the birds along the road to the south, only to hear him drumming when we returned an hour later. I listened to three drums over 10 minutes, taking a bead on his position, then circled around to the left, wanting to triangulate on him from a second position. Tiptoeing along the trail wasn't good enough — he spotted me and departed in a whir and blur of wings. Yes, a blur, as through a small opening in the birch and young pines, I *saw* where he had departed from. Without moving, I directed Harvey to the exact spot I had seen him flush.

I imagined him drumming from a log or a large rock or maybe a fine New England stone wall that the forest had reclaimed, but I think Mr. Grouse had done all those possibilities one better. Almost certainly he drummed from this very place where the moss was well worn on the raised, east rim of an old gravel pit, this very place where tiny grouse feathers were strewn about. And he almost certainly faced west, the ground dropping away 10 feet below him and to the sides, the circular pit an amphitheater, the raised rim his stage. Kneeling down, I eyed the surroundings from his perch, looking back along the forest floor through the trunks of birch and oak and maple and pine, then forward into the pit, impressed by how far in all directions he'd be able to detect the movement of any predator making a move on him. Overhead was a sufficient shield that no hawk could swoop in from above. Mr. Grouse had chosen well.

Saturday, October 7

On Saturday, in the dark well before sunrise, I had hidden the microphones in the pit beneath a pine bough a good 10 yards from his perch. The cable stretched 125 feet back to the insulated "cooler" where my recorder was kept cozy in spite of the near freezing temperature outside. At 5:45 A.M., after double-checking everything, I punched the Record button and left the area. Take no chances, I told myself. Get *something* recorded this morning. The microphones were well hidden, the recorder out of view, and I was gone, too. Mr. Grouse could not know he was bugged.

A few hundred yards down the road, in the middle of the open field and well out of range of the grouse, I sat in my lawn chair and awaited the dawn. The full moon hung above the pines to the west, highlighting a host of glowing milkweed pods all about me. A barred owl . . . two great horned owls, mates answering each other . . . migrant thrushes whistling overhead . . . a coyote chorus just to the northeast! . . . woodcock, perhaps half a dozen of them flying about, their wing-singing imperfect, their ground *peent*s uncertain, both dead giveaways that these are not adults but rather young of the year, skydancers in the making . . . geese, in perfect V-formation, about 50 of them, headed southwest, males honking low, females high . . . whistling wings of wood ducks flushed from the pond nearby, females squealing . . . the *seeet* of sparrows awakening . . . a towhee *chewink* . . . a phoebe, halfheartedly singing three *fee-bee* songs followed by a lone *fee-b-be-bee* . . . more geese, these in a single, long skein, again headed southwest . . . blue jays awakening in the forest beyond the field, all using the same harsh *jay* call. In this wilderness of Quabbin, I half expect a mountain lion to walk by.

With sunrise approaching, stars faded and colors emerged from the shadows. Maples glowed yellow or red or both, the birches yellow; pines were yellow-green as they shed their spent needles of a year or more ago. The oaks held on, still largely green. Goldenrods were truly golden. It was yet another blazing New England autumn morning, but *why*, I puzzled, was he drumming this time of year? Mating occurs in spring and early summer, not now. Was he laying claim to a territory that would serve him well next year? Or might females make some decisions during the autumn about who they'll mate with next spring? Puzzling indeed.

In the maples to the south, jays called, the harshest and most grating jay calls I've ever heard (track 2-44). Watching the flights high in the trees, I realized that never before had I heard jays being chased by sharp-shinned hawks either. The hawks and jays seemed to be playing with each other, though, the hawks darting by themselves among the treetops, followed on occasion by the jays, the hawks then reversing course and chasing the jays, the jays then always squawking.

At the pond's edge to the northwest, a young song sparrow practiced his songs, so plastic and amorphous and continuous (track 2-45), so unlike the discrete songs of the adult across the field to the south, but far better than those of the young sparrows I heard back in August (track 2-29). I winced as I listened to the high, piercing, unsteady notes of a young ruby-crowned kinglet, a migrant from the north (track 2-46). A young chickadee, too, gargled and *chick-a-dee*d and sang, not the full *hey-sweetie* song but rather an abbreviated *hey-sweet,* the last syllable perhaps to be added later (track 2-47). And how hilarious the young white-throated sparrows; as an adult, each will sing a pure whistled *poor sam peabody* song, the whistles held steady, the rhythm consistent, but these youngsters uttered single whistles, sometimes a pair that rose or fell or held on the same pitch, rarely the *peabody* triplet, and the pitch of each whistle wavered unmercifully (track 2-48).

Could Mr. Grouse be a young bird, too? I have read that young grouse occasionally begin drumming in October, when only four to five months old; that's pretty rare, but if he is a young bird, maybe I'll detect some imperfections in his drum, much like in the songs of these practicing songbirds. Or perhaps he's a yearling, hatched a year and five months ago; about half of all yearlings don't establish a territory and drum during their first possible nesting season, but perhaps they lay claim to a territory in their second autumn. Maybe. No one knows, it seems. He could be older, but not much older, given that only one out of three drummers survives from one season to the next. Drumming is apparently very risky business.

Whether or not Mr. Grouse was drumming at that point I couldn't know, and I resisted the temptation to go check lest I disturb him and spoil our mornings. Instead, I walked south, watching a cow moose and her two calves in the next open field on the left. Monarch butterflies drifted lazily past them, headed south in the still air. An otter played in a small pool beside the road on the right until he spotted me, when he retreated some and snorted at me. And just beyond him was a beaver swimming back and forth, repeatedly slapping its tail. A grouse flushed beside the road several miles to the south, but there was no drumming.

By 10:00, I couldn't resist. Slowly I approached to what was surely a safe distance, listening, waiting, and after 30 minutes I concluded that he was done for the morning. I scooped up the recording gear, hustled home, and pulled up the recordings on my computer. How wonderful to see the morning's activity at a glance! On a timeline, I could see the significant sounds against the quiet background. I listened and heard that he flew into the display area at 6:41 A.M., drummed once at 6:43, took a 16-minute break, and then drummed 32 more times before he walked away at 8:43 A.M. I was eager to study this recording, but I held off, because I wanted to study this grouse at his best, in the best-quality recording possible. I remembered Greg Budney's mantra at Cornell's sound-recording workshop: "Halve the distance, quadruple the sound." By halving my 10-yard distance from the microphone to the drumming grouse, I would improve the signal-to-noise ratio at least fourfold, with the "signal" the grouse's drum, of course, and the "noise" all other sounds. Three yards would be even better.

Sunday, October 8

On Sunday, I returned to get that best possible recording, but I was too greedy, putting the microphone up in a sapling in front of his display perch. Listening to the recordings later, I heard that he flew in and out in one continuous flight, never returning to drum that morning. He didn't like what he saw, and how could I blame him? What a sitting duck he is, so to speak, perched up there for all the world to see and hear, and how wary he must be to survive.

Monday, October 9

On Monday, Columbus Day, I wised up. This time I placed the microphones on the sloping side of the gravel pit just a few yards below his perch. After wrapping the microphones in camouflage cloth and covering them with small pine boughs, I climbed up to his perch, shining the flashlight down, trying to imagine whether he'd detect anything amiss. It looked good. I covered the nearby microphone cable with leaves, then backed out of the pit as I unrolled the rest of the cable and plugged it into the recorder 125 feet away. At 6:14 A.M., I punched Record and walked away.

Late in the morning, I sneaked back, listening, and hearing no drumming, collected the recording gear and headed home, the morning's activity soon displayed on my computer screen. Wow! He began drumming at 7:30 and finished at 10:02, 46 drums in all. I heard no flight, so apparently he walked in and walked away.

Oh, my, the questions. Now was the time to be greedy! I wallowed in drum after drum, marveling at the consistent rhythm (track 2-50; figure 38, top row). Each drum began with two soft, leisurely wing flaps, followed by a quartet in a distinctive rhythm, these 6 beats a prelude to the frenzy of wing flapping that followed. In these 46 drums, I counted either 43 or 44 wing-beats, no more, no less, for a total of 49 or 50 wingbeats over an 11-second drum. Surely, with such perfection and consistency, he was at least a year and a half old?

I could hear the rhythm and see it roughly in the sonagram, but I wanted a better feeling for how fast he flapped his wings throughout the drum, the way watching the speedometer on my car tells me how fast I am moving at any given instant. Using my Raven software, I measured the time from one wing-beat to the next throughout each of 10 midmorning drums. To determine how fast he flapped his wings, I converted my measurements of seconds per flap to flaps per second by simply inverting, then averaging the numbers for the 10 drums. Plotting the numbers on a graph, I could then see the drum signature of Mr. Grouse (figure 39), essentially the readings on his wingbeat speedometer. In the first four seconds were the 6 irregular beats; in the next four seconds, he increased from a rate of 2 to 5 flaps each second, the next two seconds from 5 to 10, and in a little over a second's time, he reached from 10 to a rate of *over 20 flaps a second* and back down to 10 again. What an absolute flurry of wing activity there at the climax of his drumroll, just a second or so before the ending.

And how precise he was. In each of the 10 drums, it was between the 35th and 36th wing flap when he reached his peak rate of over 20 flaps a second, never earlier, never later. Curious, I next checked his first 5 drums of the morning, wondering how perfect he was right from the start. Yes, perfect, as he reached over 20 flaps a second again at the precise same place in each drum.

He used his wings in flight, too, of course, but how fast did he beat his wings in drumming compared with flying? In my accumulated recordings for Mr. Grouse, I had captured the whir of his wings for one landing, one takeoff, and one flyby (tracks 2-49, 2-51). Pulling these recordings up into Raven, I measured 12 beats per second for the landing, 16 for the takeoff, and 13 for the flyby. At 21 to 22 beats per second at the peak of his drum, he was clearly extending himself.

How about the rhythm of energy in the drum? What does that look like? Minutes later, I had used my versatile Raven software to measure the relative sound energy produced by each wing flap in each of five drums. In the numbers I could then see the energy rising in the drum, until it reached a peak at eight seconds; the energy then dipped down exactly where the wing rate peaked, as if Mr. Grouse could not be both loudest and fastest simultaneously. Hmmm, if I were a female grouse prospecting for a male, could the loudness of the beats at the flapping climax tell me something of the vigor of a particular male? Possibly.

Was this a "typical" grouse drum? I hustled to Cornell's Library of Natural Sounds website, where a number of bird sounds had recently been posted online. Yes, ruffed grouse drums were included in the online collection, 14 examples from all over the continent. I worked my way west, from Ontario to New York to Ohio to Alberta to eastern Washington, finding that drums were all much alike, each male differing only in subtle details. If I had a number of local males recorded, I reasoned that I'd be able to find enough differences among them to recognize individuals, knowing then that the grouse, too, would almost certainly have enough clues to recognize one another based on their drums alone.

Figure 38: GROUSE DRUMS: Two different species?

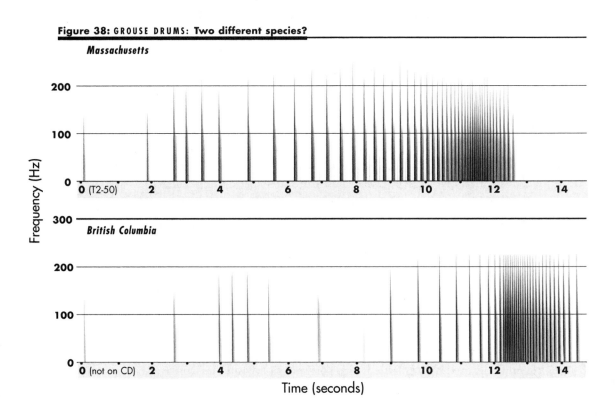

Birdsong by the Seasons

But what an extraordinarily different drum had been recorded by Bill Gunn on Vancouver Island in British Columbia (figure 38, bottom row; figure 39)! By the time my Massachusetts bird had finished all 50 of his wing flaps, this British Columbia bird had delivered only 15. The key, consistent difference between the drums, however, is in the rhythm of the climax: the British Columbia male accelerates almost instantaneously from a rate of 5 to 21 flaps a second, creating a most asymmetrical signature, whereas the signature of the Massachusetts male is beautifully symmetrical. Now what to think? Was that grouse a unique individual, or were all grouse different in the Northwest? Without more recordings, I could not know, but deep in my gut I suspected something very interesting. A grouse's drum is not learned, so local learned "dialects" don't exist; these drums are somehow encoded in the genes of the bird, and birds in a given population have both similar genes and similar drums. Any regional differences in drums would thus tell of genetic differences among grouse, and my best bet was that the unique drum from British Columbia told of a very different ruffed grouse, maybe even a different species, that lives in southwestern British Columbia and north into Alaska. These grouse are also darker and browner than grouse elsewhere, both their looks and sounds now telling of a different grouse in the Northwest. Similar differences among sage-grouse were sufficient to classify them into two species, the sage-grouse and the Gunnison sage-grouse, and the blue grouse was recently split into two also, the sooty and dusky grouse.

Having dissected the details of the drum, I began looking at the bigger picture. What an intriguing pattern I saw over the entire morning's activity. His initial drums were relatively soft, and they gradually built in intensity over

Figure 38. Top row. A sonagram of the sound produced by the Massachusetts grouse. See those first two relatively weak, well-spaced wingbeats, followed by the distinctive four beats from 2.3 to 4.0 seconds. Then, beginning at 4.9 seconds, he gradually accelerates, reaching a peak just a little after 11.0 seconds, after which he again slows. See how symmetrical the acceleration and deceleration of wingbeats is about the climax. Look next at the frequency axis and see how the energy in this drum is primarily below 150 Hz.

Bottom row. The drum from a very different grouse in British Columbia, recorded by William W. H. Gunn on May 22, 1962 (archived as catalog number 59280 at Cornell's Library of Natural Sounds). This drum begins much like the one from Massachusetts, with two soft drums and then the quartet; then, however, this western bird slows down, accelerating slowly, then finally rushing to the climax (about 12.4 seconds), with most of the wingbeats occurring after the peak, not before (see also figure 39).

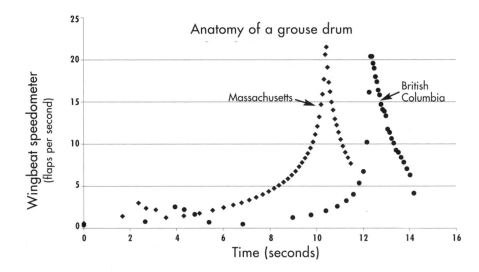

Figure 39. The drum signature of a ruffed grouse, showing how different the rate of wing-beats over time (the wingbeat speedometer) is for a Massachusetts and a British Columbia male. For Mr. Grouse at the Quabbin, in my Massachusetts backyard, see the 6 irregular wingbeats at the beginning and then how gradually he increases his flapping, reaching a peak at over 20 flaps per second just after 10 seconds, and then he gradually slows again. What a contrast that beautifully symmetrical signature is to the drum of a grouse from British Columbia; this northwestern male begins ever so slowly and methodically, and then, in one great rush of just a few wingbeats, he reaches the climax at 20 flaps per second, and far more gradually he slows. The Massachusetts male takes 19 flaps to accelerate from 5 beats per second to over 20, whereas the British Columbia male takes only 5 flaps.

the 24 drums in the first hour of activity (figure 40). They then held more or less steady, except for a couple of dips and 4 even louder drums at the end of the morning. The same gradual increase in amplitude occurred in Saturday's recordings. What was that all about? Was he incapable of hitting full stride first thing in the morning? Did his body require a warm-up period for such an intense physical activity? Mine would, I know, or I'd tear every muscle in my torso. I know some songbirds (such as the scarlet tanager, page 157, or hermit thrush, page 246) start singing softly, but only for a minute or two; then they're at peak amplitude. Perhaps these birds begin softly so as to warm up the sound-producing apparatus, but the soft beginning could also be warming up the will to drum or sing.

There was yet another puzzle I needed to sort out, and I hadn't realized the problem until I reflected back on how close I needed to be to Mr. Grouse in order to hear him drum. How soft and muffled seemed his effort and how distant he would sound even when I was close, yet his goal presumably was to broadcast his magnificence far and wide, to as many grouse as possible. I began to suspect I was missing something, because I'm used to listening to songbirds sing in the frequency range where I hear best, from 2,000 to 5,000 hertz (cycles per second), and I don't often think about how limited my hearing ability is in the lower-frequency range. Perhaps I can hear down to 16 or

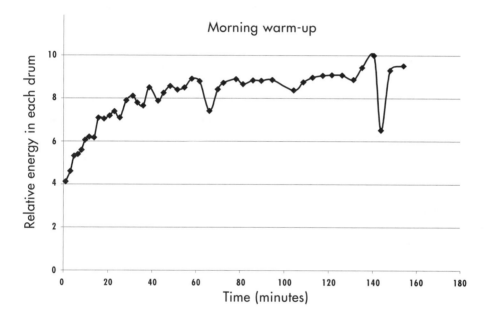

Figure 40. The morning warm-up. When this ruffed grouse begins drumming in the morning, he does so softly, the drums gradually building in intensity over the next hour or so until he is in peak performance by about the 25th drum of the morning. At the two dips in energy (at roughly 65 and 145 minutes), perhaps he faced slightly away from the microphone or he chose simply to put less energy into the drum. Nor can I explain the extra energy in 4 of the last 5 drums—perhaps he just chose to end with the most impressive flourish he could muster. Some days he began even more softly, and some days he reached peak performance in as little as 40 minutes. (The vertical axis is the relative amount of energy in the drums, graphed here with a maximum at 10, as measured with Raven Pro software.)

20 hertz, but human ears are pretty pathetic down there: a sound at 16 hertz has to be 1,000 times more intense than a sound at 50 hertz in order for a typical human to hear it, and a sound at 16 hertz has to be a million times more intense than a sound at 125 hertz (figure 41). Those are astounding numbers, as our hearing ability is so much better at the higher frequencies (until it gets much worse again beyond 10,000 hertz).

And just where was most of the energy in these drums? In the sonagram (figure 38, top row), I could see a lot of low energy, but I was astounded at the numbers my Raven software told me. In the drums I measured, the frequency with the greatest energy was only 18 hertz, essentially outside the range of my hearing. By 100 hertz, the drum's intensity had already declined 10 times, by 200 hertz, 10,000 times. It was no wonder the drum sounded muffled to me —I wasn't hearing the vast majority of the energy that was there!

And just how good was my equipment? I checked the specifications: the microphones claimed to be pretty good down to 20 hertz, the recorder to 10 hertz, the headphones to 15 hertz. All my audio gear was designed for a human's range of hearing, of course, as nothing below 15 to 20 hertz really matters to us because we can't hear it. I began to realize that at the lower frequencies, below what my audio gear could even detect, his drum is nothing

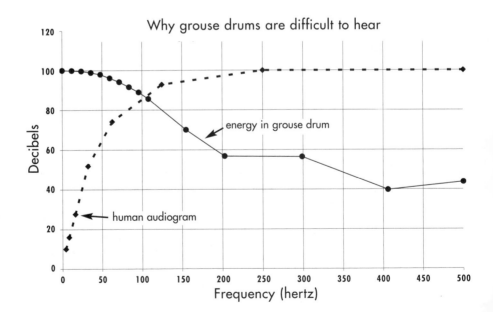

Why grouse drums are difficult to hear

energy in grouse drum

human audiogram

less than earthshaking, yet I had neither the ears nor the recording equipment to truly grasp it. I sensed that I needed a seismometer, not audio gear, to register his effort accurately.

Tuesday, October 10

All that was just yesterday. I had learned so much from Mr. Grouse, but I had yet to *see* him perform, so early this morning I put out not only the recording gear but also a blind well hidden in the trees. I then promptly left the area. Later in the morning, I collected the recording gear, discovering back home that he had accepted the blind, as he drummed 33 times from 7:06 to 8:39 A.M. As usual, there was the morning warm-up period, with his drums gradually building in intensity, but what was most exciting was that he was ready for me to be in the blind watching him!

Figure 41. In this graph one can see the reason why an earthshaking grouse drum might not seem so loud to our human ears. First look at the human audiogram; as I have drawn it here, it is intended to show how we can't hear very well at lower frequencies, and we reach our peak of best hearing at about 250 Hz, where the graph levels off. Then see how most of the energy in the grouse's drum is at those low frequencies where we can't hear well, and how the energy in the drum drops off significantly as we begin to hear better.

The two lines tell the basic story, but unless one understands decibels and the logarithmic (nonlinear) nature of this measure, the lines tell only a partial story. So, for the scientist in you, let's tackle some numbers: Decibels (dB) are on a logarithmic scale, and every 10 dB difference on the vertical axis of the graph marks a 10-fold difference in sound energy. An increase of 10 dB requires 10 times the energy, for example, and an increase of 20 dB requires $10 \times 10 = 100$ times as much energy. With that brief primer, look at roughly the lowest frequency that we humans can expect to hear, about 15 Hz, where the human audiogram is about 80 dB lower than our frequency of best hearing (scaled to 100 dB on this graph). For us to hear the grouse's drum at 15 Hz as well as we would hear it in our range of best hearing (beginning about 250 Hz), the energy at 15 Hz would have to be 100,000,000 times greater than it actually is (80 dB is 10^8, or $10 \times 10 \times 10 \times 10 \times 10 \times 10 \times 10 \times 10 = 100,000,000$)! Where we hear best, the energy in the drum is already 10,000 times lower (40 dB lower) than at its peak energy in the lowest frequencies. What a striking disadvantage we have in hearing this low-frequency drum of the grouse! It's no wonder that when we experience this drum in nature, we feel it resonate in our chests more than we hear it with our ears.

Wednesday, October 11

Day 7. And here I now sit, waiting, watching, listening, wondering whether Mr. Grouse will show today. The owls are silent; I hear a few thrushes still calling overhead, the awakening *seeet*s of sparrows, *jay*s of jays, *zhree*s of hermit thrushes. Two flocks of geese have flown by.

At 6:39 A.M., my, what a thrashing of wings I hear in the headphones, so loud in the relative silence of this October dawn. It's Mr. Grouse, I am sure, arriving by air, as I hear full flight at first and then a landing in the dry leaves, and a split second later a second landing; he must have bounced off the ground once in the darkness (track 2-49). Then he's walking in the dead, dry leaves on the forest floor, quickly, then silent, then walking some more, now more slowly. I strain to see him, but fail. And at 6:50, *there he is,* walking onto his stage. Warily he looks about and immediately departs, heading northeast. *Nooooo,* I want to scream. *Please stay.* But he's soon gone, walking out of sight.

RUFFED GROUSE

Ah, 14 minutes later, at 7:04, he's returning, now walking in from the southeast, working his way along the forest floor among the trunks of the trees and saplings. So warily, stepping slowly, cocking his head, looking this way and that, no doubt inspecting everywhere for anything amiss. Within a minute, he climbs directly to his stage and immediately flaps his wings, but just once, softly. He stands there, looking all about. What a beautiful sight! Good morning, Mr. Grouse, I want to call out. Two minutes later, there are the two initial flaps, then the quartet, and then two more flaps before he stalls, the rhythm all wrong. After another two minutes, he flaps eight times again, the rhythm improved but still wrong, and he aborts. Just 20 seconds later he begins anew, two flaps, the quartet, and then the full drum! Wow, what a blur of wings at the climax, what exertion, but so muffled, so soft compared with the louder drums that will surely follow. Still, it is a small hurricane he makes, the leaves that have fallen overnight scattering in the blast (track 2-50).

He stands on the left, on the broad lower level of his moss-covered dirt mound, looking about, then climbs up to his left, perhaps two feet over and six inches up, then immediately walks back down to the lower stage and delivers another full drum, but still soft and muffled. He repeats the performance again and again, every minute and a half to two minutes, almost always walking to the narrower high point and immediately returning, as if his stage presence required a grand entrance. More likely, though, he is taking one last look during that brief walk, checking all angles on possible approaching predators before he commits himself to another 11-second drum.

Between drums, he's on high alert. An acorn falls in the distance and he snaps to attention. Something else unsettles him and he crouches, ready to spring into takeoff, and then he slowly uncoils. A blue jay flies just overhead and he's hypervigilant again. What does he see with those ink black, beady eyes of his? When he faces me, his eyes are to the sides, and I try to imagine near-360-degree vision with a small blind spot behind.

At 7:40 A.M., a good 15 drums later, I realize how mesmerized I have been. I want to slow him down, to dissect his performance, to see how he coordinates feet and tail and body and wings and head. I concentrate on the wings. I have read all the theories of how Mr. Grouse produces his sound, from beating his body with his wings to clapping his wings together either in front or behind his back. He has been called the "carpenter bird," too, presumably because he beats the log on which he stands. Others have claimed that he simply beats the air. The latest, and most likely correct, idea is that, with each wingbeat, a ruffed grouse creates a "miniature sonic boom." As he stands nearly upright, quite penguinlike, his wings are held out nearly vertically by his sides, and so quickly does he jerk his wings back that he creates a vacuum underneath, and it is the air rushing into this vacuum that makes the noise. Yes, I can almost see that early in the drum, when he pauses between wingbeats, as I hear the *pop* when the wings are pulled back. Later, during the drumroll, there's no hope to see the cause of the sound, as the wings are a semicircular haze about his body, so rapidly do they move.

He walks now to the top of his stage and then back down, stepping slightly forward, firmly planting those silver-gray feet side by side on the green moss, flaps once, adjusts both feet once more, flaps a second time, adjusts the left foot a little, and then he's off and drumming. On the next drum, I watch the tail; at first it is horizontal, well above the ground, but after two beats he lowers and fans his tail, his rump and tail now seemingly braced against the substrate. And the body is held in typical walking posture at first, but by the third wing flap he is already nearly upright, his wings out to the sides, the body rocking about the shoulders with each flap. The head—how motionless he holds it throughout the entire drum, until the very end, when the tail springs up and every feather on the body fluffs out, the black neck ruff now showing, and only then does the head quickly jerk in one direction or another, on renewed alert.

He walks to the high point and preens the left flank, left breast, now the right, beneath the tail, then above the tail. As he works his rump, he spreads his tail vertically and I can see every feather. At the tip of each is a narrow, light gray band, then a broad black band, then narrow, alternating bands of gray and black, the entire fanned tail so gorgeous. He's finely barred on the breast and belly, too, more boldly on the flanks beneath his wings. I like that little tuft of feathers below and behind the eye, and the light eye-ring, too.

There he stands, such a handsome specimen. He's clearly a gray-phase grouse, not red (grouse come in two predominant colors). This being October, my best guess is that he is a little over a year old. He was probably one of 11 or so eggs laid in a nest by his mother during April or May of last year; she incubated him and his siblings for a little over three weeks, and then he and his brothers and sisters stayed with his mother into September, when the brood broke up and dispersed, most likely never to see one another again. Each survivor moved a mile or two or three, and the Mr. Grouse before me came to be here, sitting on this drumming stage. If he is a yearling, there's a roughly 50-50 chance he drummed this past summer, but he's clearly drumming now and, if he survives, will most likely drum here again next spring. He owns perhaps five acres that he defends against other males, and I would bet that he has exceptional hearing ability at low frequencies, which enables him to hear other male grouse drumming in the distance. Next spring, if his drums are judged satisfactory, a female will visit him and he will be chosen to father some of those 11 or so eggs in her nest, the cycle to continue.

I watch him drum again and again through the spotting scope, listening in the headphones, trying to capture the essence of his performance. He still drums every two to three minutes, though he is far louder now than he was initially, and gale-force winds scatter the freshly fallen leaves before him. How satisfying that he always faces the old gravel pit, too, always faces my microphones; it has been shown that a drum is much louder in front than to the sides, and now I can know for sure that his morning warm-up period is just that and not an artifact of how he stands on the stage.

As my hourlong videotape ends, he walks away, back to the southeast, but from my recordings on other mornings, I know to be patient, and six minutes later he returns. Now it's closer to four minutes between drums, and at 8:33 A.M. he drums and immediately runs to the south, but three minutes later he returns, drumming another eight times before walking off once more. Now, at 9:01 A.M., I see him walking off to the southeast, this time surely for good. He walks unhurriedly, foraging in the leaf litter, about to disappear behind a boulder, but then stands alert and walks quickly back to his stage, drumming immediately. Did he hear in the distance another grouse who required a reply? He's torn, it seems, between drumming and getting on with the rest of his day.

A second time he drums, then a third, the 45th of the morning, splendidly thunderous compared to his earliest drums, and now he unhesitatingly walks offstage to the southeast, disappearing behind the boulder from which he appeared over two hours ago.

NOVEMBER

22

Time Travel: Revisiting Two Hermit Thrushes in June

Late November, dreaming of June

"THREE FIFTY A.M., morning of 17 June, Quabbin Park." I listen to my voice announcing the beginning of the recording.

Though physicists may debate the idea, I know time travel for a fact. I need no futuristic machine but only one of my favorite birdsong recordings and a pair of headphones, and with closed eyes, I'm off. For this late November morning, the leaves off the trees for the winter and the woods far too quiet for my liking, I've prepared a special journey. I'm going back to that magical week in June when I just couldn't get enough of two singing hermit thrushes.

It was June 10, while I was biking the roads of the Quabbin Park, when I discovered them singing back and forth. Just two, I thought, and I realized that my dawn hours for the coming days were committed. My first and last true encounter with a hermit thrush had already been three years ago, and ever since then I had wondered. What if that first hermit was somehow a fluke? He sang so that his next song was *especially* different from the one he had just sung, but do all hermits sing like that? I needed to verify that by getting to know at least one more hermit intimately, confirming that he really organizes his repertoire of 10 or so songs on different pitches so that he can leap up and down from one distant pitch to another.

Assuming I can verify that, I really needed to know one more thing: What happens when *two* hermits sing? Just how do they respond to each other? Among many songbird species, males respond to each other with similar, or matching, songs. Good examples are northern cardinals and tufted titmice. But maybe the hermits do something really special; maybe a singing hermit chooses his next song so that it is not only especially different from the song he has just sung but also especially different from the reply of his neighbor.

On the following mornings back in June, I scouted the situation, recording thousands of songs from each bird during the dawn hour. I learned where each awoke and began singing, and for each in turn I stood in the predawn darkness, waiting, listening for his awakening growl or two before he began singing in the canopy above me, ever so softly at first, then louder and louder.

Back home, I downloaded the recordings into my computer and studied the sonagrams with my Raven software (figure 42). The first bird used 13 different songs, and I labeled them by the frequency of their introductory whistles, from highest to lowest (rounding off to the nearest 100 hertz: 43, 42, 40, 38, 36, 33, 30, 27, 23, 22, 20, 19, 17). The highest song had an introductory whistle at 4,300 hertz (or cycles per second), the lowest at 1,700 hertz, the songs differing not only by the frequency of the introductory whistle but also by all features in the flutey flourish that followed. The second bird had 11 songs: 43, 40, 38, 36, 31, 28, 23, 20, 19, 18, 17. Although the frequency of the introductory notes was in many cases the same as for Bird 1, the flutey endings were all different. I played, frolicked even, slowing the songs down to half, then quarter, then whatever speed I wished, feasting on the rollicking cascade of notes that is the hermit's song (track 2-6).

And when each male sang, did he choose his next song so that it was especially different from the one he had just sung? I needed first to confirm that the hermit of three years ago was not unique, so I plotted a sequence of songs for Bird 1 and studied how he moved from one to the next (figure 43). The jagged graph showed how he never sang the same song back-to-back and how he leaped to contrasting songs in different pitch ranges. Wow, whenever he used one of those high songs, from 3,300 to 4,300 hertz, he *always* rose to it from below and then dropped way back down again, as if singing any two successive songs in this high range would violate his singing principles. It was the same with his lower four songs. Whenever he sang one of those songs, he dropped down to it from outside this range and then immediately retreated back up. I played with the statistics, manipulating the numbers, and in the end I could be confident that, yes, successive songs were especially different, far more different from each other than if the bird had chosen his next song randomly.

I quickly ran through the same procedure for Bird 2 (figure 43). The graph was especially jagged in the high frequencies; when he sang a song with an introductory whistle above 3,000 hertz, he almost always rose to the song from below and then dropped right out of this pitch zone again. For three of the four songs at the lower frequencies (songs at 20, 18, and 17), it was the same story, as he also dropped to the song from above and then immediately

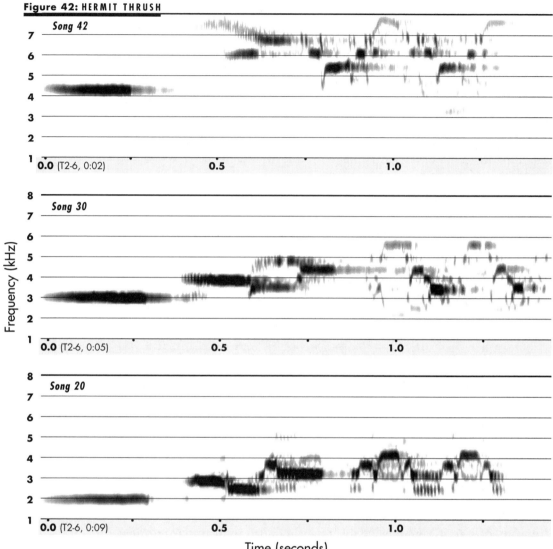

Figure 42: HERMIT THRUSH

Figure 42. Sonagrams for three songs of Bird 1: high-, middle-, and low-frequency songs (Songs 42, 30, and 20, with initial whistles at roughly 4,200, 3,000, and 2,000 Hz, respectively). See how each song begins with a pure whistle, about a third of a second long. He then rises to a flutey flourish, a striking second-long cascade of notes arising from his two voice boxes. Listen to these three songs on the CD (track 2-6) at normal speed and slowed down to half, quarter, and one-eighth speed so that you can appreciate the real music of this maestro.

rose out of this frequency zone. Song 19 was the anomaly, as he often followed Song 19 with Song 17, giving rather similar songs back-to-back. Overall, though, he also chose successive songs that were especially different.

How wonderful to know that these two hermit thrushes follow the same extraordinary singing rules as the first hermit I got to know three years ago. When each of these hermits sings, he chooses his next song so that it is not just different but rather especially different from the one he just sang. He *knows* his songs, knows how similar each is to the others, and has a taste for degrees of similarity and difference. There is nothing random, nothing left to chance in the hermit's mind as he pours out his songs. At some level in his hermit's mind, he knows very well what he is doing, and as an innocent eavesdropper collecting some numbers, I can know, too.

All that was some months ago, but for today, this bleak New England day in late November, I have saved the best. Eyes closed, headphones on, and the recorder playing, *I am there*, at 3:50 on the morning of June 17. Over the last 45 minutes, I have placed a microphone beneath the tree where each bird will begin his morning, and from each microphone I have stretched a 125-foot cable to the centrally located recorder, where I now sit in my camp chair and listen through the headphones. I want to listen, and listen some more, hearing how each bird leaps about his own repertoire and especially listening to how each bird responds to the songs of the other. I know they often take turns in their singing, as if listening and then responding in some appropriate way, so I know that each bird affects *when* the other sings. But I want to know if each bird affects *what* the other sings, and if so, in what way.

With the gain of the recorder's amplifier turned up, I hear the gentle rain of water droplets from overhead leaves falling and striking the dry leaves on the forest floor. Three eastern wood-pewees warm up with an occasional song, each on his own territory, playing tag first with their *wee-ooo* songs, then adding the *pee-a-wee* song, and finally, at 4:15 A.M., two of them launch into their frenzied dawn singing by adding the third song, the *ah-di-dee*, the third bird falling curiously silent. An ovenbird sings ecstatically in flight over to the right, a tanager and a great crested flycatcher wake up to the far left . . . a distant mourning dove . . . a chipping sparrow . . . a barred owl's *whooooo-allllllll*.

And at 4:17, in my left ear I hear the rising *zhreee* call from the first hermit

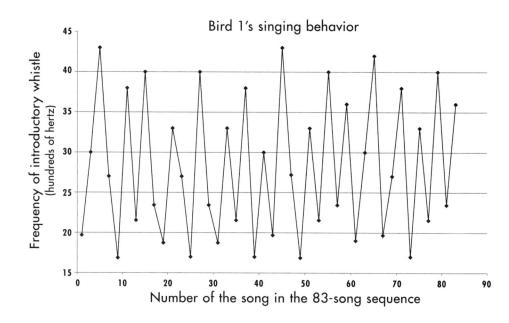

Bird 1's singing behavior

Number of the song in the 83-song sequence

thrush, whom I think of as Bird 1. He's stirring and ready to begin his day. A second *zhreee* soon follows, and then the softest of songs, and another, and gradually he builds until he is loud and clear. So far, so good, as the left microphone is placed perfectly. I listen, smiling, hearing the jagged graph I drew for him (figure 43). Birds of other species chime in, but I focus on the hermit, listening to him trampoline through his repertoire.

Minutes later, in my right ear I hear the second bird: *zhreee . . . zhreee . . .* and then the softest of songs, and soon it is back and forth, left, right, left, right, Birds 1 and 2 exchanging their songs in the predawn darkness. I check my watch: 4:21 A.M., 51 minutes before the official sunrise, and then settle back in my chair, listening, smiling.

Just listen to them now! First one, then the other, an orgy of hermit thrush songs, continuous, left, then right, left, right, so little unclaimed airtime (track 2-7). I listen to each in turn, feeling how he bounces among his songs from high to low and back again, but I struggle to hear a pattern in how they respond to each other. Do they track and match each other with similar songs, going high together and low together? No, I don't think so, as they rarely seem to be on the same pitch. Is each bird ignoring the particular song the other has just sung? I don't think I could tell that second possibility from the third, which is that each bird is singing something especially different from what the

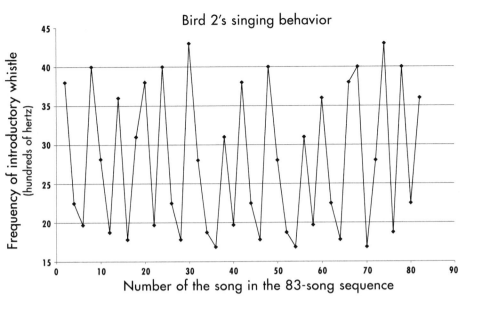

Figure 43. Just look at how each of the two hermit thrushes sang during that magical half-hour on the morning of June 17. See first how Bird 1 (facing page) begins with his song at 20 (having an introductory whistle frequency of 2,000 Hz), leaps up to 30 (3,000 Hz), then leaps as high as he can, to 43, then tumbles back down to 27 on his way to 17, back up to 38, down to 22, up to 40, and so on. The graph for Bird 2 shows much the same effect, that each male chooses his next song so that it is especially different from the one he just sang. These graphs are taken from an 83-song sequence in which the two birds perfectly alternated songs throughout, Bird 1 singing the odd-numbered songs, Bird 2 singing the even-numbered songs. Note that the horizontal axis is the total number of songs for the two birds together.

other just sang. Later, I promise myself, later I will collect the numbers I need to get to the bottom of this matter.

Timing is everything, I hear. Bird 2 pauses ever so briefly, the effect rippling to Bird 1, as if he awaits a reply. Bird 1 now gets ahead of himself, singing two songs quickly back-to-back. But mostly it is back and forth, taking turns, though one bird often doesn't wait until the other has finished before beginning his own.

By 4:53, half an hour since the singing began, Bird 2 seems to have moved away, off to the right and below the nearby ridge. He continues to sing, but he's more distant, and I wonder how well these two hermits can hear each other now. Though they both continue to sing, they are no longer engaged, no longer clearly responding to each other by taking turns in their singing. For the first time in over half an hour, I feel a bit distracted, now hearing the mourning dove, the red-eyed vireo, the oriole, the crows, the Blackburnian warbler, the ovenbird. And by 5:08, four minutes before sunrise, Bird 2 is silent. I continue, listening for the woodpeckers to awaken, listening to the local birds going about their singing business, to a young bird frantically begging for food nearby, to the increasing traffic on the highway a mile to the south, to the indefatigable Bird 1, who continues to sing on and off until I decide to call it a morning at 7:30.

Slipping the headphones off, I find myself back in November, seeing my computer before my eyes, and I know what to do next. I will focus on that special half-hour between 4:21 and 4:53 A.M., as that is when these two birds were at their best, singing and countersinging lustily.

From here on, it's a numbers game, and I buckle down to get those numbers. Using my Raven software, I advance through the half-hour of hermit music on the computer screen, collecting the numbers I need to tell me exactly when each bird sang and what he sang at that instant. A few hours later, I have the goods on about 1,000 songs in this exchange.

First, just *when* do they sing? On average, Bird 1 begins a song every 3.5 seconds, Bird 2 every 3.6 seconds, so they are singing at essentially the same pace, each bird singing about 17 songs a minute. And on average, from the beginning of Bird 1's song to the beginning of Bird 2's is 1.7 seconds, followed 1.7 seconds later by Bird 1 again. Beautiful! The numbers tell me essentially what I had heard, that the two birds take turns singing.

I'm curious about those 1.7 seconds from the beginning of one bird's song to the beginning of the other's. I measure a few songs, finding that the average song length is a little over 1.3 seconds. But about 250 feet separate the two birds, so there's a slight time lag between when one bird sings and when his neighbor hears the song. I remember that sound travels about a mile in 5 seconds, so that's about 5,000 feet in 5 seconds, or 1,000 feet in 1 second, or 250 feet in 0.25 seconds. In all of these numbers I now see that, when a hermit sings, it takes about 1.3 seconds for him to deliver his song and then an additional 0.25 seconds before the neighbor hears him finish, about 1.6 seconds overall, and only 0.1 second later the neighbor responds, at 1.7 seconds. What remarkable timing!

HERMIT
THRUSH

But just *what* does he respond with? There's the big question. I sort and resort the numbers in my large spreadsheet and methodically calculate differences in frequencies among songs. I find that, when Bird 1 sings, his song is typically 1,410 hertz different from the one he just sang but only 940 hertz different from the intervening song of his neighbor. Clearly Bird 1 is not matching the frequency of his neighbor but rather singing something different. But how different? Is 940 hertz about what would be expected if Bird 1 ignored the particular song that Bird 2 had just sung, or is it more different than would be expected

HERMIT
THRUSH

by chance? An hour later, after a tangled series of calculations, I have my answer. A difference of 940 hertz *is* significantly greater than the 760 hertz difference that would be expected if Bird 1 were simply ignoring what his neighbor had just sung.

And how does Bird 2 respond to Bird 1? When Bird 2 sings, his song averages 1,220 hertz different from his previous song and 1,130 hertz different from the intervening song of his neighbor. After manipulating the spreadsheet some more, I find that the 1,130 hertz is also significantly greater than the 870 hertz difference that would have been expected if Bird 2 were ignoring the particular song Bird 1 had just sung. How extraordinary! Each hermit thrush enhances not only the contrast between his successive songs but also, though to a lesser degree, the contrast between his song and the song he has just heard from his neighbor.

But these numbers are just abstractions. I need to *see* how these birds respond to each other, as I trust my eyes more than I do the statistics. I pick my favorite 83-song sequence, in which the two birds so perfectly alternated songs, and then graph the leaps in frequency from the song of one bird to the song of the other throughout the exchange (figure 44). Very nice, as the jagged features of the graph are retained, the two of them singing as if one bird, with successive songs especially different. I can see that. Then I rearrange the exchanges into a random sequence, as if the birds were ignoring each other, and the graph changes dramatically. Back-to-back songs are now often highly similar, and strings of songs often occur in the same narrow pitch range. My

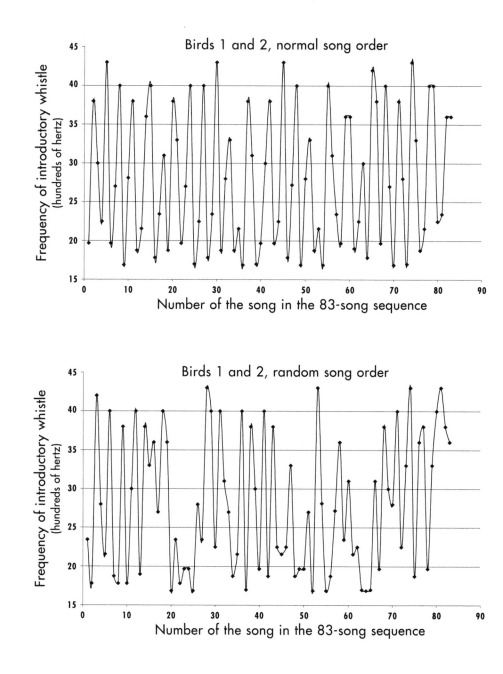

eyes confirm what the numbers have told me. This random sequence is clearly unnatural and far less exciting than true hermit exchanges.

Smiling some more, I slip the headphones on again, cue up the recording to 4:21 on the morning of June 17, 2006, punch Play on the recorder, and close my eyes (track 2-7). Yes, *I am there,* sitting in my camp chair, the half-moon behind me casting unearthly shadows onto the forest floor, the trunks of the white birches standing as sentinels in the night, my beautiful recorder on my lap, the brightly lit LEDs of orange and green and blue and red dancing about, confirming that every sound in this predawn hour is being captured so that I can return here again and again. I listen in the headphones, one ear beneath the left thrush, one beneath the right, song after song, back and forth, their performance together far better than either alone.

Figure 44. Now see exactly how these two birds respond to each other. These two graphs are more crowded than those in figure 43, because the songs of both birds are now plotted in each graph, Bird 1 with the odd-numbered songs and Bird 2 with the even-numbered songs. When the normal song order is plotted (top), see how the jagged nature of the graph is largely retained. How remarkable. How different this graph is from one that rearranges the exchanges so successive songs are chosen randomly (bottom), as if each bird were ignoring what the other had just sung. In the graph of random song order, for example, are 14 exchanges where successive songs differ by 200 Hz or less; only 4 such exchanges occur in the natural sequence. Clearly, both the statistics (see text and endnotes) and these graphs show that each hermit pays attention not only to what he has just sung but also to what his neighbor has just sung, so that the next song heard is especially different from the one just heard, no matter who sang it.

23

A Northern Mockingbird Defends Her Winter Territory

A PERFECT DAY to feast on mockingbirds, I reason, as my fellow humans should be especially quiet this morning. There's no garbage to collect; that was done yesterday, the noisy truck arriving just when the birds were awakening, the racket destroying my fun. The condo residents here are likely to sleep in this morning, enjoying the holiday and minimizing traffic on the road where I stand, just as traffic noise from Pine Ridge Road, a mile to the north, and Airport Road, a mile to the east, is likely to be lower today. And fewer residents will get a holiday paper, so the delivery period during the dawn hour will be brief. It's as good a setup as I could hope for here in this condo complex as I try to imagine for the next hour or two what it is like to be a mockingbird in late November.

And I know exactly where she is. Last night, at 6:02 P.M., 27 minutes after sunset and as it was getting too dark for me to see, I heard her settling into her roosting palm at the southwest corner of the tennis courts. It was the same routine the night before, with her slipping into her roost under cover of darkness. No cover seemed necessary, though, as she quickly sounded off, responding to the harsh calls of other mockingbirds going to their roosts nearby. After a few minutes of silence, she burst out again, just as all the others did, each confirming its place in the local mockingbird community. Then silence.

It is now 6:00 A.M., 12 hours later, and I stand here waiting for her and this whole mockingbird community to awaken. Sunrise is at 6:54, almost an hour from now, Orion still bright in the western sky, Jupiter shining brightly overhead. I expect them soon, in about 15 minutes.

She? How do I know that this bird is a "she" and some of the others are males? All I have to go on, I confess, are some educated guesses. During the spring and summer, males often sing nonstop throughout the day and sometimes the night; they sing far less in fall, when some females also sing, though far less than the males. As I have listened here the last two mornings, about half of the mockingbirds in the area sang during the first half-hour of activity, and that would be the male half of the population, I would guess. From my bird I've heard no songs, just the harsh calls, so I am guessing she's a female.

Faintly, the sounds of *kill-deer kill-deer* arrive from the north, the wild croakings of a great blue heron from the south. But the mockingbirds are quiet.

CHRRR. There's the first mockingbird, to the far east. Within a second the male behind me sounds off, a second later my female (track 2-52; figure 45), a dozen mockingbirds within earshot now all calling, all checking in. Two seconds is all it took for the wave to sweep over this mockingbird community, the wave of mockingbird growling that began on the Atlantic coast near Miami and swept westward, outracing the sun across this narrow peninsula. From the palm where I aim my parabola, I hear her four times over 5 seconds: *CHRRR CHRRR CHRRR CHRRR.* And then she is silent. Other mockingbirds continue to call, the male behind me singing briefly 10 seconds later, but within 30 seconds only a single bird continues calling, and within about a minute of when it all started, they're all silent again.

A minute later another burst comes sweeping over their roosting places, a couple of birds singing briefly at the outset, then resorting to their harsh calls. For three minutes they call, a lone neurotic bird off to the west prolonging the bout another two minutes, but my bird is curiously silent. During that calling bout, a pair of great horned owls alighted briefly in the tops of the pines, one to my left, one to my right, their muffled hooting such a contrast to the harsh calls of the mockingbirds.

After a minute of silence, the mockers call for another five minutes, all of them seeming to check in except for my female. Why is she so quiet in her roosting place? She responded to the first wave, why not the last two? I know she's still there, as I hear her shifting positions on her perch, my parabolic ear picking up her every move.

They're silent for only a minute before distant mockingbirds begin calling again; within 10 seconds, the male behind me sounds off with a harsh *CHRRR,* and a second later she responds with the same call, *CHRRR CHRRR,* then *CHAT CHAT CHAT,* 60 to 70 of them over about two minutes (track 2-53; figure 45). Here's a different call, still harsh but more explosive, as it is briefer, perhaps only $1/10$ second instead of a quarter second. When she finishes, at 6:31 A.M., I hear not a single mockingbird, as if she has had the last say.

Figure 45. Examples of the four different sounds made by the (presumably female) mockingbird on Thanksgiving morning. The three calls are all harsh, broadband sounds: the *CHRRR* is longest, up to a quarter second in duration; the *CHAT* and *CHIT* are much briefer, closer to $1/20$ second, with the *CHAT* lower in frequency (see tracks 2-52 through 2-64 for examples of these calls). And then she sings, though only briefly, but the tonal quality is a sharp contrast to the harsh calls she uses in defending her winter feeding territory.

Silence. The newspaper delivery car approaches and stops beside me, the morning's routine now being captured on my recording and playing loudly in my headphones: door squeaks open, driver jumps from car, motor left running, footsteps down the walkway, morning papers plopping onto decks and landings, footsteps, car door closing, a cough, car accelerates and drives on. Is

Figure 45: NORTHERN MOCKINGBIRD

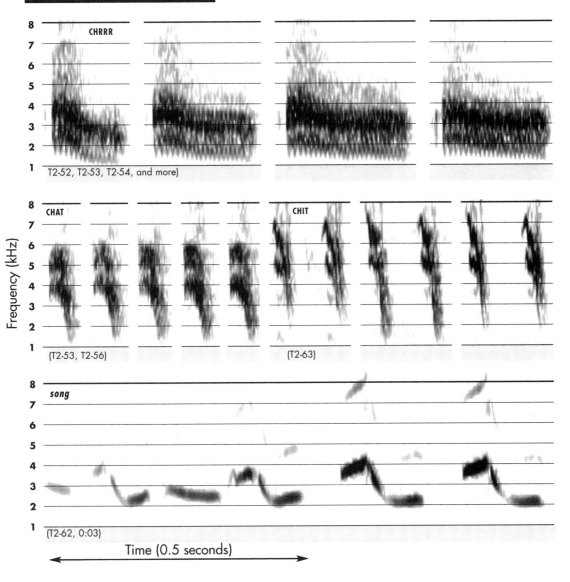

CHRRR

T2-52, T2-53, T2-54, and more)

Frequency (kHz)

CHAT

CHIT

(T2-53, T2-56)

(T2-63)

song

(T2-62, 0:03)

Time (0.5 seconds)

that a grackle awakening in the distance, a palm warbler chipping in the palm above? Herons and ibis fly west overhead from their inland roosts to their early-morning feeding grounds in the coastal bays. An osprey shrieks to my left, a kestrel calls to my right.

For 20 minutes the mockingbirds are silent, as if spent, that last bout silencing them for the day. But it's more like they've evaporated, disappeared from the planet; I've not seen a single bird moving about, not a single flash of white on gray as I've scanned the yards and isolated trees. Nothing. Where are they? What are they doing? Did she slip out of the palm when I wasn't looking? But where would she have gone? No, she must be there, because I've been aiming my parabola into her palm all these minutes, and I can detect even the slightest movements over my headphones. Surely I'd have heard her fly, rattling the dry palm fronds as she departed. No, she must still be there, as other mockingbirds must still be on their roosts. But why, more than half an hour after awakening, why aren't they moving about?

Yes! At 6:52, two minutes before sunrise, a bird calls off to the west, and 15 seconds later the calls again sweep over this neighborhood. She responds almost immediately to the CHRRRing male behind me: CHRRR   CHRRR   CHRRR   CHRRR   CHRRR, five times in 7 seconds (track 2-54).

Another two minutes pass, and at 6:54, the precise minute of official sunrise, she responds to another wave of calling, CHRRR   CHRRR (track 2-55), and departs her roost, flying toward the sunrise to an isolated cabbage palm. It is in that minute that I first hear the others, too: the *chig chig* of the red-bellied woodpecker, the loud *jay jay* of the blue jay, and the muted whistlings of a flock of starlings now gathering in the dead branches at the top of a pine 50 yards to the northeast.

For five minutes she sits there on the fruiting cluster of this palm, just watching, surveying. At 7:00, in the gathering chorus of starling whistles and gurgles, she calls (track 2-56), CHRRR   CHRRR . . . then CHAT CHAT, and up into the nearby pines she launches, a whir of gray and white scattering in all directions the starlings who had ventured from their pine to hers. A loggerhead shrike boils out of the pine canopy, too.

Down she now drops, into the fruit-laden palm beneath the pine. She eats one of the dark fruits, then a second, and flies up to a dead pine branch just above. And there she sits, above a cluster of fruiting palms, with a commanding view of them all.

Two minutes later, starlings and a red-bellied woodpecker invade her palm, and she's after them, darting, a blur of mockingbird and departing, still-

hungry visitors. The foes van-
quished, she eats another two fruits,
then perches above the palm again,
watching, surveying, preening. A
single loud CHRRR she utters (track
2-57), but otherwise she is quiet,
waiting . . .

Waiting for that next flock of starlings, and just minutes later she's after
them again (track 2-58). The starlings seem to like that particular
palm, no doubt because of the
abundant fruit so obviously clus-
tered below the fronds but probably also because it's a direct
flight from their staging pine to
the northeast. No matter what
their reason, they're unwelcome, as all
these palms belong to her.

MOCKINGBIRD

The starlings once again repelled, she returns to sit above her palm fruits,
just sitting, preening. First she works her bill under her wing on the right
side, then the left, then works into the underside of the left wing itself, running her bill the full length of the feathers, pausing to look toward her palm
fruits, then lowering her head and working up into the bend of the left wing,
then reaching with her left leg over her left wing to scratch her head, pausing
to look around, to the left, the right, back behind her, sitting, watching,
guarding. As if to make sure everyone knows, she belts out a CHRRR CHRRR
(track 2-59).

A lone starling flies into the pine tree above her. It's a harmless starling, just
perching up there and not eating her palm fruits, but she'll have none of that
and is after him, up into the canopy, the departing starling no match for her.

She returns to her perch, sitting there for seven minutes before flying down,
grabbing two more fruits, returning to her perch, and calling loudly: CHRRR
CHRRR CHRRR (track 2-60), her seemingly unprovoked calling setting off a
burst of calling among her neighbors. I study her in the binoculars. She's largely gray, lighter below and darker above, wings darker still with light fringes to
each feather. The sun's rays now peek over the nearby condos, twinkling in her
pitch-black eye.

From her perch she drops down for two more fruits, flies over to the carport across the drive, drops to the grass momentarily, and then flies back to her perch above the palms again. A lead starling, followed closely by two recruits, makes a dash for her palm, and in an instant she's off, this time just hovering beside and then above her palm, her outer white tail feathers and her white wing bars flashing; the starlings get the message, scattering in all directions.

As she perches over her domain, a red-shouldered hawk cries in the distance; on the condo to the right a flicker calls, and from the very top of the starling's staging pine a loggerhead shrike now sings. What sharp, precise, mechanical two-syllable songs they are, *krrDI krrDI*, one song every two seconds, maybe 10 or 20 of them, and then another song, *JEEuk JEEuk*. A pileated woodpecker calls nearby, too.

To the sounds of sirens on Pine Ridge Road, she again chases off a flock of starlings, then returns to her perch. A minute later, the male neighbor to the south calls loudly, and she responds within half a second: CHRRR. The two take turns calling, she calling four times to his five, and then they're silent (track 2-61).

She's relentless, as a little over a minute later she's after them again, chasing the starlings from above her in the canopy of the pine. As she does so, a second group advances on her palm, and there she hastens next, giving them hell. Thirty-five seconds of frenzy it takes, but her small territory is again starling-free. This area now secure, she snatches another berry or two for the gullet and flies to the lone palm at the south end of her territory. There she perches, looking, guarding, then calling CHIT-CHIT-CHIT . . . CHIT-CHIT . . . CHIT-CHIT . . . CHIT-CHIT . . . CHIT-CHIT . . . CHIT-CHIT . . . CHIT-CHIT . . . CHIT-CHIT (figure 45). It's her third type of call this morning, even sharper than the CHAT, and given in pairs or threes. The male just to the south responds to her, calling almost continuously, five or more CHITs in a burst.

Just 20 seconds later, she sings (track 2-62)! Remarkable. She *sings*. It's only a second of song, but it's clearly song. Was it set off by the intense CHIT-ting encounter with the neighboring male who does a fair amount of singing? Fascinating. As if in exclamation, a pileated woodpecker sings nearby, KU-KU-KUK-KUK-KUK-KUK-KUK-KUK-KUK-KUK-KU-KU.

Six minutes later, while still perched in that same palm, she calls CHRRR CHRRR CHRRR (track 2-63). Half a minute later, it's CHIT-CHIT-CHIT and then eight CHIT-CHIT calls in midair as she flies back to the east, to the cluster of palms and pines that she has been so obsessed with protecting.

She sits again on her perch above the palms, six minutes later dropping down to eat, flying across to the carport, then flying back to her lone palm on the south end of her territory, where she sits, waiting, watching. A starling enters the no-fly zone overhead, and she intercepts it in midair, catching up with it in the canopy of the pines, where she inflicts some bodily harm.

Then she drops to one of her palms below and perches there momentarily, seemingly ensuring that the palm and all of its fruits are secure. But it's soon back to that lone palm south of the tennis courts, where she silently evicts the mockingbird who has intruded from the south. Silently? Why so? Why none of the vocal venom I would have expected? How well does she know this singer from just across the road to the south? Is he special, perhaps her mate of last year, or a potential mate?

Six minutes later she spots a lone starling in the top of the pines above her fruiting palms, and she's off on yet another mission to defend her winter's food supply. No match for her speed and agility, the starling departs, and she again drops to her favorite perch low in the pine, just above the palms. A minute and a half later she yet again proclaims herself, CHRRR CHRRR CHRRR, in immediate response to her neighbor, who also CHRRRs (track 2-64). What a harsh, angry-sounding growl, a bark as intense and threatening as any I've ever heard. Were this mockingbird more my size, I would be running for cover at the very sound of it.

I watch one more cycle. She drops into the palm, eats two fruits, returns to her perch, chases a lone starling out of the canopy, and drops back to her perch.

It is there, at 8:10 A.M., that I leave her surveying her kingdom. About two hours ago she stirred 40 yards away in her roost at the southwest corner of the tennis courts, and here she now sits in the cluster of pines and palms nearby. It is the palms that she cares deeply about, as they have the abundant fruits that will see her through the winter, nourishing her until spring, when she will rely more on insects. She will defend these palms against all comers, whether they be another mockingbird or a single red-bellied woodpecker or a flock of starlings.

And how does she defend? She barks and growls, using at least three different calls that I've heard this morning. Her CHRRR sounds the harshest, so angry, so threatening, a full quarter-second growl. No less intimidating are her CHAT and CHIT, both briefer and more explosive. And she *sang,* though for only a second. Does the song somehow help in this defense, as if a little bit of maleness thrown in is a stronger defense? Four distinctive sounds—CHRRR, CHAT, CHIT, and song—and I hear each playing over and over in my mind. Why four? Why not more, or fewer? Does each serve a different purpose? With her bark is plenty of bite, too, as any intruder into her territory soon discovers. She's the total package.

But why? Why is she so aggressive? Why has the mockingbird come to be so attentive to what other species are doing? During the spring and summer, when males sing abundantly, so much of what they proclaim consists of songs pilfered from other species. Now, midwinter, I hear little of that mimicry, but these mockers are ultra-aggressive, not only against other mockingbirds but especially against other species. The mocker is off scale on both aggressiveness and mimicry, so almost certainly the two are related, I reason. Perhaps it's even the fall and winter aggressiveness toward other species that has led to the mimicry expressed predominantly during the spring and summer.

I think back to when she left her roost this morning, the very minute in which I first heard and saw the starlings. She had heard them, too, and no doubt before I did. I bet she waited until she heard the threat to her food and then emerged, ready for action. And action it was, a total of 11 defensive sallies in 70 minutes, roughly one rout of the intruders every 6 to 7 minutes. A number of strikes were preemptive, too, chasing the starlings from the pines before they had a chance to descend on her palms, even intercepting one starling in midair as it entered her space.

Why wait so long before emerging from the roost? My mind flashes to some other birds I know, like a chickadee trying to survive a New England winter. The chickadee is early to leave the roost, as it must search all day for tiny morsels of food hidden throughout its foraging range. But this mockingbird's challenge is different. There's no shortage of food in her palms, so she's in no hurry to depart her roost and can save her energy until it is needed to defend what she has claimed as hers. How unlike the chickadee; most of this mockingbird's day is spent sitting, watching, and waiting to protect her palm fruits.

I wonder what the cabbage palms would think of all this if they could voice an opinion. The mockingbird eats the fruits, and I saw her regurgitate one of the large pits, inside of which is the seed, the palm's future. The mockingbird's territory is small, only 40 or so yards across, and if the palm were to rely solely on the mockingbird, its offspring would disperse such a short distance. Nothing personal, I can almost hear the palm saying, but bring on the starlings, who fly all over creation and disperse my seeds far and wide.

I wish I could see into her past and into her future. She's unpaired and all alone on this territory, but it's not atypical for each mockingbird to defend its own winter territory. Maybe she's a young bird, just a half year or so old, holding her first winter territory; or she could be the community matriarch, splitting from her mate to hold her own feeding grounds for the winter. Will her mate for the coming season come from an adjacent territory or from elsewhere? I'd love to be here daily, to follow her progress through the winter.

There's one question I'd like to ask of her, though it seems a little mean. About 15 minutes before her usual roost departure and before the starlings show up, I'd love to broadcast a recording of starlings from her nearby fruiting palm. My bet is that she'd emerge from her roost in a flash, rising to the challenge of these early marauders. To the palm she'd fly, finding nothing but an old black speaker box perched there with a wire leading down to my recorder. I bet, too, that she'd snarl a few times, *CHRRR CHRRR*, before moving on with her day.

Yes, I'll do that sometime, well before she pairs with a male in the spring —perhaps on Christmas morning or New Year's Day, keeping our holiday tradition intact.

December

24

The Winter Solstice Is the First Day of Spring

December 21, 6 A.M., Amherst, Massachusetts

AWAKENING EARLY, an hour and a quarter before sunrise, I dress and head downstairs for a quick breakfast.

It's the winter solstice, the shortest day of the year, the day I so eagerly anticipate, as it is the day when the sun begins its return north. Longer days lie ahead. I know it by my calendar, but the birds know it, too, for deep in their bodies lie systems dedicated to knowing these things. It is the length of the day that governs their annual activities, guiding the ebb and flow of hormones and mating activities, initiating the vast migration movements over the globe, inducing feather molt and replacement, indeed, affecting almost every feature of their lives.

For years, no, decades, a few of us birdsong enthusiasts have remarked to each other about the great burst of singing that begins at the winter solstice. It just had to be so, we reasoned, and we had all heard it, to be sure; and someday, we all agreed, we would prove it by a good listen during midwinter. We used that word "prove" lightly, because we knew good science can only disprove an idea, or "falsify a hypothesis," and scientists who try to prove a hypothesis usually get into trouble because they become blinded to any facts opposed to their favorite idea. But we also knew that rigorously testing our cherished belief had its dangers, lest we find it not to be so, and perhaps it was just as well that our midwinter busyness kept us indoors at our desks. Studying birdsong, after all, was a spring and summer affair.

But what excuse did I have now that I had retired from the university? There were no classes to teach, no papers to grade, no end-of-semester franticness—only birdsong to contemplate. In early December, I remember looking at the calendar and seeing the winter solstice bearing down on me. I knew, then, that I had no excuse.

I devised a plan. The question was simple: Do the winter birds begin to sing more on the winter solstice? Do they know that this shortest of days is in fact not the first day of winter but instead the first day of spring, and do they announce it in song? I needed to focus on *song,* not just calling; the *chick-a-dee-dee-dee* calls of the black-capped chickadee are used to moderate social interactions throughout the year, for example, but it is the whistled *hey-sweet-ie* song that signals spring. I'd listen for the unmistakable songs of other songbirds, too, such as those of tufted titmice, white-breasted nuthatches, Carolina wrens, robins, sparrows, and goldfinches. For the woodpeckers, I'd monitor their drumming, which is essentially a mechanical song. All of these songs tell of desire, of the desire to defend a territory and the desire to mate, all sure signs of spring.

Looking at the calendar, I decided that December 11 to December 31 was a good time frame. My goal would be to listen on at least five days before the solstice and five days after, plus the solstice itself, trying to keep the weather factor constant by choosing relatively calm days with no inclement weather.

Beginning at sunrise, about 7:15 A.M., I'd take an hourlong walk, simply listening for birdsong. Tough job, my working friends commented, but when I explained the significance of this task, they readily agreed that someone had to do it. I plotted the route on the map: I'd walk from my house down to Heatherstone Road and take a left, then a right on Stony Hill Road, left on Hickory Lane, right through the woods to Stony Hill again, left to Harkness Road, and left on Harkness to the end, about two miles from my home. There I'd reverse the route and listen on the return, and near home take a loop around Aubinwood Road before heading up to my house again.

Yes, today is December 21, the day of truth, as it is on this very day that the sun lies poised far to the south and begins its comeback. While I down my cereal breakfast, I study my notes for my six outings so far.

DECEMBER 11, SUNDAY. 20°F, clear and calm as I leave home; a foot of snow lingers from Friday's snowstorm. A pileated woodpecker drums and "sings" a loud *kuk kuk kuk-kuk-kuk-kuk-kuk-kuk-kuk-kuk-kuk-kuk-kuk kuk kuk.* From a single chickadee, a faint *hey,* then another, then a weak *hey-sweetie.* A titmouse sings a slowly down-slurred whistle, *heere,* sometimes *heere hre,* the second note unstable and incomplete, higher-pitched than it should be, about 10 song attempts in all; perhaps he's a young bird, or possibly an adult who doesn't quite yet care about getting it right.

DECEMBER 12, MONDAY. 25°F, clear, calm. A pileated woodpecker drums and sings. No other songs.

DECEMBER 13, TUESDAY. 5°F, clear, calm, and cold. A lone white-throated sparrow practices his songs; what wonderful variations he sings, not the bold *poor poor sam peabody peabody peabody* of springtime, but each whistle now wavers, the song delivered in bits and pieces, ever so softly, and he seemingly can't decide whether the *poor* should be higher- or lower-pitched than the *sam* (see track 2-48 for similar white-throat songs during October).

DECEMBER 15, THURSDAY. −5°F, clear, calm, even colder; smoke and steam rise vertically from the chimneys, soon swallowed by the cold; the air bites at my cheeks and nostrils. The pileated woodpecker is undeterred, drumming and singing. Before my walk, as I was putting the garbage at curbside, a single titmouse sang *heere heere*, then *heere*. I shouldn't really count him, as he was before my scheduled walk, but I choose to let his voice be heard anyway.

DECEMBER 17, SATURDAY. 15°F, clear, calm. From a pileated, I hear three drums. A Carolina wren belts out five of his loud, ringing *tea-kettle* songs, and on the fifth song his mate adds her buzzy rattle. As I linger, marveling at the wrens, a chickadee in the distance sings three *hey-sweetie*s, a brown creeper behind me his jumbled cascade of whistles.

DECEMBER 19, MONDAY. 15°F, partial clouds, calm; I'm grateful for the continuing good weather. I hear four pileated woodpeckers, presumably two pairs, with both drumming and singing. Nothing else.

That was the extent of singing on those six outings before today, the magical solstice. The pileated woodpeckers were regulars, but other than that, I heard "song" from a total of only seven birds: two chickadees, two titmice, a creeper, a Carolina wren, and a white-throated sparrow. Each was a solitary effort by a single bird.

From most of the other regulars, I heard no song but lots of calling, such as the simple *yank yank* of the white-breasted nuthatches, the *chig chig* calls of the red-bellied woodpeckers, and the sharp *pik* calls of the downy and hairy woodpeckers (I'm still not confident I can tell them apart). Goldfinches routinely flew overhead, their *per-chick-o-ree* flight call giving them away; house finches called from the treetops, *vweet, vweet.* Near fruiting trees, robins often called *tut tut,* or more sharply, *piik, piik.* From the bushes, the sharp, hard *tik, tik* informed of cardinals. On the ground, juncos twittered in their flocks, and from the treetops the high, thin *zee-zee-zee* notes told of golden-crowned kinglets. Only two chickadees sang a *hey-sweetie,* but almost always I was within earshot of their typical winter calls, the *chick-a-dee* call, the "gargle" (a descending jumble of rapidly delivered notes), and often their "alarm" notes (high, thin notes, *teeteeteeteetee*). Titmice were abundant, too, with a variety of sounds, my favorite being what sounds to me like an angry snarl of nasal, rising notes. For the crows and jays, I heard lots of standard calls; I didn't expect anything like a song, as these songbirds don't normally "sing," but females have a rattle call that I associate with spring and summer—I heard none of those. Mourning doves were silent.

Yes, here it is, December 21, in my mind the most significant date on the bird-year calendar, and with breakfast finished, the sun minutes away from rising, I'm ready. Check the thermometer: cold, at 4°F, but clear and calm. Hiking boots on, wool balaclava next, a fleece and shell layer on the torso, the heavy-duty gloves, and I'm out the door.

At Heatherstone Road, I hear the *zee-zee-zee* of kinglets from the tops of the pines. A hundred yards down the road is the usual flock, as I hear the calls of titmice, chickadees, white-breasted nuthatches, a woodpecker (downy or hairy?), and more kinglets. Two miles into my walk, at the end of Harkness, a titmouse sings three songs. Pretty slow so far. Don't these birds know what day it is?

On my return, off to the left at South Valley Road, a white-breasted nuthatch sings a slow version of his song, *haah-haah-haah-haah-haah*, and one to my right responds with the faster version, *hah-hah-hah-hah-hah-hah-hah-hah-hah* (track 2-65; figure 46). I had read about these nuthatches having two versions of their songs, one slow and one fast, and there they are, now that I am truly paying attention to them for the first time. Here's a first for my outings, too: two birds of the same species are singing at the same time, engaging each other with their songs, hurling them back and forth across the road. The one on the left falls silent, but the male on the right continues from a branch just a foot or so below the top of the tallest ash tree. Another bird, presumably his mate, calls *yank yank* just off to the side and a little lower. Abruptly, he switches to the slower version of his song.

He sings . . . and sings . . . and sings, 5 minutes, pushing 10. My walking rule before this has been to linger when a bird sings, to let him have his say

NUTHATCHES

before I move on, but I now grow impatient. A chickadee sings off to the east — another first, males of two species singing at the same time. I must move on — yet another first, breaking my rule of engagement with a singing bird.

Along Stony Hill, off to the right, I hear a melodious rumble. Whaaat? Animal? Human? Music, as from a radio? At this distance, the sounds are unrecognizable, but I pick up the pace, taking my trail back through the woods, and as I approach, I realize the source: robins! In the treetops, now awash with the reddish rays of the rising sun, is a flock of *robins,* and many of them are *singing!* Yes, there are the usual calls, too, the *tut*s and *piik*s, but I hear song, two to four whistled carols at a time before a pause, and clearly from a number of birds. How many? Twenty? Thirty? There's no single bird belting out a sustained spring song, but these robins are feeling something. I listen, dumbfounded, scanning through my binoculars the tops of the ashes and hickories and oaks, trying to pick out the reddish robins among the brownish leaves lingering on the branches.

To my left are the high, thin notes of cedar waxwings, a large flock of them

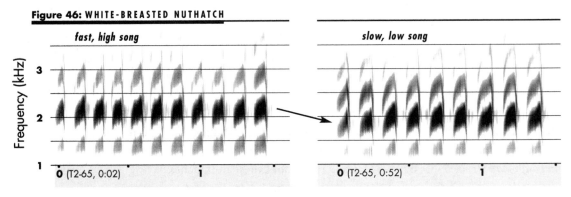

Figure 46: WHITE-BREASTED NUTHATCH

Time (seconds)

Figure 46. A male white-breasted nuthatch has two different songs, both with their characteristic nasal quality, but one is higher and faster than the other. In the song on the left, count seven brief phrases each second, each phrase consisting of a "harmonic stack" (for explanation of this term, see page xiv and endnote), i.e., a fundamental note together with all of the harmonics above it. The song on the right has about six notes per second. The arrow connects the corresponding notes in the two songs, showing how much higher the faster *hah-hah-hah-hah-hah-hah* song on the left is than the slower *haah-haah-haah-haah-haah* song on the right (track 2-65).

in the treetops, somewhere between 60 and 70 birds. They're using the same sounds I'd expect from them throughout the year, high *seeee*s and buzzy *bzeee*s; I don't think of them as having a song that is used exclusively during the breeding season (see page 178). Counting robins and waxwings alone, that's about 100 birds here.

I'm drawn to the robins again. They're singing. *Singing.* I roll the word off my tongue, saying it aloud, as if to make sure I'm here, among singing robins on December 21, the winter solstice. I close my eyes, trying to take in this entire scene, trying to focus on the listening. It's the sound of spring that I hear, no doubt about it. This is no first day of winter. With eyes closed, I can see and hear and smell and imagine a spring day, the understory fully leafed out, the tree buds bursting overhead, flowers everywhere, robins singing all around.

Off to the right, a tufted titmouse sings, *heere heere,* two confident, down-slurred whistles, repeated, and again, when a little beyond him a second bird chimes in, *heere heere hre hre,* the last two phrases poorly formed. Back and forth, they seemingly take turns singing. An adult and a youngster, maybe, perhaps father and son, both from the same winter flock. It won't be long before the youngster is sent off to fend for himself on a spring territory of his own. Two titmice singing, simultaneously! Another first. Never have I had two titmice singing on the same day, let alone together.

Tea-kettle tea-kettle tea-kettle! resounds from the underbrush, just below the adult titmouse. A Carolina wren. Again, two, three, and during his fourth song the female chimes in, giving her rough chatter. I've never heard this pair of wrens before.

High above, among the robins, a woodpecker drums, so rapidly I can't count the number of strikes — it's a hairy woodpecker. I see him, too, the red patch on the back of his head glowing in the morning sun. Again he drums, and again.

Hey-sweetie, hey-sweetie — a chickadee chimes in, near the woodpecker. To the left another chickadee sings, and to the right a third. Three chickadees singing, more than I had heard on all six outings before this. The bird above me shifts his pitch downward, now singing at a lower frequency, but he seems to stall partway through the song, *hey-sweet . . . hey-sweet . . .* and then he falls silent.

And from the right, from a bird well hidden in the pines, comes the rattle of a crow. It's not a *caw* — it's nothing like what I've been hearing before today. No, it's a rattle, like that of a female crow.

No cardinal songs? What's with you cardinals? Everyone else is singing! And that downy woodpecker over there, and the red-bellied woodpecker. Why aren't you drumming, too? Get with the program. How can I not feel just a little greedy for more spring song?

The robins continue. I see numerous chases in the treetops, these "harbingers of spring" clearly energized. I stand here, motionless, incredulous, as the cold of the morning slowly penetrates my layers. I must move on, breaking my "linger as they sing" rule yet again. My cold legs move stiffly at first, my balance unsteady, but soon I regain my stride.

Around Aubinwood, another chickadee sings, *hey-sweetie,* the full-blown version of the spring song, and several times.

Just a few hundred yards from home, a titmouse sings, then another, and a third chimes in! Three titmice singing, all the same song, the rapidly down-slurred whistle, like *here here, here here.* At first they're well separated, about 50 yards between them, but soon I see three birds swirling about the top of an oak. Perhaps it's the adult chasing the youngsters, suggesting that they should start thinking about leaving the family flock and heading out on their own. Three titmice! Never have I heard more than one titmouse on my outings before, and today I have heard six. Onward.

Home, at last. I check my watch. I'm about 20 minutes later than usual, delayed by singing birds.

My head spins giddily. What did I just witness? How extraordinary an outing. The early pair of singing white-breasted nuthatches and the late trio of titmice were special, but back there between Stony Hill and Hickory Lane was the ultimate solstice party, a grand gathering of a few dozen robins, many of them singing, joined by the titmice, the Carolina wrens, the hairy woodpecker, and the chickadees, all in spring *song*. And there was that odd crow rattle, too.

It is a day of firsts, unlike any of the days from December 11 to December 20. Robins are singing, a whole flock of them. A woodpecker drums. Neighboring males of the same species countersing with each other: two nuthatches, three chickadees, and two sets of titmice. At least 25 birds are heard singing, far more than on all previous outings combined (figure 47).

The solstice is special, and these birds know it. Or so I want to conclude. Though it seems anticlimactic, I need to know if the singing continues, and I must continue with my plan to listen through December 31.

DECEMBER 22, THURSDAY. 15°F, cloudy, calm. A total of eight singing birds, better than any day before the solstice, but not as active as the solstice itself. I hear the crow rattle from the same group of pines, and a female blue jay also rattles, the first I've heard. One robin sings, continuously but ever so softly, from a fruiting tree beside a house along Aubinwood Road; he sings with his bill closed, with rarely even a trace of movement in the throat feathers, though with each phrase he sings I can see through the binoculars that his tail nudges upward and his wings downward. Other than that he sits there, motionless, just singing until he pauses to eat or until a jay or another robin approaches the tree; he then springs into action, chasing the competitor from what he has claimed as his own winter food supply (track 2-66; figure 48).

DECEMBER 23, FRIDAY. 28°F, clear, calm. Five singing birds, including the same robin in his fruiting tree. I also see one male cardinal chasing another, the first sign that these generally amiable winter flocks will soon be breaking up.

DECEMBER 24, SATURDAY. 28°F, clear, calm. I could skip a day, but I'm eager to know who's about. Nine singing birds, including the crow rattle and the same singing robin. For the first time, I hear the drums of a downy woodpecker.

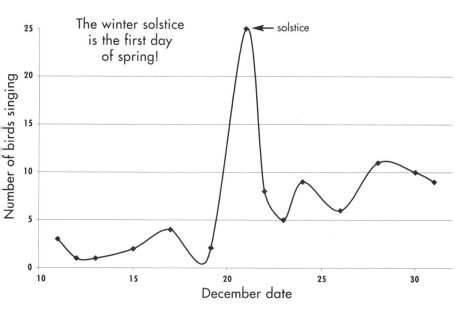

Figure 47. This figure lifts my spirits, as I can see the burst of birdsong on the winter solstice and the rising enthusiasm for singing in the days that follow.

The Christmas Robin

He was just one robin, sitting peacefully in his fruiting tree and minding his own business. Arriving about sunrise, he chuckled the familiar robin *tut* and *piik* calls; he offered an occasional series of *quiquiqui* notes, and at one point he also slipped in what sounded like a high-pitched "hawk alarm." Those calls were familiar and expected, but it was his singing that so puzzled me, because I couldn't tell when he was singing his lower-pitched carols or higher-pitched *hisselly*s (track 2-66).

The more familiar of the robin's two adult song forms is a melodious stream of low-pitched "carols," a "variable *cheerily cheer-up cheerio*," according to Peterson; a typical robin has 15 or so of these carols in his repertoire. The less familiar song is a much higher-pitched, flutey flourish, dubbed a *hisselly* by Bent in his classic life history series, and each robin sings a bewildering variety of these high notes. At dawn, a male robin often sings a series of caroled notes followed by a single *hisselly*. Given how songbirds use their two voice boxes to produce songs, it's probable that a robin uses mostly his left voice box to produce the lower-pitched carols and mostly the right to produce the higher *hisselly*s.

As expected, the muted songs of this winter robin were not in peak form. No two caroled phrases were the same, as he was just beginning to tune up for his spring singing. During "winter," hormone levels and motivation to sing are low; even the singing centers in the brain are in idle mode and regressed. As spring approaches, however, the singing phrases for this robin will become increasingly stable, until he settles on his well-practiced repertoire of carols and *hisselly*s.

What was unexpected, no, what absolutely floored me, was what I saw in his practice routines: he was singing a high-pitched *hisselly* and a low-pitched carol *simultaneously!* As an adult, he'd sing either one or the other, never the two together. How fascinating to see him babbling away, practicing a caroled song below 5 kilohertz most likely with his left voice box and a totally different *hisselly* song well above 5 kilohertz with his right voice box (figure 48). Here is robin song in the making, a mix of low and high sounds that will eventually separate and crystallize into distinct carols and *hisselly*s. It's no wonder I couldn't tell on Christmas morning which kind of song he was singing, as he was doing both at the same time.

How puzzling. Singing is really precision breathing, gating the air through the left and right voice boxes in measured puffs, tightening and relaxing membranes in split-second routines to produce the desired effect, yet here is this winter robin playfully testing both voice boxes together — not alternately, but *simultaneously*. It's all wrong by adult standards, but so deliciously and delightfully wrong.

Why does he practice this way? Do other songbirds exercise their two voice boxes

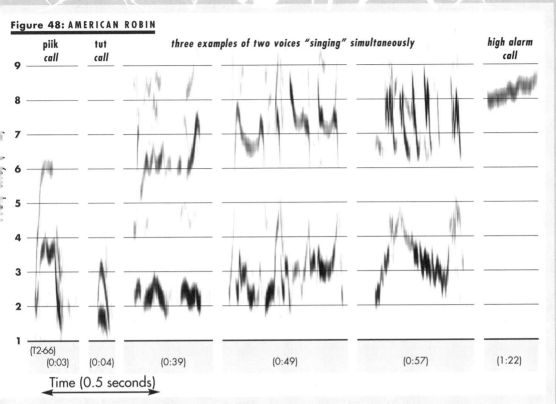

Figure 48: AMERICAN ROBIN

| piik call | tut call | *three examples of two voices "singing" simultaneously* | high alarm call |

Time (0.5 seconds)

(T2-66)
(0:03)   (0:04)   (0:39)   (0:49)   (0:57)   (1:22)

Figure 48. I like what I see in the practice songs of this Christmas robin. He gives the usual *piik* and *tut* calls (track 2-66), and a note that may well be what is called his "hawk alarm," but it is his attempted song phrases that so enthrall me. It is clear that he uses both voice boxes simultaneously, practicing different phrases above and below 5,000 Hz, because if he were using only one voice box to produce these sounds, the upper sound would be an exact frequency multiple of the lower sound, as in the phrases of the white-breasted nuthatch (figure 46).

like this, too? Is such practice a necessary part of mastering control of a dual brain and dual voice boxes? And how I'd love to follow this robin through to spring, to see how he isolates and perfects his two song forms.

But I find myself a bit sad, too, as I like "wrong" better. Here is the Jonathan Livingston Seagull of robins, the robin who does it all, singing his carols and *hissellys* with abandon, revealing an artistry unmatched by anything I've seen from a seasoned robin doing it the "right way." I'll have to settle for the sheer joy of simply knowing this playful side of robins, of knowing the roots of the carols and *hissellys*, of knowing how the American robin and his song come to be the way they are.

DECEMBER 25, SUNDAY. 25°F, clear, calm. I forgo the usual walking route and just visit the singing robin. He arrives about sunrise, eats a few fruits, and then begins calling, chuckling as a friend described it, and three minutes into his chuckles he begins singing, again ever so softly. For minutes on end he whispers his song, stopping only to eat and chase other birds from his tree. An hour later I leave him, still singing, but I take him with me, too, as I have stood in the relative quiet of Christmas morning and captured in my recording all that he said (see sidebar).

DECEMBER 26, MONDAY. 35°F, cloudy, calm. Goldfinches are singing! I heard a brief song from one, just two phrases. From another perched in the treetop, I heard that thin, rising call, *toweeeowee,* nonstop for well over a minute; it's the first I've heard that sound, one that is often included in the goldfinch's song. And I could swear that I heard the flight whistle of a brown-headed cowbird, another sign of spring. A total of six singing birds.

DECEMBER 28, WEDNESDAY. 22°F, partial clouds, calm. Eleven singing birds!

DECEMBER 30, FRIDAY. Ten singing birds, including the first cardinals.

DECEMBER 31, SATURDAY. Nine singing birds. The one regular since December 22 has been the lone singing robin along Aubinwood Road, still singing ever so softly.

I look now at the simple numbers I've accumulated over the past 20 days. Before the solstice, the number of singing birds on each day was 3, 1, 1, 2, 4, 2; on the solstice itself, at least 25 birds were singing; after the solstice, 8, 5, 9, 6, 11, 10, 9. The simple answer to my question is clear: *Spring arrives on the winter solstice!* Look at that party on the winter solstice itself and how the numbers of singing birds after the solstice clearly exceeded the numbers before. When graphed, those numbers are all the more appealing, because I can see the winter solstice launching me into spring (figure 47).

These convincing numbers alone don't tell the whole story, though, because it wasn't just the number of birds singing but their exuberance, too. One of those two nuthatches on the solstice, for example, seemed to sing forever, and he continued singing when I walked out of earshot. In contrast, all singing before the solstice consisted of at most a few songs from a single individual.

Inevitably, as scientists are trained to do, I search for all possible explanations for what I have heard.

I think first of the weather. I don't think there was anything special about the weather on the solstice itself, as it was calm, clear, and cold, much like most of the other days. Could the warmer temperatures after the solstice have been a factor? Perhaps, but that doesn't explain the solstice singing on the second coldest day of them all.

I worry about my biases and reluctance to challenge a cherished belief. I know how much I did not want to hear song before the solstice and how much I wanted to hear it after. It's dangerous knowing the results one wants in order to support some favorite idea, and the bias that desire can introduce into data collection is significant. Perhaps I lingered a little longer at some places after the solstice, for example, giving more birds a chance to sing. Also, the more I walked the route, the more I would know where to "pick up" a singing bird. The lone robin singing so softly was always in his fruiting tree after the solstice, for example, and I might have missed him had I not known to look for him there.

I realize that the only way to truly test this idea about a solstice effect is to listen again during other years and, preferably, at several locations. Listening over several years is the only way to be sure that it is the solstice itself and not some other factor, such as weather, that causes any increase in singing. I'd also need a better way to collect my data. The person who counts the singing birds must somehow be blind, so to speak, blind to the question being asked. I could hire someone to walk the route and listen for singing birds, not telling that person what idea is being tested. Better yet, I could deploy a microphone and recorder at several locations on each day; later, without knowing which day I was listening to, I could objectively tally the amount of singing as I listened to the recordings.

That's next year. For now, though, I'm satisfied. The calendar may tell me that the toughest days of winter are yet to come, but I know in my heart that on December 21 it is already spring. I have heard it in the air. I have heard it in the lusty singing of nuthatches and titmice and chickadees. The woodpeckers are drumming, female jays and crows rattling. In the grand cycle through the seasons, these birds know what time it is. They know that the winter solstice is the turning point. Here is "the first day with promise, the first day that is longer, if ever so slightly, than the one before, our first day of winter that in reality is their first day of spring."

Appendix 1: *The Audio Book*

How to Listen to the Bird Sounds on the Two Compact Discs

HERE IS THE TEXT that describes in detail how to listen to the sounds on the two CDs that are referenced throughout the book. Many of these sound tracks have accompanying sonagram figures, and to aid your listening, I encourage you to watch along in the sonagrams as you listen to the sounds.

I can imagine several approaches to listening. Some readers will read the account of each species in the main text of the book and turn here and to the appropriate track on the CD as each is referenced. Others will read the entire account of a species before coming here to listen to all of the sounds for that species. I think I know where I'd be tempted to begin — I'd forgo all text initially and just feast on the sounds, playing the two CDs back-to-back and probably over and over again, marveling at the diversity of sounds and the variety of avian minds that produce them. Then I'd dive into the 24 accounts that are the heart of the book's text.

For a truly special listening experience, I repeat a message from the introduction, just in case you missed it there, as I so heartily recommend it. Go to the website at Cornell's Lab of Ornithology and download Raven Lite to your computer (www.birds.cornell.edu/brp/raven/RavenOverview.html). Once Raven Lite is on your computer, you can open any track on the two CDs and watch the sounds dance across your monitor as you listen to them. Using Raven Lite, you can also slow the sounds down to any speed you wish and watch them again. It's a whole new way of listening, as seeing and hearing these bird sounds simultaneously takes you one step closer to imagining what it must be like to be one of these birds, and that, after all, is the goal, to come to identify with these remarkable creatures that share our planet with us.

Additional listening is available at Cornell's Macaulay Library of Natural Sounds. You can explore their entire online collection of sounds (at www.birds.cornell.edu/macaulaylibrary/) and listen to almost any bird you could ever ask to hear. Here's just one example. In the account of the ruffed grouse, I mention a bird from British Columbia that likely represents a different species just waiting to be "discovered"; you can hear him for yourself in Cornell's catalog number 59280. On the website, just go to the archive and search for "59280." Or simply view all the "ruffed grouse" recordings and feast, as I did, on grouse drums across the continent. On this website is unlimited listening pleasure.

Most of the sounds on the two CDs were recorded in "stereo." For most of the recordings, I used two microphones inside a parabolic reflector, with a plastic shield separating the microphones (Telinga Pro5W); this device allows the focal bird to be loud in both left and right tracks, and background sounds are heard appropriately to the left and right, in simulated stereo. For some other recordings, I mounted two microphones into a device simulating a human head (two Sennheiser MKH20 mikes in a Crown SASS setup), the microphones then recording the sounds much as we would hear them. Less commonly used microphone systems are described where relevant.

Several different tape recorders were used, too. In January 2004, I favored my stereo minidisc recorder (HHB Portadisc MDP500). Shortly after that, I switched to my (currently) favorite recorder, one that records sounds in WAV file format directly to a computer hard drive (Sound Devices 722). As needed, a few other recorders were occasionally used along the way, too.

The sounds you hear on the two CDs are the sounds that I heard (and recorded) as I listened throughout the year. So that these sounds and the text here could best tell the story of the seasons, I have on occasion rearranged the sequence of sounds from that reported in the main text of the book (the hermit thrushes of November are moved to a sequence in June, for example). That rearrangement allows you to read here and listen independently of the main text, inviting you to listen continuously to the sounds of birds through the seasons.

Come now and listen to our planet sing, beginning with the sounds of a young female pileated woodpecker going to roost on New Year's Day and on through late December with the promise of spring on the winter solstice.

January

A PILEATED WOODPECKER GOES TO HER ROOST ON NEW YEAR'S DAY

January 1, 2004. Hear this young female pileated woodpecker announce the day's end as she approaches and enters her winter nesting cavity on New Year's Day.

Track 1-1: Initially she is perched about 100 yards away, calling sporadically there. She surveys her domain in silence for some seconds before, with a flurry of calling, she launches and in 6 seconds lands about 10 yards from her nest cavity; about 10 seconds after that she's airborne again, making her final approach to the nest cavity (figure 1, page 6). Once on the cavity entrance, she calls six more times in a second and a half, and then the scuffling of her feet on the entrance provides the last sounds as she settles into her winter roost for the next 15½ hours.

THE HARBINGERS OF SPRING (ROBINS) IN THEIR WINTER ROOST

During January nights, in the toughest of New England winter conditions, tens of thousands of robins gather from all over the Connecticut River Valley to huddle together in their winter roost. Listen to them here and to those who feed on them.

Track 1-2: January 2, 2006, 4:30 P.M. At dusk and under relatively mild winter conditions, thousands of robins jockey for position in the dense firs; hear their *tut*s and *piik*s and squeals and bill snaps as each searches for the perfect perch where it will spend the night. Listen, too, for the occasional high, thin whistles of brown-headed cowbirds and the whistling of mourning dove wings. A great horned owl hoots ominously in the background.

Track 1-3: January 15, 4:55 P.M. In the toughest of winter conditions, these robins have been out foraging throughout the Connecticut River Valley all day, and they now return after sunset. Feel the plummeting temperature as you listen to the raging winds; hear the *swoosh* of wings and calls of stressed robins as they arrive at the roost.

Track 1-4: January 15, 6:32 P.M. Footsteps in the night. Who has come to dine on the robins? Bobcat? Fox? Coyote?

Track 1-5: January 15, 7:45 P.M. Mayhem! The relative quiet of the early evening gives way to mass unrest. As the wind howls, hordes of robins take to the air, scattering and resettling about the roost. They *tut* and *piik* and squeal, some of those squeals no doubt robins in their death throes.

Track 1-6: January 16, 12:02 A.M. Just after midnight, the wind has calmed but the unrest continues, with robins resettling about the roost. Now, however, the source of the unrest is clear, as a great horned owl chortles nearby.

Track 1-7: January 16, 6:44 A.M. In the relative calm before sunrise, amid gentle *tut*s, the whir of wings tells of a contagious departure, the irresistible urge to depart en masse with those roosting nearby.

Track 1-8: January 16, 6:50 A.M. Once the robins are out of the firs and boiling overhead, the airspace is limited, and as they head out to feed for the day in their favorite places, they squawk and squeal, sometimes one bird chasing another, driving it toward the ground. Hear also the blue jays who have taken advantage of this communal roost.

AN ALL-NIGHTER AMONG THE WADING BIRDS IN THE EVERGLADES

Follow the winter sun south to Florida; come spend the night and listen to the symphony of sounds in the nightly wading bird roost at the end of the tram road in Shark Valley, Everglades National Park.

Track 1-9: As the day birds arrive at their night roost, listen to the black-crowned night-herons depart their day roost. Hear their *quork*s and *quark*s and *what*s as they fly by, fanning out to forage by night. Common yellowthroats sing in the background, a limpkin begins sounding off at 0:23 (for more limpkins, see tracks 1-17 to 1-20), and a pair of king rails duets during the last 10 seconds of this track.

Track 1-10: Birds of a feather leave together, it seems, the black-crowned night-herons in track 1-9 soon followed by these yellow-crowned night-herons. Hear the higher pitch of their calls, more of a *koak* or *kaow* than the deeper *quark*s of the black-crowns.

Track 1-11: In the waning light, see the great blue herons perched high and scattered about the roost. During the night, they sound off sporadically but contagiously, their harsh *fraaahnk, fraaahnk, fraak, fra* echoing throughout the roost. In this sequence are concentrated some of the louder sounds heard from nearby birds throughout the night. Last is one of these herons near sunrise, launching into the air, its wings flapping about four times a second, the *fraaahnk, fraaahnk, fraak, fra* fading into the distance as he flies by. See sonagrams of these sounds in figure 3 (page 28).

Track 1-12: A male eastern screech-owl calls softly off to the right, giving three of his bounce songs in this brief excerpt of his nighttime singing. If you listen carefully, just before his second call you'll hear the female answering in the far distance off to the left. Do you hear the difference in pitch? The whistles in his bounce call are at about 650 Hz, hers noticeably higher, at 750 Hz, roughly the difference between middle E and F sharp on a piano keyboard.

Track 1-13: In the dead of night, a common moorhen pipes its *pep pep pep* notes followed by its characteristic whines, which seems to prompt a limpkin and then a great blue heron to sound off, all in the first 15 seconds. Another great blue heron then replies, followed by more moorhen and limpkin calls.

Track 1-14: In the night, a few white ibis bleat in the roost. Then, at dawn, hear the commotion build until a thousand or more take to the air at once, lifting out of the roost and streaming past the tower, most of the birds heading to the north to forage for the day.

Track 1-15: Again, birds of a feather call together; the hundreds of white ibis having departed, the lower-pitched, more piglike grunts of the less numerous glossy ibis can be heard, and they soon depart, too, all together.

Track 1-16: Last to leave the roost is a magnificent wood stork. Storks are mute, making no vocal sounds as adults (though they clatter their bills), but hear the whistling of its wings as it launches directly out in front of the tower, flies briefly to the left and then across to the right, fading off into the distance.

February

THE LIMPKINS OF CORKSCREW SWAMP

The quiet of an early February night at Corkscrew Swamp near Naples, Florida, is shattered by the cries of a male limpkin just a few yards away.

Track 1-17: Spectacular, beyond belief, the male limpkin calls from the small island so near. With the parabolic microphone aimed at him, listen to the 12 ear-shattering *kur-r-ee-ow*s in this sequence, with the female adding her simple *gon* four times during his first four calls (figure 4, row 1, page 38).

Track 1-18: Nine minutes later he calls out again, but this time it's a series of simpler calls, not the longer *kur-r-ee-ow* but instead a briefer *keoow*. He clucks and stutters for about four seconds before offering eight *keoow*s, then stutters some more before finishing with six more *keeow*s. Hear her three *gon*s during the first series.

Track 1-19: Here he pulls out all the stops, this time calling for well over four minutes. Just listen to his *keeow*s interspersed with some stuttering and pauses of a few seconds, and he ends it all with two of the longer, more complex *kur-r-ee-ow*s, as if they are the fitting conclusion to such a fine performance. His pure *keeow*s at times become hoarse, raising all kinds of questions. Even more intriguing is the female contribution to this performance. The female off to the left calls occasionally from high in the cypress trees, but at about 1:50 a second female offers a single *gon*, this one at a lower frequency and seemingly closer to the calling male. That *gon* prompts a rapid series of the higher-frequency calls from the (perhaps younger?) female high in the trees to the left. Who are these females, and what are their relationships to him (figure 4, row 3, page 38)?

Track 1-20: Liftoff! Five minutes after his last *kur-r-ee-ow*, he lifts off from his singing place on the small island, the labored wingbeats lifting him high into the cypress to the left. Before he even lands, the nearby female offers a *gon*, followed by 20 of his calls, many seemingly crosses between a pure *keeow* and a *kur-r-ee-ow*, the last of which seems but a whimper. How intriguing that his last call is offered from the highest vantage point, and that she calls more intensely now than ever, calling *gon* 12 times during his first 14 calls. Soon both birds glide down and slip away into the marsh (figure 4, row 4, page 38).

FLORIDA SCRUB-JAY FAMILIES

Florida scrub-jays don't have long, extended songs by which they enthrall either themselves or us humans; rather, they use a variety of brief calls, the subtle differences among them no doubt conveying a variety of important messages to the jays. Listen in on some of these calls, trying to identify with these remarkable birds in the scrub oak communities at the Archbold Biological Station. The family consists of Al and Betty, the parents; Cindy, the nearly two-year-old daughter; and Lily, Linda, Ron, and Roy, the yearlings.

Track 1-21: The *hiccup*. Big Sister Cindy is courting the unpaired male who holds a territory to the north. Listen here as the male calls *weep weep weep weep weep* in the distance from his territory, and by the sixth *weep*, within two seconds, Cindy is responding from her family's territory with her sexy *hiccup* call (figure 5, page 48).

Track 1-22: Off by himself on the northern end of the family territory, young Ron begins calling, though for what purpose is anyone's guess. In this brief excerpt of one minute and 16 seconds from his five-and-a-half-minute soliloquy, listen carefully to successive *weep* sounds. The majority of sounds in the first half minute seem to be of one kind, the majority in the last half minute of another kind, but within and especially between those series successive sounds sometimes vary in subtle ways. His slightly wavering voice suggests that he may be off here by himself just to practice the subtle intonations required for accomplished jay-speak. But, then, given how much I have come to admire these jays, I wouldn't be surprised if Ron were discussing matters of great significance with the neighboring widower who has designs on Ron's older sister.

Track 1-23: Calls of the sentinel. As the scrub-jays forage on the ground, they're particularly vulnerable to hawks that might suddenly arrive on the scene, so one jay is often perched above them and alert for possible danger. Sometimes these sentinels call, as if to assert that all is well. In the first 48 seconds here, listen to Betty as she calls from her perch, the occasional wings of family members heard as they fly about foraging below her (in the background can be heard calls of towhees, robins, and palm warblers); hear how consistently she calls, successive *weep*s varying little except for emphasis. Then, for another 15 seconds, listen to the calls of her daughter Lily while she perches above the family. Hear again how the tonal quality of successive calls is similar, but how they vary slightly in duration and emphasis.

Track 1-24: Not all calls are loud and harsh. Betty here gives soft, low-pitched, guttural *churr*s when she drops down from her sentinel duty and greets other members of her family. At the end of this sequence, listen to the blue and red metal bands jingle on her right leg as she scratches her head.

Track 1-25: Al is king of the family, dominant over all, and as peanuts are tossed to the group, he lets it be known who is boss. To the sounds of jays fluttering for the best position, he calls loudly, not once but twice, asserting that he has first rights.

Track 1-26: These scrub-jays appear able to produce an astounding variety of *weep* calls, so when the kids all give what seems to be the same call in rapid succession (figure 6, page 52), something special must be going on — it's just that we humans have no idea what it is. Listen here first to Lily (15 seconds), then Roy (15 seconds), then Linda with the jay I believe to be Ron giving the same call in the background (14 seconds).

THE ANHINGAS OF ANHINGA TRAIL, EVERGLADES NATIONAL PARK

Beginning two hours before a February sunrise, come listen to the life along the Everglades' Anhinga Trail. Anhingas themselves are not known for "singing," but the young birds in the nest certainly wow those walking by whom I invite to listen over the headphones.

Track 1-27: Two hours before sunrise, stand in the darkness on the boardwalk and feel the love in the growling of courting alligators just below.

Track 1-28: Just 15 or so yards off the boardwalk to the north and roosting in the island of pond apples are the double-crested cormorants. Hear their guttural, piglike grunts, their snarls and moans, how some also seem to cough and sneeze. In the background, red-winged blackbirds sing *konk-la-ree*, catbirds *meow*, and barred owls *who-who-who-who-all*.

Track 1-29: Watch (in figure 7, page 57) and listen as the incubating male anhinga stretches his neck out to the female who roosts nearby, the two of them erupting simultaneously into their clicking and chattering greeting ceremony. As their necks arch back and with open bills swaying like two dancing snakes, their *chitter-chitter-chitter-chee-cheer-chitter-chitter-chitter* keeps pace, rising and falling, undulating, keeping tune to the dancing snake. In the background are the footsteps and voices of potential victims who will soon don my headphones and pronounce the world such a beautiful place.

Track 1-30: How continuously this lone, young anhinga calls from the nest, cycling once a second as if a metronome, sounding as if he breathes out on his rapid chatter and then catches his breath on his lower, tonal note (figure 7, page 57).

Track 1-31: As an adult anhinga arrives near the nest, the youngster calls more frantically, his chatter now often much higher-pitched and more modulated, his lower tonal notes higher in frequency, too, all of which is designed to make him sound excruciatingly hungry, just desperate for food. As the adult leaves, he quiets, though only momentarily (figure 7, page 57).

Track 1-32: Imagine walking along the Anhinga Trail boardwalk and encountering someone like me with headphones, tape recorder, and parabolic reflector on a tripod. We strike up a conversation, about birds, of course, and soon we talk about listening, after which I invite you to try listening over the headphones. To the striking sounds of a chorus of these nestling anhingas, you'd probably respond as others did on the boardwalk: *"fabulous . . . fantastic . . . cool . . . awesome . . . sensational . . . you've changed my life . . ."* Amplified and focused, the world of bird sound suddenly comes alive, and now not only do you see but also you hear and feel and smell. You're more alert overall, hearing in the background the *chitter* and *chatter* of adult anhingas in the trees, the *quark* and *skeow* of herons all about, and all the little sounds that went unnoticed before.

Track 1-33: Well below the higher-pitched calls of a few songbirds and nestling anhingas, hear the soft, low warble of the male anhinga as he courts his mate. How striking is his display as he erects the feathers on his neck and head, waves his wings slowly, bows deeply forward and then backward with head on his back, the body wavering from side to side, feathers slightly quivering, all as he warbles.

March

SANDHILL CRANES ON THE PLATTE RIVER

How could any life be complete without a visit to one of the greatest wildlife spectacles in all of North America, the spring migration of half a million cranes through Nebraska?

Track 1-34: The cranes having streamed into their roosting places in the Platte River, listen to the general clamor from tens of thousands of these magnificent creatures about an hour after sunset, around 8:00 P.M. Complementing the incessant bugling and trumpeting of the adults are the occasional bleats of the colts, yearling cranes who have yet to develop their adult voices. Geese cackle and yelp overhead, too, as they mill about.

Track 1-35: Only half an hour later, about 8:30 P.M., the general clamor dies and more individual voices can be heard as the cranes settle in for the night. Listen especially for the male-female duets, typically the male bugling first, followed quickly by a higher-pitched female. These are ancient sounds from ancient times; fossils of these cranes date back over 2 million years throughout North America. Listen to voices from the crowd as individual males and females affirm their lifelong commitment to each other, as they mate for life, their "till death do us part" far more literal than the weaker human bonds.

Track 1-36: After another half-hour, about 9:00 P.M., a flock of cranes arrives from the left, circling over the colony as they no doubt search for a place to roost. When they pass over the first time, flying to the right, and then the second time, flying back to the left, listen for the bleating of the colts below them. The bleating continues in the relative silence after the flock has passed. It is at this time of the annual cycle that the parents and yearling colts separate for good, and perhaps it is the calling of the colts here that best signifies that initial feeling of a lonely youngster setting out all on his own.

Track 1-37: Liftoff by thousands upon thousands of cranes! It is a sight and a sound beyond belief, deafening, mind-boggling, as so many of these ancient creatures take to the air. Neighboring birds, especially those in small family units, watch one another carefully, all facing the same direction and making "intention movements," signaling with their bodies that they are soon to depart. And then they're off, launching from the river and fanning out over the Nebraska farmlands in search of fuel for their eventual migratory flight far to the north.

April

A TROPICAL PILGRIMAGE

So many of "our" North American birds return to their ancestral home each year during our northern winter. I try to make my own tropical pilgrimage each year, and during 2006, I toured by bicycle from Managua, Nicaragua, to San José, Costa Rica, listening all along the way.

Track 1-38: GREAT KISKADEE. PART 1 (0:00–0:25). Isla de Ometepe, Lake Nicaragua. To the dawn sounds of night-herons and a giant marine toad, a great kiskadee calls in the distance, answered immediately with a *weeer* by the kiskadee overhead. Two seconds later, it's a slightly longer call, *weeeer*, followed immediately by *weeer*, *weee-eep* (a two-part, emphatic note ending high), *zikikikikikik* (a raucous chatter), *weee-eep zikikikikik*, *weee-eep weee-eep zikikikikik*, and after a slight pause *weee-eep weee-eep . . . weee-eep* (figure 8, page 78). These sounds were recorded with two binaural microphones mounted just in front of my ears on my eyeglasses; by wearing headphones, you hear the morning awaken as I heard it standing there. I yearned for my parabolic reflector so that I could capture the songs as he sang them rather than as I heard them, but for this bicycle tour I had to leave the more cumbersome gear at home.

PART 2 (0:25–1:15). The kiskadee continues to sing overhead, but the mnemonics fail to capture the nuances of his calls. Hear the subtle differences in pitch, inflection, loudness, and duration of the "simple" *weeer* calls. This sequence begins with *weeer*, followed in rapid succession by *weee-eep zikikikikikik weee-eep*, then *weeer weee-eep weee-eep zikikikikikik*, with more calling throughout this selection.

PART 3 (1:15–1:35). He continues, in this section with a *chick-weeer*, then *chick-weeer weee-eep weeeer zikikikikikik weee-eep*, another *weeer*, followed soon after by *weeeer weee-eep zikikikikikik*.

PART 4 (1:35–2:02). Finally, as if he had just been warming up during all of the previous sounds, he launches into a series of *kis-ka-dee* calls. Then he's gone, as this bird—actually either male or female—seems to fly off into the distance and greet others of its kind with a raucous chorus of *kis-ka-dee*s.

Track 1-39: BANDED WREN. For two minutes this banded wren is in fine dawn form as he sings a varied sequence of delightfully beautiful songs (figure 9, page 81). Hear the variety, trying to follow along in the sequence (which arbitrarily starts with the letter "M") M N M N M P P P Q R R S S S. At first he alternates two different songs, M and N, then he offers Song P three times, becoming increasingly repetitive as he delivers Songs R and S. At about two minutes into this sequence, the interaction with his neighbor escalates, as summarized in the following table; try to follow along in the table as you listen, marking the double songs of the neighbor in the background as you monitor the exchange. Over the next minute and 20 seconds, this wren sings 11 A songs in the foreground (some in double or triple songs), and as you listen to the bird in the background, you'll hear 13 A songs in response, as summarized in the following table (see text):

Near bird	A	B		A		A		A	B	AA		AAA		A		A
Neighbor			AA		AA		AA			A	AA		AA		AA	

If you listen to this selection several times, you begin to hear more and more of how these neighboring territorial wrens interact, both during the first two minutes and during the escalation. (Recorded with a short, "shotgun" microphone and minidisc recorder—not the best combination to capture a singing neighborhood, but it's what I could carry on my bike.)

Track 1-40: THREE-WATTLED BELLBIRD. Not only does a male bellbird learn his songs but he must relearn them continually as he keeps pace with the changing songs in the population. In this track, I have *simulated* how the whistles in the "four-whistle" song from the Monteverde, Costa Rica, dialect have changed from 1974 to 2006. The four songs illustrated represent the years 1974, 1987, 2002, and 2006 (spans of 13, 15, and 4 years), with whistle frequencies of 5,600 Hz, 4,600 Hz, 3,610 Hz, and 3,400 Hz (differences of 1,000 Hz, 1,010 Hz, and 210 Hz for the three time spans). I constructed these songs by taking a song from the year 2001 and adjusting the whistle frequencies to match the frequencies that we have measured for each year. Listen especially to the change from 2002 to 2006, as this is the change that I heard when I stood beneath the bellbirds in the Reserva Bosque Nuboso, Santa Elena, Monteverde.

Track 1-41: CLAY-COLORED ROBIN. While I was packing my bicycle into its suitcase for the return trip home, the national bird of Costa Rica began singing in the courtyard. Mesmerized, I laid the microphone down on the windowsill and captured the songs much as I heard them, with all of the echo and reverberation one would expect under such conditions (and so unlike the sharp, crisp songs that would be recorded with a parabolic reflector aimed at the bird). Just like the daytime singing of the American robin, this bird sings a series of caroled phrases and then pauses briefly before moving on to the next series.

As he sang, I listened especially for two phrases I could distinguish from all the others, a down-slurred *phew* (A) and a *chu-wi* (B) that rapidly fell and then rose. In the selection on the CD, try to pick out those two phrases. I offer the following guide for the first five series of caroled phrases (with a dash representing a caroled phrase that is neither A nor B):

- - - - - A - B - - A - -
- - - - - - - B A - A - - - - - - -

```
- - - - - - - - A
- - - B A
- - - - B - - A - - - - - -
```

From there you're on your own. Try to pick out more of the *phew* and *chu-wi* phrases in the sequences that follow, but listen for others that you might be able to identify, too, and listen also for the ubiquitous great kiskadee in the background.

May

TWO VIRGINIA MIMICS: BROWN THRASHER, WHITE-EYED VIREO

Immerse yourself in the songs of a fine spring morning, and inevitably a few birds will speak to you in some special way. So it was with me during this first weekend in May in western Virginia, as a brown thrasher and a white-eyed vireo caught my ear.

Track 1-42: *I'm here I'm here, listen up listen up, record me record me* this brown thrasher seems to be singing, couplet after couplet raining down on me from just overhead. Accepting the invitation, I raise the parabolic reflector and slip the headphones over my ears, bedazzled as this brown thrasher speaks his mind. As he sings, I accept each couplet for what it is, but I also strain to identify the possible source of his sounds. Those for which I am most confident are as follows: song sparrow phrase at 0:33, Carolina chickadee song 0:44, American goldfinch 0:51, Carolina chickadee *chick-a-dee* call 1:14, American robin call 1:45, female red-winged blackbird call 1:49, northern flicker song 2:13, northern cardinal whistle 2:21, Carolina chickadee song 2:30. For sonagrams of the chickadee mimicry, see figure 10 (page 92).

Track 1-43: The male white-eyed vireo is a remarkable mimic (figure 11, pages 94–95). He sings with "eventual variety," repeating one of his songs dozens of times before switching to another, and most of the snappy little notes within his songs are pilfered from the calls of other species. Listen here to three examples of each of the 10 different songs from the male who sang to me. In the following list, I describe how I came to recognize each of these songs (usually by a mimicked element).

A (0:02) 4 *whit* notes of wood thrush at beginning
B (0:26) nasal *chew* at beginning, unknown origin
C (0:48) *piiik* note of American robin at beginning of song

D (1:04)   *whit whit* of wood thrush, mid-song
E (1:23)   *klear* note of northern flicker
F (1:40)   *chewink* of eastern towhee
G (2:04)   *nyeeh* of red-eyed vireo
H (2:23)   *tut* of American robin at beginning of song
I (2:44)   *jay* of blue jay
J (3:02)   *jeeer* of Carolina wren

Track 1-44: A singing bird wouldn't want to waste his effort, so he tends to sing when other birds don't interfere with his message. In the 70 seconds of singing in this track are a total of 28 songs from a white-eyed vireo, Carolina wren, and eastern towhee. Listen to how each bird inserts its songs into the silent intervals between the others' songs in the following sequence: *vireo, towhee, vireo, towhee, vireo, towhee, wren, vireo, wren, towhee, wren, vireo, wren, towhee, vireo, wren, vireo, towhee, v/wren, vireo, towhee, wren, vireo, towhee, wren, vireo, wren, towhee.* The loud, aggressive wren seems to control the tempo, and once (at *v/wren*) the vireo begins his song but is interrupted by the wren; the vireo immediately stops and resumes after the wren has finished his song.

BALTIMORE ORIOLE—SHE SINGS, TOO

Among most North American songbirds, only the males sing, but the females of a few species also sing.

Track 1-45: Listen here as the incubating female Baltimore oriole responds to the song of her mate nearby. In these exchanges, excerpted from several hours of listening and recording, hear how the male typically first offers part or all of his four-note song, the last two notes higher than the first two: *tew tew twe twe*. She responds, sometimes with a single note but often with her entire song, a wonderfully rhythmic *we-chew-dle-wee-dle-wee-dle-weet*. (Sonagrams of representative sounds from tracks 1-45 to 1-47 are in figure 12, page 103.)

Track 1-46: Sometimes a male and female have almost identical songs, as illustrated here. Listen to the male, while he chatters first, then chatters briefly again before singing his full six-note song. She responds a few seconds later from high in the canopy where she sits on the nest; her four-note song is essentially identical to the first four notes of his (figure 12, page 103).

Track 1-47: Often it seems that the male's song is far more complex than that of his mate. In this selection, listen to the male's rich, complex songs, not all of which are complete, and then to the female's relatively simple song at the end, consisting of five low notes and one high note, as in *tew tew tew tew tew twe* (figure 12, page 103).

A PRAIRIE DAWN ON OUR PAWNEE NATIONAL GRASSLAND

Come travel with me to our Pawnee National Grassland, in north-central Colorado, during the early-morning hours of late May. A horned lark sings from the ground in the predawn darkness, but without trees or other elevated perches from which to sing, a sparrow and bunting and longspur sing on the wing.

Track 1-48: A horned lark perches nearby on the ground and sings nonstop four to five tinkling notes a second, on and on, occasionally punctuating his message with a slurred flourish in which seemingly stuttered notes rise rapidly (figure 13, page 110). (Hear these flourishes at 0:50, 1:26, 1:30, 1:33, 2:17, 2:40, and 2:57.) Stored in his memory and fully at his command are about 200 of these tinkling notes and about 10 different flourishes, and they are combined in what must be an endless variety of song, perhaps even the bird not knowing exactly what is coming next. In the background, a lark bunting sings, but if you listen to the metronomic rhythm of the horned lark, you come to distinguish easily which notes belong to the horned lark and which to the lark bunting (nighthawk "booms" are prominent in the background).

Track 1-49: This Cassin's sparrow has been singing from a perch much of the night, but now, against the glow of the eastern horizon, see him launch upward, flying at a 45-degree angle and beginning his song just before he reaches his peak of about five yards, then setting his wings and continuing his song as he glides back to earth. In this selection, as he skylarks about his territory, he sings his three different songs in the sequence A A B B B C A A A B (figure 14, page 115). In the background are songs of horned larks, lark buntings, western meadowlarks, and mourning doves.

Track 1-50: Listen to the wings of this lark bunting as he takes flight and then, on the wing, offers his bold, clear, eight-second song (figure 15, page 118). He lands and sings briefly from his perch before launching again, singing alternately from land and air in this sequence. Hear how each song, no matter its duration, always begins with the same phrase. Other birds sing in the background, including another lark bunting, horned larks, and a nighthawk.

Track 1-51: What a spectacular sight and sound is this group song flight by three male lark buntings as they twist and fly about one another and gradually fade into the distance. During a brief lull midflight, only one male seems to be singing, but then they all surge again.

Track 1-52: The McCown's longspur perches on the ground and then takes flight into the wind, rising steeply to about 50 feet before he begins his tinkling song, which then continues as he floats back to earth. He perches briefly, then flies again, repeating this cycle. Some songs are short but some far longer as he glides into the wind and stays aloft longer. Try to hear how each song begins in the same way, with the first one to two seconds similar, but then diverges to its own unique conclusion (figure 16, page 120).

June

BELTED KINGFISHERS ON THE CONNECTICUT RIVER

Heaven is sitting on the banks of the Connecticut River and listening to a spring morning, with a special focus on the kingfishers.

Track 1-53: A beaver swims by, notices me, and registers its protest by slapping its tail on the water, first nearby and then, 10 seconds later, a little farther downstream.

Tracks 1-54, 1-55: Swimming slowly upstream is a female wood duck followed closely by a mostly silent male. Hear her off to the right, then just offshore, then upstream to the left. Shortly after that (track 1-55), they're up in the tree above. She calls nearly continuously, a long series of simple calls often ending in a high squeal so reminiscent of her loud, squealing *oo-eek* alarm call, which is the only call most of us associate with wood ducks.

Track 1-56: The kingfishers arrive on their favorite perches, the emerging limbs of dead trees lying in the river just out from their nest cavity. First it is the female who arrives, landing just a little off to the left (as heard especially well if you listen with headphones); shortly after that, the male calls in the distance and arrives with a flurry of calling, landing a little farther away and to the right. What follows is a gentle banter, the female close by, the male slightly farther away, until the male flies to the female and they call together nearby. He then calls as he flies from perch to perch, and soon both take flight, fading off into the distance (figure 17, page 128).

Track 1-57: The male kingfisher flies in, landing just off to the right on a perch in front of the nest cavity. He calls there a few times, makes a loud vocal approach to a perch just outside the cavity, calls three more times, and then calls while flying into the nest cavity itself. In the background are a titmouse, a cardinal, a song sparrow, and, faintly, the female wood duck. Fifty minutes later (shortened to 10 seconds on the CD), the titmouse now having changed its song and a Carolina wren singing, too, the male emerges with a loud rattle and flies downstream to a favored perch. He calls there a few times before flying off downstream.

Track 1-58: The female's approach and departure are much the same as the male's. She flies in quietly, perches just outside the nest cavity, and calls softly. The female wood duck calls below in the water; she and her mate eventually fly off, leaving the female kingfisher and in the background a singing titmouse. She probably knows the male is in the nest cavity, but in she then flies, rattling on entry. Two minutes later he rattles as he departs (see track 1-57). And over an hour later (eight seconds here), she departs as he did, with a loud rattle and flying downstream to the same perch where he had paused before flying downstream and then over the trees, probably to the feeding grounds on nearby Great Pond.

LISTENING WITH DAVE: A JUNE DAWN IN HATFIELD CEMETERY

Cemeteries are birdy places and offer fine listening opportunities in peaceful settings. Here are the songbird stories overheard in a cemetery in western Massachusetts near the gravesite of my longtime friend and listening partner Dave Stemple.

Track 1-59: One of the first singers of the morning is the eastern bluebird. Hear how varied his songs are, all beginning with the typical predawn chatter. While the parabola is trained on the bluebird at eye level, a northern cardinal sings overhead; listen to the background as the cardinal sings one of the songs in his repertoire three times, then switches to another.

Track 1-60: The cardinal is irresistible, and I swing the parabola from the bluebird to the cardinal overhead. Listen to the first song, a song that might be phrased *wheet-wheet-wheet-wheet-chew-chew-chew-chew*, the *wheet* rising in frequency, the *chew* falling (Song A). The second and third songs are the same, except to the second the cardinal appends what sounds like the chatter of a red squirrel. Next are three examples of a simpler song (B), which consists mostly of four to six down-slurred whistles. Listen on for three examples of another song (C) and then two of still another (D), so that in this brief sample the cardinal sings A A A B B B C C C D D. These songs are part of a longer series of 63 songs in which the cardinal sang 6 examples of one type, then switched to another song and sang 13 of it, then 11 of another, then 8, 12, 3, 5, and 5 songs of other types before flying off.

Track 2-1: The chipping sparrow who owns the birch tree where I stand has now flown in from his distant discussions with two neighboring chippies to the east, and he sings just off to the south. His songs are no longer the staccato, spitfire songs of the predawn darkness, but he still sings fairly rapidly, delivering a song every three to five seconds. On the fifth song, hear the distant crow, who flies closer and closer, the parabolic microphone following him until he lands in the birch tree overhead.

The crow now calls from the treetop while the chipping sparrow continues in the background. At first it's a leisurely *ca ca ca*, up to seven at a time, but then there's a sudden franticness to his calling (at 1:27), a rapid burst of these same sharp calls, a good dozen in all before the pace slows again (figure 19A and B, page 139). A second crow arrives (2:32), and they dance about in silence atop the birch, no doubt listening to the other crows in the distance. For nearly 30 seconds they are silent, and then, in a 2-second burst of calling, they reveal so much of what I love about crows. As the second crow delivers a typical *caaw caaw caaw caaw* series, the first crow calls sharply *ca-ca* and then switches midstream to match the throaty quality of the second crow's *caaw*s (figure 19C, page 139).

In the following minutes, the first bird typically uses a throaty *caw*, the second bird a slightly longer *caaw* of the same throaty quality. Throughout this selection, the two crows call, and every minute or so the second bird shortens the duration of his *caaw* to match the *caw* of the first bird. Listen here to the entire sequence at normal speed, and then listen to some of the highlights of this interaction at half speed on track 2-2.

Track 2-2: Crow calls at half speed are far more easily deciphered by our ears. In this track are selected calls from the two crows in track 2-1.

A (0:00–0:07). Six calls of the first crow to land in the birch tree. These are not the throaty *caw*s of a typical crow call but instead are much sharper, as in *ca-ca-ca-ca-ca-ca* (figure 19A, page 139).

B (0:11–0:20). The same crow almost doubles the pace now, calling frantically; the calls are still not throaty, as the quality and duration of each call is pretty much the same as when he called more slowly (figure 19B, page 139).

C (0:24–0:29). Two crows now call simultaneously. The second crow to arrive in the tree utters a throaty *caaw-caaw-caaw-caaw*, four in all. Simultaneously, the first bird utters two sharp *ca* notes and then switches to a more throaty *caw*, of the same quality as the second bird's *caaw* but not quite as long: *ca-ca-caw-caw* (figure 19C, page 139). Try to follow along in this schematic as you listen:

Bird 1:   *ca*   *ca*   *caw*   *caw*
Bird 2: *caaw*   *caaw*   *caaw*   *caaw*

D (0:33–0:44). Here are the typical calls of these two crows, uttered in succession, the throaty *caw-caw-caw* of the first crow followed by the slightly longer *caaw-caaw-caaw* of the second bird (figure 19D, page 139).

Bird 1: *caw caw caw*
Bird 2:   *caaw*   *caaw*   *caaw*

E (0:48–0:55). Most of the time the two crows call with their distinctive voices, but here the second crow matches the first, each of them using the shorter *caw*. But alas, I do not know which bird is which! If I use A to designate one bird and B the other, hear what I believe is the following sequence of *caw*s: A A AB AB AB AB AB A. Bird A calls eight times, Bird B five (not illustrated in figure).

Bird A: *caw*   *caw*   *caw*   *caw*   *caw*   *caw*   *caw*   *caw*
Bird B: *caw*   *caw*   *caw*   *caw*   *caw*

F (0:59–1:07). Again the second crow shifts from his longer *caaw* to match the shorter *caw* of the first bird. Listen carefully and you'll hear how this sequence begins unmistakably with the second crow's longer *caaw*; what follow are two more of those long *caaw* notes, but simultaneously the first crow offers three shorter *caw* notes. On the next two notes, the two crows *caw* simultaneously, the second crow having now shortened the duration of his longer *caaw* to match the *caw* of the first crow. I think the last three *caw*s are from the first crow, but I can't be sure (not illustrated).

Bird 1:   *caw*   *caw caw caw*   *caw caw caw caw*
Bird 2: *caaw*   *caaw*   *caaw*   *caw*   *caw*

G (1:12–1:25). It's much easier to hear how the second crow matches the first in this sequence. First, there are three of the longer *caaw* notes from the second crow. Next, the first bird calls seven times, *caw-caw-caw-caw-caw-caw-caw*, followed immediately by the second bird adding three identical notes of its own, *caw-caw-caw*, the entire 10-*caw* sequence sounding as if it were one bird (figure 19E, page 139).

Bird 1:   *caw caw caw caw caw caw caw*
Bird 2: *caaw*   *caaw*   *caaw*   *caw caw caw*

H (1:28–1:36). And just before the second crow departs, he matches the first crow one more time. The second crow begins the sequence with a long *caaw*. During its next two *caaw* notes, the first crow *caw*s twice. The first crow then offers a solo *caw* before the two birds *caw* in unison three times. I believe Bird 2 contributes that solo *caw* on the end (not illustrated).

Bird 1:   *caw*   *caw caw caw*   *caw caw*
Bird 2: *caaw*   *caaw*   *caaw*   *caw caw caw caw*

Track 2-3: Here are the sounds of a male house finch who is excited by a nearby female. Listen to him sputter at first, and then he launches into a song followed by two high notes, the songs and high notes then alternating for about a minute before he slows to a sputter again (figure 20, page 140).

Track 2-4: A starling, one of the most extraordinary singers in North America, though he's so underrated, mostly because his songs are so softly and subtly given (and, of course, because many listeners simply hate this introduced bird that ousts native birds from their nesting cavities). He begins with a low, throaty whistle, *weeeeoooooo,* rising and falling over two seconds, the sure sign that the show is about to begin, and then he's off! Please see pages 139–140 in the text for the details of this recording. Listen especially for the sequence of *jay jay caw jay jay caw jay jay caw* (0:18–0:21), when he mimics American crows and blue jays.

Track 2-5: The male savannah sparrow arrives after most of the other singers have had their say. Listen to how he stutters at the beginning, then offers a high buzz followed by a lower one. He seems to sing *take take take take-it eeeeeeeaaaaa-ssssssyyyyyyyyy* (figure 21, page 141). Over and over he delivers the only song that he knows, at a leisurely pace of about six songs a minute.

TIME TRAVEL: REVISITING TWO HERMIT THRUSHES IN JUNE

(Note: In the text, this hermit thrush story takes place during November. I have moved the songs to this place on the CD, however, so that they occur in the correct seasonal context.)

The only song better than a singing hermit thrush is two singing hermit thrushes. When a male sings, he chooses his next song so that it is especially different not only from his previous song but also from the previous song of his neighbor. The effect is stunning.

Track 2-6: Three songs of a hermit thrush (Bird 1 from Quabbin Park, Massachusetts), with the introductory whistles at about 4,200, 3,000, and

2,000 Hz (see figure 42, page 244). Listen to a typical sequence at normal speed first and then to the same three songs slowed down to half, quarter, and one-eighth speed. What extraordinary activity in those two voice boxes as he tumbles through the flourish, and what delightfully unearthly sounds.

Track 2-7: Come sit with me in the predawn darkness and listen to these two hermit thrushes. The left microphone is beneath Bird 1, the right beneath Bird 2, the two birds about 250 feet apart. Listen as they take turns singing, first a song from the left, then the right, back and forth, filling almost all available airtime. Listen to how each male bounces about the frequency spectrum of his songs so that successive songs are especially different, and then listen to how the two birds respond to each other, each male seeming to sing a song that is especially different not only from his own previous song but also from the previous song of his neighbor (see figures 43, 44, pages 246–247 and 250). (My original field recording in which I documented the exchanges between these two birds was of relatively poor quality, so I simulated this exchange by taking high-quality recordings for each of the two males and splicing them into a sequence that simulates the real interaction.)

BLACKBURNIAN WARBLERS OF MOUNT GREYLOCK

Stunningly beautiful, the Blackburnian warblers sing from high in the treetops of boreal coniferous forests. Come spend the morning and listen to these birds on Mount Greylock, the highest point in Massachusetts; the birds chip and sing frenetically during the dawn chorus, and just before sunrise switch to their daytime songs.

Track 2-8: When a male Blackburnian warbler sings in the predawn darkness, he usually chips vigorously, pausing to sing every few seconds. Here Bird 5 offers seven renditions of his standard dawn songs, each preceded and followed by his dawn chipping. Contrast this male's dawn singing with his daytime singing in track 2-10.

Track 2-9: A sample song (or two) and chipping from 11 Blackburnian warblers singing during the dawn chorus. Listen to the variety of expressions here among the birds, hearing not only each male's unique song but also how he chips (or doesn't) between songs. Sample sonagrams for four of these birds are in figure 23, page 147.

Bird 1, 0:00–0:16, with typical dawn frenetic chipping before and after the song.

Bird 2, 0:18–0:46. This male has two different dawn songs. In the first selection, he chips vigorously, then offers his unique song of descending notes.

In the second, he delivers a song that is more typical of the other warblers in the neighborhood; it was recorded later in the morning, without the dawn chip notes.

Bird 3, 0:48–0:55.

Bird 4, 0:57–1:12.

Bird 5, 1:13–1:21.

Bird 6. No dawn song recorded from this male.

Bird 7, 1:23–1:31.

Bird 8, 1:33–1:43.

Bird 9, 1:45–1:59.

Bird 10, 2:00–2:12.

Quabbin 1, 2:14–2:30. Listen especially to the two end notes, as those were not heard at Mount Greylock, just 50 miles to the west.

Quabbin 3, 2:32–2:47.

Track 2-10: Daytime singing by Greylock Male 5, with five songs over about 50 seconds; never does a male chip between these daytime songs. These are the *wee-see-wee-see-wee-see-wee-see-weeeeee* songs so similar to the daytime songs of the black-and-white warbler. Two chipping sparrows sing nearby in the background. Contrast this male's daytime singing with his dawn singing in track 2-8.

Track 2-11: Sample daytime songs from 10 Blackburnian warblers, all of the same basic *wee-see-wee-see-wee-see-wee-see-weeeeee* format. Songs of Mount Greylock birds: Bird 2's song occurs at 0:02; 3, 0:08; 5, 0:13; 6, 0:18; 8, 0:22; 9, 0:27; 10, 0:33 (daytime song of Birds 1 and 4 were too poorly recorded to include here, and no daytime song was recorded for Bird 7). Songs of Quabbin birds: 1, 0:38; 2, 0:42; 3, 0:48. In figure 24 (page 149) one can see the differences between the songs of Mount Greylock and Quabbin birds; test your ears to determine if you can hear them, too.

July

THE DAWN AND DAY SONGS OF SCARLET TANAGERS

Tropical jewels in a temperate forest, scarlet tanagers are better known for their looks than for their "hoarse robin" song. How fascinating, though, to hear them greet the day with their methodical dawn singing, such a contrast to the typical song of later in the day.

Track 2-12: Dawn singing by the scarlet tanager (figure 25, page 158). Listen to the halting performance by this male singing in his lofty perch in the ash tree. He delivers five song phrases, then a *chip-burr* call; then seven phrases and a *chip-burr;* five phrases, *chip-burr;* five more phrases and a *chip-burr;* and so on, ending this selection on the CD with two *chip-burr*s. Follow along for the two minutes, feeling the rhythm of his singing, perhaps counting the number of song phrases between successive *chip-burr* calls, perhaps trying to identify a particular song phrase to see if you can recognize it when it occurs again.

Track 2-13: How different is the daytime singing of this same scarlet tanager (figure 25, page 158). Now after sunrise, he sings four or five phrases in a discrete package and then pauses several seconds before singing again. Listen to how all of the songs begin with the same two song phrases (A B). Sounds in the background include a red squirrel calling repeatedly, perhaps disturbed at my presence; a pileated woodpecker drumroll in the distance at 0:12 and 0:51; as well as a few distant songbirds.

YEARLING INDIGO BUNTINGS LEARN THE LOCAL MICRODIALECT

Yearling indigo buntings can be identified by the splotches of brown in their plumage, and older birds are typically a resplendent indigo. Early in the season, when the birds are just back from migration, their songs differ, too: Older birds have stable, well-formed songs that they learned in previous years, but the songs of a yearling vary wildly as he comes to learn the song of an older neighbor.

Track 2-14: Five songs of Ol' Blue, the bird who was two years or older at the Enfield Lookout, Quabbin Park. Feel the rhythm, the *fire fire where where heeerre my my run run run faster faster safe safe pheewww*, the paired phrases at the beginning followed by the single up-slurred buzzy *heeerre*, then more paired (or triple) phrases, ending with the *pheewww* buzzy phrase on the end. Or try to follow along by simply counting phrases: 2 2 *buzz* 2 3 2 2 *buzz*. In the background are the songs of Li'l Brown, the yearling who learned almost the entire song of Ol' Blue (see figure 26, page 167).

Track 2-15: Ten songs of Li'l Brown, recorded June 17, by which time he had copied most of the song of Ol' Blue. The song of Ol' Blue contains the phrases A B C D E F G H, the song of Li'l Brown now A B D E F G I J, omitting the two buzzy phrases (C and H) and adding two other phrases (I J) to the end. I confess I was frustrated trying to record the songs of Li'l Brown, as he seemed to stay so distant, so I played one of his songs to him; he then flew to a tree nearby and sang at twice the usual rate, chipping between songs (see figure 26, page 167).

Track 2-16: The songs of Li'l Brown two weeks earlier, on June 5, were still in the making. On June 17 he would be consistently singing the phrases A B D E F G I J, but on June 5 the sequence in these ten songs is more variable: A B <u>N</u> E F G, A <u>KL</u> E F G, A B <u>N</u> E F G, A B <u>N</u> E F G, A <u>KL</u> J F, A B <u>N</u> E F G, A B <u>M N</u> E F G J, A <u>KL</u> J F, A B <u>N</u> E F, A B <u>L</u> E F G. Notice that Li'l Brown will eventually jettison the underlined phrases K, L, M, and N (not found in the song of his tutor, Ol' Blue), and he'll add D (copied from Ol' Blue) and I (source unknown). Try to hear the inconsistencies as you compare successive songs (see figure 26, page 167).

Track 2-17: Songs of an older bunting, Blue-2, at Quabbin Hill, just a half mile away from the Enfield Lookout. His first song is complete, consisting of Phrases A K T U H F V, with Phrases U and H making up the three distinctive buzzy phrases in the middle of the song. More typically, he stops the song after just one or two buzzy phrases, as he does with the other four songs here. A prairie warbler sings in the background, his rising buzzy song distinctive (see figure 27, page 172).

Track 2-18: Songs of the other older bunting, Blue-1, at Quabbin Hill. His first song is complete, with Phrases P K L J Q R S. He is somewhat "excited" in this sequence, his second song being a double song (P K L J Q S R K P K L J Q R), a couple of the phrases (S R K) out of order between the songs. Other songs are incomplete, leaving Phrase S or both R and S off the end (see figure 27, page 172).

Track 2-19: Sample songs from the one yearling who settled next to adult male Blue-1 on Quabbin Hill and adopted his song almost perfectly, singing the same sequence of song phrases: P K L J Q R S (see figure 27, page 172).

Track 2-20: When a yearling returns from his first migration, he resumes work on getting the right song for the neighborhood where he will settle. As illustrated here, he can ramble on and on, revealing that he has memorized far more song phrases than he could possibly use in the song that he eventually perfects. In roughly the first 16 seconds here, this bunting sings 16 different phrases, in the following sequence: L J Q R d W V H S R K X <u>K L J Q R S</u> H Y Z K X C J Q R S H J a b J Q R L J. Many of these phrases are sung by his adult neighbors, and the underlined sequence already is almost a complete match for the songs of the adult with whom this yearling is battling for a territory (Blue-1, whose standard song is P K L J Q R S). See sonagrams in figure 28 (page 174).

THE CEDAR WAXWING: A SONGBIRD WITHOUT A SONG?

Although these waxwings may not have what we typically think of as a "song," they certainly produce a variety of calls, from pure whistled *seee*s to raspy *bzeee*s and everything in between.

Track 2-21: At Plum Island in northeastern Massachusetts, with the dull roar of the Atlantic Ocean in the background, listen to the trilled *bzeee* calls of frantic young waxwings begging for food from their parents. Nearby, an eastern towhee sings his *drink-your-tea* song and a few robins call; near the very end, an adult waxwing calls with a high, thin *seee*. See figure 29A (page 182).

Track 2-22: The calls of an adult female demanding (or begging) food from her mate are also the trilled *bzeee*s, similar to the *bzeee* call of the fledgling (figure 29B, page 182). In the background are songs of a common yellowthroat, then the calls and songs of an eastern phoebe.

Track 2-23: Two waxwings, presumably male and female, forage together before the nesting season, their conversational *bzeee* calls sharp and crisp (figure 29C, page 182).

Track 2-24: A flock of waxwings becomes more and more restless in the top of a tree, the intense *seee* calls announcing an imminent departure (figure 29D, page 182).

Track 2-25: A female incubates her eggs in her nest high in the oak tree. She is silent most of the time; were it not for the parabolic microphone aimed at her, the tiny *peep* notes that she utters from time to time would go undetected. Here are seven calls over half a minute's time. Perhaps these brief, downslurred notes reveal an increasing restlessness and hunger, a signal to the male that she's about to leave the nest or would appreciate having some food delivered (figure 29E, page 182).

Track 2-26: Mid-November, a flock of waxwings gathers in the leafless trees, a continuous stream of them flying down to and returning from the bittersweet berries below. Birds call continuously, and every few minutes, a brief squabble breaks out, one bird apparently confronting another face-to-face; one of the birds, presumably the one attacked, calls out with what has been labeled an "injury call," an especially intense, raspy *bzeee* call that spans a wide frequency spectrum (figure 29G, page 182).

Track 2-27: The *bzeee* and *seee* calls are two ends of what seems to be a continuum, with all manner and combinations of these calls in between. Here are just a few samples of those in-between calls that are part *bzeee* and part *seee* (see, for example, figure 30, page 186). This track consists of multiple brief recordings taken from birds calling throughout the year (to see these calls, import them into your free Raven Lite program on your computer).

YOUNG OF THE YEAR PRACTICE THEIR SONGS

During early August, after the nesting and singing season, the air is alive with the sounds of young birds; some are still begging for food from their parents, but most are fully independent, the males now practicing their songs, which will play such an important role in their adult lives.

Track 2-28: With the familiar sounds of August's night insects everywhere, listen to a young great horned owl screech in the distance and to youngish, nonbreeding great blue herons squawking loudly nearby. Frogs call in the water, and if you listen ever so carefully, you'll hear the overhead flight calls of veeries (at 0:03, for example), some of the earliest migrants (for more veery sounds, see track 2-42).

Track 2-29: A young song sparrow calls several times before blurting out practice attempts at his songs. Here is the beginning, his first effort at what will eventually emerge as 8 to 10 fully formed, impressively complex, and superbly performed songs by the time this young sparrow reaches adulthood. (To hear how much he might improve by October, listen to track 2-46.)

Track 2-30: In the foreground, a young black-capped chickadee calls repeatedly, *chick-a-dee-dee-dee*, the call for which this species is named. Soon the chickadee begins to gargle his complex calls, and toward the end of this selection is an abbreviated song, a single high whistle followed by a lower one, the first two syllables of the *hey-sweetie*. Initially in the background are somewhat similar calls and a brief song of a young tufted titmouse.

Track 2-31: Listen to what the parabolic microphone captures from the treetops a good hundred yards away. The low-frequency sounds suggest it is a largish bird, and the tonal quality and rhythm of the attempted song are much like those of a Baltimore oriole; the mystery is solved when he gives himself away with the typical oriole chatter.

Track 2-32: The common yellowthroat in the cattails clearly identifies itself with its *djerp* call, but then there's that scratchy attempt at a song, revealing that he's a male. The second and third attempts contain the typical rhythm of the *witchity-witchity* song, though he has some months to go before he perfects the characteristic yellowthroat rhythm and tonal quality (see figure 31, page 193).

Track 2-33: Through the binoculars, it is clear that down below in the marsh the young eastern kingbirds open and close their bills as if they are calling, but with the unaided ear we hear nothing. With the parabolic microphone aimed at them and the gain turned high, their sharp *tzeet* calls rise out of the background noise. The kingbirds are flycatchers, which don't learn their songs, and the calls of young birds are often already similar to the sounds that adults will use as songs throughout their lives.

Track 2-34: Yes, it *is* a young warbling vireo overhead. Hear his distinctive call and then the unmistakable attempts at his song. The overall rhythm and quality are already surprisingly good, though the details are unformed. Successive songs are never the same, with some short and some long, the component notes and their arrangements all uncertain. At times he hurries from one song to the next, too, blurting out hastily all that he knows (see figure 32, page 196).

Track 2-35: From low in the dense underbrush beside the rail trail, a young Carolina wren calls, the bubbly, down-slurred *jeeer, jeeer, jeeer*. And he then sings, successive phrases in his *teakettle-teakettle* song so uneven. Three times he seems to try one particular song, and then midsong in the fourth (at 0:14) he changes his tune to another of the 30 or 40 songs that he will eventually perfect. He alternates these two songs, then switches (at 0:38) to yet another song, which he practices for the last half minute of this selection. He seems unfazed by the bicyclist who passes at 0:53 (see figure 31, page 193).

(Throughout this selection, I never see him, and I cry for him to come up and show himself, or at least hold still. My parabola is effective only if I can aim it directly at a visible bird or if the bird sings from one place and I can aim the parabola where the songs are loudest. But this bird keeps moving, sight unseen, and I keep searching for him with the parabola, focusing on him for a few seconds, then losing him. As a result, my recording is spotty, the quality uneven.)

Track 2-36: From a tree perhaps 70 yards away, a young tufted titmouse sings a few phrases of one song and then another, and another, phrases of what could be five different songs in the first 30 seconds of this selection. How different from what he will do as an adult, when he sings one of his songs up to 500 times before switching to another. Beginning at 0:30, listen to yet another tufted titmouse, this one just overhead as he escorts me down the bicycle path. His attempts at song are mixed with sharp notes and *chick-a-dee*-like calls. This second titmouse seems younger than the first, his songs less well formed (see figure 31, page 193).

Track 2-37: The calling insects of an August morning still reign, but from the insect din emerge the practice songs of a sassy young male house wren. Based on the sound alone, one would be hard-pressed to identify the singer, so scratchy and unformed are these early attempts at his adult songs. Had I not seen him, I would not have known who he was.

Track 2-38: Uncertain of his sounds in almost every way, a young red-eyed vireo practices his songs overhead. Just like an adult, he offers a song phrase every second or two, but the rhythm is uncertain, just as is the quality of the individual phrases (see figure 32, page 196). When he returns next spring, he'll have 20 or so distinct phrases, each one recognizable and repeated with precision, but now no two attempts are alike. Twice he calls *myaah* (at 0:33, 0:48), the distinctive call of the red-eyed vireo. In the background are *hey-sweetie* songs and calls of a black-capped chickadee.

Track 2-39: American goldfinches! In the foreground are the calls of a single young goldfinch, isolated as much as possible from the calls of other young goldfinches nearby. It's a constant stream of calling, *tew, tew tew twweeeeee tew tew teweee tew, tew tew*, several simple, low *tew* notes followed by the wiry, ascending *twweeeeee*, no two of which sound alike (see figure 33, page 198). Then, after 40 seconds, listen to this goldfinch as it rejoins its flock mates, the calls of this small family flock seeming to come from a far larger group than is actually flitting about in the treetops.

Track 2-40: As I listened in the early-morning hours, veeries were clearly migrating in the night, their loud *veeeer* calls overhead unmistakable (see track 2-28). On one of my return trips to the bike path, one of those young migrant veeries did sing midmorning. With drops of a recent rain falling from the trees, this veery calls sharply, a descending *veeeer,* but then three times he blurts out an attempt at his song, this attempt having little resemblance to the breezy, wheeling, downward spiral of three to five flutey yet nasal phrases that he will sing as an adult.

September

A WOOD THRUSH GOES TO ROOST

The evening symphony of song has ended for the season, and some night soon these wood thrushes will depart for the South. Now, though, in early September, they still announce roosting time with their gentle *tut* and sharper *whit* calls.

Track 2-41: Two wood thrushes call shortly after sunset in their early September going-to-roost routine. In the foreground is a bird initially giving a series of soft *tut tut tut* sounds, but at 0:16 it gives a five-note call that begins with a soft *tut* and ends with a sharp *whit*, the notes in between a transition between the two extremes (figure 34, page 203). He continues to call sharply with a series of *whit* notes, and the bird in the background offers an occasional series of soft *tut* notes. In a single six-note call, the first of which is a sharp *whit* and the last a soft *tut*, the foreground bird transitions back to his milder *tut* calls (1:51). The two birds then *tut* softly back and forth before silently going to roost.

THE FLIGHT CALLS OF NOCTURNAL MIGRANTS

Beginning in mid-August and continuing into October, migrants stream south overhead. On many (but not all) nights they call, our only clue as to what is passing. Imagine yourself on your favorite hilltop in early to mid-September; with stars overhead and a gentle north wind blowing the migrants south, just listen to all that passes.

Track 2-42: During early September, the veeries are still migrating, and here they fly by night above the Connecticut River a little more than an hour before sunrise. The recording is made with a stereo parabolic microphone aiming to the sky; most of the veeries are distant, but occasionally a bird calls loudly nearby or directly in the focus of the parabola. Listen to the variety of calls in this small flock of veeries and, by wearing headphones, try to pick out individuals in the dispersed flock overhead. See figure 35 (page 210) for sample sonagrams.

Track 2-43: Just listen to the variety of calls here from the night migrants! For this track, I have extracted one or two examples of a call for each of the species listed and then played the calls in rapid succession, giving only a few seconds to each. I prefer to listen to these sounds by importing this track into Raven Lite (see page xv) and then selectively listening to each isolated call; that way I can match each call with the sonagrams in figures 36 (page 212) and 37 (page 220) and not be confused by some of the background calls (such as the low thrush calls).

> American redstart (two calls can be heard, at 0:03 and 0:07)
> common yellowthroat (0:12, 0:17)
> northern parula (0:21, 0:26)
> northern waterthrush (0:31, 0:37)
> *zeep* (0:41, 0:46)
> mourning warbler (0:51)
> black-and-white warbler (0:57, 1:01)

Canada warbler (1:07, 1:11)
black-throated blue warbler (1:16, 1:20)
chestnut-sided warbler (1:25, 1:30)
double-up (1:32, 1:38)
Lincoln's or swamp sparrow (1:42)
savannah sparrow (1:46, 1:51)
white-throated sparrow (1:54, 1:58)
indigo bunting (2:02)
gray-cheeked thrush (2:06)
Swainson's thrush (2:09–2:20)

October

THE AUTUMNAL DRUMMING OF A RUFFED GROUSE

How puzzling that this ruffed grouse should drum during the fall, when no females are mating and no offspring are to be sired. But drum he does, in a striking New England autumnal scene, with the trees in their finest colors and young birds everywhere practicing their songs for next year.

Track 2-44: As I settle into my lawn chair a few hundred yards from where I hope an undisturbed Mr. Grouse will soon be booming into my microphones, a New England autumn morning comes alive around me (here through track 2-48). How curious this circus of blue jays and sharp-shinned hawks who seem to fly about in circles in the treetops, with me (and perhaps they, too?) uncertain as to who is chasing whom. At the outset, the tonal *ke-ke-ke* calls of the hawk are followed by the harsh squawk of a jay, then *jay jay jay* in the distance. Soon there are sounds of jays and hawks fluttering through the treetops, followed by another ultraharsh jay call and muted hawk calls, then more flights and calls, hawks and jays spiraling around the treetops, all ending as the jays fly off.

Track 2-45: Loud and bold, this young song sparrow has asserted himself on his territory, where he may stay for the winter. He's about four months old, but his songs are still a jumble of uncertainty, not the discrete packages that will constitute the eight or so songs he'll perfect as an adult but far better than his song would have been back in August (compare track 2-29). As I view the sonagrams of this youngster's effort in Raven, I love seeing how variable are his successive attempts at the same sound and how the various sounds fall into seemingly random sequences. (You can do this, too, of course, with your free version of Raven Lite; see page 277.)

Track 2-46: The ruby-crowned kinglets have arrived from the north country, and here a young male runs through his practice routine. He begins with the double *di-dit* call, then sings, first with the typical high whistles; but hear them wavering, nothing pure and certain as he will sing when an adult. And then it's a continuous chatter of a song as he babbles on for another 40 seconds. The wind picks up, but he continues, a young song sparrow practicing his songs in the background, too.

Track 2-47: A young black-capped chickadee struts his stuff. In this sequence, he flits about the foliage as he gargles his complex aggressive calls, offers three incomplete songs (just a high and a low whistle, giving a *hey-sweet* instead of the full *hey-sweetie*), and there's a *chick-a-dee-dee* call in there, too, for good measure. All three of these sounds need to be learned from adult chickadees. For comparison, listen to young chickadees during August on track 2-30.

Track 2-48: A young white-throated sparrow practices his songs. As an adult, he'll sing two or three long, pure whistles, followed by a series of triplets, his *poor sam peabody peabody peabody* song. Now, however, his whistles are uncertain and wavering, successive attempts at his song all different. In each of his first six attempts, he offers only two longish whistles, but he's undecided as to whether the first should be lower or higher than the second. In his last try here, there's a hint of the *peabody* triplet, the longer whistles broken into at least two shorter ones. Other birds call in the background, including a great horned owl at this early-morning hour.

Track 2-49: In the quiet of the early morning, Mr. Grouse arrives at his display arena by air. Hear him maneuver the obstacles, then bounce to a landing and walk about in the dry leaves.

Track 2-50: On Tuesday, October 10, Mr. Grouse begins with a relatively gentle, low-energy drum, the slow start perhaps necessary lest he rip every muscle in his chest. As he warms up, successive drums build in energy (figure 40, page 233), the hurricane generated by his whirring wings soon blowing the dry leaves in all directions. In this track, the normal time of two or more minutes between drums is reduced to about 10 seconds so that seven different drums during the morning could be included here. As you listen, feel the rhythm of each drum, how he begins with two wingbeats, then a quartet of beats in a distinctive rhythm, and then the frenzy of the whirring wings as he completes his display (figure 38, page 230). Hear how precise he is, how consistent from one drum to the next (figure 39, page 232). And realize, too, that what you are hearing with your ears is only a small part of the energy in his drum, and that if you were standing there beside him, you'd *feel* so much more as the low-frequency energy of the drum resonated in your chest (figure 41, page 234).

Track 2-51: Our grouse usually departs his display perch by walking away, but this time he was spooked, and he departs by air, flying off to the left.

November

TIME TRAVEL: REVISITING TWO HERMIT THRUSHES IN JUNE

In the text, the story of the hermit thrushes occurs here, in November; for the audio on the two CDs, however, I have moved the thrushes to June so that the sounds of singing hermit thrushes can be heard "in season."

A NORTHERN MOCKINGBIRD DEFENDS HER WINTER TERRITORY

Come listen to this (presumed) female northern mockingbird for her first two waking hours on Thanksgiving morning. Her every sound of the morning is described in the text, so please refer there for more details. Four different kinds of sounds are heard from this mockingbird — the CHRRR, CHAT, CHIT, and song (figure 45, page 255) — though how the mockingbird classifies her calls or encodes her messages is unknown.

Track 2-52: At 6:14 A.M., 40 minutes before sunrise, a wave of calling sweeps through the mockingbird community. Hear some of the neighboring mockingbirds calling first, and then within two seconds this mockingbird calls CHRRR loudly four times from her roost. Other mockingbirds continue to call, the male nearby even singing a little.

Track 2-53: At 6:28 A.M., another wave of calling sweeps among the mockingbirds. She responds within 10 seconds, first with two harsh CHRRR calls, then 60 to 70 equally harsh CHAT calls over two minutes and 15 seconds (shortened to 1:38 here); in this series, she is the last mockingbird calling. Listen to her sound off, but listen to all that goes on in the background, too, including some singing again by the nearby male.

In the following series, I describe only briefly the context. For details, please follow along in the main text, and enjoy listening to the background birds here, too:

Track 2-54: 6:52 A.M.: Five CHRRR calls from the night roost.

Track 2-55: 6:54 A.M.: Two *CHRRR* calls, and then hear her flight as she departs her roost.

Track 2-56: 7:00 A.M.: *CHRRR CHRRR...CHAT CHAT*, all from the fruiting cluster on the palm tree. Just listen to the gathering starlings in the background!

Track 2-57: 7:05 A.M.: A single *CHRRR* from her perch where she vigilantly watches.

Track 2-58: 7:08 A.M.: And the chase is on! A red-bellied woodpecker innocently calls *chig chig*, but the starlings have arrived, and now she launches her attack. Hear the rustling of dry palm fronds and squawks of starlings as she attacks and the starlings scurry for cover.

Track 2-59: 7:10 A.M.: Two *CHRRR* calls from her perch above the palm fruits.

Track 2-60: 7:19 A.M.: Three *CHRRR* calls, again from her perch.

Track 2-61: 7:41 A.M.: Four *CHRRR* calls, from her perch, in response to the five calls of the male just across the street; in the background is a familiar sound of the city.

Track 2-62: 7:45 A.M.: After a series of *CHIT* calls (not on CD), she follows with a brief song, delivered from the southern end of her territory, where she seldom goes as little fruit is there.

Track 2-63: 7:51 A.M.: Three *CHRRR* calls and a half minute later (compressed to seven seconds here), a series of *CHIT* calls.

Track 2-64: 8:06 A.M.: Three *CHRRR* calls; she has returned to the perch just above her palm fruits.

December

THE WINTER SOLSTICE IS THE FIRST DAY OF SPRING

The shortest day of the year, the winter solstice, marks the first day of winter on our calendars, but I'm convinced that the birds view it as their first day of spring. The sun is on its way back, and it is the sun and day length that govern their lives. The birds announce this first day of spring in song, and I've adopted their calendar for myself.

Track 2-65: On the solstice itself, unlike the two weeks before, white-breasted nuthatches sang, and it wasn't with just a whimper or two but instead with a full-blown, exuberant performance that proclaimed unmistakably the first day of spring, or so I felt. To a background of winter wind and leafless tree branches striking each other, listen to the rapid *hah-hah-hah-hah-hah-hah-hah-hah-hah* songs of this enthusiastic nuthatch. After six songs and a few nasal *yank-yank* calls, he abruptly switches to his other song, lower-pitched and delivered more slowly, *haah-haah-haah-haah-haah* (figure 46, page 268).

Track 2-66: American robins sang on the solstice, too, a whole flock of them high in the trees. A day later, low in a fruiting tree beside a house in my neighborhood, one robin sang continuous, though muted songs. Arriving about sunrise, he'd begin (as here) with the familiar *tut* and *piik* notes, then launch into what seemed a never-ending soliloquy. He did not sing as a springtime robin, with a string of low, rich caroled phrases sometimes followed by a high-pitched *hisselly* or two, but instead he seemed to practice both forms of his song simultaneously (figure 48, page 273). As you listen here, see the winter scene in your mind's eye while he sits on his leafless perch, his bill closed, and when he squeezes out each split-second phrase, see his tail nudge upward ever so slightly and his wings downward. In the background, crows caw, and twice, at 0:45 and 1:18, a pileated woodpecker drums in the distance.

Appendix 2:

How to Record a Singing Bird

WITHOUT RECORDING GEAR, I can enjoy listening to birdsong anytime and anywhere, but there's a special joy in capturing the voice of a bird and then taking the sound home with me. At home I can import the recording into my Raven software and study the details of the sound, thereby learning so much about the bird itself. Or by simply listening to that recording, I can be transported back to the very place where I recorded it, seeing and smelling and feeling and hearing the entire scene (see, for example, the November story "Time Travel: Revisiting Two Hermit Thrushes in June"). And, with the voice of the bird itself, I can share these experiences with others.

If you feel even the slightest urge to record birds, I encourage you to go to the highly informative website at the Cornell Lab of Ornithology, www.birds.cornell.edu/macaulaylibrary/record. There you can learn all about the latest gear, how to use it, and where to get it. (Check out the sound recording workshop, too, a fabulous opportunity to learn from the experts.) In my 2005 book, *The Singing Life of Birds,* I shared everything that I knew about how to record bird songs, offering ideas about recorders, microphones, headphones, and the like. I'll not reproduce that information here, but instead offer a few introductory thoughts.

I'm often asked this basic question: "What do you recommend if I can't afford much?" I'm reluctant to suggest the following, as the experience is so inferior to what better gear can offer (see below), but a system that I used for several years while working in a marsh included an inexpensive cassette recorder and microphone from RadioShack, with the microphone mounted in a plastic funnel (after an occasional dunking, I'd simply buy a new system). This setup involves some serious compromises in sound quality and little joy in enhancing one's listening experiences in nature, but it's cheap and does capture some semblance of the bird's sound. For less than $50, I could get an adequate recording, take it home for study, and learn a bit about the birds. Today, the free Raven Lite software from Cornell's Lab of Ornithology could be used to see a sonagram of what was recorded.

For the "you've changed my life" kinds of experiences (page 62), however, and for the sheer joy of listening in nature to all that birds have to say, I think you can't afford *not* to get a parabolic microphone. The highly directional reflector physically amplifies a sound by concentrating it at the microphone. Then the recorder electronically amplifies it further. The songs can be so sharp and loud in the headphones that I feel I'm plucking the songs directly from the bird's bill. And that's special!

For the recordings on the two CDs with this book, I used a variety of microphone systems. When I wanted a sharp recording of a single vocalizing bird, I used a parabolic microphone (tracks 2-1 through 2-41, for example). When I wanted a parabola but had none, I settled for a recording made with a simpler microphone (see tracks 1-38, 1-39, 1-41); the difference in sound quality with and without the parabola is evident. Sometimes I wanted to capture a broader soundscape, so I used two microphones mounted in a device that captures a sound environment in stereo. This kind of "you are there" listening experience is captured best in the sounds of large numbers of roosting robins (tracks 1-3 through 1-7), wading birds (tracks 1-9 through 1-16), and cranes (tracks 1-34 through 1-37).

So what system should you buy? That depends, of course, on what kind of experience you want and how much money you want to spend. For just a few dollars you could have some fun with a cassette recorder, microphone, and a funnel. If you are handy, you can buy a small "parabolic reflector" from Edmund Scientific (www.scientificsonline.com) and assemble your own parabolic microphone, perhaps following the inspiration provided on "A Web Page Dedicated to the Recording of Bird Vocalizations with Simple, Inexpensive Equipment" (www.bio.umass.edu/biology/kunkel/gjk/homepage.htm).

Most recordists now use digital recorders, rather than the more cumbersome analog cassette recorders. A current, rather inexpensive favorite of mine is the M-Audio MicroTrack II, which records sounds (as WAV files) directly to compact flash cards; those WAV files can then be imported directly into Raven software. This small digital recorder, coupled with a directional "shotgun microphone" or (preferably, in my opinion) a parabolic microphone (see Cornell website for examples) can make truly stunning recordings. The system I use these days (early 2009) is a Telinga "stereo" parabolic microphone and Sound Devices 722 recorder, which records directly to a hard drive, compact flash card, or both; my backups are a MicroTrack II recorder and a second microphone that I can insert into the Telinga parabola. And my Sennheiser HD 25-1 II headphones are indispensable, not only because they are needed to aim the parabola accurately but also because hearing a bird well as he sings is one of the truly great pleasures in life.

Most importantly, don't worry about getting the perfect system. Go ahead and try something. If what you are using isn't giving you enough fun, upgrade. Keep in mind that it's all about enjoying the sounds of nature; you're not running a professional sound-recording business, unless, of course, you get hooked — and that *is* a possibility.

Notes

INTRODUCTION

xv **how the bird uses his two voice boxes** For luscious, unimaginable delights about how singing birds use their two voice boxes, see papers by Rod Suthers (e.g., Suthers and Zollinger 2004).

xv **details in the songs that the birds themselves hear** Birds can resolve the temporal fine structure of their sounds far better than we can, hearing tiny changes in sounds over about 1.225 milliseconds; we need 3 to 4 milliseconds to hear similar changes. In other words, the scientific evidence shows that birds can hear three to four times better than we can, but my hunch is that they're far better than that—we just haven't been able to show it yet. See Lohr, Dooling, and Bartone 2006; Dooling et al. 2002.

xvi **the words "song" and "call"** For a full discussion of how to define a "song," see Spector 1994.

January

A PILEATED WOODPECKER GOES TO HER ROOST ON NEW YEAR'S DAY

3 **the oddest time of year** It's widely believed that young great horned owls hatch in late winter so that they have a long summer and fall season to learn how to hunt for themselves. See Houston, Smith, and Rohner 1998.

8 **the sight of my parabolic microphone** The parabolic microphone consists of both the parabola and the microphone, but for shorthand hereafter I'll simply refer to them as "the parabola."

13 **fleas that have little fleas upon them** From the 17th-century writer Jonathan Swift's ditty

> So nat'ralists observe, a flea
> Hath smaller fleas that on him prey,
> And these have smaller fleas that bite 'em,
> And so proceed *ad infinitum.*

13 **a great horned owl . . . it is a female** Houston, Smith, and Rohner 1998.

18 **microphones are perched** For this purpose, I am using two Sennheiser MKH20 omnidirectional mikes in a Crown SASS setup, so that I can listen in stereo as if I were among the robins myself.

18 **demons of Pandemonium** Quotations are from page 18 in Black 1932.

18 **in robin-time this roost is quite recent** The year 2006 seems to have been special for some unknown reason, as only hundreds rather than tens of thousands of robins used this roost in the two following years.

18 **Christmas Bird Count** See www.audubon.org/bird/cbc/ for the source of these data.

21 **This is the moment!** I feel a bit like David Johnston must have felt back in 1980 as he excitedly reported the much-awaited eruption of Mount St. Helens; sadly, my elation endured longer than his.

AN ALL-NIGHTER AMONG THE WADING BIRDS IN THE EVERGLADES

25 **fraaahnk, fraaahnk, fraak, fra** From Sibley 2000.

25 **chitter chitter chitter chee cheur chitter chitter** The late Bud Owre's mnemonic, in Frederick and Siegel-Causey 2000.

29 **Leopard frogs** Thank you, Lang Elliott, for identifying these frog sounds.

30 **southern birds adding an extra syllable** Borror 1967.

February

THE LIMPKINS OF CORKSCREW SWAMP

40 **person being strangled** Brewster 1881. "A hoarse rattling cry like the sound of a person being strangled, at the same time shaking his head so violently that his neck seemed in imminent danger of dislocation."

40 **large bronchial box** Ruppell 1933.

40 **relatives of these limpkins** Livezey 1998.

40 **For four full minutes they carry on** Here's my best attempt to write it down: *Kkkkkkkkk keoow keoow kkkk keoow keoow kkkk keoow keoow kkkk keoow* [pause] *kkkk keoow keoow kkkkk keoow* [pause] *kkkk keoow keoow kkkk* [pause] *kkkk keoow keoow kkkk keoow keoow kkkk* [pause] *kkkk keoow kkkk keoow keoow keoow keoow keoow keoow keoow keoow keoow keoow keoow keoow keoow keoow keoow kkk keoow keoow keoow keoow kkkk keoow keoow keoow kkkk keoow keoow keoow keoow kkkk keoow keoow keoow kkkk keoow keoow keoow keoow keoow kkkk keoow keoow keoow kkkk keoow keoow keoow* [pause] *keoow keoow keoow kkkk keoow keoow keoow keoow keoow kkkk keoow keoow keoow keoow keoow keoow keoow keoow kkkk keoow keoow kkkk keoow keoow keoow keoow keoow* [pause] *keoow keoow keoow keoow keoow kkkk keoow keoow keoow keoow keoow keoow keoow kkkk keoow keoow keoow keoow keoow keoow keoow keoow keoow keoow keoow keoow keoow kur-r-ee-ow kur-r-ee-ow*

43 **slowly moving off into the swamp** For additional reading, see Truslow 1958.

45 **"Family"** For a discussion of human and other families, see Emlen 1995a; Emlen 1995b.

45 **Glen Woolfenden since 1969** Facts throughout this chapter are gleaned from two summaries written by Glen Woolfenden and John Fitzpatrick: Woolfenden and Fitzpatrick 1984; Woolfenden and Fitzpatrick 1996.

45 **raising siblings "counts" in evolutionary currency** An individual's evolutionary success is measured by how much it contributes genetically to the next generation. Leaving a son or daughter is a *direct* contribution to the next generation, but helping to raise close kin is also a contribution, although an *indirect* one. When the probability of raising one's own offspring is low, it's sometimes to one's advantage, such as in this scrub-jay system, to stay at home and become a "helper."

45 **widow or widower** On average, each scrub-jay faces about a one in five chance of dying in any given year, so in the 20 or so territories within easy dispersal distance of a young bird, one would expect about four vacancies for males and four for females. Among those 20 territories there's perhaps one divorce each year, too, with one of the mates leaving the territory to seek better conditions elsewhere; that's one more opening for an opportunist, but such divorces typically occur on poor terri-

tories, so a young bird might do better to wait for a death in a better situation than to take the poor territory. It's all a matter of probabilities, but over time evolution molds a wise scrub-jay that can, on average, make good choices.

48 **find mates by the time they are two** Finding an opening isn't all that easy, and about a third of the birds wait until they are three years old, 1 in 10 waiting four or five years before breeding.

49 **a sentinel ready to alert** How the jays look out for one another is nicely described in McGowan and Woolfenden 1989.

50 **incest in family lines is strictly avoided** The babies in the nest are the offspring of the two adults in the territory, and in 960 pairs over the years, never have any father-daughter or brother-sister pairings been found. Three examples of mother-son pairings have been reported, however, cases in which an older son stayed on the home territory after Dad died and repelled courting males, eventually pairing with his mother.

THE ANHINGAS OF ANHINGA TRAIL, EVERGLADES NATIONAL PARK

58 **males [incubate] most of the time** Frederick and Siegel-Causey 2000.

63 **parents and their offspring recognizing one another's voices** A fascinating example is in colony-living penguins (Aubin, Jouventin, and Hildebrand 2000).

March

SANDHILL CRANES ON THE PLATTE RIVER

66 **Platte River Crane Trust** The full name is the Platte River Whooping Crane Maintenance Trust, Inc., a nonprofit group dedicated to conserving habitat for migratory birds on the Platte River, along an 80-mile stretch of the Big Bend region from Overton to Chapman in central Nebraska. I'm deeply grateful to Dr. Felipe Chavez-Ramirez for scheduling me in his blinds for three evenings and two mornings.

66 **Paul Johnsgard** Just a small bit of the passion of Paul Johnsgard is illustrated in his two books about cranes: Johnsgard 1981; Johnsgard 1991.

66 **north blind . . . south blind** These are two blinds maintained by the Platte River Crane Trust.

69 **may live up to 20 years** A wealth of good information on sandhill cranes is in Tacha, Nesbitt, and Vohs 1992.

71 **several million years** Fossils almost 2 million years old have been found throughout North America. See Tacha, Nesbitt, and Vohs 1992.

72 **identify family and . . . acquaintances by voice alone** Such individual recognition has been shown to occur among many bird species. Among my favorites are studies on barn and cliff swallows (Medvin and Beecher 1986; Beecher 1989; Beecher, Stoddard, and Loesche 1985).

73 **knowing that I'll be back** Two years later, during March 2008, I did return, at the kind invitation of Felipe Chavez-Ramirez to take part in the Rivers and Wildlife Celebration hosted every year by Audubon Nebraska (www.nebraska.audubon.org/ne-rwc.htm). Nor is twice enough.

April

A TROPICAL PILGRIMAGE

77 **what I have read kiskadees do at dawn** The chatter is described in Ffrench 1991. Another source (Howell and Webb 1995) describes this dawn vocalization as *kyah k-yah zzk-zzik kyar*. Describing bird sounds is tough!

78 **encoded in the genetic material** See Kroodsma and Konishi 1991.

80 **inner feelings or "thoughts"** I use those terms loosely but make no apologies to my hard-core scientific colleagues who might shun such words. As these birds sing, they interact with others and adjust what they sing accordingly; in my opinion, there's a thought process of some kind going on, though I make no claim that they think consciously about what they are doing.

80 **from my readings I know** Molles and Vehrencamp 1999.

82 **I yearn for my computer** I also yearn for my parabolic microphone; it was too bulky to carry on the bicycle, but I would have loved to have had the parabola focused on him, his songs then so loud and crisp in the headphones over my ears.

84 **field guide describes them so perfectly** Stiles and Skutch 1989.

85 **birds of the Monteverde dialect** Because bellbirds learn their songs, birds from different geographic areas sing different "dialects." In addition to the Monteverde dialect heard in mid–Costa Rica, there's the Nicaraguan dialect to the north and the Talamanca (or Panamanian) dialect to the south.

85 **having dropped about as much as I would have expected** Back home, I used

Raven software to determine the frequency of 35 whistles from these three bellbirds, and the median frequency was about 3,400 Hz, a drop of 210 Hz from the 3,610 Hz of 2002.

85 **bellbird research team** Deborah Hamilton currently heads the bellbird research team that was begun by George Powell in the Monteverde area.

86 **cotinga relatives** The three-wattled bellbird belongs to a group of roughly 70 birds called "cotingas," which includes a wonderful assortment of Neotropical birds with names like fruiteaters, purpletufts, pihas, fruitcrows, umbrellabirds, cock-of-the-rocks, and others.

87 **the American robin** The clay-colored robin is every bit as much of an "American robin" as the one so designated to the north, of course, as are all robins from Central and South America. We should all bristle a bit at the name "American robin," as if the others don't really count, as if any bird "south of the border" (of the United States) isn't really American.

May

TWO VIRGINIA MIMICS: BROWN THRASHER, WHITE-EYED VIREO

90 **four times louder in my ears** It's the physicists' law of spherical spreading, or the inverse square law, that applies here. As a sound spreads out in all directions from a source, there will be less and less energy on the surface of the expanding sphere. That's semitechnical jargon for a general rule that reminds me to get the microphone as close to the bird as possible, that halving the distance will quadruple the amount of energy that strikes the microphone (i.e., in more technical language, the signal-to-noise ratio is increased by 6 dB).

91 **thousands of different songs** Kroodsma and Parker 1977.

92 **calls pilfered from other species** For details, see Adkisson and Conner 1978.

93 **neither ever interfering with the song of the other** For a well-documented example in nightingales, see Brumm 2006.

96 **about a 1 in 45 probability** If one makes a few minor assumptions, one can calculate the rough probability of the vireo choosing his next two songs so that they address the towhee and the wren. If he has 10 different songs in his repertoire, he must choose either the *chewink* or the *jeeer* song for his first effort; he thus has a 2 in 10 chance of choosing one of those songs next if he chooses at random. On his next effort, he must

choose the other song from the 9 remaining choices, and he has only a 1 in 9 chance of choosing the correct song at random. Multiplying $^2/_{10} \times$ $^1/_9 = ^1/_{45}$, so that if he chooses the next song at random, only 2 percent of the time will he address the wren and the towhee on his next two singing bouts. That's pretty rare. Scientists often use a 5 percent "rule," claiming an event is "significant" if it occurs but it's likely to occur by chance less than 5 percent of the time, and 2 percent is well below that cutoff. I think this vireo knows exactly what he's doing, but a scientific test of this idea would require far more rigorous testing, of course.

96 **average Virginia male has about 13** Hopp, Kirby, and Boone 1995.

97 **16 species whose calls are known** Thank you to Gene Morton, Ed Talbot, and Roger Mayhorn, three friends who helped me think about the mimicry in these songs.

98 **up to 75 percent of these vireo song components are mimicked** Percentage of mimicked notes in songs of individuals ranged from 35 percent to 78 percent, with an average of 55 percent. Adkisson and Conner 1978.

98 **Why he mimics in this way** Why songbirds often mimic other species has remained largely a mystery. One recent paper stated that there is "little evidence for vocal mimicry having evolved to serve important functions in most birds" (Garamszegi et al. 2007). Yet careful studies, such as by Eben Goodale (Goodale and Kotagama 2006a; Goodale and Kotagama 2006b), show purposeful imitation, with mimics knowing exactly which of their mimicked sounds to use in which contexts. My opinion? My vote is with the birds, that they "know" what they're doing and that mimicry serves some (though usually unexplained) purpose.

98 **mobbing the owl** A white-eyed vireo used alarm calls of chickadee, thrush, flycatcher, wren, catbird, warbler, and towhee when mobbing a screech-owl (Adkisson and Conner 1978). A few other species, such as thick-billed euphonias of the Tropics (Morton 1976), do this also. Lawrence's and lesser goldfinches from western North America also sing mimicked call notes of other species (Remsen, Garrett, and Erickson 1982).

BALTIMORE ORIOLE—SHE SINGS, TOO

99 **One paper in the journal *Condor*** Beletsky 1982a.

106 **male's song is identical to that of his neighbor** This phenomenon has been reported before; of 18 males studied by Les Beletsky, 10 had unique repertoires, but four pairs of neighboring males had almost identical repertoires. Beletsky 1982b.

106 **among chipping sparrows** See Liu and Kroodsma 2006.

106 **older females sing more** See discussion in Byers and King 2000.

109 **these horned larks can also sing from the heavens** Beason 1995.

111 **where I am staying in Sterling** Thank you, Colorado Field Ornithologists, for hosting me for a long, glorious weekend in the "other Colorado."

112 **my stereo microphone** Two Sennheiser MKH20 mikes in Crown SASS.

113 **three different songs in his repertoire** I expect three based on my reading of Schnase and Maxwell 1989.

116 **the higher-frequency** *pzeeents* **. . . are lost** Sound attenuates over distance, but low-frequency sounds (such as the booming *hooov* of the flight display) attenuate far less than higher-frequency sounds (such as the higher, vocal *pzeeent*).

117 **successive phrases contrasting sharply** Some birds seem to alternate contrasting phrases like this so that they can catch their breath during the more slowly delivered phrases; during the fast buzzes, this lark bunting is probably exhaling continuously, but between the lower, slower notes he can take mini-breaths, thus replenishing the air in his lungs (Suthers and Zollinger 2004).

119 **"It saves going to heaven"** Words of the poet Emily Dickinson, of course.

June

125 **Dan, a former graduate student** Thank you, Dan Albano, for introducing me to kingfishers. His Ph.D. thesis is Albano 2000.

127 **what banter it was, so expressive** The rattles can be altered in many ways, presumably to convey subtle differences in meaning, as described by Davis 1988.

133 **I don't know the author** But everything is available on the web, where I discover that the author of "Morning Has Broken" was Eleanor Farjeon (1881–1965). I also confirm that she was English.

141 **different from those of his neighbors** It's a different story out west, where neighboring birds often have identical songs in their repertoires. The western birds are typically resident, not migratory, and learn the songs of their particular neighborhoods. See Beecher 1996.

142 **how a life should be lived** Patrick, a visitor to a website run by Teresa Nielsen Hayden, said it best: "David Stemple — scientist, outdoorsman, world traveler and paterfamilias — was sharp, funny, irascible, generous, kindly, impassioned, profane, and great company. He could talk your ear off about Scottish history, growl terrifyingly about the iniquity of bad database design, and in the presence of a bird he wanted to observe, he could bend reality itself. He believed in knowing things. He was a man who, when you met him, you thought 'That's right, that's how a human life should be lived.'"

BLACKBURNIAN WARBLERS OF MOUNT GREYLOCK

145 **each male can sing two types of songs** Douglass Morse wrote some of the early papers on warblers, including the Blackburnian (Morse 1967). Later, he wrote a book summarizing all that he had learned about this marvelous group of birds (Morse 1989).

145 **I will use "dawn" and "day"** I vastly oversimplify with these labels, but they help me keep track of the two song categories. The "dawn song" is the one that males sing during the intense dawn chorus. The "day song" is the one that a male sings all day long when he is unpaired. Dawn songs can be sung in aggressive contexts during the day, but day songs are not sung at dawn unless the bird is unpaired. It's a little confusing, but give it a try. (I could use the terms that scientists use, such as type 1 and type 2 songs, or accented and unaccented, or A and B — that's more objective, perhaps, but I don't think such objectivity helps to remember them and the way they are used.)

145 **obsessed with warblers** See the chestnut-sided warbler story in Kroodsma 2005.

150 **what . . . Bruce Byers has found** Bruce began studying chestnut-sided warblers with me in the mid-1980s and 20 years later is still obsessed with them. One of his first papers — Byers 1995 — is most relevant here.

151 **chipping sparrows and American redstarts** For sample references, see Secunda and Sherry 1991; Liu 2001.

July

THE DAWN AND DAY SONGS OF SCARLET TANAGERS

156 **just inside Gate 51** Thanks to a Quabbin research permit, I have access to the reservation at all hours.

157 **"robin with a sore throat"** Peterson 1980.

159 **greatest energy at dawn** For lots of examples of energetic dawn singing, see Kroodsma 2005.

160 **particular combination of burry phrases** Each male has a unique combination of about 10 burry phrases in his repertoire. Other features of daytime singing described here are consistent with those described earlier in Shy 1984.

161 **typical repertoire size for a scarlet tanager** Again, as determined by Shy 1984.

164 **scarlet tanager is not a tanager** See Klicka, Burns, and Spellman 2007.

YEARLING INDIGO BUNTINGS LEARN THE LOCAL MICRODIALECT

165 **Enfield Lookout, Quabbin Park** Enfield was one of four towns that were discontinued when Boston took this watershed; the center of the town was at the junction of the west and east branches of the Swift River, now under the reservoir below me.

166 *fire fire where where* Thanks to David Sibley for the mnemonic (Sibley 2000).

168 **based on my readings** As summarized by Robert Payne in Payne 1996.

170 **where he eventually settled** About 80 percent of yearlings learn the songs of a neighbor, who is usually an older adult. See Payne 1996.

171 **throughout the geographic range** Thompson 1970.

173 **no change in ownership** For a discussion of this idea, see McGregor and Krebs 1984.

175 **songs appear essentially identical to us** Ample evidence shows that birds can hear differences in songs that look identical to us in sonagrams (Blumenrath, Dabelsteen, and Pedersen 2007). Songbirds have remarkable memories, too, and are able to recognize many more songs than they actually sing (Stoddard et al. 1992).

175 **fathered not by the male attending the nest** The source of so much good information on buntings is Payne 1992.

175 **father more offspring as a result** In the related lazuli bunting, an adult male is especially aggressive toward brightly colored yearlings, and the adult fathers more young in a neighboring territory if that neighboring male is dull-colored. Greene et al. 2000.

THE CEDAR WAXWING: A SONGBIRD WITHOUT A SONG?

178 **Jim's doctoral thesis** Howell 1973.

178 **Another waxwing enthusiast . . . concluded the same** Putnam 1949.

178 **Pete Dunne echoed "No song"** Dunne 2006.

178 **Golden Guide and the National Geographic Guide** Robbins et al. 1983; National Geographic Society 1987.

178 **Kaufman and Peterson** Kaufman 2000; Peterson 1980.

178 **Sibley adds some confusion** Sibley 2000.

179 **with all of the specialized songbird . . . anatomy** Gahr, Güttinger, and Kroodsma 1993.

179 **last few hundred thousand years** The entire Pleistocene period seems to have been an important time of radiation among birds, with many new species arising during the last 250,000 years (Johnson and Cicero 2004).

179 **series of defining moments** These are stories of self-discovery, guided by the journeys of other inquisitive naturalists who have enjoyed waxwings before me. I especially thank James Clayton Howell for his meticulous work with waxwings (Howell 1973). Jim, you left this earth some 20 years ago, but I remember well the fun we had thinking about bird sounds together. Thank you for introducing me to waxwings, although I'm a bit embarrassed that I've taken this long to follow your encouraging words.

180 **It's just a guess at this point** I dream about how I could move beyond the guess. I'd love to know what part of the brain controls the trills and what part the tonal notes. If the tonal notes are more learned, they should be controlled by the intricate network of forebrain neurons and control centers that enable song learning in other songbirds. Perhaps the innate trill notes are controlled by a more primitive part of the brain. Or perhaps I could raise some young birds and determine if the tonal *see* notes seem to require learning from other waxwings. Or, I wonder, if waxwings have no song, does a young waxwing still engage in "subsong"? At three to four weeks of age, other songbirds begin to whisper and warble and babble a jumble of sounds (i.e., subsong) as they practice what will eventually be their song (see page 189). Does a "songless" waxwing still "subsing"? If so, what is the young bird practicing?

181 **a female ornithologist friend** Dr. Susan M. Smith, Professor Emeritus, Mount Holyoke College. Smith 1980.

183 **the *Birds of North America* account** Witmer, Mountjoy, and Elliot 1997.

YOUNG OF THE YEAR PRACTICE THEIR SONGS

189 **special place on the bike path** The bike path is officially the Norwottuck Rail Trail, the mileage markers beginning on Station Road in Amherst; just before the one-mile sign is the bridge over the wetland formed by beavers damming little Hop Brook.

189 **these insects . . . make good August sounds** Now, with the publication of a new book, *The Songs of Insects,* I can begin learning these August sounds (Elliott and Hershberger 2007).

194 **sound so much like those of the adults** My friend John Smith wrote years ago that, at two weeks of age, the young kingbirds already sound much like the adults. Smith 1966.

195 **encoded in the genetic material** Kroodsma and Konishi 1991. See also the story on flycatchers in Kroodsma 2005.

195 **Bewick's wren is like that** See story on Bewick's wren in Kroodsma 2005.

197 **white noise** White noise is a broadband hissy sound, defined as a signal that contains sound at the same loudness at all audible frequencies. We tested other sounds with our laboratory birds, too, such as human music, but nothing worked like a vacuum cleaner to stimulate the birds to sing.

September

A WOOD THRUSH GOES TO ROOST

205 **perhaps fidgeting all night long** During migration season, birds *are* restless on their perches. In English, it's called "migratory restlessness," in German *Zugunruhe;* caged birds during this season are active in their cages all night long, spending most time at the south end of their cages during the fall migratory season and at the north end during the spring season.

THE FLIGHT CALLS OF NOCTURNAL MIGRANTS

207 ***Flight Calls of Migratory Birds*** Evans and O'Brien 2002.

208 **my stereo microphone system** For the technically inclined, what I use here

are two Sennheiser MKH20 mikes in a Crown SASS, aimed to the north, hoping to capture birds to the west in the left channel and birds to the east in the right channel. Microphones were powered with a MixPre from Sound Devices.

221 **two-month obsession** For a wonderful read of another man's obsession, see Tyler 1916. More recent studies of these night flight calls are summarized in Withgott 2002; Farnsworth 2005; Floyd 2007.

October

THE AUTUMNAL DRUMMING OF A RUFFED GROUSE

225 **confirming a drummer just where my friend Tom** Tom Gagnon is a fellow member of the Hampshire Bird Club, and a number of its members are on my "Birding Consultants" team, eager to relay good information to me about where they hear and see birds.

227 **four to five months old** Gullion 1967.

227 **about half of all yearlings** Rusch et al. 2000.

228 **to see the morning's activity at a glance** I use a program called Adobe Audition, which provides a waveform of a long recording, thus revealing where significant sounds were recorded.

228 **"halve the distance, quadruple the sound"** See note on page 318 for an explanation of this law of spherical spreading, or the inverse square law, which applies here.

229 **Using my Raven software** To measure features of sonagrams, one needs Raven Pro, the Raven software program used by professional biologists. For most people I recommend the free Raven Lite. Only if one gets obsessed with measuring sound would one need the professional (not-free) program.

229 **each of five drums** For this analysis, I chose five drums of overall equal loudness as measured in the Raven software.

230 **Library of Natural Sounds website** What fun to go to this website and listen to sounds not only of ruffed grouse but of so many other species. Go ahead — explore the online collection of sounds at www.birds .cornell.edu/macaulaylibrary/. First, though, listen to each of the grouse that I listened to on my virtual trip across the country, and hear that "new species" in British Columbia. To hear that particular drum, find 59280, the catalog number of the recording made by William W. H.

Gunn on May 22, 1962, in British Columbia. When the professionals eventually discover this different grouse, they'll almost certainly call it a new species, well after you already knew.

231 **darker and browner than grouse elsewhere** Rusch et al. 2000.

231 **sooty and dusky grouse** See Young et al. 2000; Barrowclough et al. 2004.

237 **how Mr. Grouse produces his sound** Bent 1932.

237 **"miniature sonic boom"** Rusch et al. 2000.

238 **exceptional hearing ability at low frequencies** Pigeons can hear frequencies so low that we call them infrasound (Yodlowski, Kreithen, and Keeton 1977), so why shouldn't these ruffed grouse?

238 **much louder in front** Archibald 1974.

November

TIME TRAVEL: REVISITING TWO HERMIT THRUSHES IN JUNE

242 **first and last true encounter** In my book *The Singing Life of Birds,* I tell of this experience. Kroodsma 2005.

242 **especially different from the reply of his neighbor** Such a possibility is not so far-fetched. A close relative of the hermit thrush, the wood thrush, chooses his next song so that it is different from what he just sang *and* different from what his neighbor just sang. With the hermit thrush, though, I want to know not just whether the next song is different (neighboring hermit thrushes rarely have identical songs in their repertoires) but whether it is especially different, i.e., more different than would be expected by chance. See Whitney 1990, and the chapter on wood thrushes in Kroodsma 2005.

243 **than if the bird had chosen his next song randomly** Statistics confirm that statement for both males. In a half-hour recording of 600 songs, I show that Bird 1 typically (i.e., median value) leaps 1,410 Hz to his next song, but if his sequence is arranged in random order, the typical leap would be only 940 Hz; also, in his natural sequence, 536 leaps are greater than one would expect by chance, 62 are fewer. Using a binomial statistical test, I can state with considerable confidence (being right more than 999,999 times out of a million!) that Bird 1 is choosing his next song so that it is especially different from the one he just sang (ratio of 536:62 is so different from expected ratio of 299:299). The same conclusion is reached for Bird 2.

245 **frenzied dawn singing** For more about how eastern wood-pewees sing, see Kroodsma 2005.

248 **collecting the numbers I need** The Raven Pro (but not the free Raven Lite) software automatically collects numbers in a table that can be analyzed with a program like Excel. All I have to do is draw a little box around the introductory whistle for a song, and the two numbers I need—when the song began and the frequency of the whistle, which tells me which of the male's songs it is—are placed into the table.

249 **typically 1,410 hertz different** I use median values for all calculations. I should also say that I was very selective about the interactions I used. I wanted to make sure that each bird had sufficient time to hear what the other had sung, so I included only those song exchanges that gave at least 0.5 second from the beginning of one bird's song to the beginning of the other's.

249 **A difference of 940 hertz *is* significantly greater** How confident can I be in that statement? Given the statistics that I used, I would be right more than 999 times out of 1,000, a pretty sure bet. I found that out of 427 times that Bird 1 followed Bird 2, 253 songs made a greater frequency leap than expected, 174 a smaller leap. Using a binomial statistical test, I find that an observed ratio of 253:174 is significantly different from the expected ratio of 214:214 ($p < 0.001$).

Somewhat doubting myself and the ability of these hermits, I try another approach, playing yet another numbers game. This time I take all of the song sequences from these two birds and rearrange them in a random order. The frequency difference between successive songs in the normal sequence is 1,030 Hz, but in this random sequence only 840 Hz, 190 Hz less (significantly different at $p < 0.001$ again, binomial test). At this point, I rest. I am confident in my claim.

December

THE WINTER SOLSTICE IS THE FIRST DAY OF SPRING

264 **the length of the day that governs** For a discussion of how the photoperiod controls the annual cycle of birds, see Gwinner 2003.

264 **scientists who try to prove a hypothesis** The perils of having a favorite idea and trying to prove it are explained well by a geologist in a paper originally published in the late 1800s. Facts contrary to one's pet hypothesis

are ignored or discarded, for example, and only the favorite idea is tested, so when facts are "consistent with" the favored idea, it's considered proven, even though the facts are also consistent with many other ideas. Reprinted in Chamberlin 1965.

268 **harmonic stack** The astute observer might look at the harmonics in these songs and realize that the numbers don't quite add up. In the left song, measurements of the primary frequency of the three visible notes in the harmonic stack are about 1,500, 2,250, and 3,000 Hz. The fundamental note can't be 1,500 Hz, because 2 × 1,500 is 3,000 Hz, not 2,250 Hz. If we halve 1,500, however, we get 750; if we then multiply 750 by 2, 3, and 4, we get the observed frequencies of 1,500, 2,250, and 3,000. So the fundamental note of the faster, higher song is about 750 Hz, even though that fundamental note seems to be suppressed by the bird and doesn't appear in the sonagram. Applying the same logic to the note of the slower, lower song gives a noticeably lower fundamental frequency, of about 650 Hz.

272 **The Christmas Robin** The quietest morning of the week to record birds, especially in a housing development, is typically a Sunday, and in this particular year (2005), Christmas was on Sunday, making for the quietest (and therefore most joyful) morning of the entire year when I recorded this robin.

272 *cheerily cheer-up cheerio* Here is the mnemonic from the master. See Peterson 1991.

272 *hisselly* For the origins of this name, see Bent 1949.

272 **two voice boxes to produce songs** For examples of how wood thrushes and brown thrashers use their two voice boxes, see pages 246–250 and 199–202, respectively, in Kroodsma 2005.

272 **singing centers in the brain are in idle mode** It wasn't all that long ago that the groups of neurons responsible for song in songbird brains were found to undergo drastic seasonal changes (Nottebohm 1981).

273 **Jonathan Livingston Seagull** In pursuit of self-perfection, this special seagull excelled in flying (Bach 1970), just as I'd like to think this young robin, if he persisted in singing his two songs simultaneously, would be a special robin indeed.

275 **"the first day with promise"** From page 135, Kroodsma 2005.

Bibliography

Adkisson, C. S., and R. N. Conner. 1978. Interspecific vocal imitation in white-eyed vireos. *Auk* 95: 602–606.

Albano, D. J. 2000. A behavioral ecology of the belted kingfisher (*Ceryle alcyon*). Ph.D. thesis, University of Massachusetts.

Archibald, H. L. 1974. Directional differences in the sound intensity of ruffed grouse drumming. *Auk* 91: 517–521.

Aubin, T., P. Jouventin, and C. Hildebrand. 2000. Penguins use the two-voice system to recognize each other. *Proceedings of the Royal Society of London Series B: Biological Sciences* 267: 1081–1087.

Bach, R. 1970. *Jonathan Livingston Seagull.* New York: Macmillan.

Barrowclough, G. F., J. G. Groth, L. A. Mertz, and R. J. Gutierrez. 2004. Phylogeographic structure, gene flow and species status in blue grouse (*Dendragapus obscurus*). *Molecular Ecology* 13: 1911–1922.

Beason, R. C. 1995. Horned lark (*Eremophila alpestris*). In *The Birds of North America, no. 195* (ed. by Poole, A., and F. Gill), pp. 1–32. Philadelphia and Washington, D.C.: The Academy of Natural Sciences, The American Ornithologists' Union.

Beecher, M. D. 1989. Signalling systems for individual recognition: an information theory approach. *Animal Behaviour* 38: 248–261.

———. 1996. Birdsong learning in the laboratory and field. In *Ecology and Evolution of Acoustic Communication in Birds* (ed. by Kroodsma, D. E., and E. H. Miller), pp. 61–78. Ithaca, New York: Cornell University Press.

Beecher, M. D., P. K. Stoddard, and P. Loesche. 1985. Recognition of parents' voices by young cliff swallows. *Auk* 102: 600–605.

Beletsky, L.D. 1982a. Vocalizations of female northern orioles. *Condor* 84: 445–447.

———. 1982b. Vocal behavior of the northern oriole. *Wilson Bulletin* 94: 372–381.

Bent, A. C. 1932. *Life Histories of North American Gallinaceous Birds: Orders*

Galliformes and Columbiformes. Washington, D.C.: *Smithsonian Institution United States National Museum Bulletin* 162.

————. 1949. *Life Histories of North American Thrushes, Kinglets, and Their Allies*. Washington, D.C.: *Smithsonian Institution United States National Museum Bulletin* 196.

Black, J. D. 1932. A winter robin roost in Arkansas. *Wilson Bulletin* 29: 13–19.

Blumenrath, S. H., T. Dabelsteen, and S. B. Pedersen. 2007. Vocal neighbour-mate discrimination in female great tits despite high song similarity. *Animal Behaviour* 73: 789–796.

Borror, D. J. 1967. Song of the yellowthroat. *The Living Bird* 6: 141–161.

Brewster, W. 1881. With the birds on a Florida river. *Bulletin of the Nuttall Ornithological Club* 6: 38–44.

Brumm, H. 2006. Signalling through acoustic windows: nightingales avoid interspecific competition by short-term adjustment of song timing. *Journal of Comparative Physiology A: Neuroethology, Sensory, Neural, and Behavioral Physiology* 192: 1279–1285.

Byers, B. E. 1995. Song types, repertoires and song variability in a population of chestnut-sided warblers. *Condor* 97: 390–401.

Byers, B. E., and D. I. King. 2000. Singing by female chestnut-sided warblers. *Wilson Bulletin* 112: 547–550.

Chamberlin, T. C. 1965. The method of multiple working hypotheses; with this method the dangers of parental affection for a favorite theory can be circumvented. *Science* 148: 754–759.

Davis, W. J. 1988. Acoustic communication in the belted kingfisher: an example of temporal coding. *Behaviour* 125: 1–24.

Dooling, R. J., M. R. Leek, O. Gleich, and M. L. Dent. 2002. Auditory resolution in birds: discrimination of harmonic complexes. *Journal of the Acoustical Society of America* 112: 748–759.

Dunne, P. 2006. *Pete Dunne's Essential Field Guide Companion*. Boston: Houghton Mifflin Company.

Elliott, L., and W. Hershberger. 2007. *The Songs of Insects*. Boston: Houghton Mifflin Company.

Emlen, S. T. 1995a. An evolutionary theory of the family. *Proceedings of the National Academy of Sciences USA* 92: 8092–8099.

————. 1995b. Making decisions in the family. *American Scientist* 83: 148–157.

Evans, W. R., and M. O'Brien. 2002. *Flight Calls of Migratory Birds: Eastern North American Landbirds*. Ithaca, New York: Old Bird Inc.

Farnsworth, A. 2005. Flight calls and their value for future ornithological studies and conservation research. *Auk* 122: 733–746.

Ffrench, R. 1991. *Birds of Trinidad and Tobago.* Ithaca, New York: Cornell University Press.

Floyd, T. 2007. Detecting and documenting nocturnal migration in Colorado. *Colorado Birds* 41: 16–28.

Frederick, P. C., and D. Siegel-Causey. 2000. Anhinga (*Anhinga anhinga*). In *The Birds of North America, no. 522* (ed. by Poole, A., and F. Gill), pp. 1–24. Philadelphia and Washington, D.C.: The Academy of Natural Sciences, The American Ornithologists' Union.

Gahr, M., H.-R. Güttinger, and D. E. Kroodsma. 1993. Estrogen receptors in the avian brain: survey reveals general distribution and forebrain areas unique to songbirds. *Journal of Comparative Neurology* 327: 112–122.

Garamszegi, L. Z., M. Eens, D. Z. Pavlova, J. Aviles, and A. P. Moller. 2007. A comparative study of the function of heterospecific vocal mimicry in European passerines. *Behavioral Ecology* 18: 1001–1009.

Goodale, E., and S. W. Kotagama. 2006a. Context-dependent vocal mimicry in a passerine bird. *Proceedings of the Royal Society* Series B: *Biological Sciences* 273: 875–880.

———. 2006b. Vocal mimicry by a passerine bird attracts other species involved in mixed-species flocks. *Animal Behaviour* 72: 471–477.

Greene, E., B. E. Lyon, V. R. Muehter, L. Ratcliffe, S. J. Oliver, and P. T. Boag. 2000. Disruptive sexual selection for plumage coloration in a passerine bird. *Nature* 407: 1000–1003.

Gullion, G. W. 1967. Selection and use of drumming sites by male ruffed grouse. *Auk* 84: 87–112.

Gwinner, E. 2003. Circannual rhythms in birds. *Current Opinion in Neurobiology* 13: 770–778.

Hopp, S. L., A. Kirby, and C. A. Boone. 1995. White-eyed vireo (*Vireo griseus*). In *The Birds of North America, no. 168* (ed. by Poole, A., and F. Gill), pp. 1–20. Philadelphia and Washington, D.C.: The Academy of Natural Sciences, The American Ornithologists' Union.

Houston, C. S., D. G. Smith, and C. Rohner. 1998. Great horned owl (*Bubo virginianus*). In *The Birds of North America Online* (ed. by Poole, A.). Ithaca, New York: The Cornell Lab of Ornithology.

Howell, J. C. 1973. Communicative behavior in the cedar waxwing (*Bombycilla cedrorum*) and the Bohemian waxwing (*Bombycilla garrulus*). Ph.D. thesis, University of Michigan.

Howell, S. N. G., and S. Webb. 1995. *A Guide to the Birds of Mexico and Northern Central America.* New York: Oxford University Press.

Johnsgard, P. A. 1981. *Those of the Gray Wind: The Sandhill Cranes.* New York: St. Martin's Press.

———. 1991. *Crane Music: A Natural History of American Cranes.* Washington, D.C.: Smithsonian Institution Press.

Johnson, N. K., and C. Cicero. 2004. New mitochondrial DNA data affirm the importance of Pleistocene speciation in North American birds. *Evolution* 58: 1122–1130.

Kaufman, K. 2000. *Birds of North America.* Boston: Houghton Mifflin Company.

Klicka, J., K. Burns, and G. M. Spellman. 2007. Defining a monophyletic cardinalini: A molecular perspective. *Molecular Phylogenetics and Evolution* 45: 1014–1032.

Kroodsma, D. E. 2005. *The Singing Life of Birds: The Art and Science of Listening to Birdsong.* Boston: Houghton Mifflin Company.

Kroodsma, D. E., and M. Konishi. 1991. A suboscine bird (eastern phoebe, *Sayornis phoebe*) develops normal song without auditory feedback. *Animal Behaviour* 42: 477–488.

Kroodsma, D. E., and L. D. Parker. 1977. Vocal virtuosity in the brown thrasher. *Auk* 94: 783–785.

Liu, W.-c. 2001. Song development and singing behavior of the chipping sparrow (*Spizella passerina*) in western Massachusetts. Ph.D. thesis, University of Massachusetts.

Liu, W.-c., and D. E. Kroodsma. 2006. Song learning by chipping sparrows: when, where, and from whom. *Condor* 108: 509–517.

Livezey, B. C. 1998. A phylogenetic analysis of the Gruiformes (Aves) based on morphological characters, with an emphasis on the rails (Rallidae). *Transactions of the Royal Society London,* Series B 353: 2077–2151.

Lohr, B., R. J. Dooling, and S. Bartone. 2006. The discrimination of temporal fine structure in call-like harmonic sounds by birds. *Journal of Comparative Psychology* 120: 239–251.

McGowan, K. J., and G. E. Woolfenden. 1989. A sentinel system in the Florida scrub jay. *Animal Behaviour* 37: 1000–1006.

McGregor, P. K., and J. R. Krebs. 1984. Song learning and deceptive mimicry. *Animal Behaviour* 32: 280–287.

Medvin, M. B., and M. D. Beecher. 1986. Parent-offspring recognition in the barn swallow (*Hirundo rustica*). *Animal Behaviour* 34: 1627–1639.

Molles, L. E., and S. L. Vehrencamp. 1999. Repertoire size, repertoire overlap, and singing modes in the banded wren (*Thryothorus pleurostictus*). *Auk* 116: 677–689.

Morse, D. H. 1967. The contexts of songs in black-throated green and Blackburnian warblers. *Wilson Bulletin* 79: 64–74.

———. 1989. *American Warblers: An Ecological and Behavioral Perspective.* Cambridge, Massachusetts: Harvard University Press.

Morton, E. S. 1976. Vocal mimicry in the thick-billed euphonia. *Wilson Bulletin* 88: 485–487.

National Geographic Society. 1987. *Field Guide to the Birds of North America.* Washington, D.C.: National Geographic Society.

Nottebohm, F. 1981. A brain for all seasons: cyclical anatomical changes in song control nuclei of the canary brain. *Science* 214: 1368–1370.

Payne, R. B. 1992. Indigo bunting. In *Birds of North America, no. 4* (ed. by Poole, A., P. Stettenheim, and F. Gill), pp. 1–24. Philadelphia and Washington, D.C.: The Academy of Natural Sciences, The American Ornithologists' Union.

———. 1996. Song traditions in indigo buntings: origin, improvisation, dispersal, and extinction in cultural evolution. In *Ecology and Evolution of Acoustic Communication in Birds* (ed. by Kroodsma, D. E., and E. H. Miller), pp. 198–200. Ithaca, New York: Cornell University Press.

Peterson, R. T. 1980. *A Field Guide to the Birds East of the Rockies.* Boston: Houghton Mifflin Company.

———. 1991. *A Field Guide to Western Bird Song.* Boston: Houghton Mifflin Company.

Putnam, L. S. 1949. The life history of the cedar waxwing. *Wilson Bulletin* 61: 141–182.

Remsen, J. V., K. Garrett, and R. A. Erickson. 1982. Vocal copying in Lawrence's and lesser goldfinches. *Western Birds* 13: 29–33.

Robbins, C. S., B. Bruun, H. S. Zim, and A. Singer. 1983. *A Guide to Field Identification: Birds of North America.* New York: Golden Press.

Ruppell, W. 1933. *Physiologic und Akustik der Vogelstimme. Journal für Ornithologie* 81: 3.

Rusch, D. H., S. DeStefano, M. C. Reynolds, and D. Lauten. 2000. Ruffed grouse (*Bonasa umbellus*). In *The Birds of North America, no. 515* (ed. by Poole, A., and F. Gill), pp. 1–28. Philadelphia and Washington, D.C.: The Academy of Natural Sciences, The American Ornithologists' Union.

Schnase, J. L., and T. C. Maxwell. 1989. Use of song patterns to identify individual male Cassin's sparrows. *Journal of Field Ornithology* 60: 12–19.

Secunda, R. C., and T. W. Sherry. 1991. Polyterritorial polygyny in the American redstart. *Wilson Bulletin* 103: 190–203.

Shy, E. 1984. The structure of song and its geographical variation in the scarlet tanager (*Piranga olivacea*). *The American Midland Naturalist* 112: 119–130.

Sibley, D. A. 2000. *The Sibley Guide to Birds.* New York: Alfred A. Knopf.

Smith, S. M. 1980. Demand behavior: a new interpretation of courtship feeding. *Condor* 82: 291–295.

Smith, W. J. 1966. Communications and relationships in the genus *Tyrannus. Publication of the Nuttall Ornithological Club* 6: 1–250.

Spector, D. A. 1994. Definition in biology: the case of "bird song." *Journal of Theoretical Biology* 168: 373–381.

Stiles, F. G., and A. F. Skutch. 1989. *A Guide to the Birds of Costa Rica.* Ithaca, New York: Cornell University Press.

Stoddard, P. K., M. D. Beecher, P. Loesche, and S. E. Campbell. 1992. Memory does not constrain individual recognition in a bird with song repertoires. *Behaviour* 122: 274–287.

Suthers, R. A., and S. A. Zollinger. 2004. Producing song: the vocal apparatus. In *Behavioral Neurobiology of Birdsong* (ed. by Ziegler, H. P., and P. Marler), pp. 109–129. New York: Annals of the New York Academy of Sciences, vol. 1016.

Tacha, T. C., S. A. Nesbitt, and P. A. Vohs. 1992. Sandhill crane (*Grus canadensis*). In *The Birds of North America, no. 31* (ed. by Poole, A., P. Stettenheim, and F. Gill), pp. 1–24. Philadelphia and Washington, D.C.: The Academy of Natural Sciences, The American Ornithologists' Union.

Thompson, W. L. 1970. Song variation in a population of indigo buntings. *Auk* 87: 58–71.

Truslow, F. K. 1958. Limpkin, the "crying bird" that haunts Florida swamps. *National Geographic* 113: 114–121.

Tyler, W. M. 1916. The call-notes of some nocturnal migrating birds. *Auk* 33: 132–141.

Whitney, C. L. 1990. Avoidance of song matching in the wood thrush: a field experiment. *Wilson Bulletin* 103: 96–101.

Withgott, J. 2002. Night voices revealed: a new guide to flight calls sheds light on nocturnal migration. *Birding* 34: 546–553.

Witmer, M. C., D. J. Mountjoy, and L. Elliot. 1997. Cedar waxwing (*Bombycilla cedrorum*). In *The Birds of North America, no. 309* (ed. by Poole, A., and F. Gill), Philadelphia and Washington, D.C.: The Academy of Natural Sciences, The American Ornithologists' Union.

Woolfenden, G. E., and J. W. Fitzpatrick. 1984. *The Florida Scrub Jay: Demography of a Cooperatively-breeding Bird.* Princeton, New Jersey: Princeton University Press.

———. 1996. Florida scrub-jay (*Aphelocoma coerulescens*). In *The Birds of North America, no. 228* (ed. by Poole, A., and F. Gill), pp. 1–28. Philadelphia and Washington, D.C.: The Academy of Natural Sciences, The American Ornithologists' Union.

Yodlowski, M. L., M. L. Kreithen, and W. T. Keeton. 1977. Detection of atmospheric infrasound by homing pigeons. *Nature* 265: 725–726.

Young, J. R., C. E. Braun, S. J. Oyler-McCance, J. W. Hupp, and T. W. Quinn. 2000. A new species of sage-grouse (Phasianidae: Centrocercus) from southwestern Colorado. *Wilson Bulletin* 112: 445–453.

Index

Note: In **bold** type is the most important information in the book: the track number(s) where a particular species can be heard on the CDs, the range of pages for the section that focuses on that particular species or topic, and the text that describes the CD track(s). In *italics* is the page number for sonagrams.

Accipiter striatus. See hawk, sharp-shinned
acorns, 47, 49, 53
Adirondack Mountains, 214
adrenaline, 28, 34
Agelaius phoeniceus. See blackbird, red-
    winged
Aimophila
    aestivalis. See sparrow, Bachman's
    cassinii. See sparrow, Cassin's
Aix sponsa. See duck, wood
alarm, warning calls, 98, 129, 179, 184, 203,
    266, 272, 273
Alaska, 71
Alauda arvensis. See lark, sky
Albano, Dan, 125
Alberta, 230
Allen, Harvey, 225
alligator, American, **track 1-27,** 24, 27
    roar of, 28, 31, 55, **283**
"American" defined, 318
Amherst, Massachusetts, 3, 10, 12, 99, 145,
    184
Anas
    acuta. See pintail, northern
    americana. See wigeon, American

    platyrhynchos. See mallard
    strepera. See gadwall
ancestral home
    migrants, xi, 76, 205
    tanagers, 163
anhinga (*Anhinga anhinga*), **tracks 1-29**
    through 1-33, xi, 31, 36, *57,*
    55–64, 283–84
    appearance of, 58, 59, 60
    begging calls of young, 56, 57, 59, 61–64,
    284
    calls described, 25, 30
    courtship, 63, **284**
    duetting, 57
    exclamations about, 62–64, 284
    families, 61
    incubating, 58
    nestling appearance, 59
    recognizing family, 63
    siblicide, 59
Anhinga anhinga. See anhinga
Anhinga Trail, 55, 283
antbird, 142, 194
antelope, 111, 121
anthropomorphism, 46

nest helpers, 315, 345
scrub-jay mating system, 45
song learning, 84, 86, 194
speech, 84

Falco sparverius. See kestrel, American
family
  anhingas, 61, 62
  bunting, indigo, 166
  crane, sandhill, 72, 285
  crow, American, 137
  goldfinch, American, 199, **303**
  human, compared to birds', 50
  oriole, Baltimore, 105
  scrub-jay, Florida, **44–54,** 282
  thrush, wood, 203
  titmouse, tufted, 270
  warbler, Blackburnian, 151
  waxwing, cedar, 183
  woodpecker, pileated, 4
family dynasty, 49, 53
Farmer's Almanac, 202
female song. *See also* duetting
  finch, purple, 143
  mockingbird, northern, 252
field note notations, 83, 87, 103, 113
finch, house (*Carpodacus mexicanus*),
      track 2-3, *140*, 142
  calls, 266
  courtship song, **137, 295**
finch, purple (*Carpodacus purpureus*), 143,
      150, 153
fire, 44
fireflies, 26
fish
  anhinga, 63
  kingfisher, 125
  sounds of, 27

flicker, northern (*Colaptes auratus*), 5, 124,
      129, 258
  calls, 124, 258
  drum, 129
  imitated by thrasher, 91, 92, **288**
  imitated by white-eyed vireo, 93, 97, 98,
      289
  nesting cavities, 5
flight calling. *See also* flight singing
  cowbird, brown-headed, 110, 274
  crane, sandhill, 70, 72
  crow, American, 136
  goldfinch, American, 8, 9, 138, 176, 209,
      266
  nocturnal migrants, **207–221**
  scrub-jay, Florida, 51
  waxwing, cedar, 183
  woodpecker, pileated, 5, 11
flight singing. *See also* flight calling
  bunting, lark, 117, 118
  kingbird, eastern, 101
  lark, horned, 109
  longspur, McCown's, 119, 120
  ovenbird, 146, 245
  sparrow, Cassin's, 114
  woodcock, American, 226
Florida, xi, 23, 34, 44, 254
flycatcher
  distribution of, 76, 80, 133, 142
  evolution of, 194
  great crested (*Myiarchus crinitus*), 97,
      245
  mimicked by white-eyed vireo, 319
  singing energy at dawn, 158, 189
  suboscine relatives of, 194
  willow (*Empidonax traillii*), 100, 101
frog, 35–37, 100, 188
  contagious calling, 30

frog (*cont.*)

  green, 100, 133, 157, 165, 189

  leopard, 27, 29

  pig, 30, 55

fruitcrow, 318

fruiteater, 318

fun. *See also* joy

  decoding white-eyed vireo songs, 98

  Internet listening, 325

  listening to anhingas, 64

  listening to slowed-down songs, 243

  recognizing individuals by voice, 69

  recording birdsong, 310

  ruined by traffic noise, 252

  self-discovery, 323

  sharing birdsong with others, 62, 64

  syrinx and two voices, xiv

gadwall (*Anas strepera*), 69

Gagnon, Tom, 225, 325

Gallinula chloropus. See moorhen, common

gallinule, purple (*Porphyrio martinica*), 24,
    30

Gallus gallus. See rooster

Gavia immer. See loon, common

geographic song variation. *See also* dialects

  bunting, indigo, 171

  lack of in flycatcher, 79

  yellowthroat, common, 30

Geothlypis trichas. See yellowthroat,
    common

gnatcatcher, blue-gray (*Polioptila caerulea*),
    25, 160

goldfinch, American (*Carduelis tristis*),
    track 2-39, 142

  babbling, 130, 198

  begging calls, *198,* 199, **303**

  flight calling, 8, 9, 138, 176, 209, 266

  imitated by brown thrasher, 91, **288**

  song, 265, 274

goldfinch, Lawrence's (*Carduelis lawrencei*),
    319

goldfinch, lesser (*Carduelis psaltria*), 319

gonads, xi

"good birds" (starlings and cowbirds), 138,
    139, 142

goose, Canada (*Branta canadensis*), 226, 236

goose, snow (*Chen caerulescens*), **track
    1-34,** 67–70, 73

grackle, boat-tailed (*Quiscalus major*), 79

grackle, common (*Quiscalus quiscula*), 138,
    141, 256

  calls, 25, 138, 256

  one-song repertoire, 141

  song, 138

Grand Island, Nebraska, 71

Green, John, 10

grosbeak, rose-breasted (*Pheucticus ludovi-
    cianus*), 100

groundhog, 34

grouse, blue (*Dendragapus* spp.), 231

grouse, dusky (*Dendragapus obscurus*), 231

grouse, ruffed (*Bonasa umbellus*), **tracks
    2-49 through 2-51,** xii, 224–39,
    230, **306, 307**

  appearance of, 237

  dispersal and survival, 238

  drum signature, 230–32

  energy in drum, 234, 235

  morning warm-up, 232, 233

  precision in drum, 229

  rate of wing flapping, 229

  recordings at Cornell Lab of
      Ornithology, 278

  two species, 230, 231, 325

grouse, sage. *See* sage-grouse

Kearney, Nebraska, 71

Keller, Geoff, 79

kestrel, American (*Falco sparverius*), 4, 256

killdeer (*Charadrius vociferus*), 4, 25, 46, 91, 253

kingbird, 80

kingbird, eastern (*Tyrannus tyrannus*), **track 2-33, 302**

    begging calls, 194, 197, 199

    fledgling calls and innate song, 194, 195

    flight singing, 100, 101

kingfisher, belted (*Ceryle alcyon*), **tracks 1-56 through 1-58, 2-30,** xii, 24, 47, **124–32,** *128,* **291, 292, 301**

    appearance of, 127

    banter, 127

    calling at nest, 130, 131

    expressive voice, 127

    flooded out, 131

    nesting cycle, 131

    rhythm in calls, 127

    winter territory, 125

kinglet, golden-crowned (*Regulus satrapa*), 266, 267

kinglet, ruby-crowned (*Regulus calendula*), **track 2-46, 306**

    babbling, 227

kiskadee, great (*Pitangus sulphuratus*), **tracks 1-38, 1-41,** xiv, **77–80,** *78,* **286**

    countersinging, 77

    dawn singing, 77, 80

    expressive voice, 78, 80

    innate songs, 78

    intelligence of, 78

kite, snail, 25, 31

Kroodsma, David, 76, 86

Lake Nicaragua, 77

Lake Placid, Florida, 44

lambs, 30

Lanius ludovicianus. See shrike, loggerhead

lark, horned (*Eremophila alpestris*), **tracks 1-48 through 1-50,** xii, **108–12,** *110,* 113, 116, 121, **290**

    compared to sky lark, 109

    continous dawn singing, 109

    flight singing, 109

    repertoire of song flourishes, 111

    repertoire of song phrases, 112

    song flourishes, 111

lark, sky (*Alauda arvensis*), 108, 114

learned songs. *See* call learning; improvised song; innate calls; innate song; song learning; song matching; song sharing

lettering game, 82, 87, 114

Library of Natural Sounds, 79, 230, 231

Limnothlypis swainsonii. See warbler, Swainson's

limpkin (*Aramus guarauna*), **tracks 1-9, 1-13, 1-17 through 1-20,** xi, **34–44,** *38,* **280–82**

    appearance of, 42

    bronchial box, 40

    contagious calling, 27

    duetting, 27, 36, 37, **281**

    expressive voice, 39

    harmonics in sounds, 39

    preening, 43

    sound production, 40

    sound quality of, 40

    sounds of young males, 40

Lincoln's Homestead Act, 108

lion, mountain, 226

Liu, Wan-chun, 106

lizard, 188

longspur, McCown's (*Calcarius mccownii*), **track 1-52,** xii, **116–21,** *120,* **291**

   appearance of, 119

   flight singing, 119

   rapid, complex songs, 120

loon, common (*Gavia immer*), 157, 208, 215

Loxia curvirostra. See crossbill, red

mallard (*Anas platyrhynchos*), 69, 101, 189

Managua, Nicaragua, 76

Marcum, Jim, 105

martin, purple (*Progne subis*), 91

Massachusetts, 231, 232

mating system and song

   bunting, indigo, 173, 175

   grouse, ruffed, 226

Mayhorn, Roger and Lynda, 90

meadowlark, eastern (*Sturnella magna*), 91

meadowlark, western (*Sturnella neglecta*), **track 1-49,** 110, 113, 114, **290**

Megascops asio. See screech-owl, eastern

Melanerpes carolinus. See woodpecker, red-bellied

Meleagris gallopavo. See turkey, wild

Melospiza

   georgiana. See sparrow, swamp

   lincolnii. See sparrow, Lincoln's

   melodia. See sparrow, song

memory for song

   beginnings, 180

   bunting, indigo, 170

   lark, horned, 290

   songbirds, 322

   thrasher, brown, 91, 92

merganser, common (*Mergus merganser*), 126

Mergus merganser. See merganser, common

Mexico, 71

Miami, Florida, 26, 56, 254

Miccosukee village, 26

Michigan, 50

microdialect. *See* dialects

Milky Way, 108

mimicry

   catbird, gray, 101, 137

   evolution of, 319

   mockingbird, northern, 260

   starling, European, 4, 140

   thrasher, brown, **90–92,** 98, **288**

   vireo, white-eyed, 90, **92–98, 288,** 319

Mimus polyglottos. See mockingbird, northern

Minear, Deedee, 105, 194, 195

Mniotilta varia. See warbler, black-and-white

mockingbird, northern (*Mimus polyglottos*), **tracks 2-52 through 2-64,** xii, **252–61,** *255,* **307, 308**

   attacking starlings, 256–59, 261

   calling from roost, 254

   call repertoire, 254

   dawn calling, 254

   defending palm fruits, 260

   female song, 258

   harsh calls, xiv

   male song, 46, 178

   mimicked by white-eyed vireo, 97

   mimicry, 98, 260

   mimicry and aggression, 260

   starling relative, 139

   winter roost, 252, 260

Molothrus ater. See cowbird, brown-headed

monkey, howler, 77

otter, 227

ovenbird (*Seiurus aurocapilla*)
  flight singing, 146, 245
  nocturnal migrant calls, 216, 217
  song, 143, 248

owl, 98, 142, 236

owl, barred (*Strix varia*), **track 1-28,** 29, 36,
    42, 146, 208, 225, 226, 245, **283**
  duetting, 36, 37, 55
  eating robins, 18
  expressive voice, 55
  unearthly sounds, 18

owl, eastern screech. *See* screech-owl,
    eastern

owl, great horned (*Bubo virginianus*),
    tracks 1-2, 1-6, 2-28, 2-48, 279,
    301, 306
  begging screeches, 190, 197, 207
  breeding in winter, 3
  duetting, 3, 226, 254
  eating robins, 18, 20, 21, 22
  female hooting, 13
  hooting, 8, 199, 208, 225
  in robin roost, 17, 21

Panamanian land bridge, 163

Pandion haliaetus. See osprey

parabolic microphone ("parabola")
  aiming, 10, 109
  recording in stereo, 278
  sensitivity of, 254, 256, 313

parrot, 77

parula, northern (*Parula americana*), **track**
    2-43, *212*, 216, 217, 219, **304**

Parula americana. See parula, northern

Passerculus sandwichensis. See sparrow,
    savannah

Passer domesticus. See sparrow, house

Passerina
  amoena. See bunting, lazuli
  cyanea. See bunting, indigo

Pavo cristatus. See peacock

Pawnee Grasslands, xii, 121

peacock (*Pavo cristatus*), 40

peeper, spring, 133, 204, 208

Pelham, Massachusetts, 17

Peterson, Roger Tory, 178, 272

Petrochelidon pyrrhonota. See swallow, cliff

pewee, eastern wood. *See* wood-pewee,
    eastern

phainopepla (*Phainopepla nitens*), 179

Phainopepla nitens. See phainopepla

Phalacrocorax auritus. See cormorant,
    double-crested

Pharomachrus mocinno. See quetzal,
    resplendent

Pheucticus ludovicianus. See grosbeak, rose-
    breasted

phoebe, eastern (*Sayornis phoebe*), **track**
    2-22, 101, 129, 141, 150, 189,
    226, **300**

photographers seeing, not hearing, 62

piano, xiv, 85

Picoides
  pubescens. See woodpecker, downy
  villosus. See woodpecker, hairy

pig, 49

pigeon, rock (*Columba livia*), 326

piha, 318

pintail (*Anas acuta*), 69

Pipilo erythrophthalmus. See towhee, eastern

Piranga
  flava. See tanager, hepatic
  ludoviciana. See tanager, western
  olivacea. See tanager, scarlet
  rubra. See tanager, summer

sparrow, swamp (*Melospiza georgiana*),
    track 2-43, 100, 101, 218, *220,*
    305
sparrow, white-crowned (*Zonotrichia*
    leucophrys), 217
sparrow, white-throated (*Zonotrichia*
    albicollis), **tracks 2-43, 2-48,**
    220, **305, 306**
    babbling, 227, 266
    nocturnal migrant calls, 216, 218, 219,
        220
speech, evolution of, 84
spherical spreading law, 90, 228, 325
Sphyrapicus varius. See sapsucker, yellow-
    bellied
spider web, 35
Spizella
    arborea. See sparrow, American tree
    breweri. See sparrow, Brewer's
    pallida. See sparrow, clay-colored
    passerina. See sparrow, chipping
    pusilla. See sparrow, field
spring
    first day of, xii, 264
    harbingers of, 12
    sounds of, 269
squirrel, red, **track 2-13,** 4, 8, 9, 21, **292, 298**
stars, 34
    Aldeberan, 213
    Capella, 213
    Castor, 213
    Pollux, 213
    Procyon, 213
    Rigel, 213
    Sirius, 213
starling, European (*Sturnus vulgaris*), **tracks**
    2-4, 2-56, 2-58, 9, **139–40, 295,**
    308

attacked by mockingbird, 256–61
complex song, 140, 142
mimicked by brown thrasher, 91
mimicry, 4, 140
repertoire, 141
syrinx and two voices, 140
statistics. *See* numbers games
Stemple, David
    counting robins, 17
    listening with, **133–42**
    in memory of, 133
Stemple, Jason, 17
Sterling, Colorado, 111
stork, wood (*Mycteria americana*), **track**
    1-16, 23, 31, **281**
Strix varia. See owl, barred
Sturnella
    magna. See meadowlark, eastern
    neglecta. See meadowlark, western
Sturnus vulgaris. See starling, European
stuttering, 39
suboscines, 194
subsong. *See* babbling
Sunderland, Massachusetts, 12
sunrise. *See also* dawn singing
    birds singing before, 8
sun's seasons, xi, 189, 202, 264, 308
survival
    grouse, ruffed, 238
    scrub-jay, Florida, 53
swallow, barn (*Hirundo rustica*), 317
swallow, cliff (*Petrochelidon pyrrhonota*),
    317
swallow, tree (*Tachycineta bicolor*), 101, 189
swift, chimney (*Chaetura pelagica*), 138, 142
Swift River, 165
syrinx
    crane, sandhill, 69

trumpet, 39

Turdus

    grayi. See robin, clay-colored

    merula. See blackbird, Eurasian

    migratorius. See robin, American

turkey, wild (*Meleagris gallopavo*), 7

turtle, 24

Tyrannus tyrannus. See kingbird, eastern

umbrellabird, 318

University of Michigan, 178

Utah, 71

veery (*Catharus fuscescens*), **tracks 2-28,**
    2-40, 2-42, *210,* 301, 303, 304

    babbling, 199

    call, 159

    mimicked by white-eyed vireo, 97

    muted vocalizations, 160

    nocturnal migrant calls, 208, 209, 211,
        213, 215–17, 219, 221

Venezuela, 79

Vermivora

    celata. See warbler, orange-crowned

    chrysoptera. See warbler, golden-winged

    peregrina. See warbler, Tennessee

    pinus. See warbler, blue-winged

    ruficapilla. See warbler, Nashville

Vireo

    flavifrons. See vireo, yellow-throated

    gilvus. See vireo, warbling

    griseus. See vireo, white-eyed

    olivaceus. See vireo, red-eyed

    solitarius. See vireo, blue-headed

vireo, blue-headed (*Vireo solitarius*), 143,
    151

vireo, red-eyed (*Vireo olivaceus*), **track 2-38,**
    196, **303**

babbling, 196, 197, 199

late risers, 176

mimicked by white-eyed vireo, 93, 96, 97

song, 124, 143, 151, 160, 248

vireo, warbling (*Vireo gilvus*), **track 2-34,**
    196, **302**

    babbling, 194–97, 199

    song, 124

vireo, white-eyed (*Vireo griseus*), **tracks
    1-43, 1-44,** xii, 90, **92–98,** *94, 95,*
    288, 289

    appearance of, 96

    babbling, 196

    coordinated singing with wren and
        towhee, 93

    function of mimicry, 95, 98

    list of species mimicked, 96, 97

    mimicry of calls, 92, 98, **288,** 319

    mimicry and mobbing, 98

    rhythm in song, xv

    thinking? 95

vireo, yellow-throated (*Vireo flavifrons*), 97,
    105

Virginia, xii

Virginia Society for Ornithology, 90

voice box. *See* syrinx

Volcan Barva, Costa Rica, 133

vulture, turkey (*Cathartes aura*), 24

wading birds, xi, **23–31,** 68

warbler, 133, 143

    chip notes, 97

    dawn songs defined, 321

    daytime songs defined, 321

    mimicked by white-eyed vireo, 319

    nocturnal migrant calls, *212,* 213, 215–19

    singing behavior of, 145

    singing energy at dawn, 158, 189